designing
THE HAMPTONS

portraits of interiors

introduction by
mayer
RUS

edited by
diana
LIND

designing
THE HAMPTONS

portraits of interiors

photography by
laurie LAMBRECHT
charles MAYER
joshua McHUGH
toni MENEGUZZO
MINH + WASS
eric PIASECKI
laura RESEN
paul WARCHOL

EDIZIONI
press

joe NAHEM 12
steven GAMBREL 38
thomas O'BRIEN 56
jamie DRAKE 72
jack CEGLIC 86
waldo FERNANDEZ 102
mark ZEFF 120
tony INGRAO &
randy KEMPER 134
tom FLYNN 152
bill SOFIELD &
dennis ANDERSON 166
robert STILIN 186
enrico BONETTI &
dominic KOZERSKI 200
arthur DUNNAM 214
michael HAVERLAND &
philip GALANES 226
thom FILICIA 246
john BARMAN &
kelly GRAHAM 260
vicente WOLF 276
jonathan ADLER &
simon DOONAN 298

Share the Fantasy

Ninety miles from Manhattan, on the easternmost tip of Long Island, Shangri-la spreads out along the Atlantic Ocean. Welcome to the Hamptons—playground of the rich and powerful, symbol of modern American leisure, and non-denominational temple of luxury. Natural splendor, enormous wealth, Old Guard society, social climbers, publicity whores, renowned artists, and fancy decorators all converge in this crucible of fantasy and fortune.

The hoi polloi get to share the Hamptons fantasy vicariously, by way of endless magazine articles, books, and movies. In the past decade, the popular media's appetite for Hamptons dish has become ravenous. Celebrity gossip rags and society journals obsessively chronicle the lifestyles of Hamptons swells—rappers and debutantes alike. Between Memorial Day and Labor Day, television camera crews are a fixture on the East End. Tabloid newspaper reporters prowl the streets looking for boozed-up celebrities and contemptuous rich kids behaving badly. Three years ago, Barbara Kopple, the documentary filmmaker best known for *Harlan County, USA*, a movie about the struggles of coal miners in Kentucky, directed an exposé on life in the Hamptons for ABC.

Hollywood also has a piece of the action. Movies like *Annie Hall* and *Wall Street* served up archetypal images of life in the Hamptons as it was popularly perceived in two earlier decades: in the former, 1970s New York intellectuals cooked lobsters in a charming, weatherworn shack; in the latter, a 1980s-era arbitrageur exercised his greed in a sinister, oceanfront mansion of glass and steel. More recently, *Something's Gotta Give* (the 2004 Diane Keaton vehicle) distilled a contemporary picture of the good life in the Hamptons: a large, Shingle-style house tricked out in blue-and-white fabrics, seagrass carpets, glass hurricanes, and odd bits of coral and twig.

Like its predecessors, the home in *Something's Gotta Give* looks perfectly natural and appropriate to the region. Current sales catalogs for luxury real estate in the Hamptons suggest a consensus on the question of architectural style—an overwhelming majority of houses built in recent years, particularly developer spec houses, mimic the classic Shingle aesthetic, with varying degrees of finesse. This historical redux is the standard dress uniform throughout the Hamptons. Modernism continues to be a marginal presence on today's swinging Shingle scene, despite the area's rich tradition of avant-garde architecture.

Mercifully, what you see is not always what you get. The tired, conservative architecture of so many houses on the East End masks the real face of great Hamptons design in the early twenty-first century. Inside those cookie-cutter walls, polite consensus gives way to daring, idiosyncratic personal taste of every flavor. Razor-sharp modernism, Belle Epoque grandeur, Orientalist fantasy, New Age tranquility—when it comes to interior design, anything goes. Judgments on issues of taste and artistry are based on individual connoisseurial vision, not adherence to a predominant style.

The money and attention lavished on interiors signifies a reversal of fortunes among the design disciplines. In the past, Hamptons homeowners used architecture to express the status and spirit of their families. Houses were not so much "decorated" as they were furnished—typically with cast-offs, junk store finds, and family hand-me-downs. Today, many well-heeled pleasure seekers don't have the patience or inclination to make architecture. Why waste two or three years on construction when you can conjure an instant fantasy within the walls of a "luxury" spec house in a matter of months?

Of course, successful conjuring requires magic. In the new world order of Hamptons design, homeowners typically rely on the wizardry of decorators to make their dreams come true. Competition is fierce in the dream fulfillment business. Elite decorators at the top of the pack become celebrities on the Hamptons social scene. They each speak a different, highly personal language of style, which they project not only through their design work but also in the clothes they wear and the cars they drive. They are bon vivants, society gadabouts, ironic dandies, and sometimes, when the mood strikes, leather queens—chintz by day, chaps by night. Like Chanel or Valentino, they are also recognizable brand names in the luxury marketplace. Clients will spend a little more for an imprimatur of taste, quality, and discernment.

Indeed, the worlds of high fashion and high design in the Hamptons have much in common. Both of these rarefied demimondes arouse the voyeuristic curiosity of people confounded by the idea of a $50,000 dress or a $50,000,000 weekend getaway. Furthermore, the popular media's frequent attempts to expose (or ridicule) the "real" face of high fashion and design—Robert Altman's tedious *Ready to Wear*, and Kopple's Hamptons documentary, for starters—always seem to miss the mark. They fail to capture the true depths of vulgarity and decadence, as well as the transcendent moments of beauty and wonder that make the Hamptons so fascinating. To fully appreciate the kaleidoscopic brilliance of Hamptons design today, you can't just peek at the stately houses through the tall hedges. The real drama is happening inside.

—*Mayer Rus*

joe NAHEM

"This house was built by Joe D'Urso, my mentor, so it was both very exciting and intimidating to work on its interior design. My clients decided that they didn't want the interiors to have a lot of bright colors, but they wanted the furniture and fabrics to soften the space and to make it comfortable and inviting. When you have a view of the ocean like this house does, you don't want the interiors to compete with that."

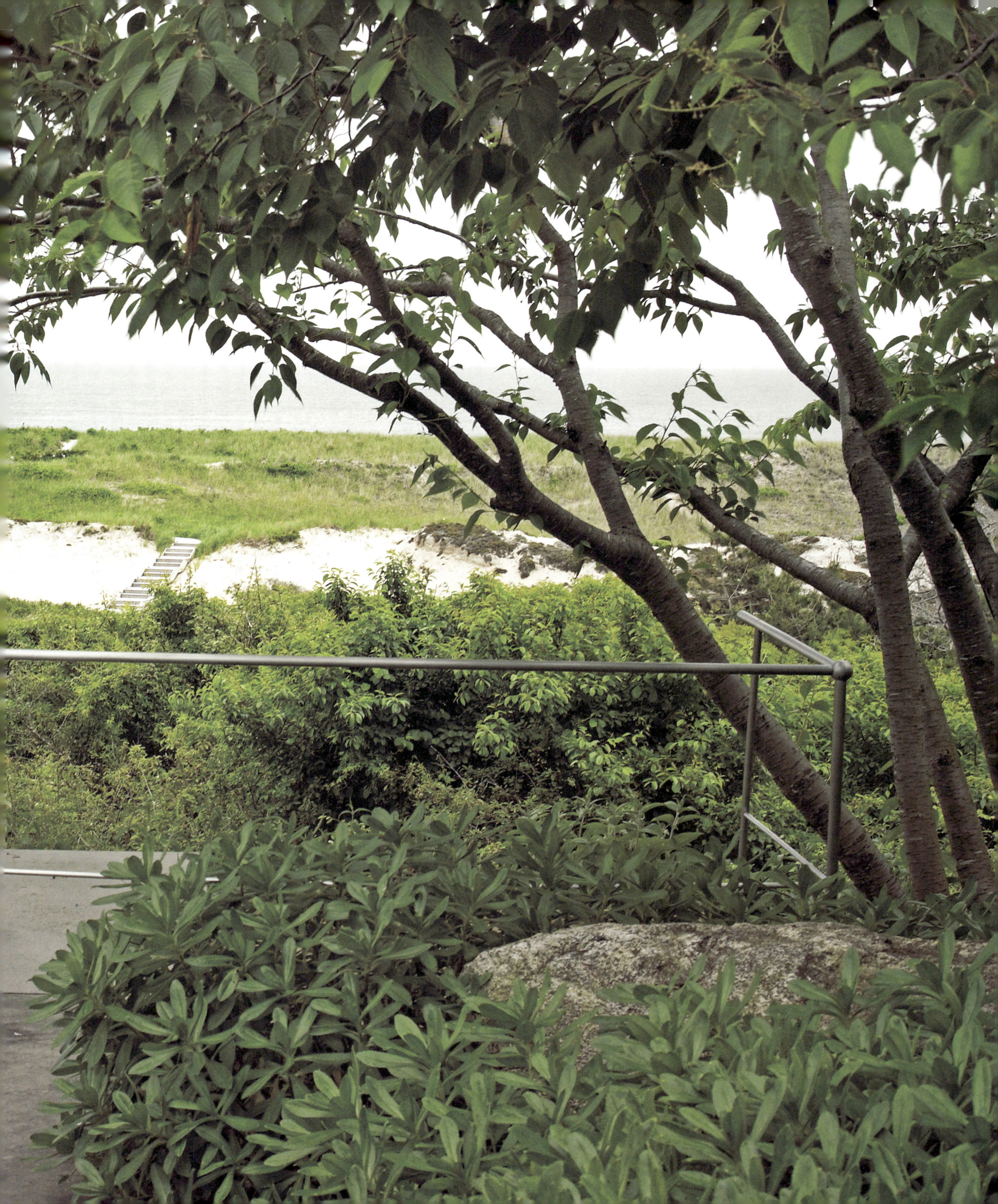

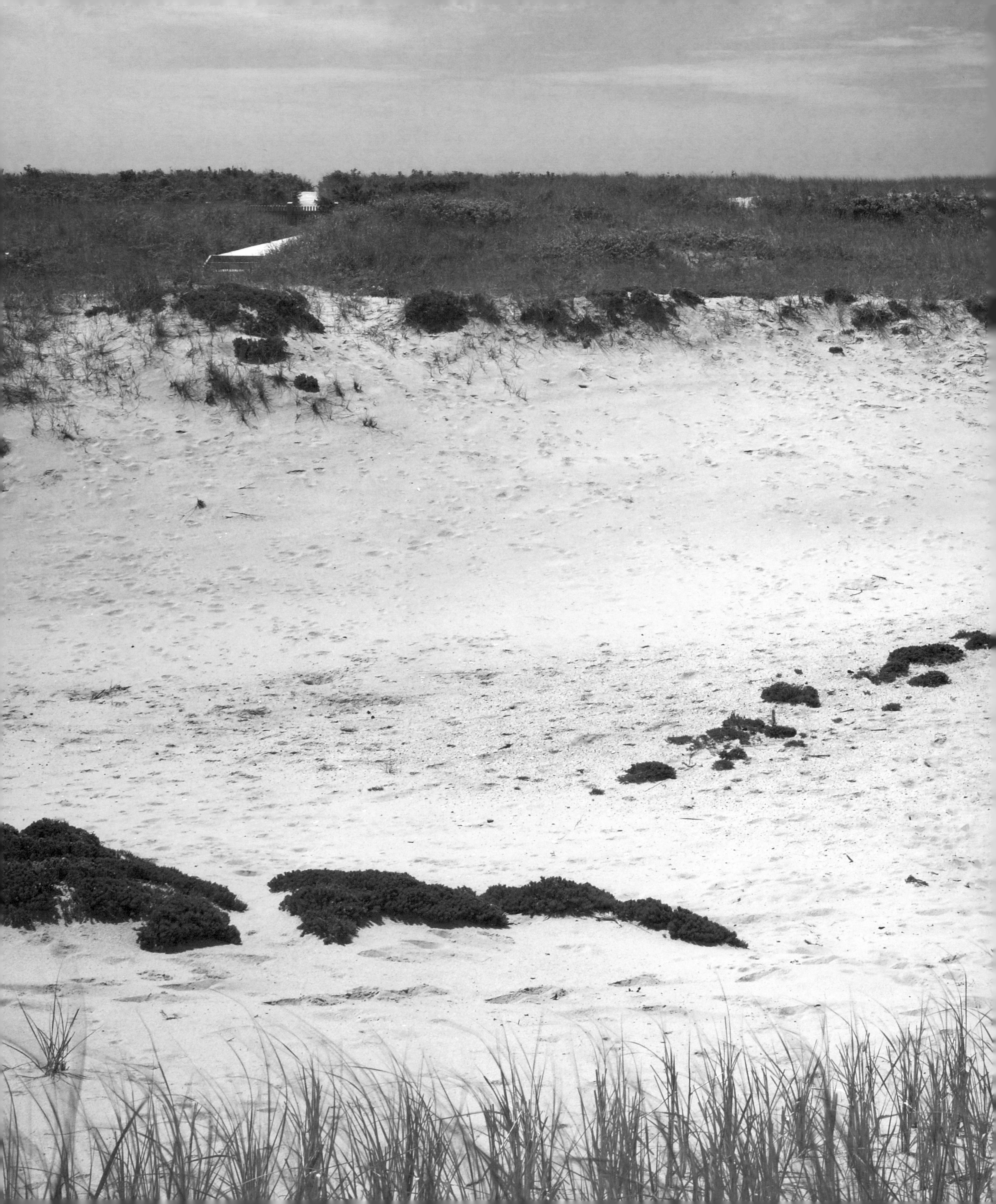

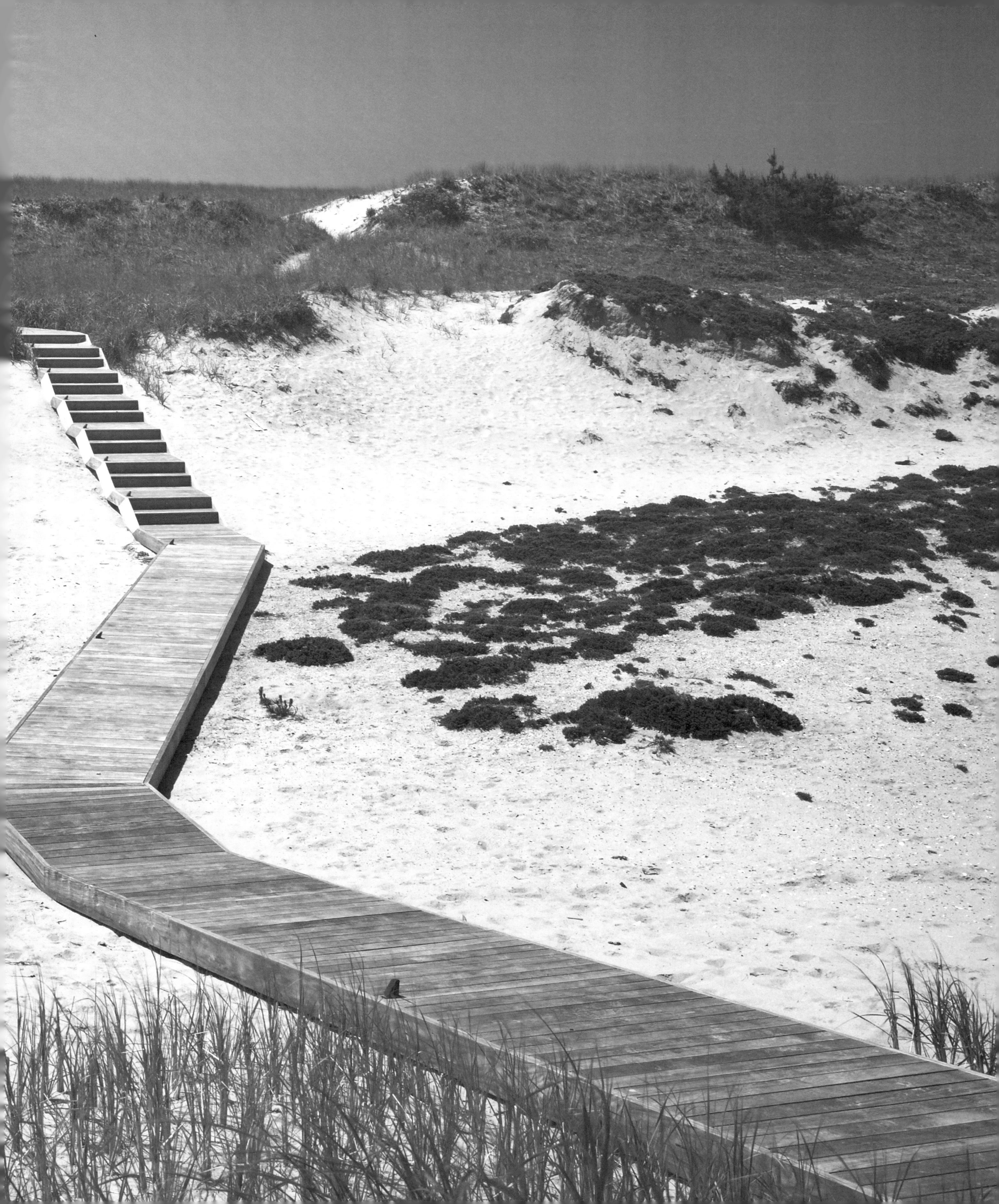

steven
GAMBREL

"In the 19th century, when sea captains returned to Sag Harbor after a year of whaling they were flush with ideas—and cash—and often remodeled and redecorated their homes. Their houses sometimes showcased Cantonese cabinets, collections of German porcelain or French clocks, all considered very modern at the time. Like those sea captains, I am inspired by travel; I love finding and assembling new collections and dragging them back to their new home. I have never understood why many equate the term 'modern' with 'spare.'"

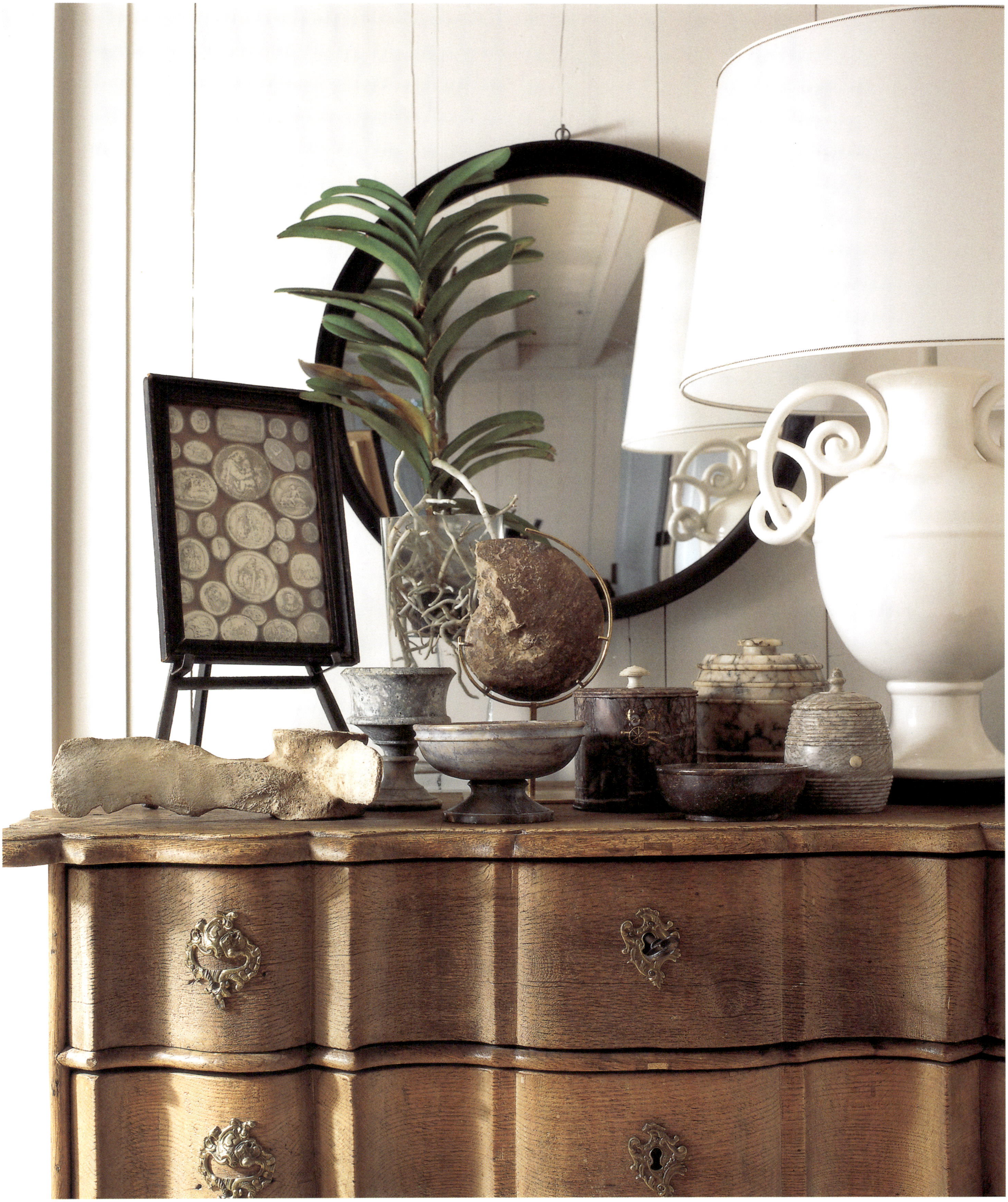

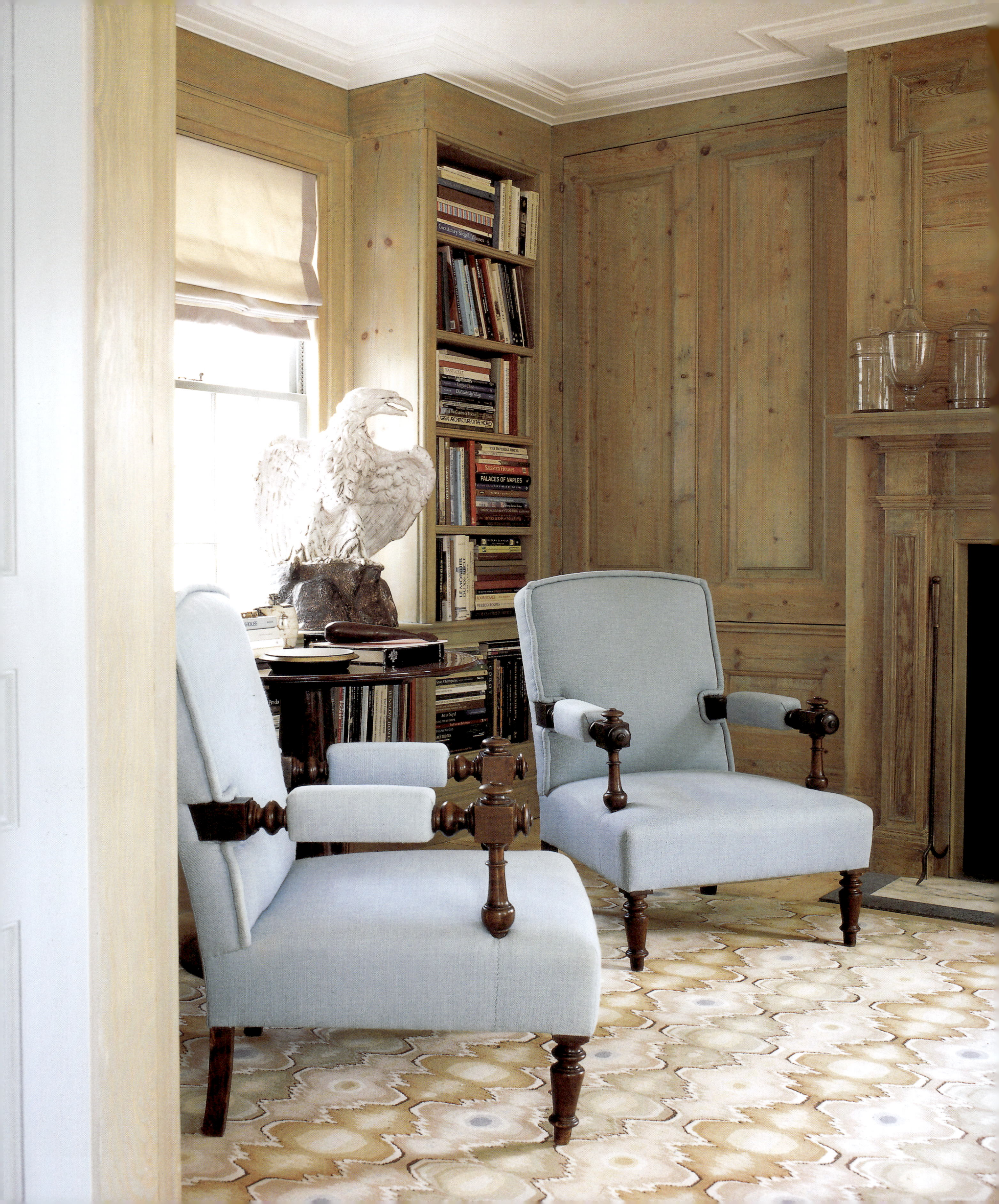

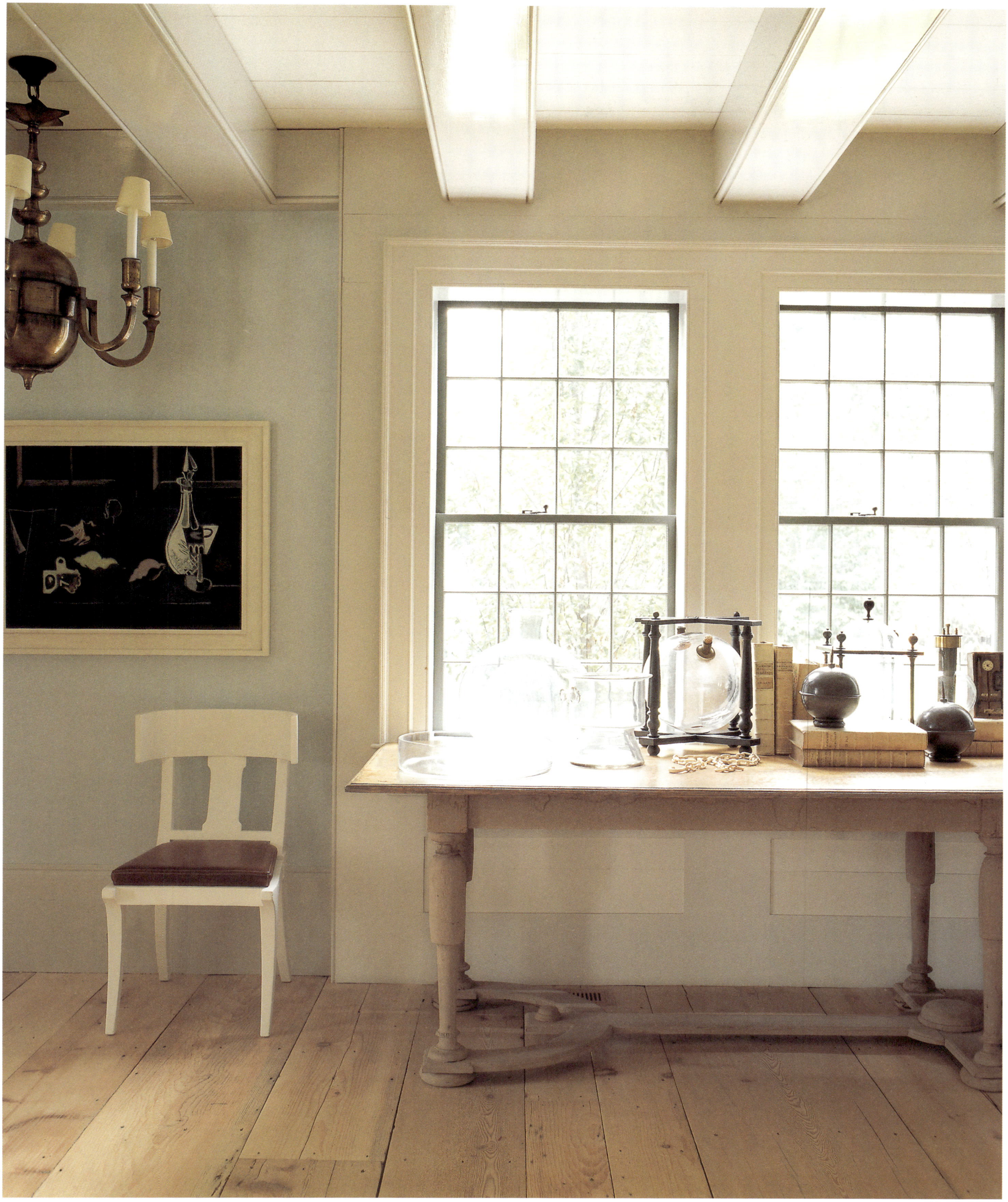

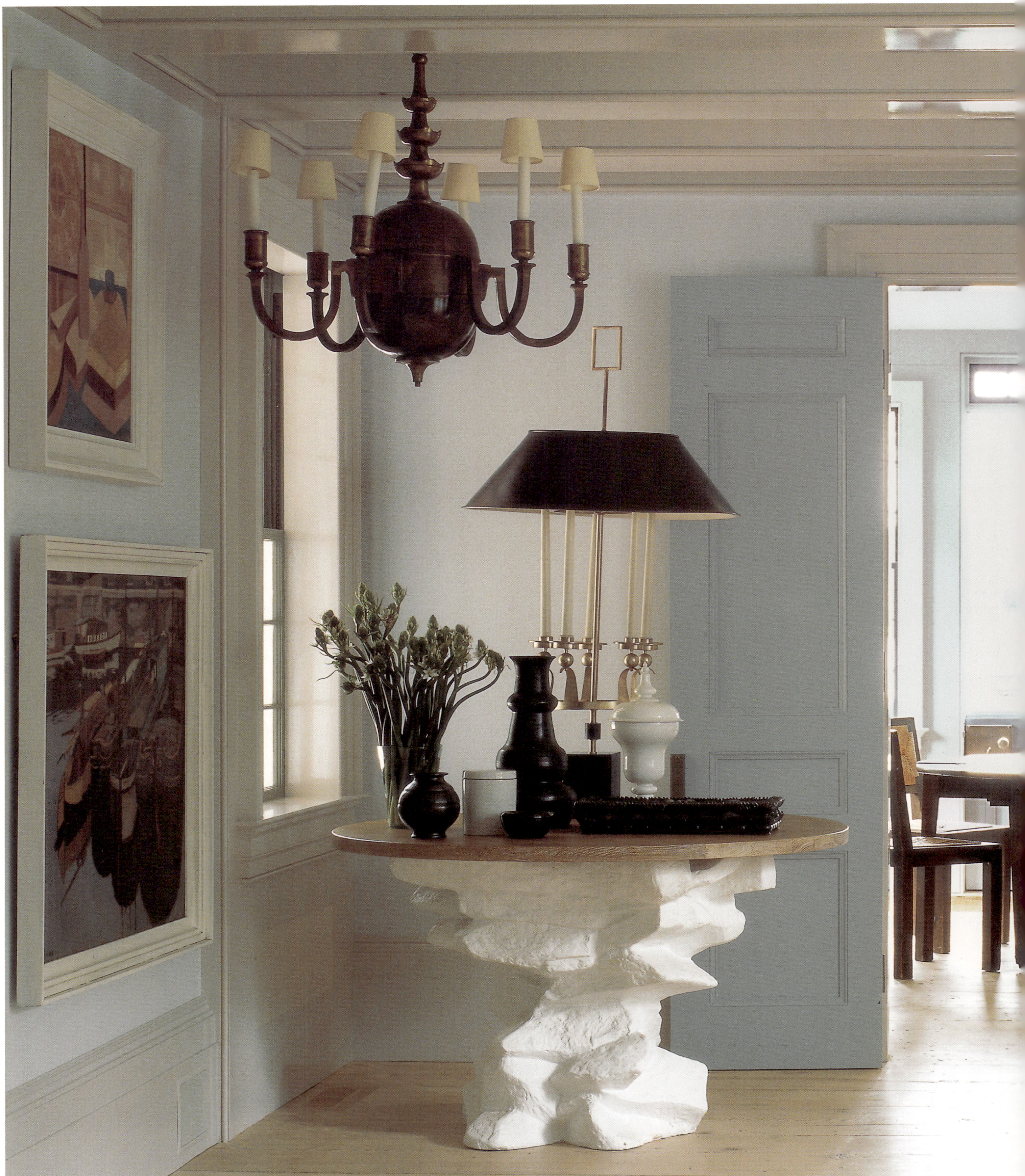

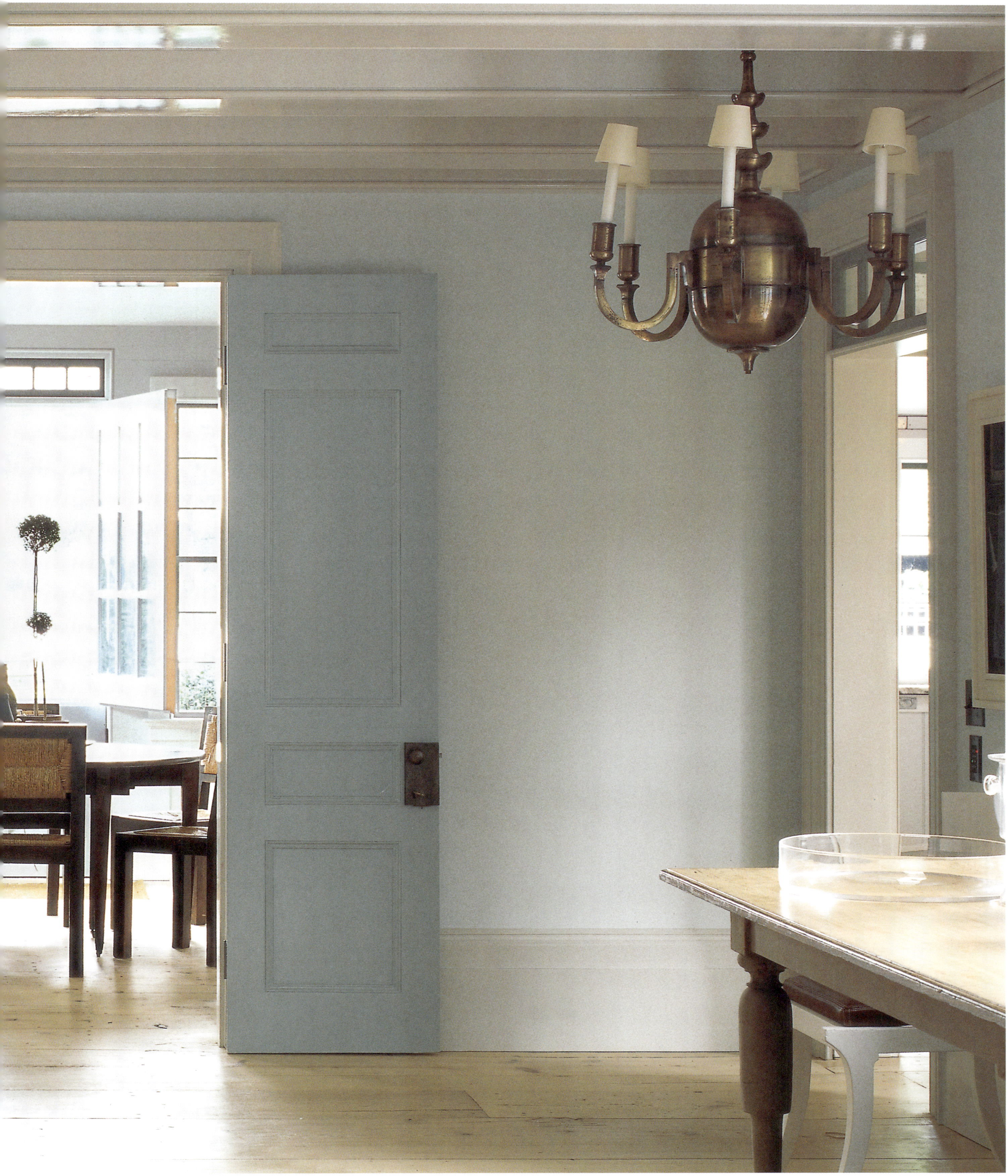

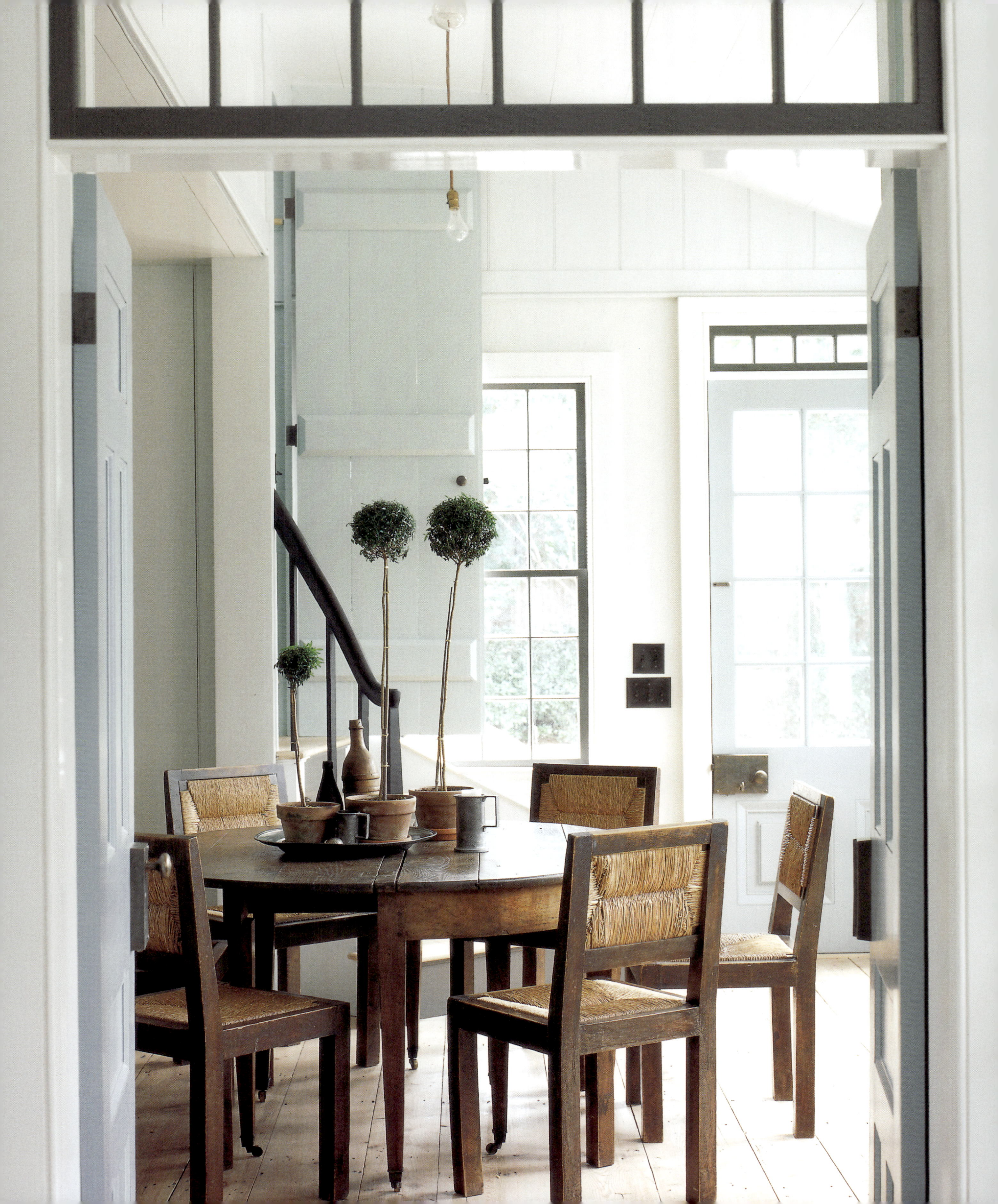

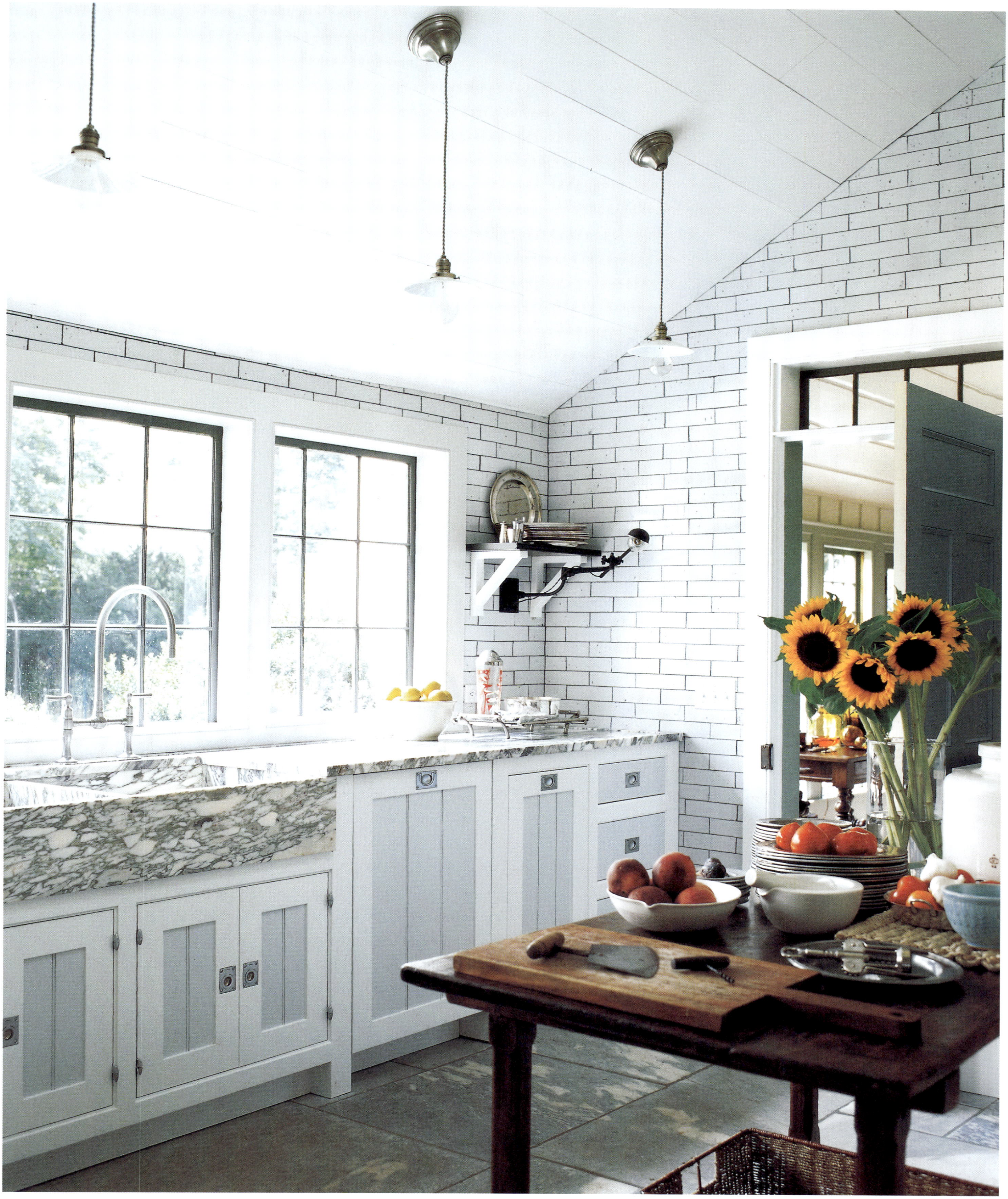

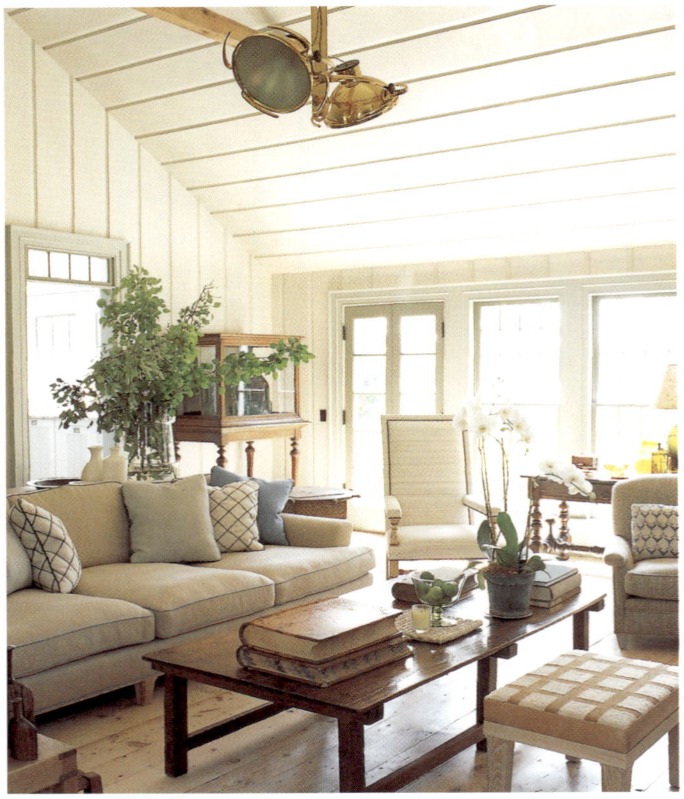

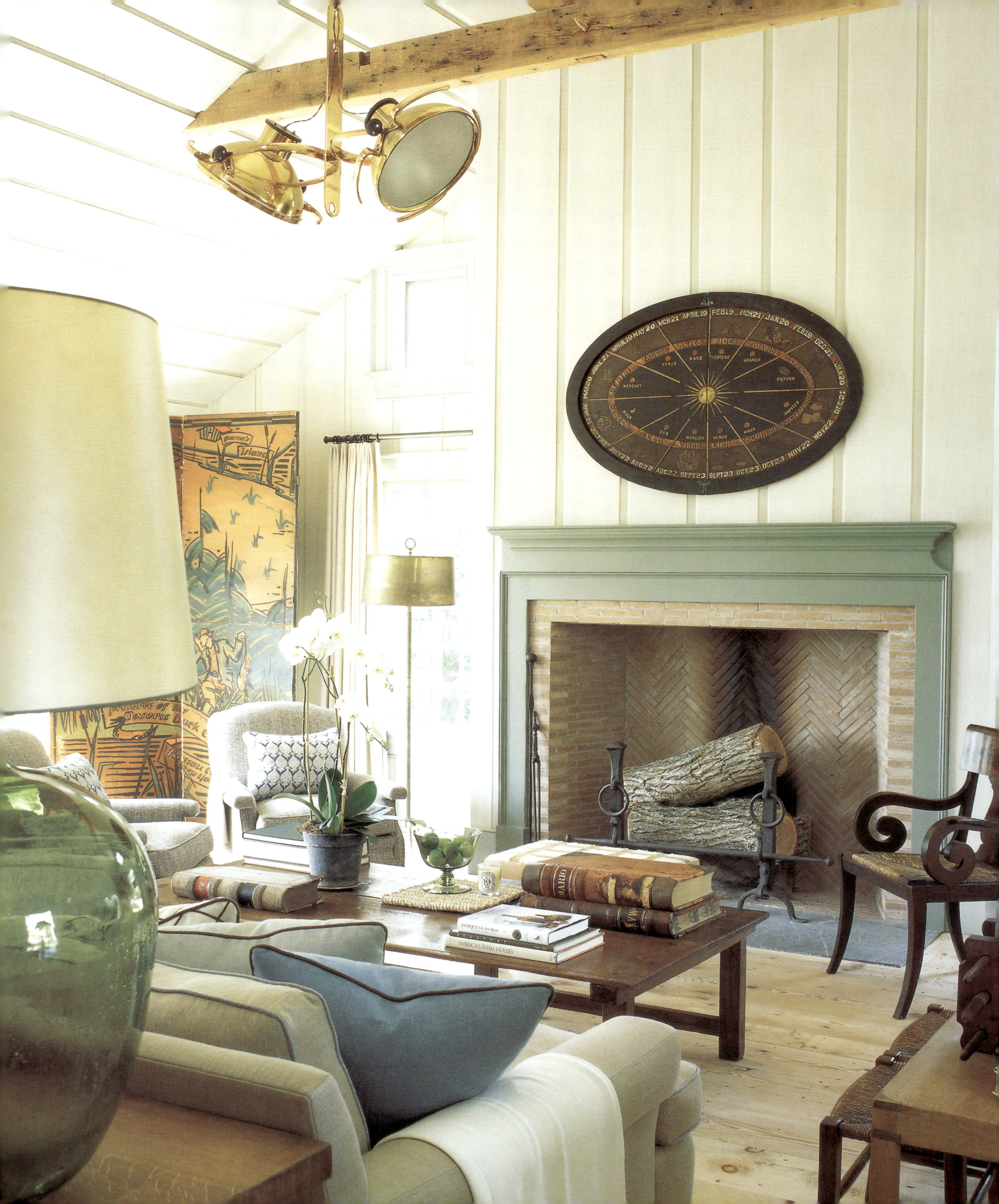

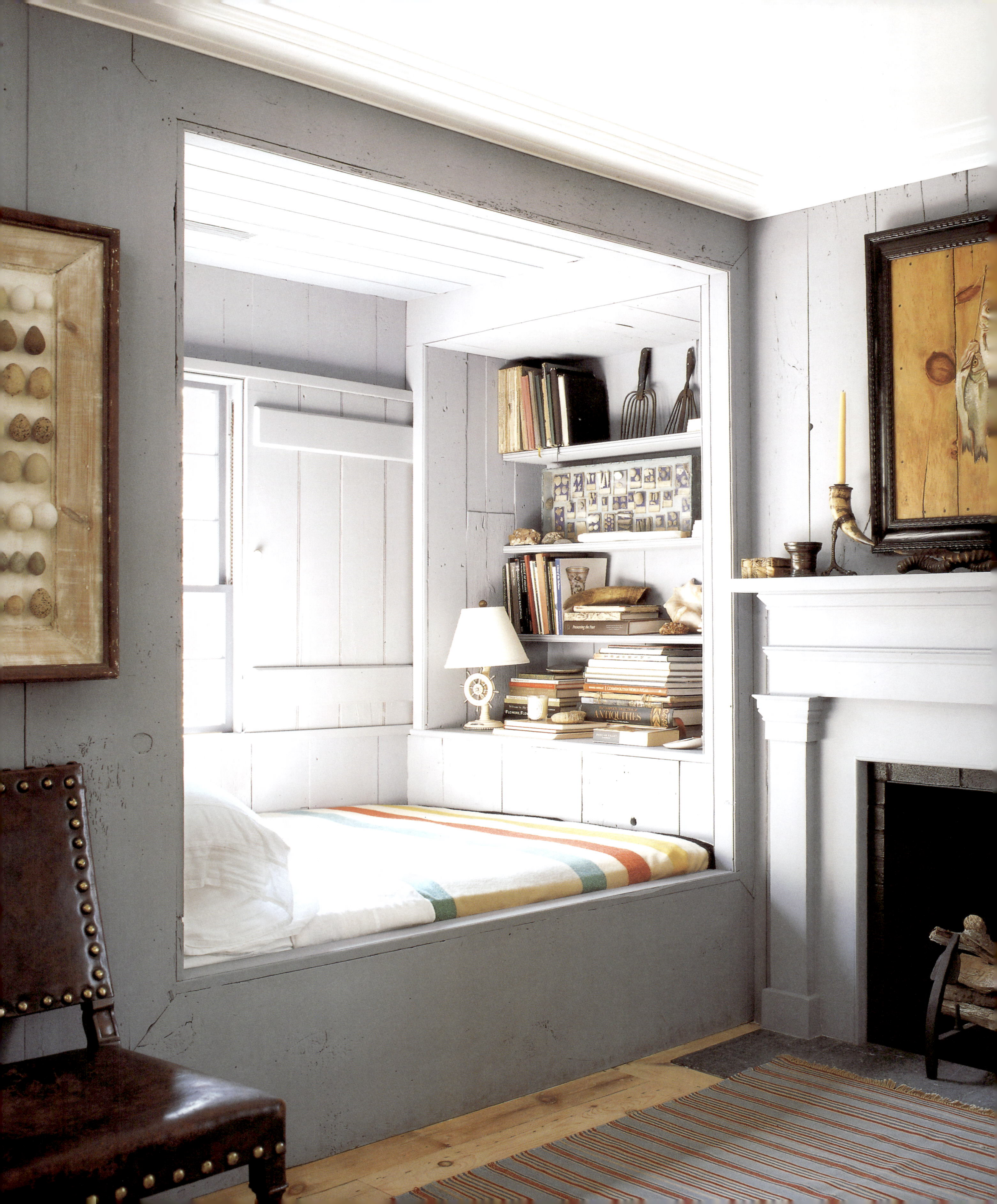

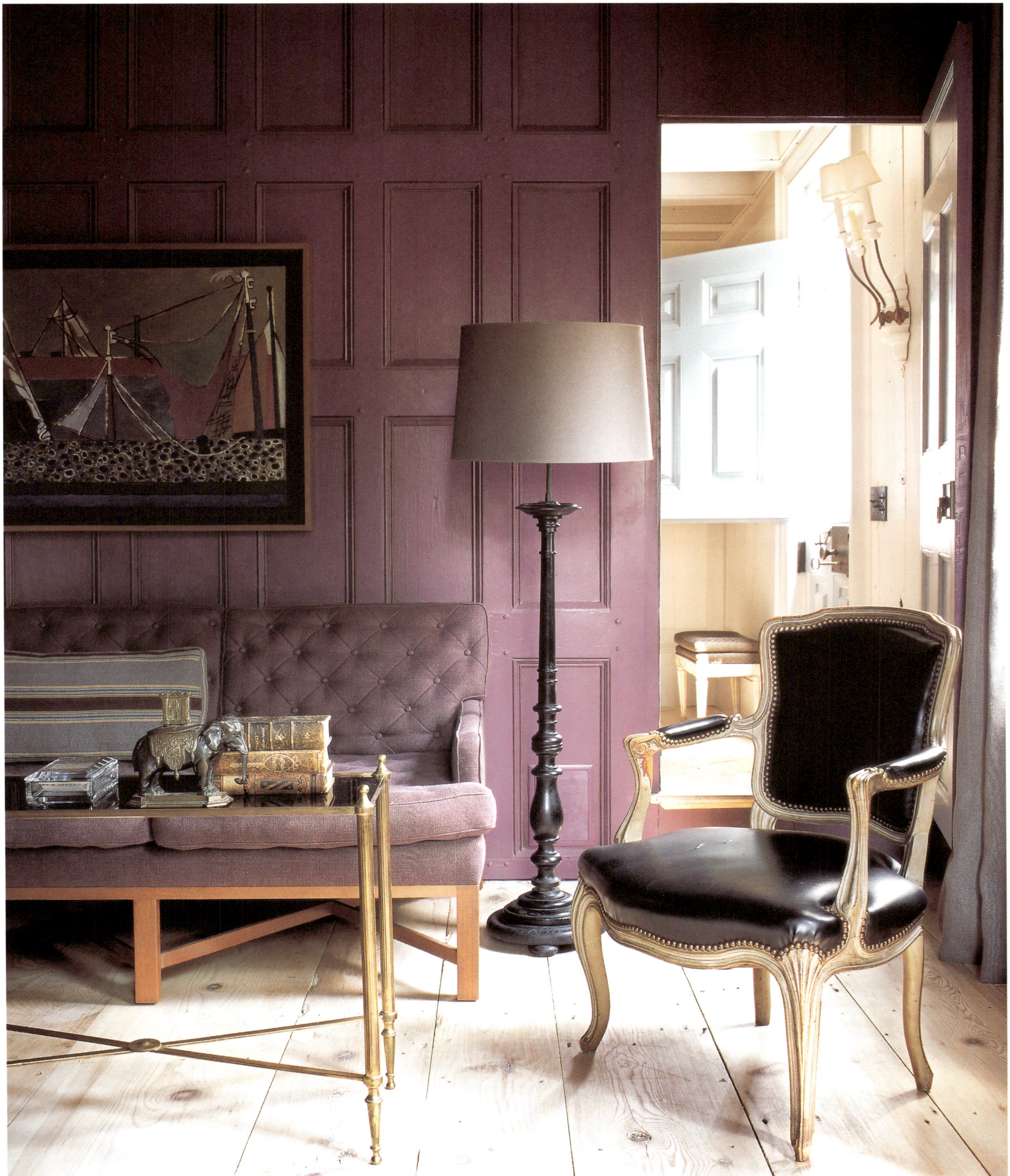

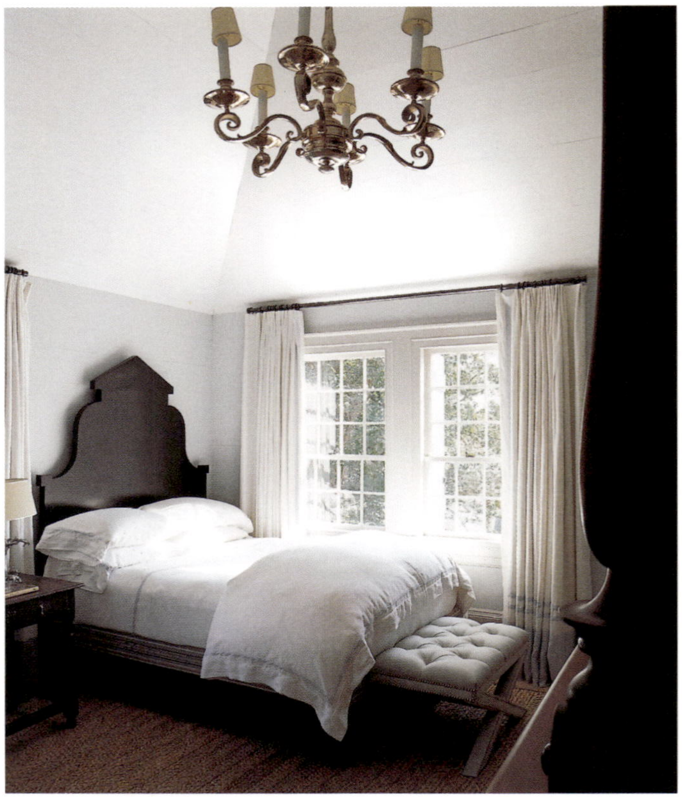

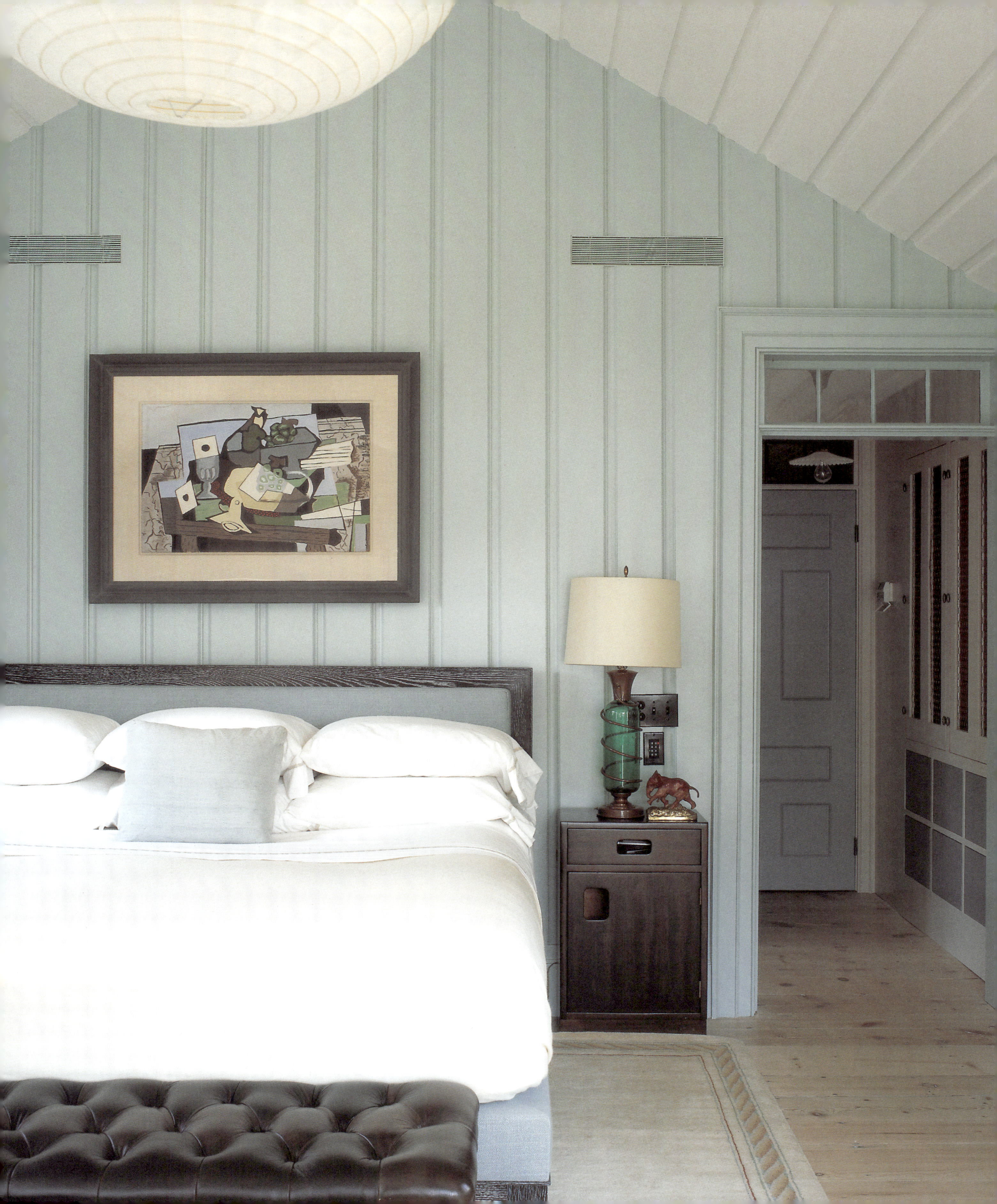

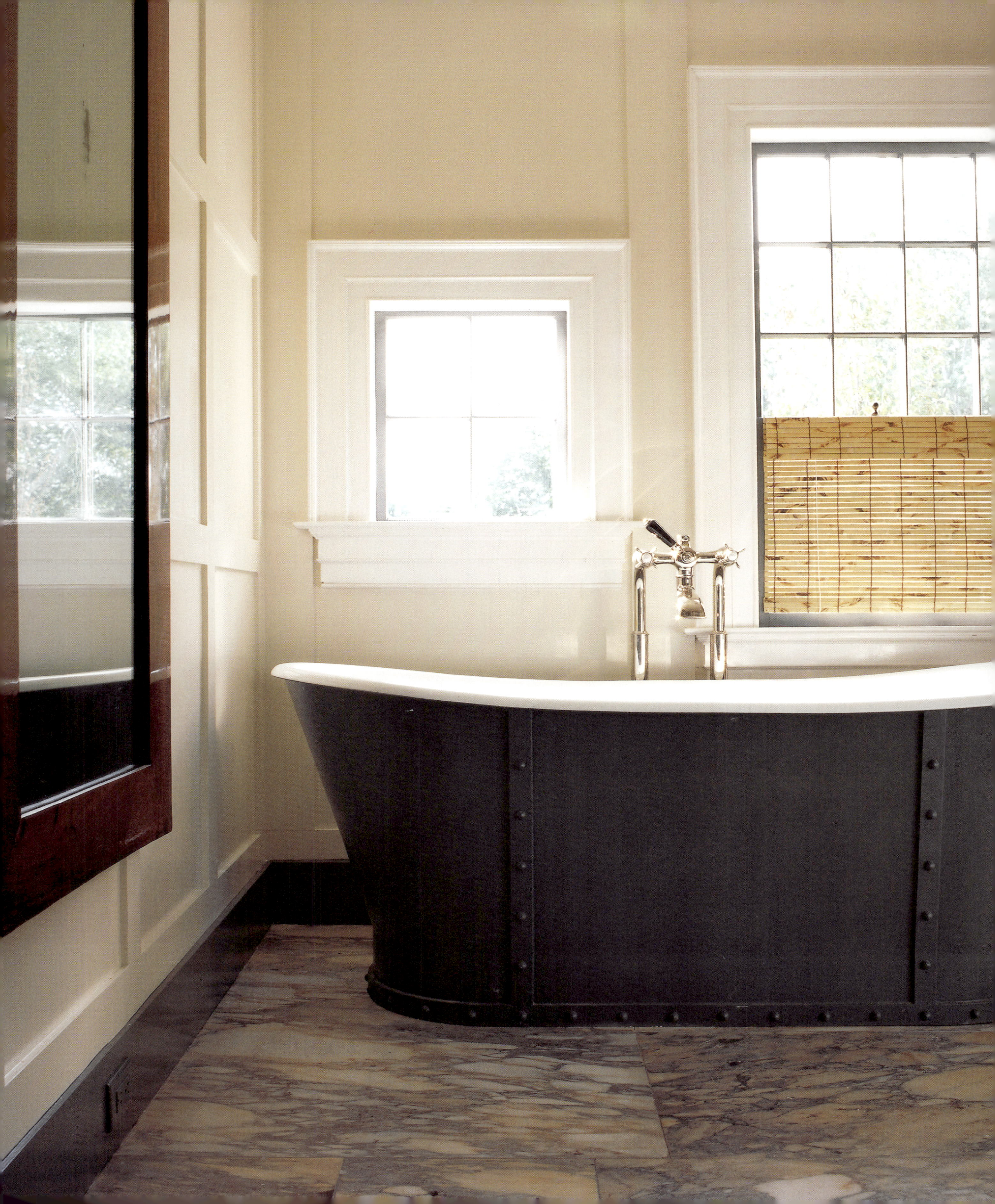

thomas
O'BRIEN

"I was thrilled to have the opportunity to work on a Norman Jaffe house with clients who have impeccable and eclectic taste in 20th-century furniture. My goal was to combine the interests of both the husband and the wife into one cohesive house—a house that is both handsome and distinguished, but also comfortable. The quality of the light and atmosphere in the Hamptons encourages one to create interiors that reverberate with warmth and an understated glamour."

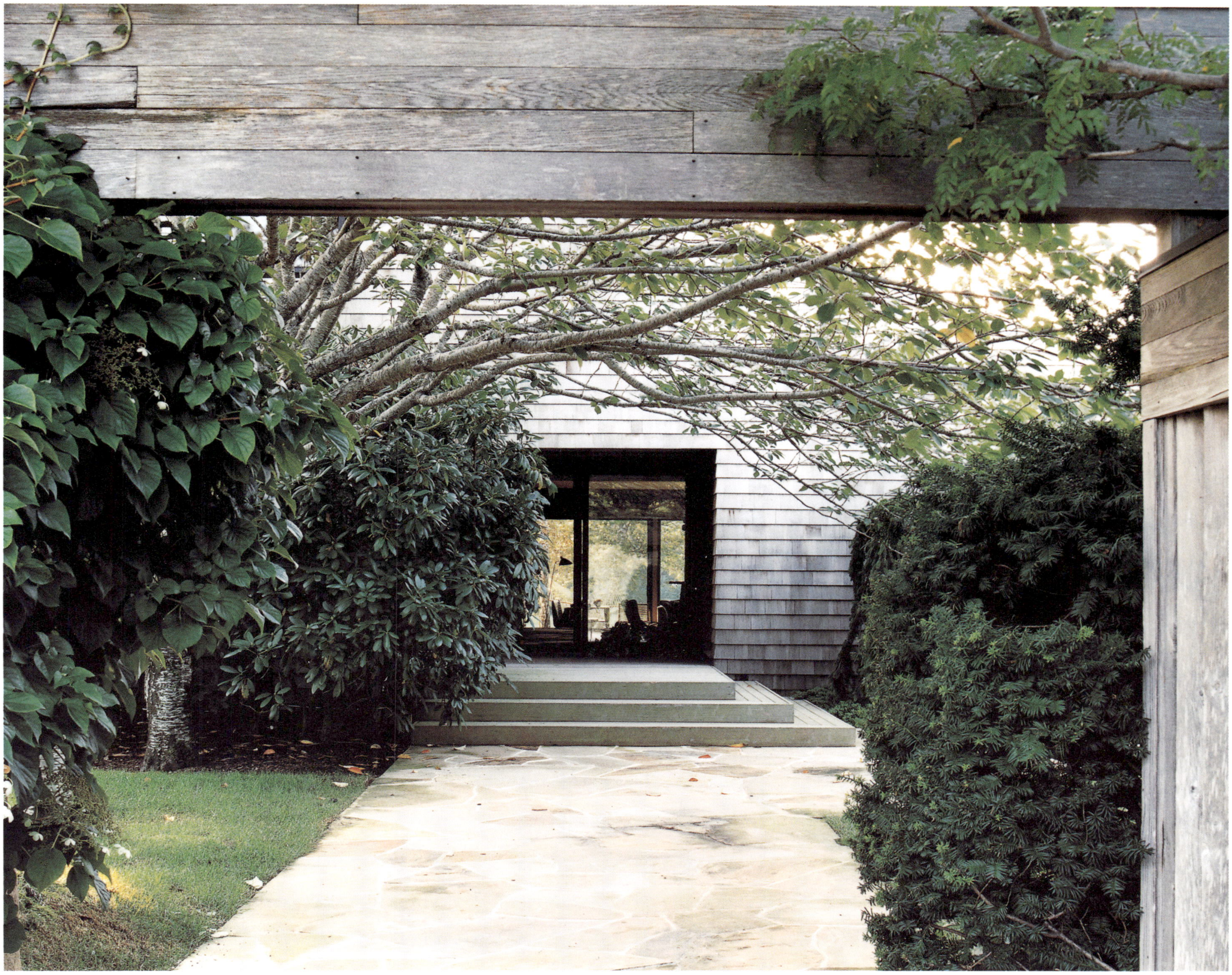

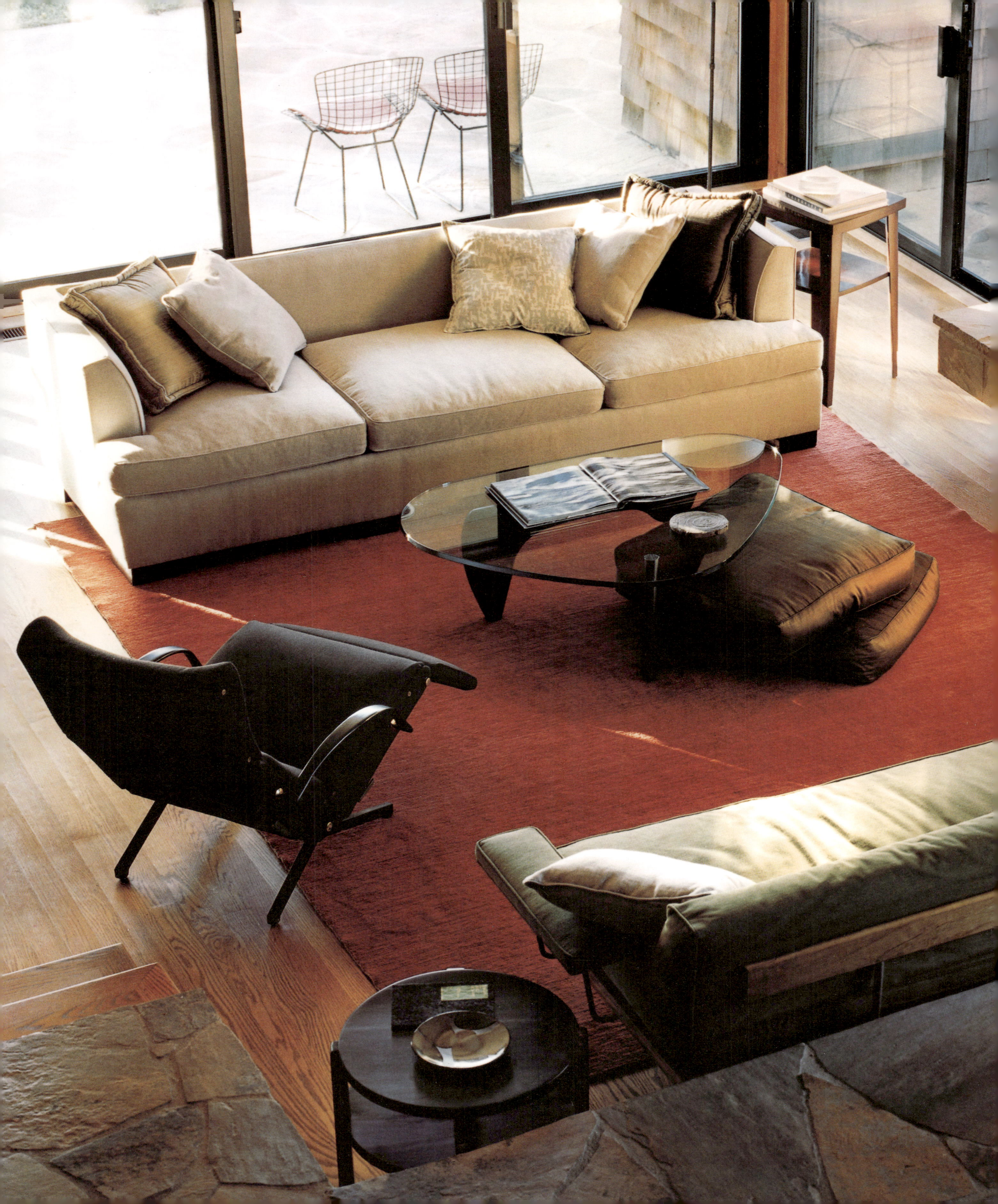

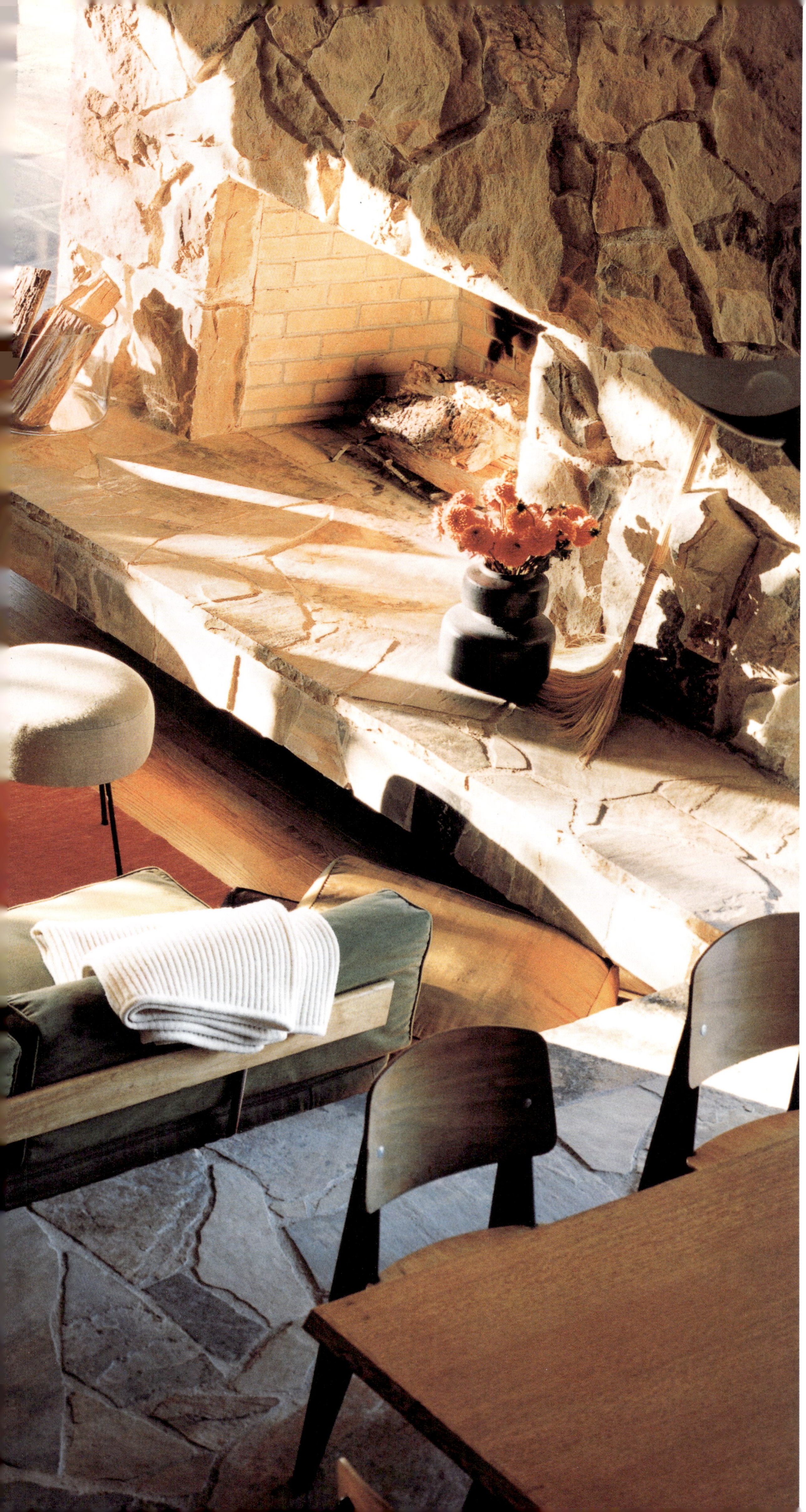

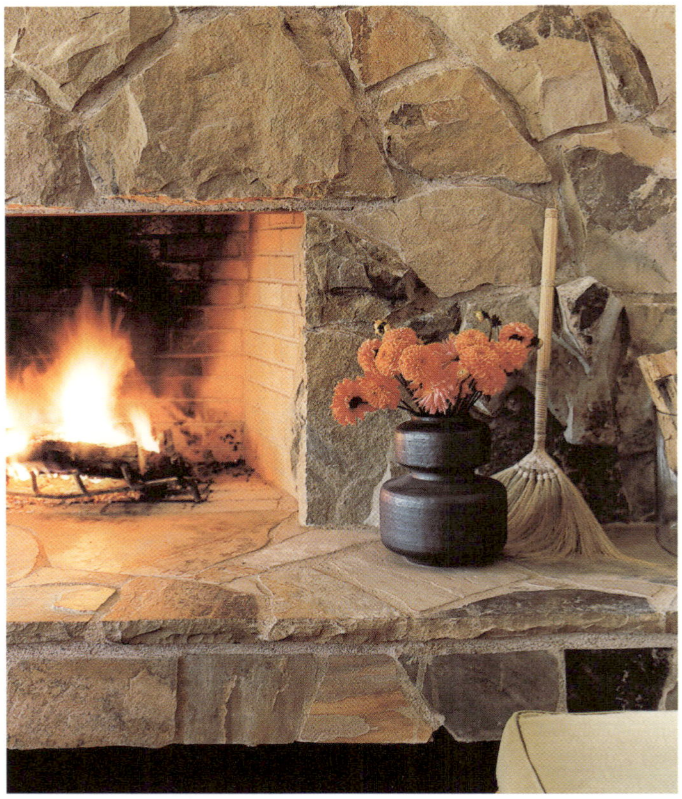

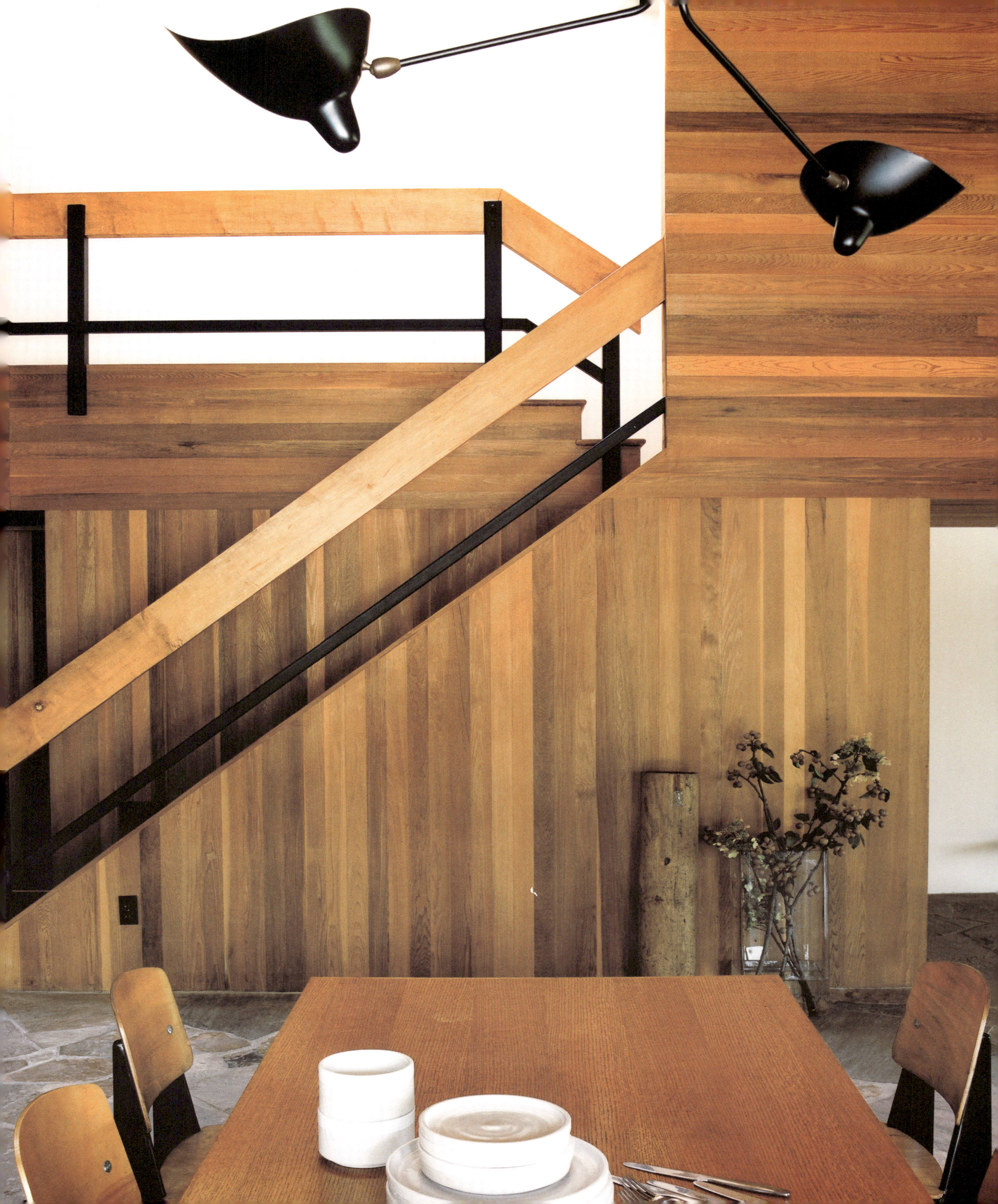

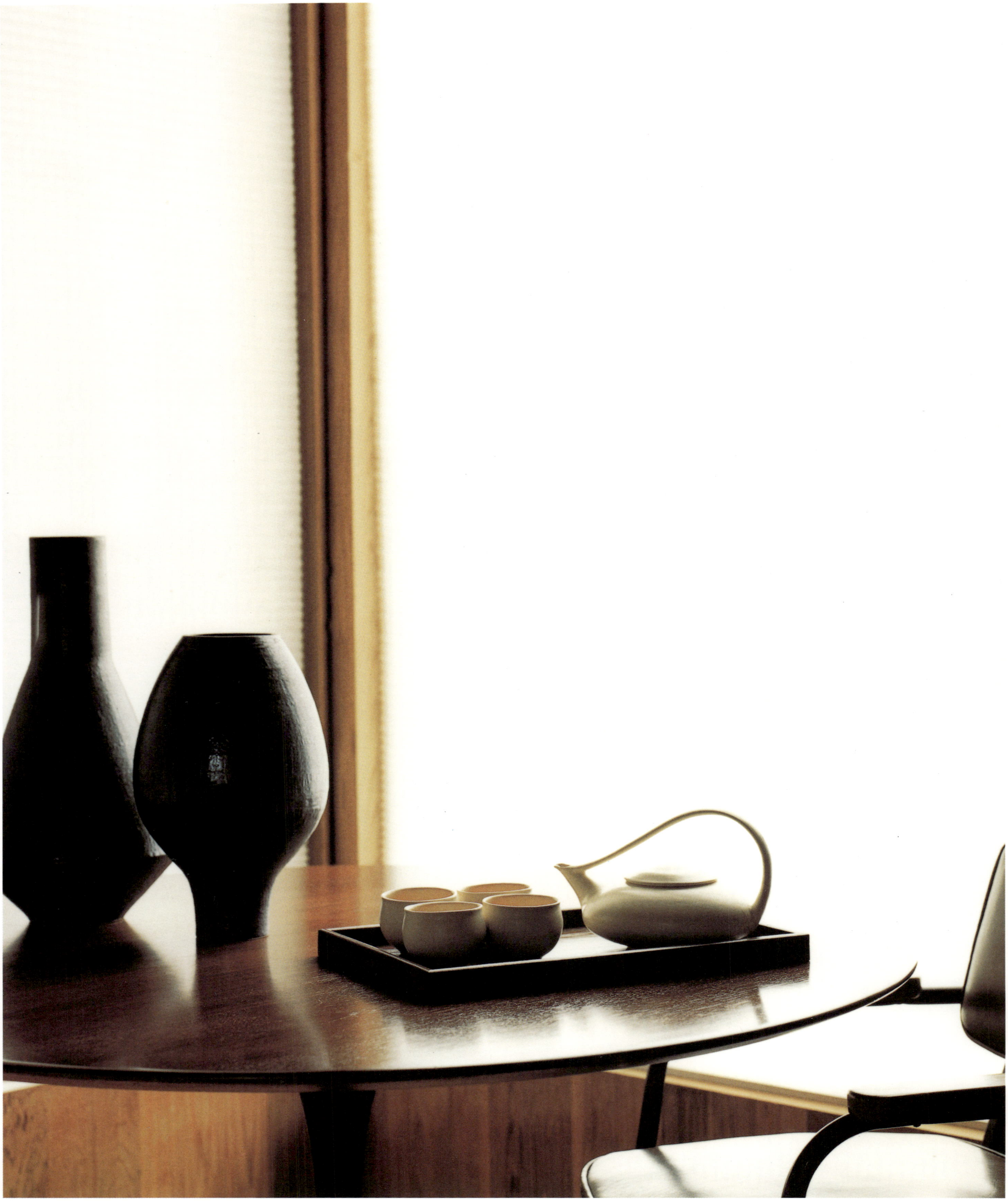

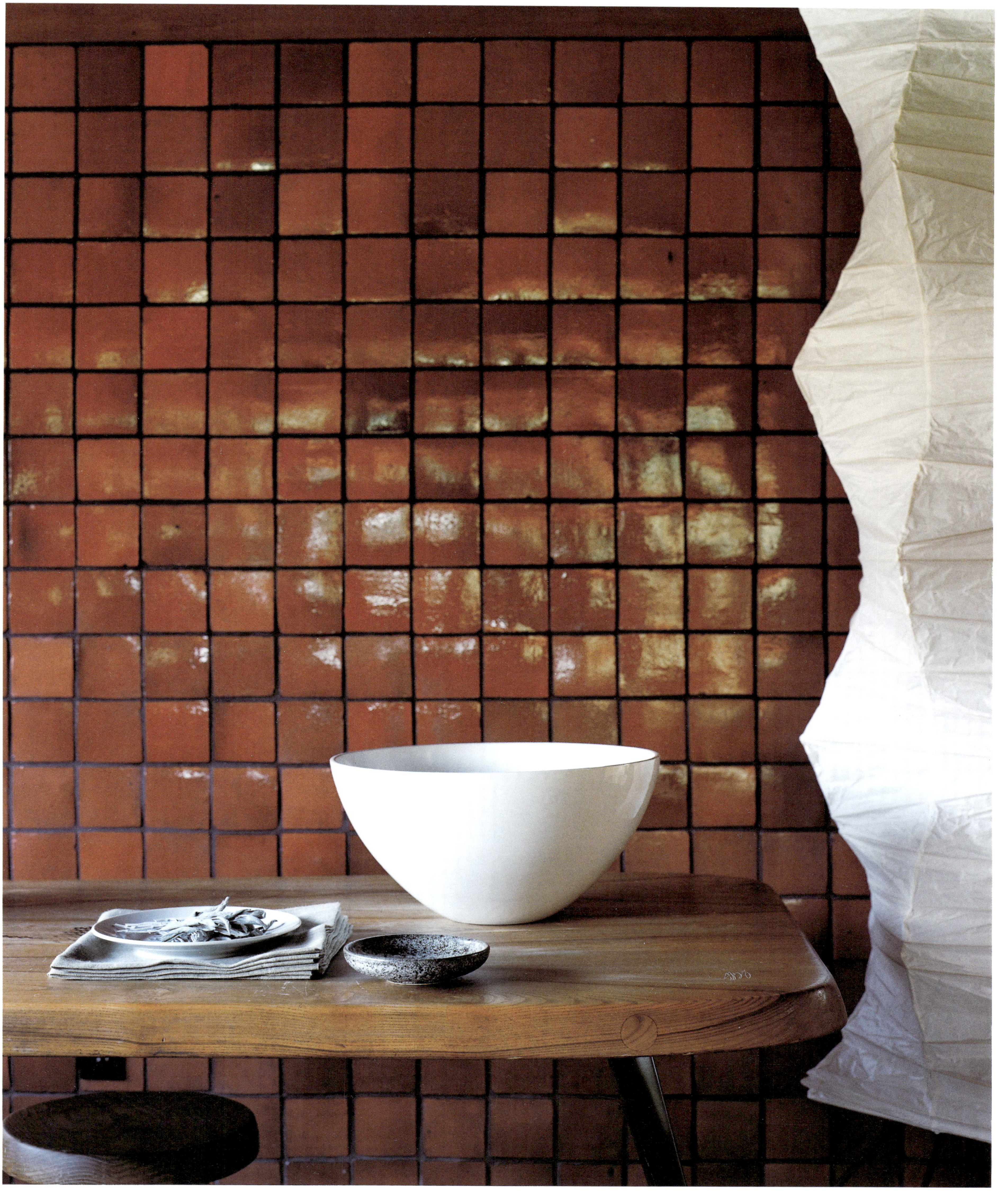

LITERARY OUTLAW
TED MORGAN
ENDURANCE
THE INFERNO OF DANTE
ROBERT PINSKY
Best Loved Poems of the American People
THE WORKS OF OSCAR WILDE
COLLINS
Jack Kerouac
On the Road
JFK
THE POWER BROKER
ROBERT A. CARO

PALACE WALK
NAGUIB MAHFOUZ
GREAT BOOKS
The Noonday Demon
American Poetry
CAMILLE
PAGLIA
MICHAEL ONDAATJE
ALICE MUNRO
TO KILL A Mockingbird

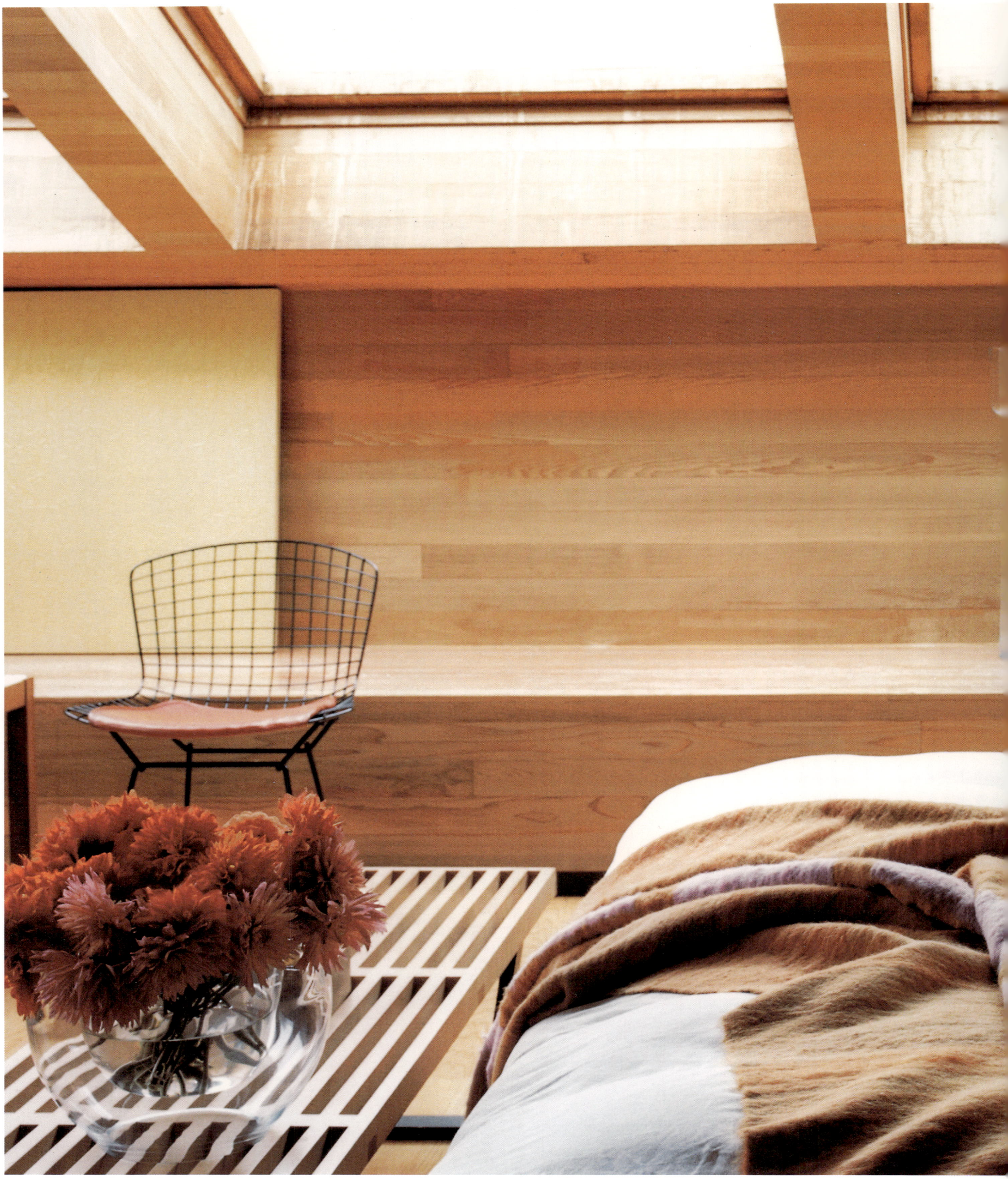

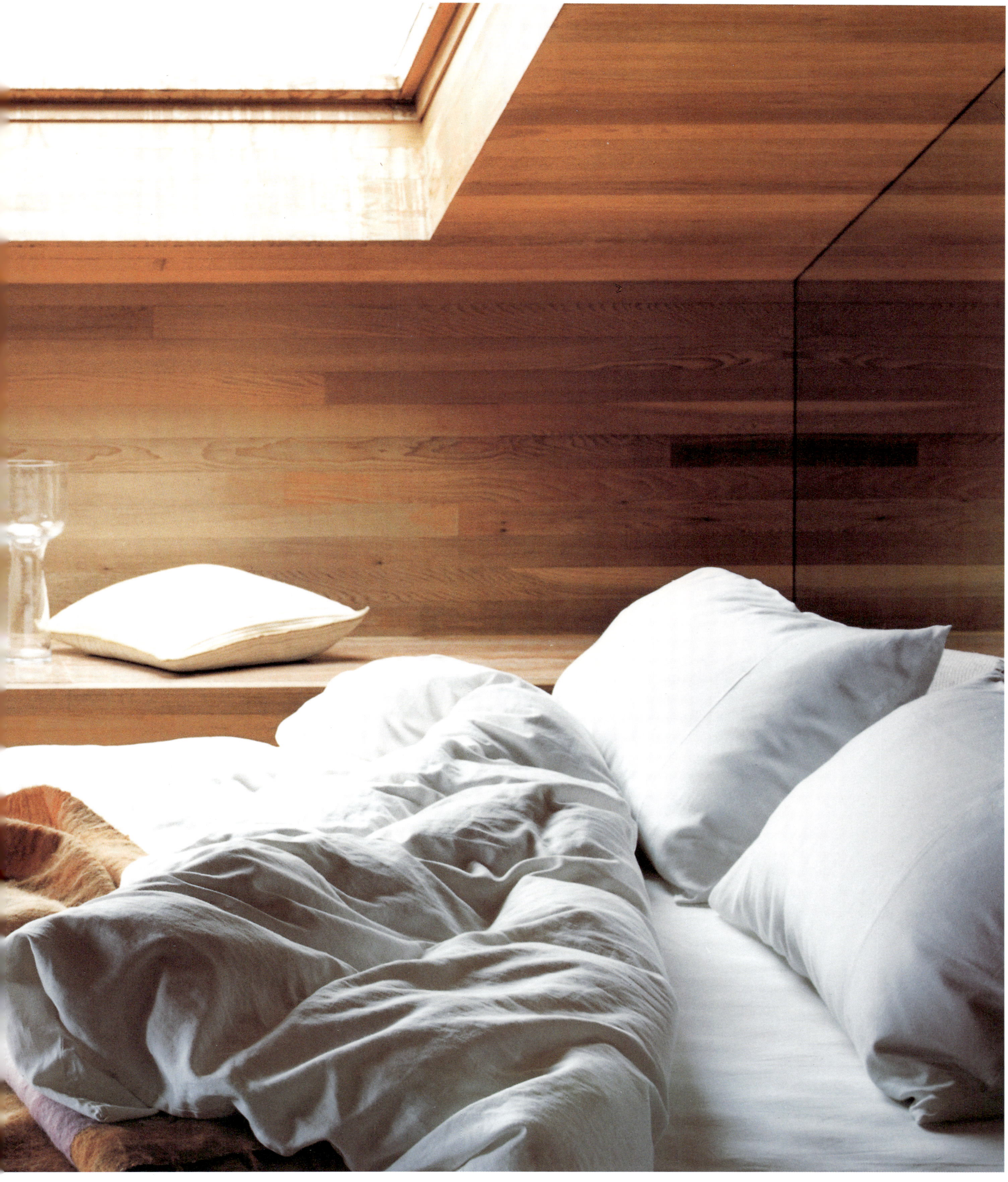

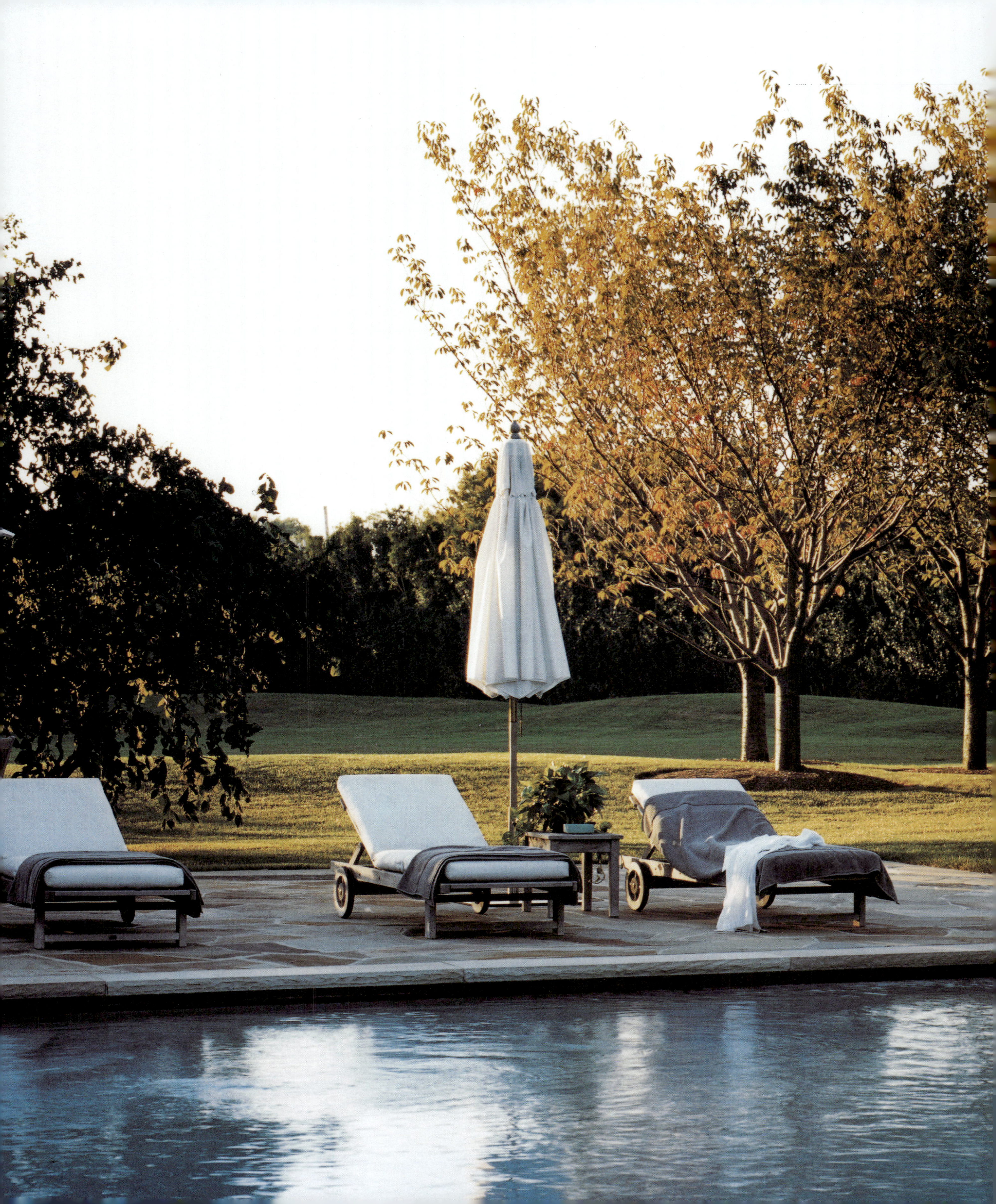

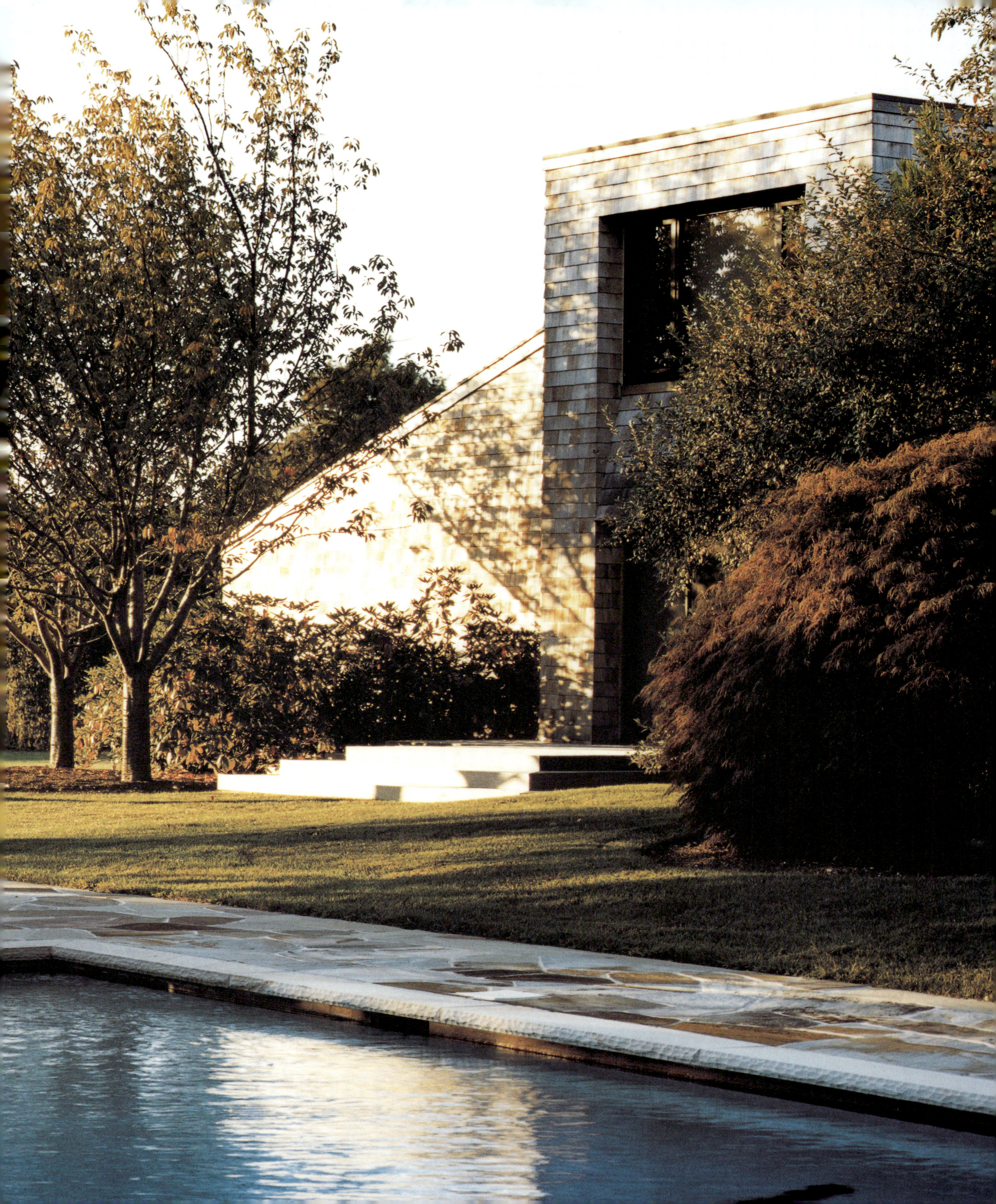

jamie
DRAKE

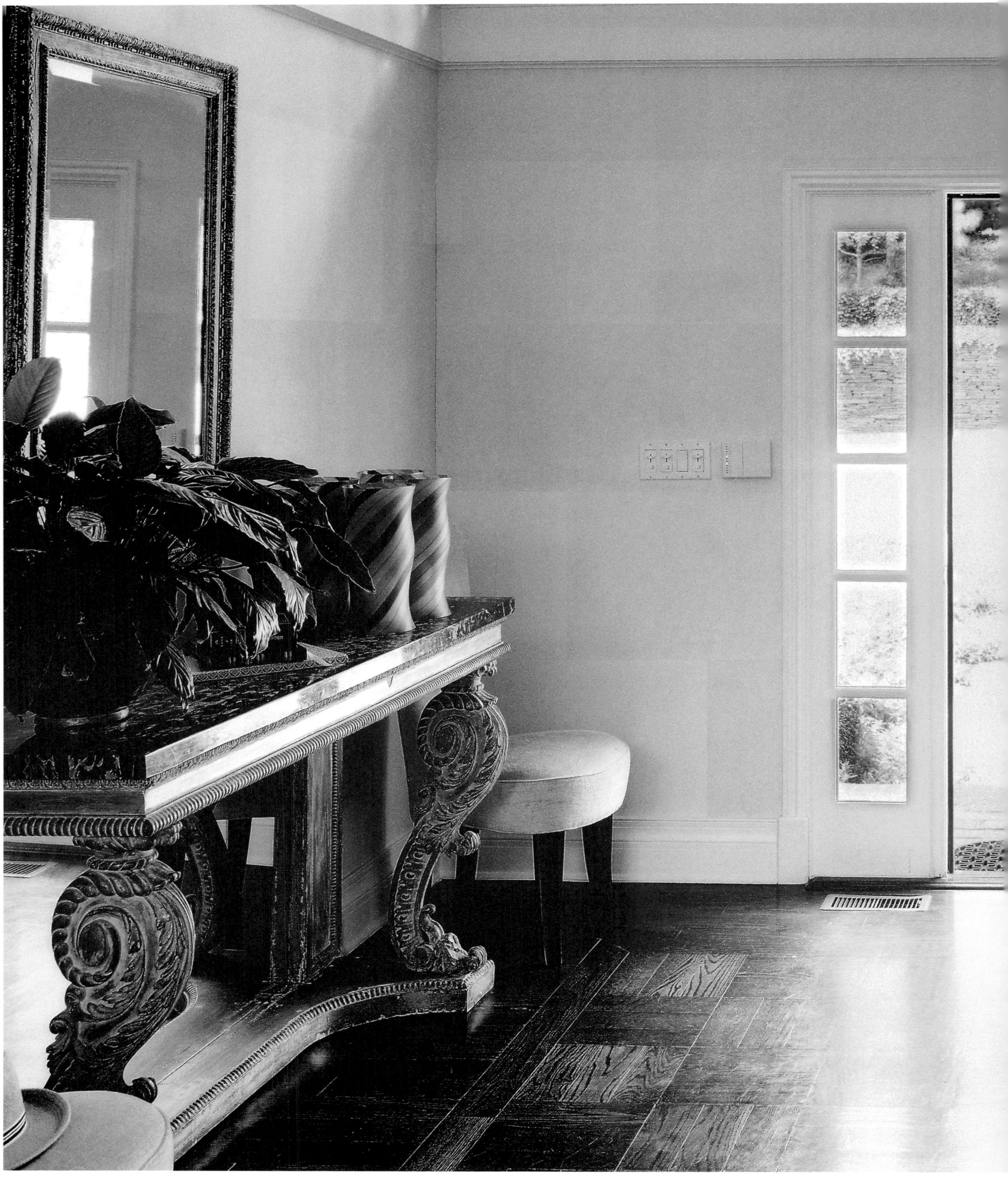

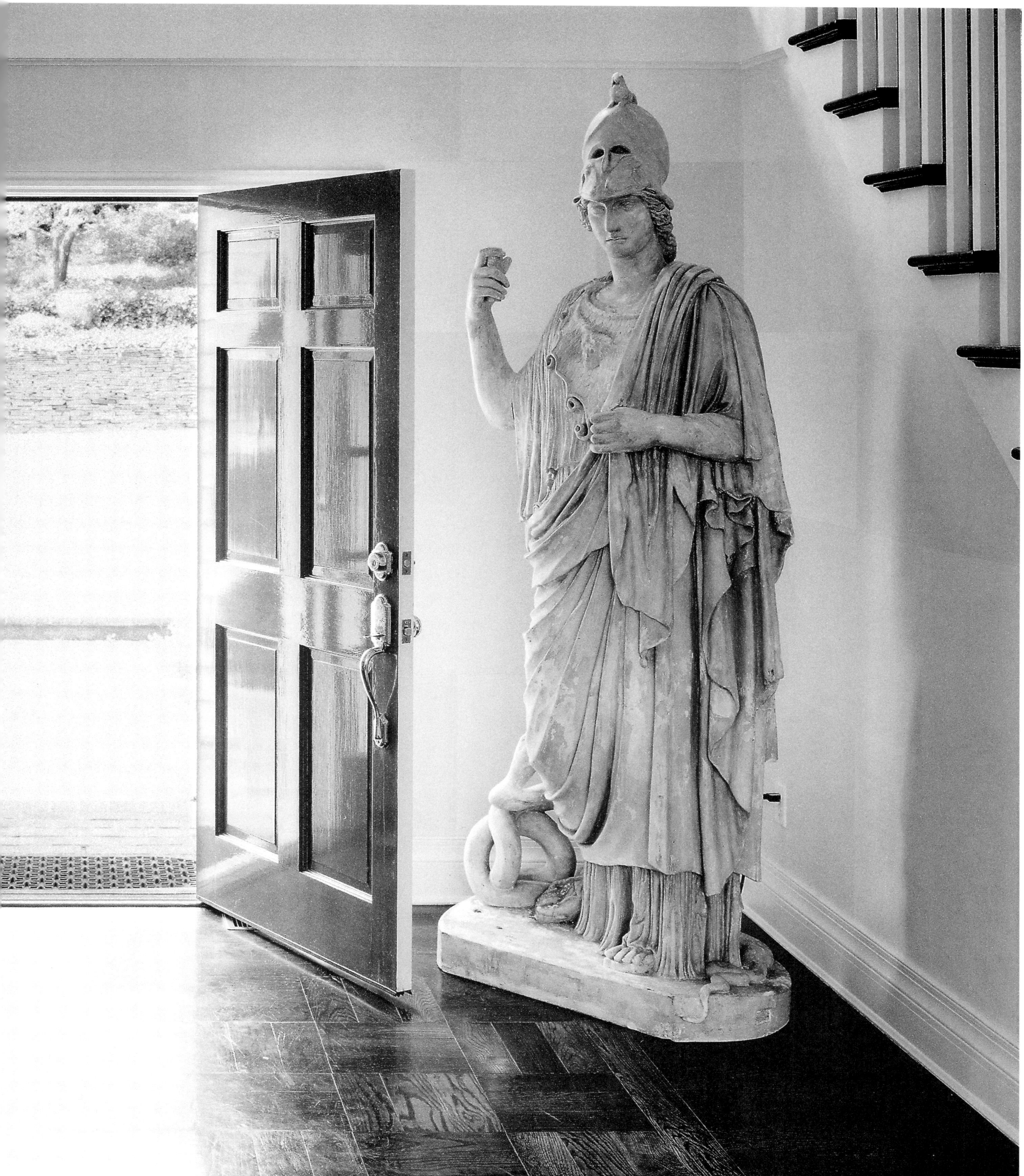

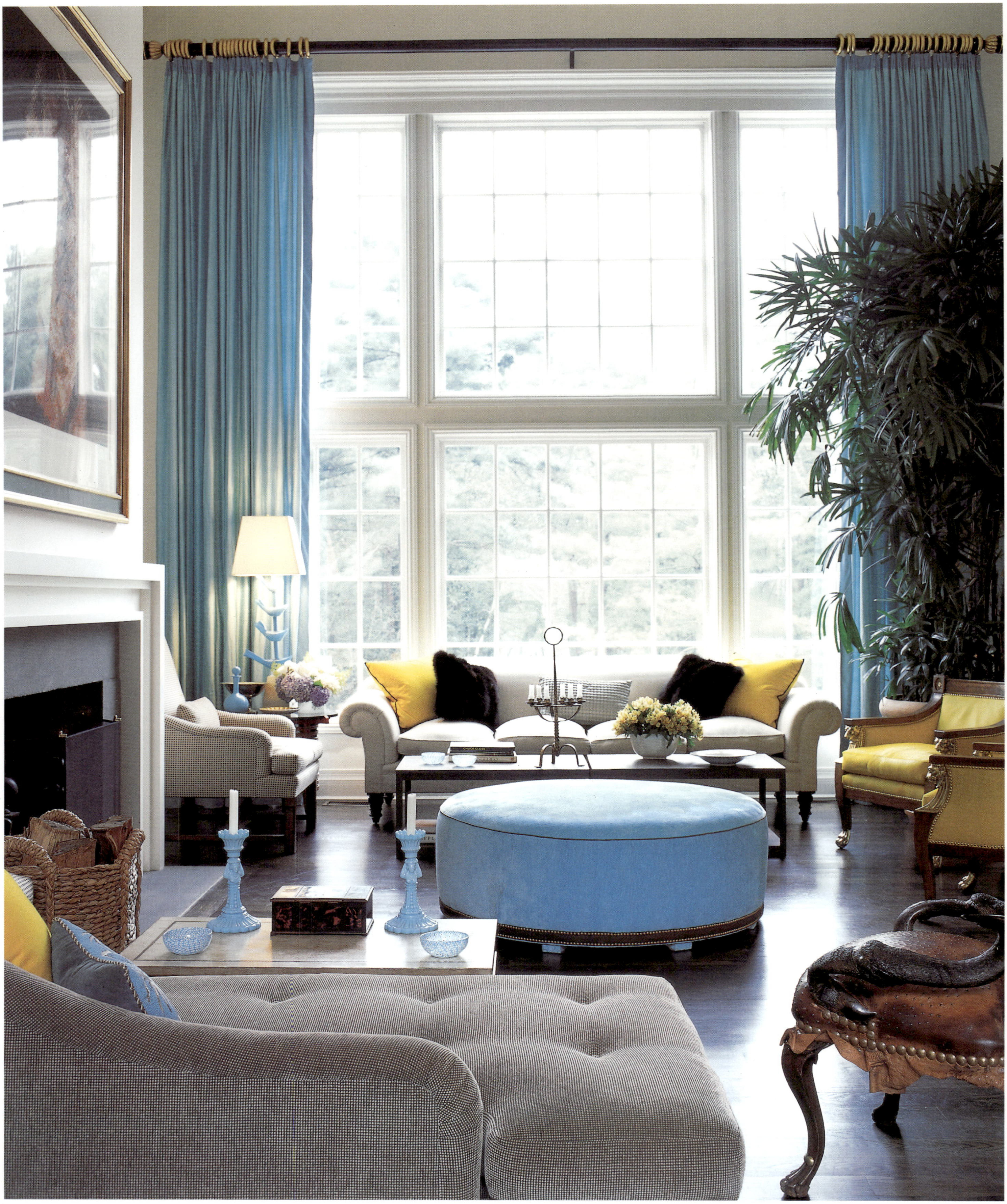

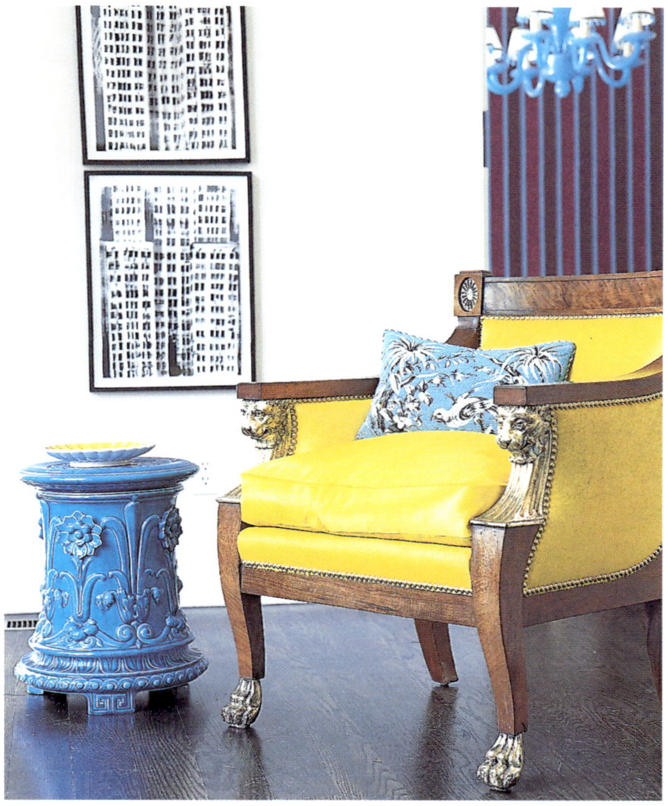

"Everyone calls it the beach, but for me the Hamptons have always been the country… more eccentric English, than farmer-in-the-dell. On my way to the Hamptons, I wind down into the lush forestry and shed my city slicker for a more relaxed but no less colorful repose: a Corniche convertible instead of a tractor, chrome yellow pony skin rather than gingham."

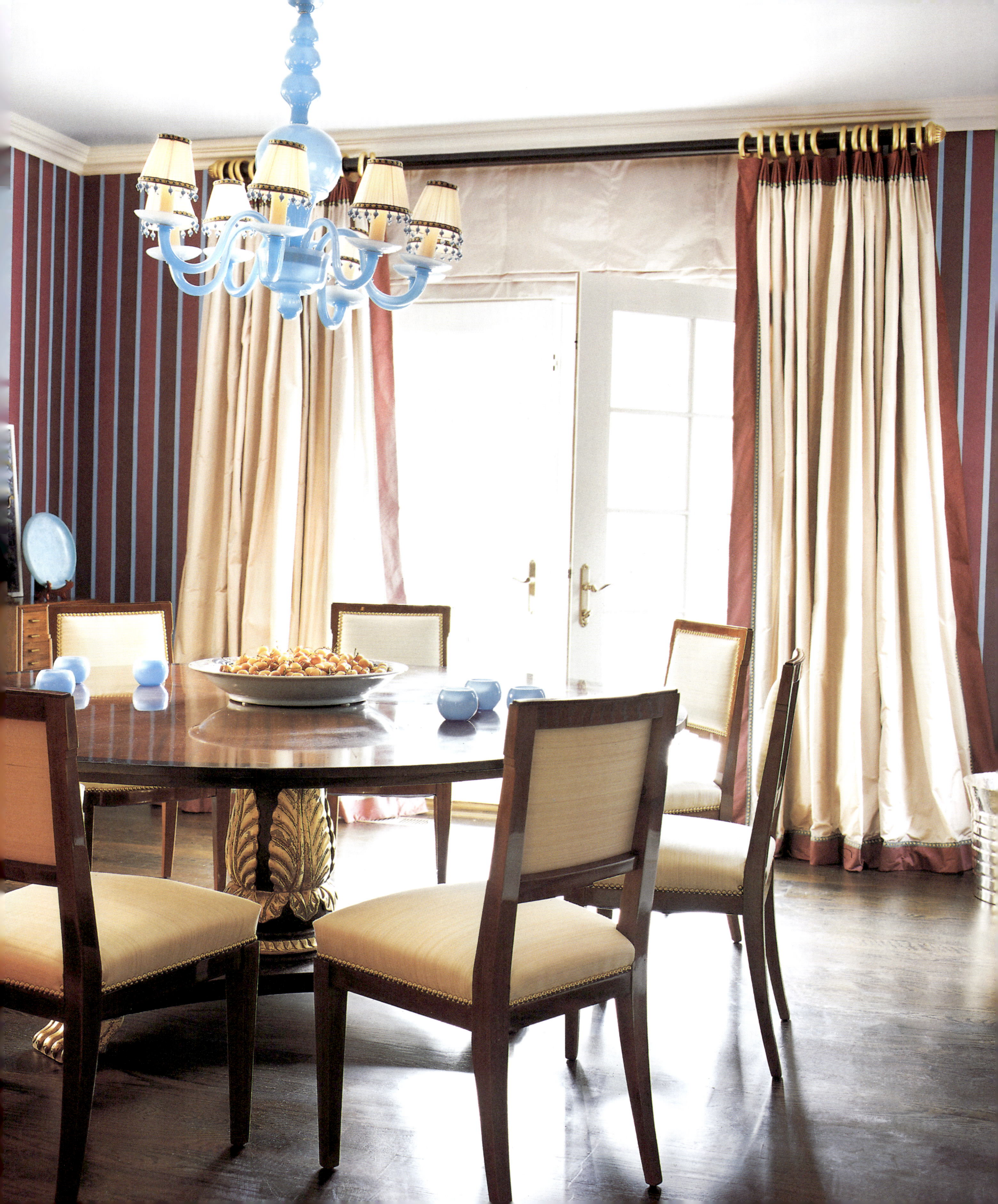

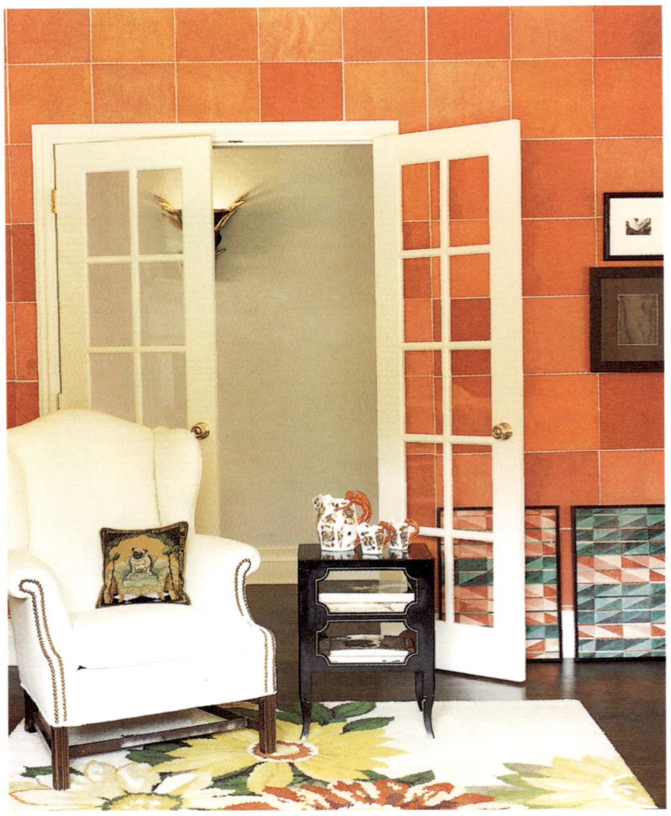

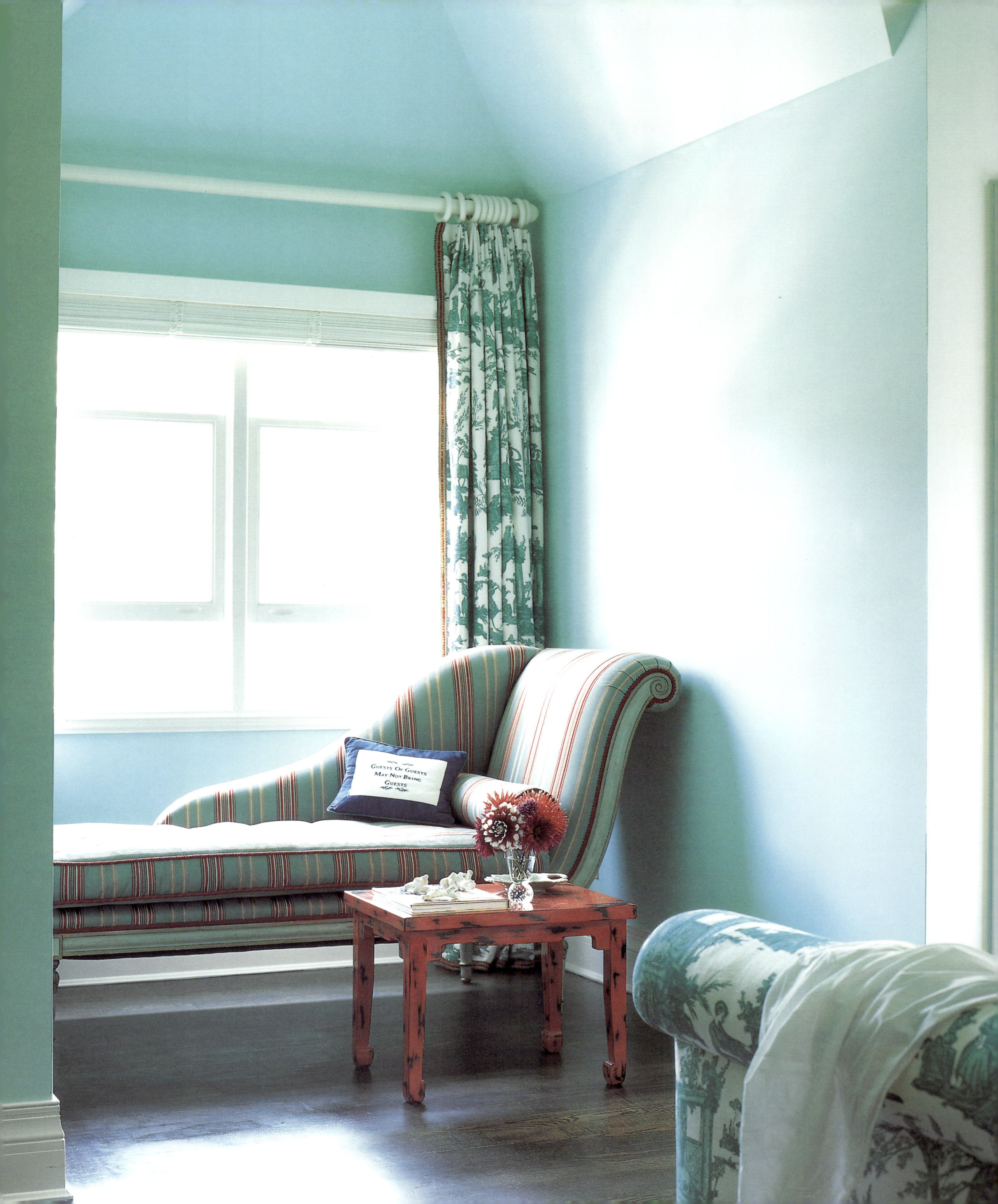
Guests Of Guests
May Not Bring
Guests

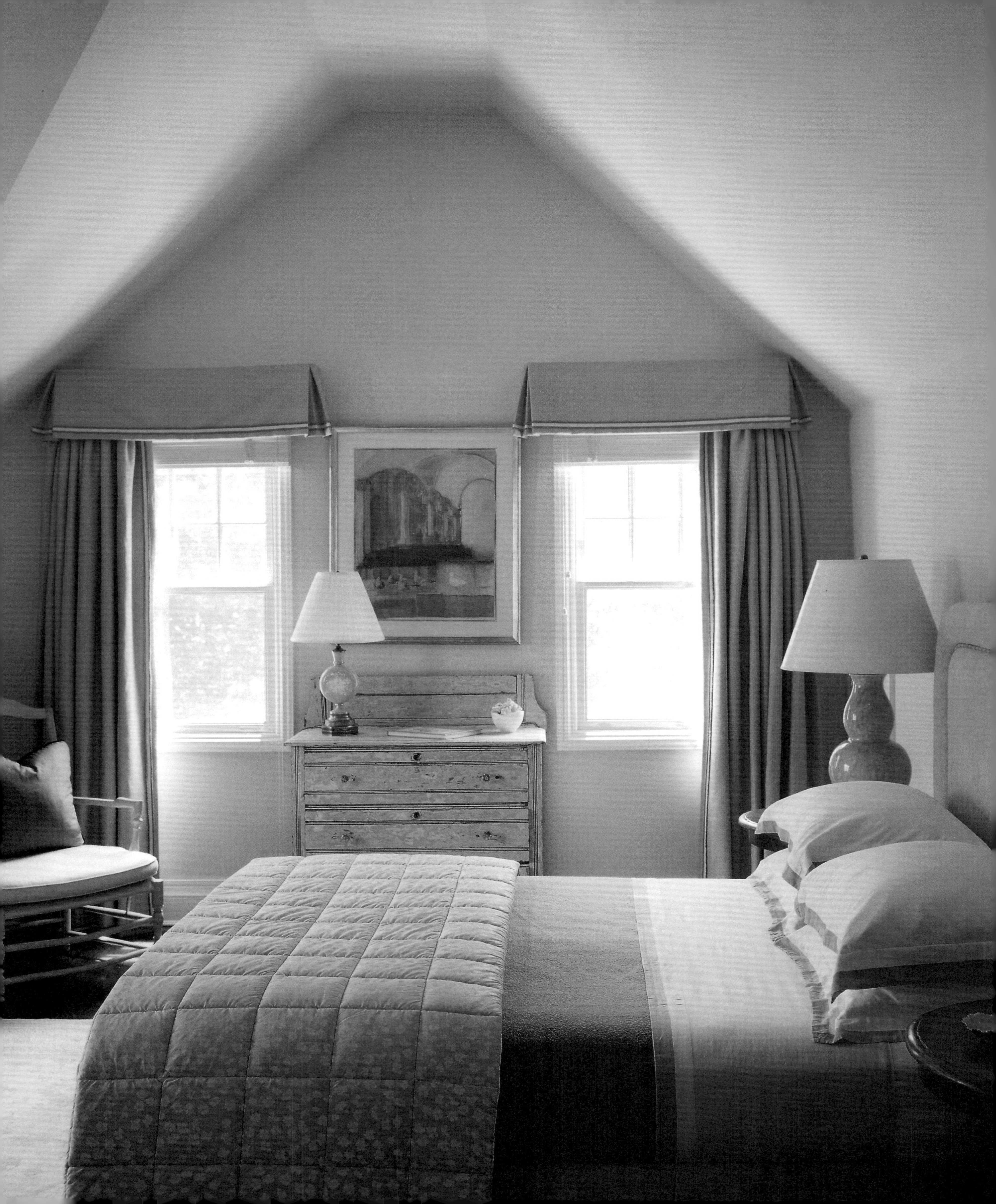

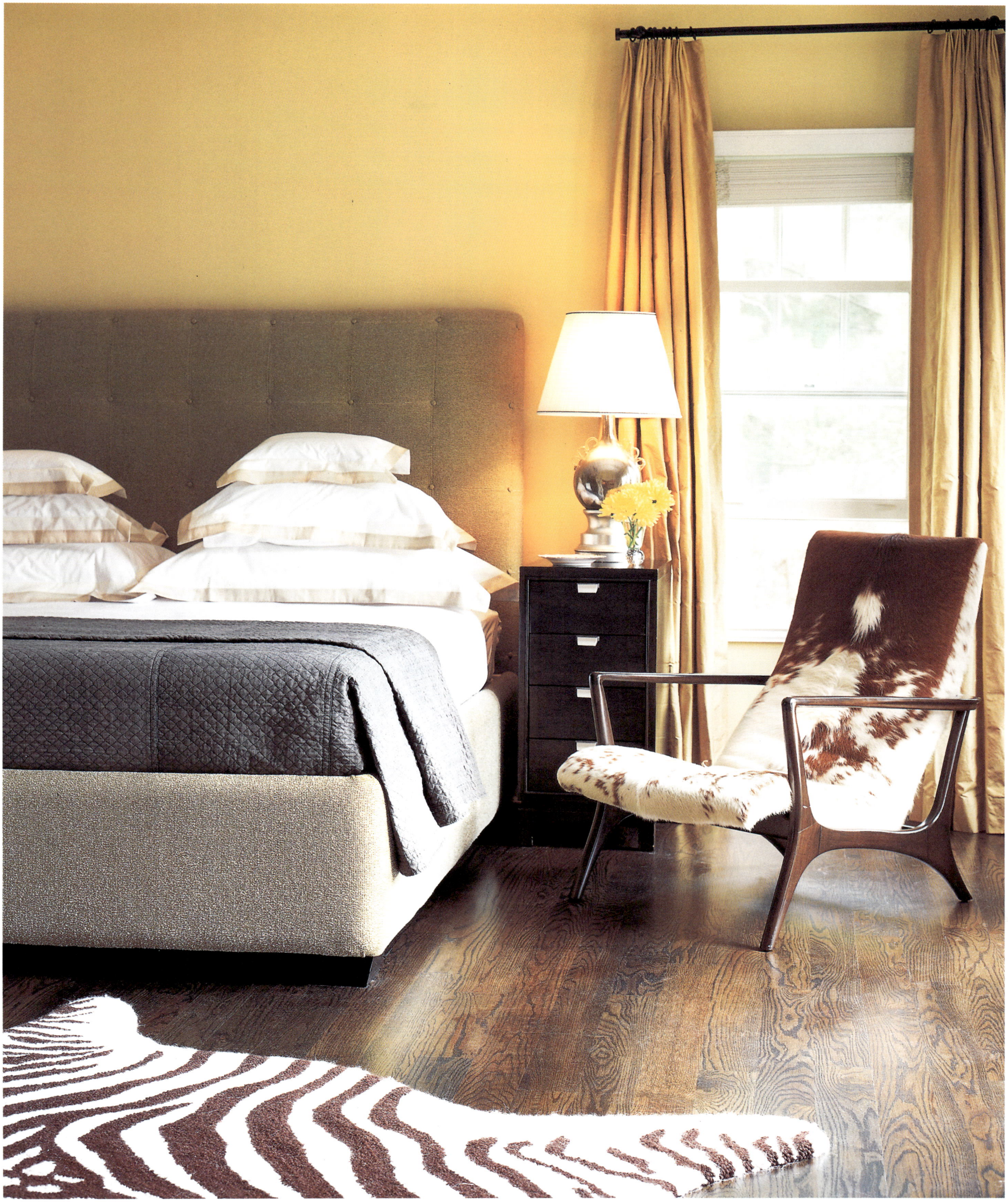

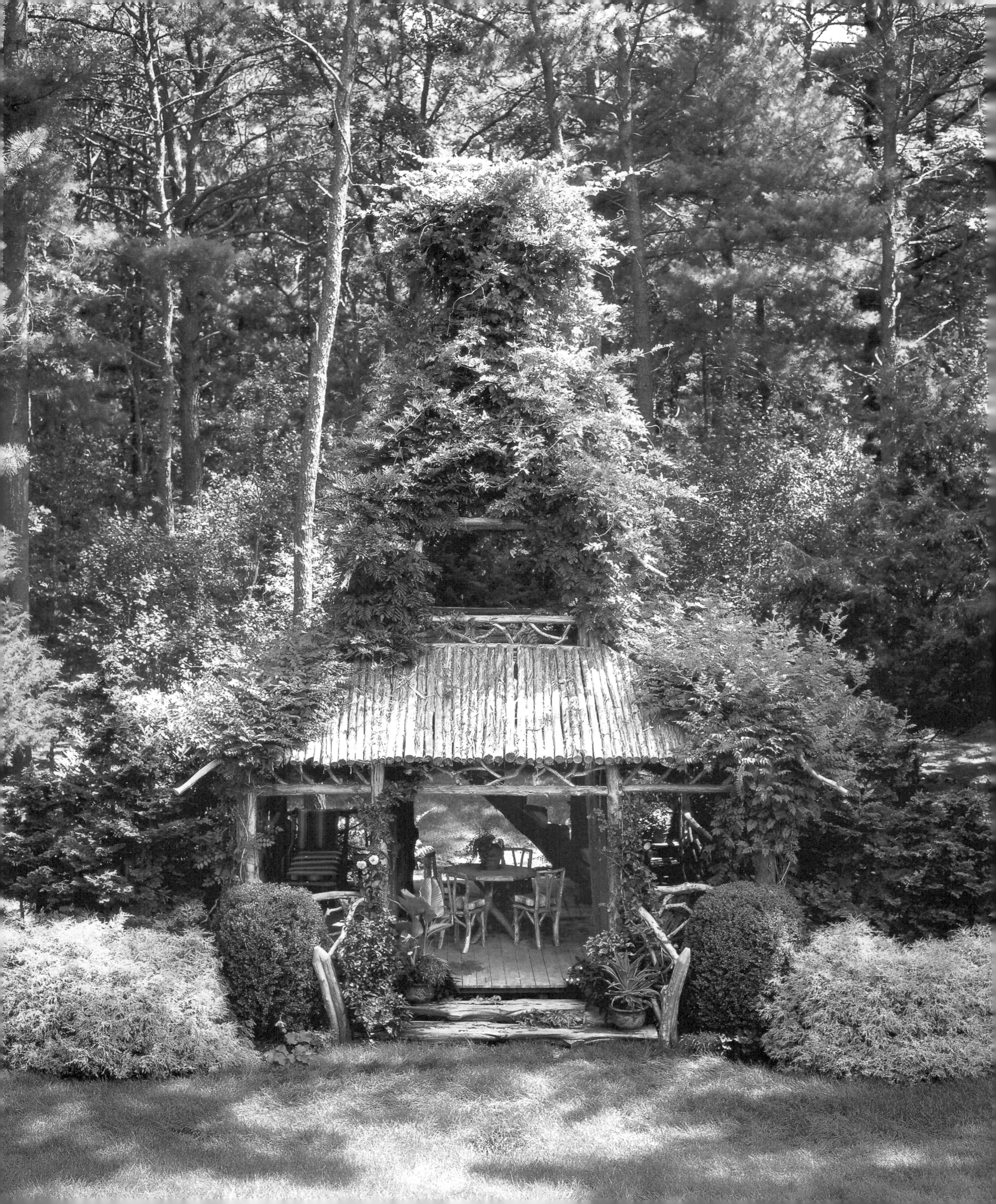

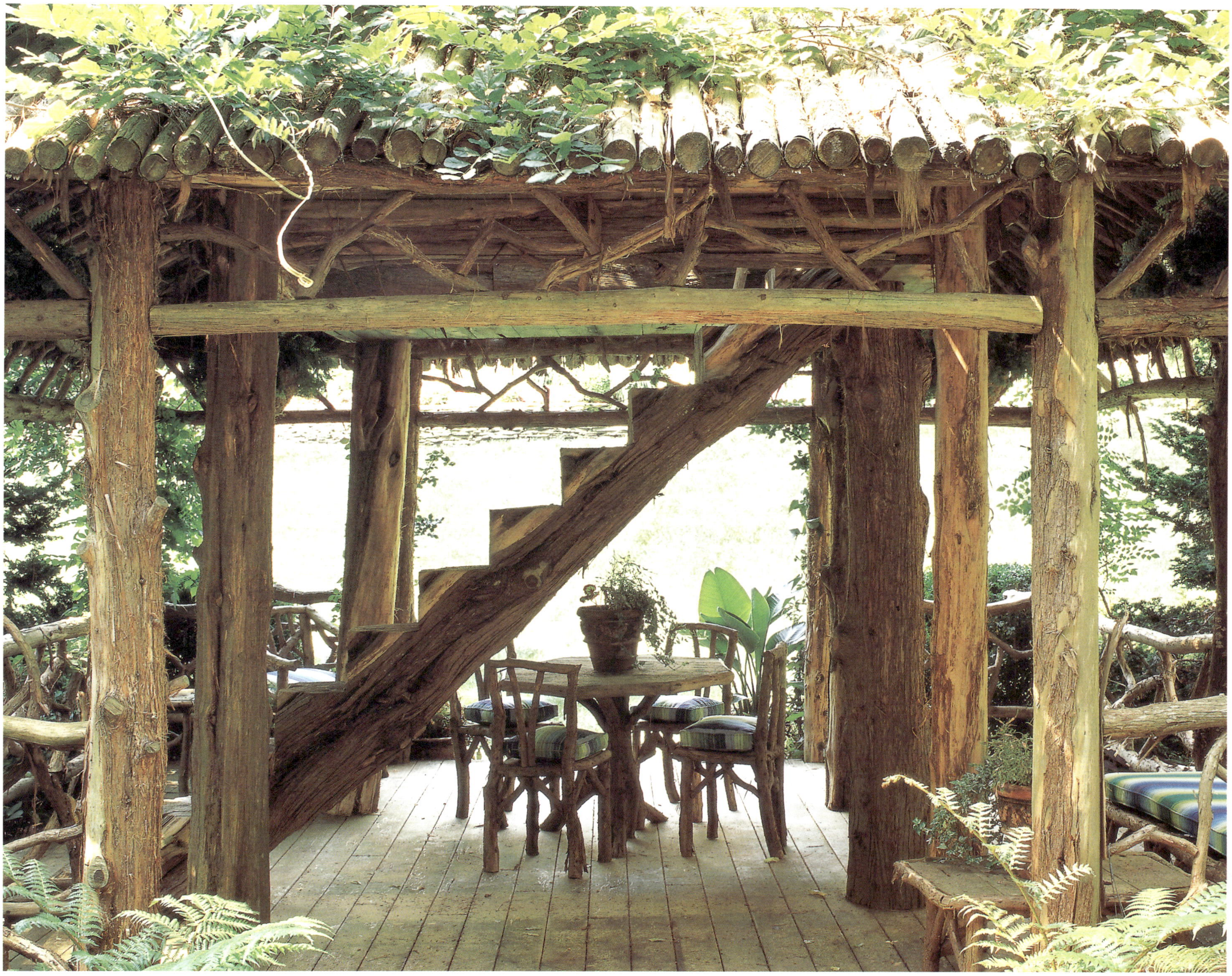

jack CEGLIC

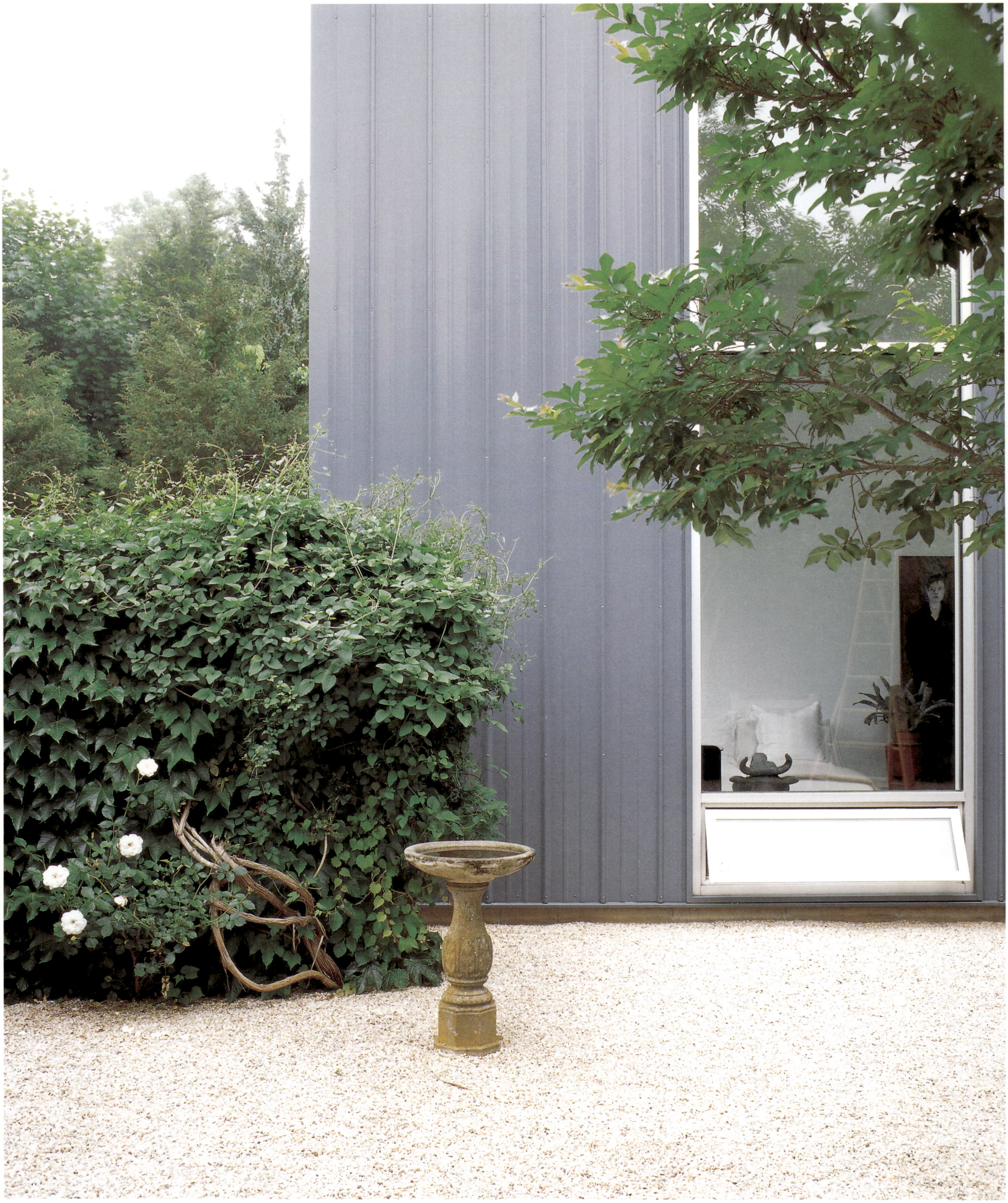

"Our houses, which are made of pre-engineered parts, are often inspired by found objects and recycled materials. We keep them practical and unadorned, trying to stay 'on this side of design' and 'the right side of the sun.' The *New York Times* called our design sensibility, 'poetic functionalism,' and that sounds just about right."

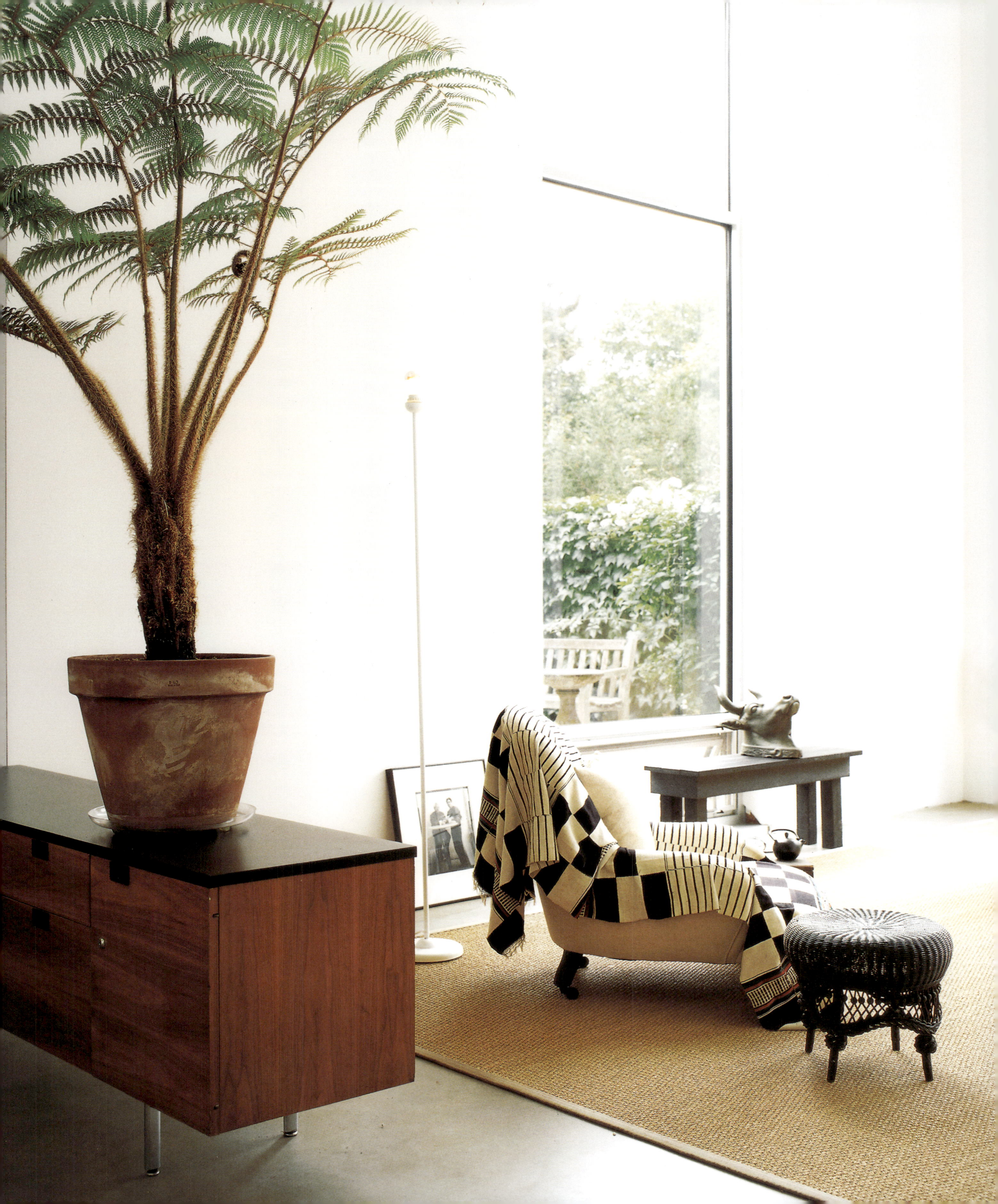

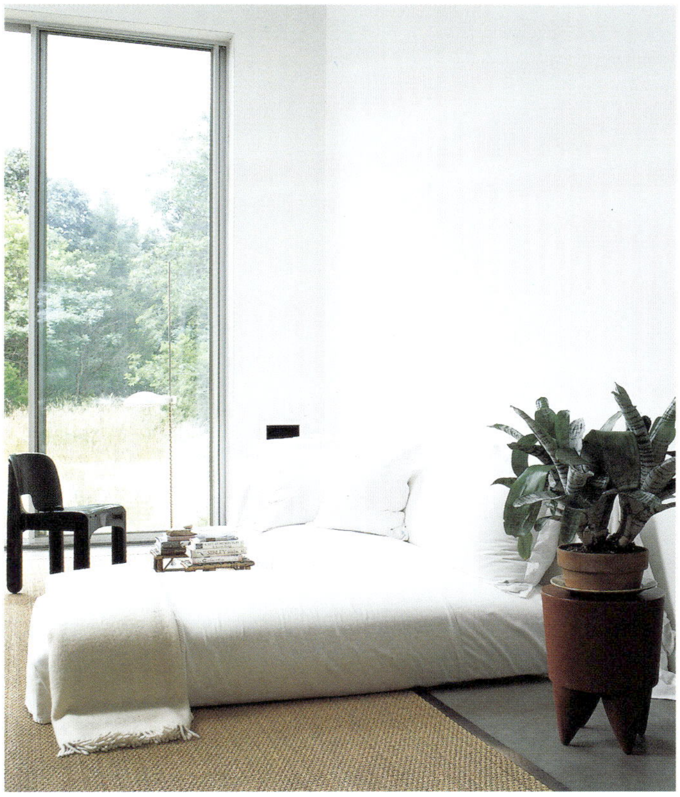

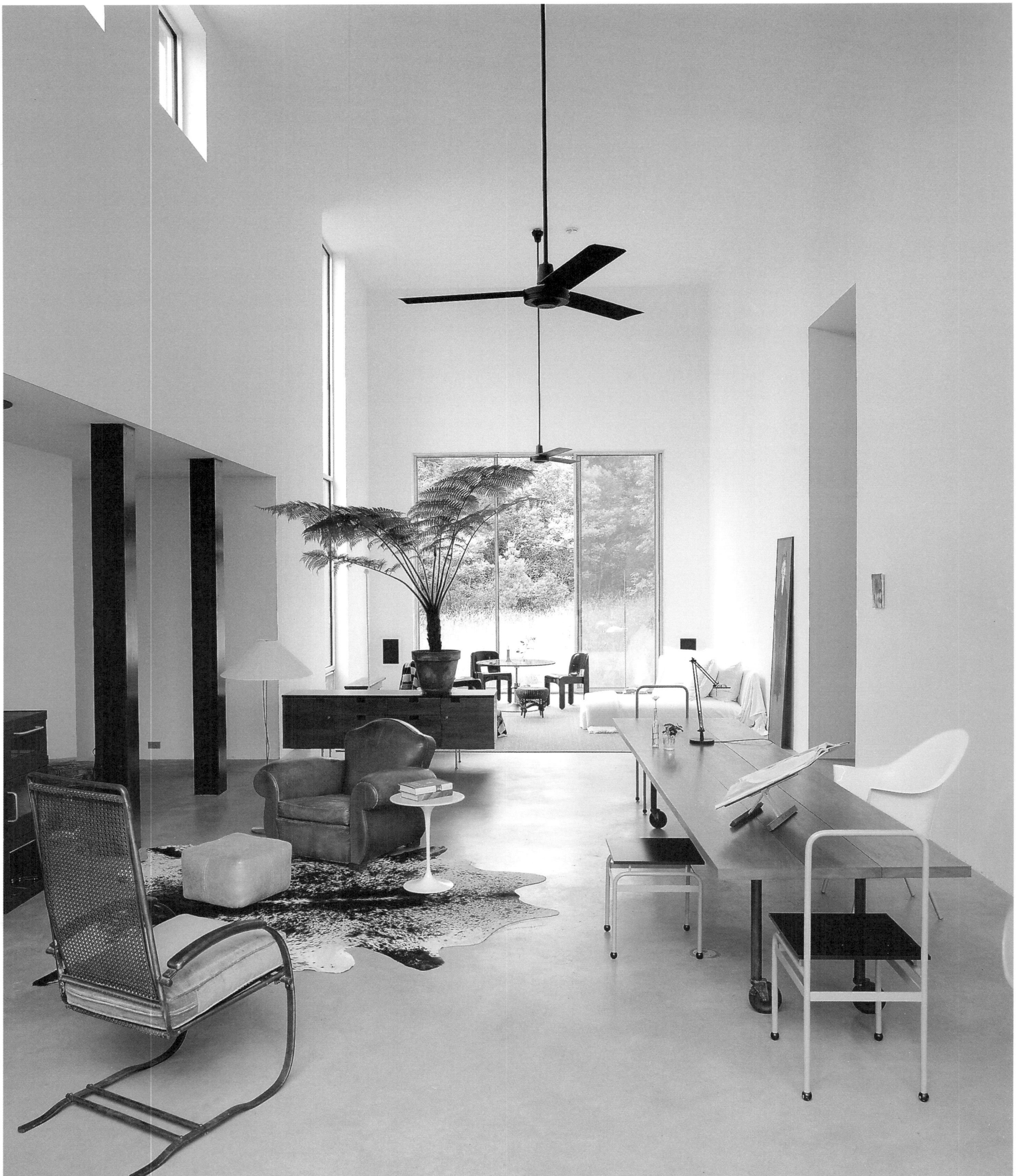

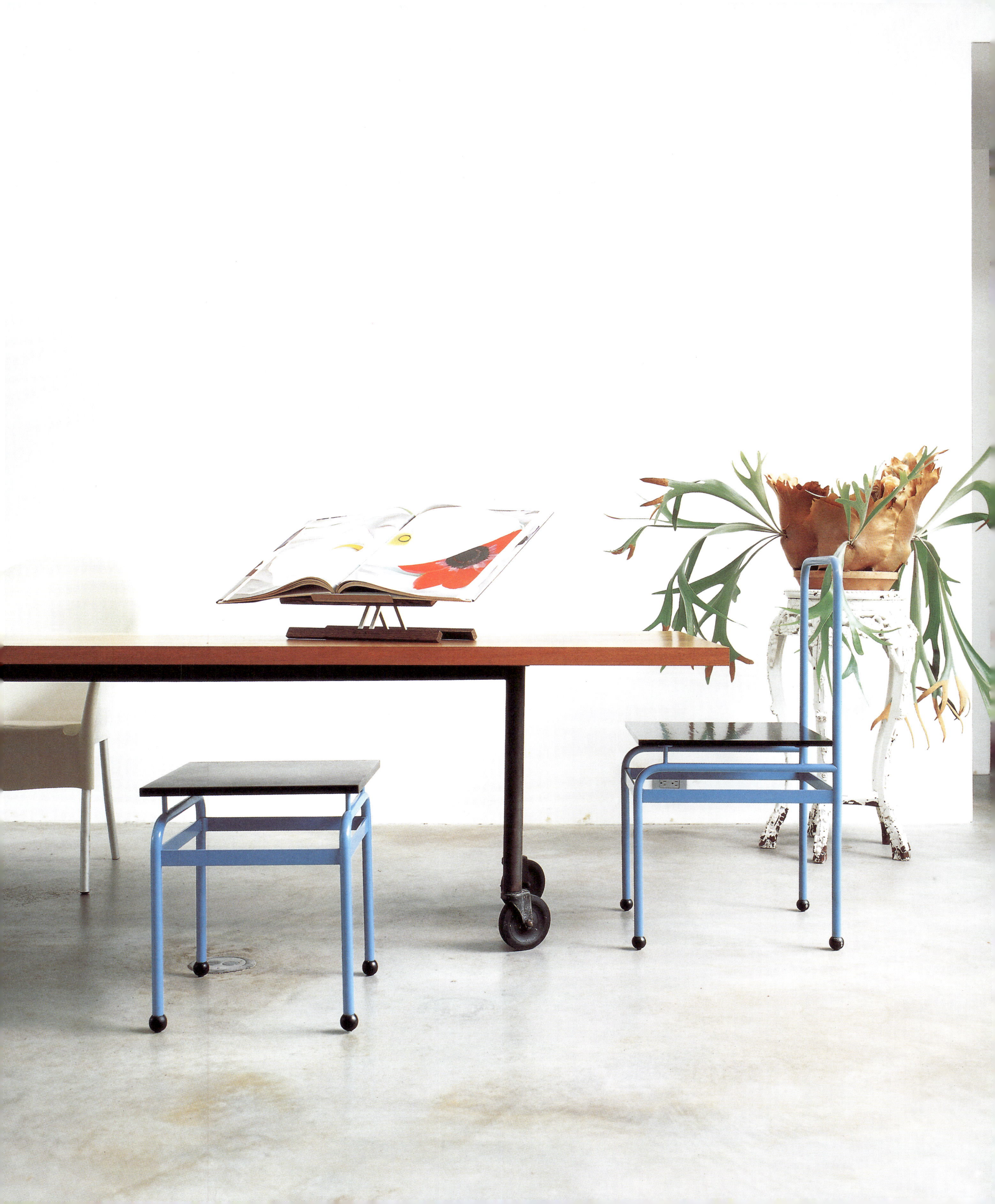

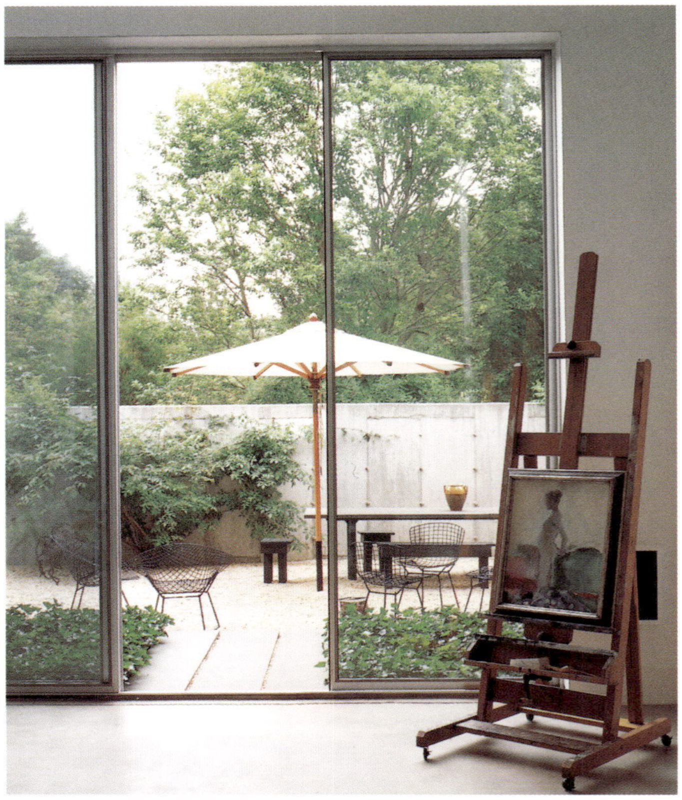

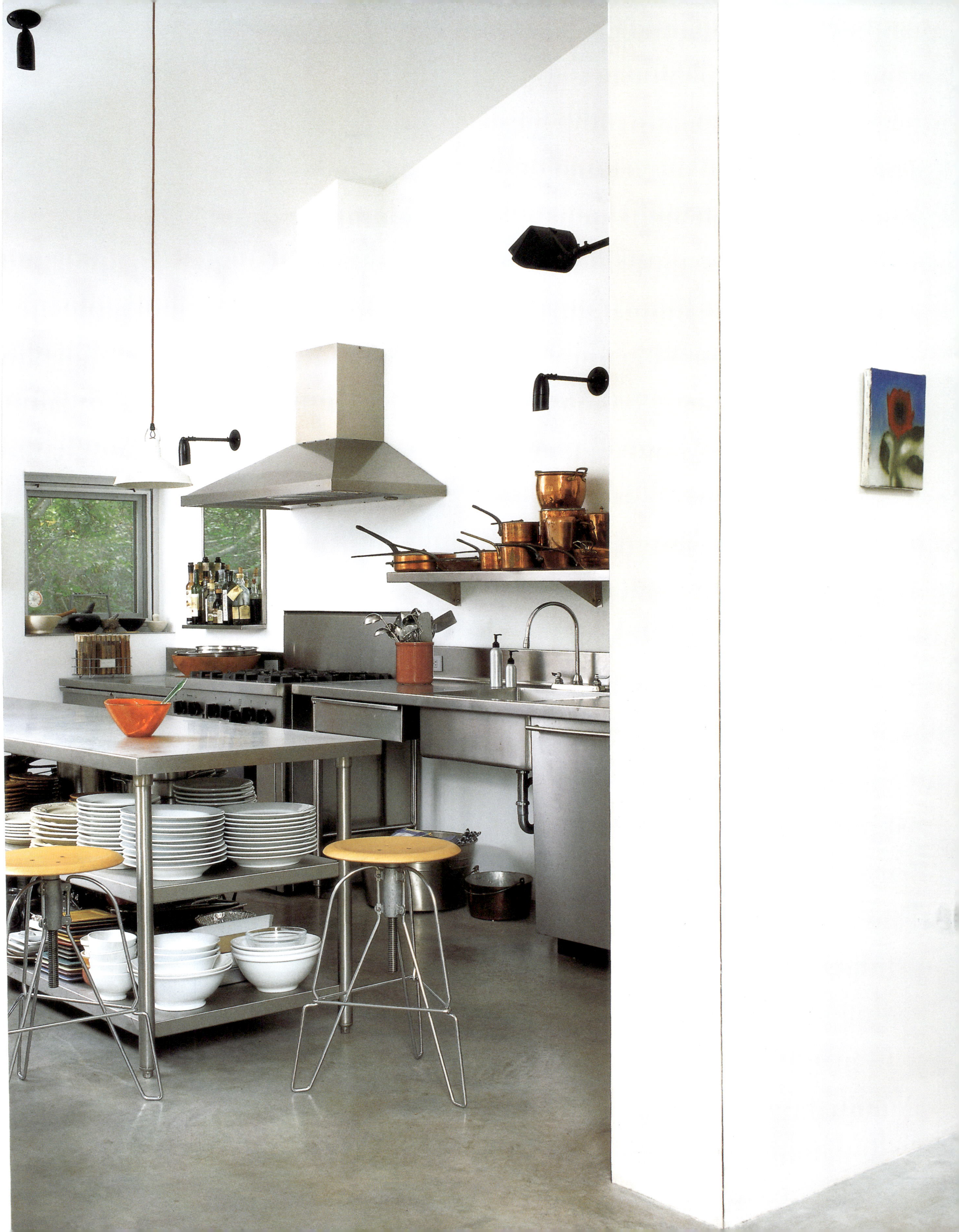

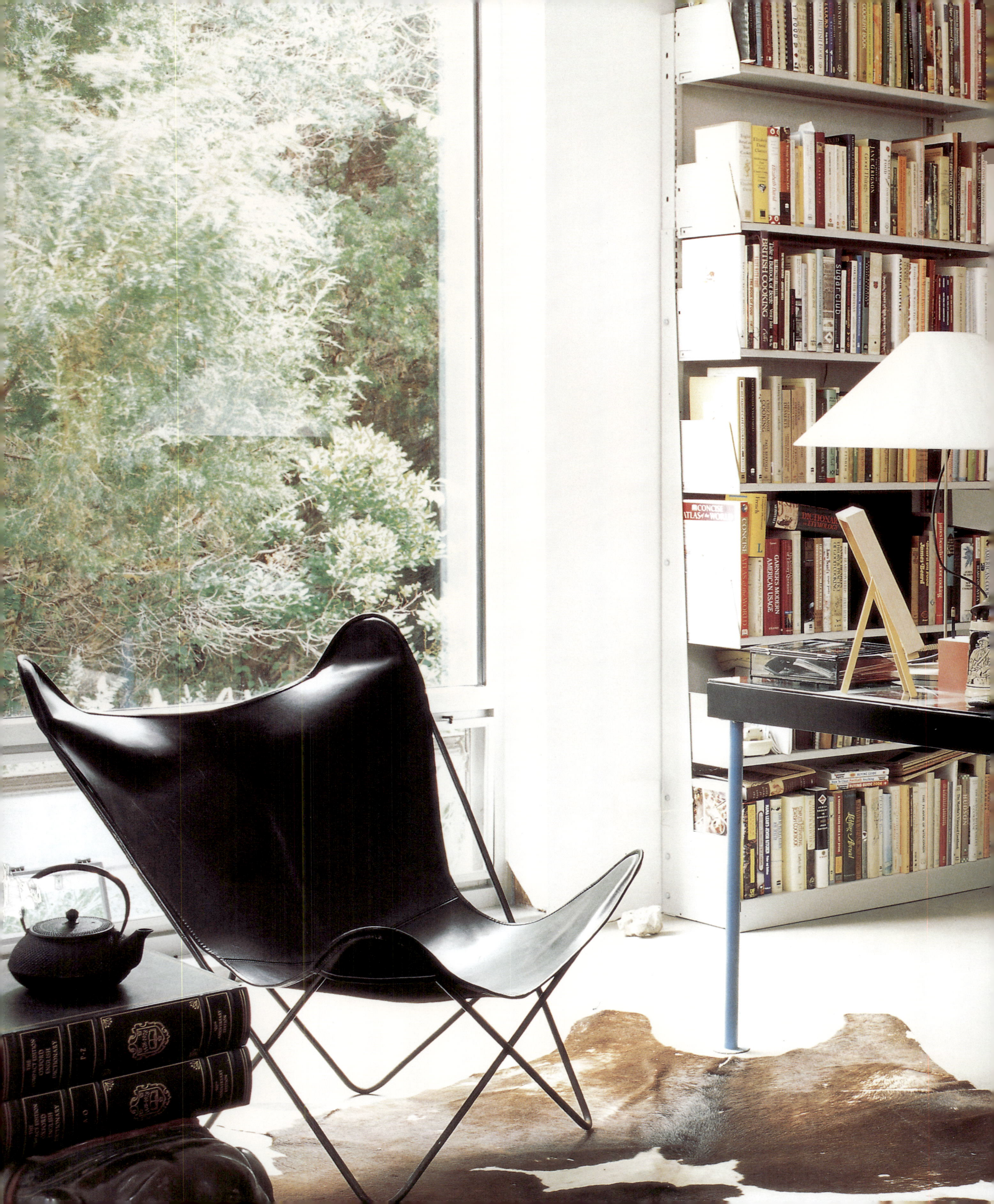

A TASTE OF ITALY
THE WAY TO COOK
JACQUES PÉPIN'S TABLE
THE ART OF FRENCH COOKING
SIMPLE CUISINE
CUCINA RUSTICA
POLISH HERITAGE COOKERY
THE CUISINE OF HUNGARY
VIENNESE CUISINE
FEASTS OF PROVENCE
GREAT EUROPEAN CHEFS
EUROPEAN FESTIVAL FOOD
THE OLD WORLD KITCHEN
RAYMOND BLANC
marie claire

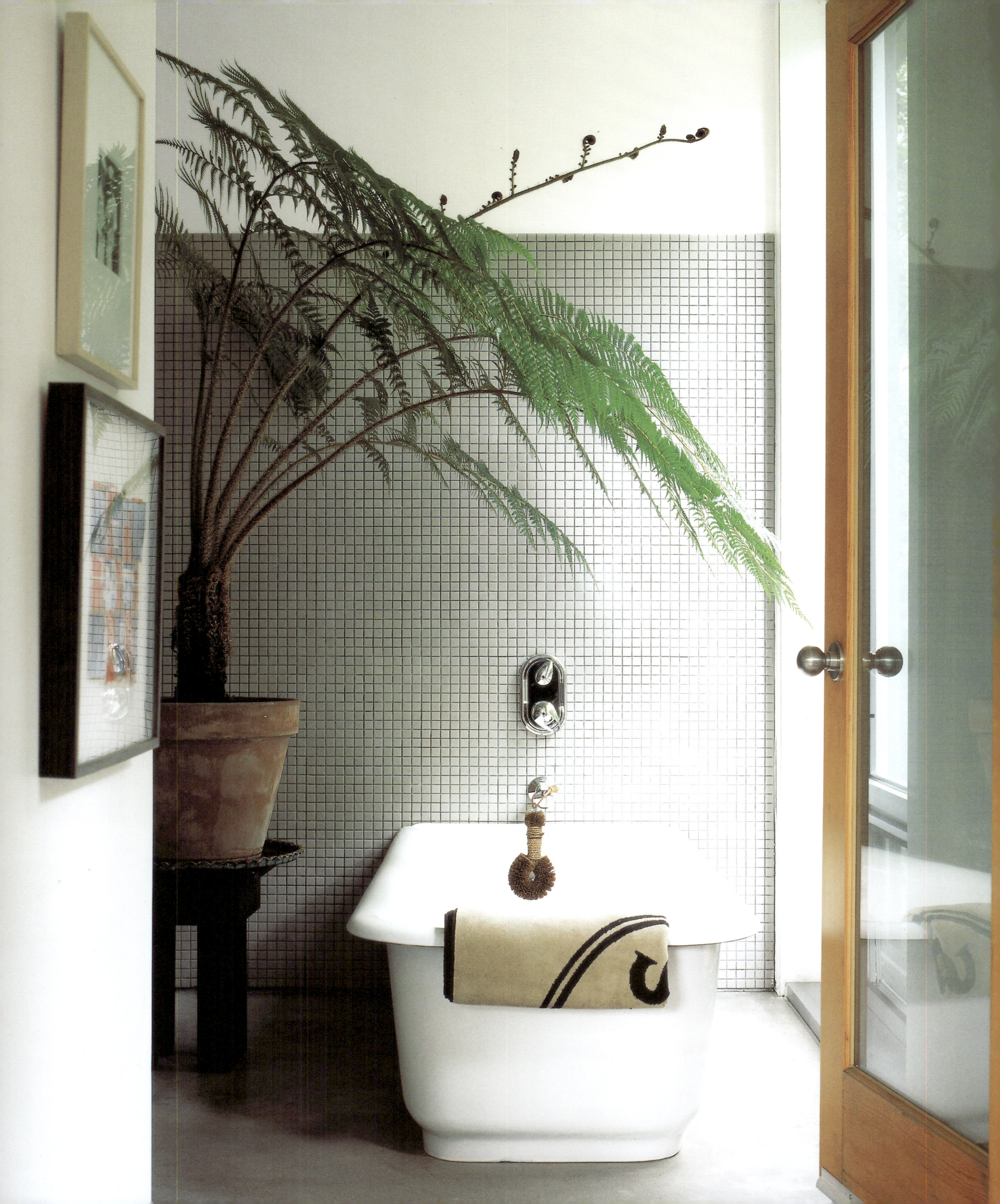

SONY
EDITH WHARTON: An Extraordinary Life
Hockney's People
THE BRITANNICA ENCYCLOPEDIA OF AMERICAN ART
Reflections in a Glass Eye
A HOUSE IS NOT A HOME Bruce Weber

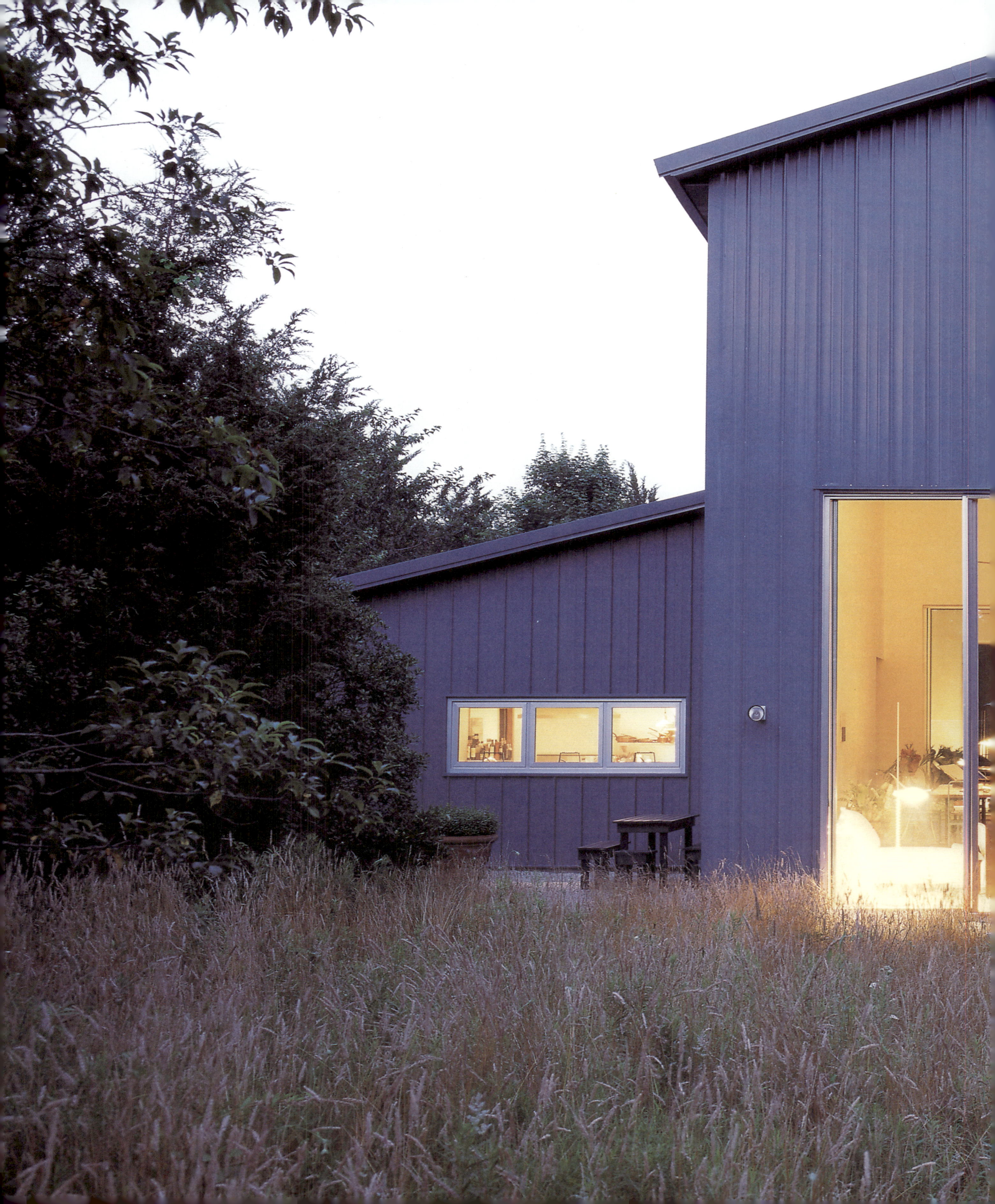

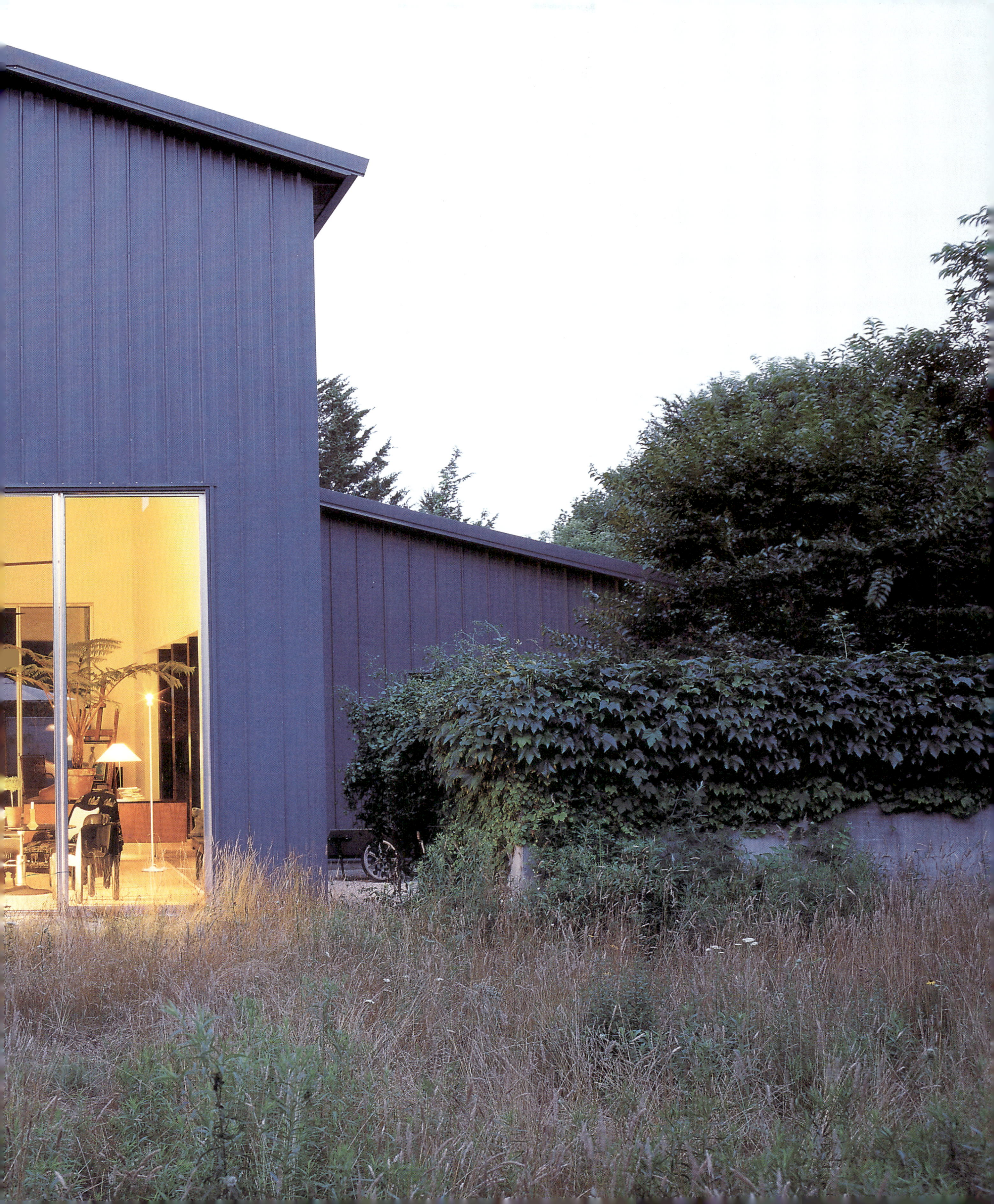

waldo FERNANDEZ

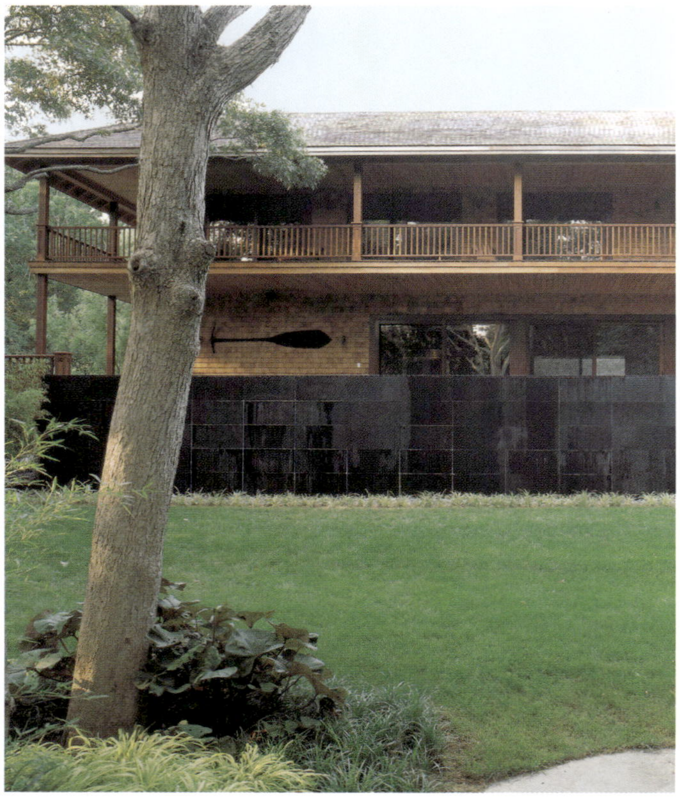

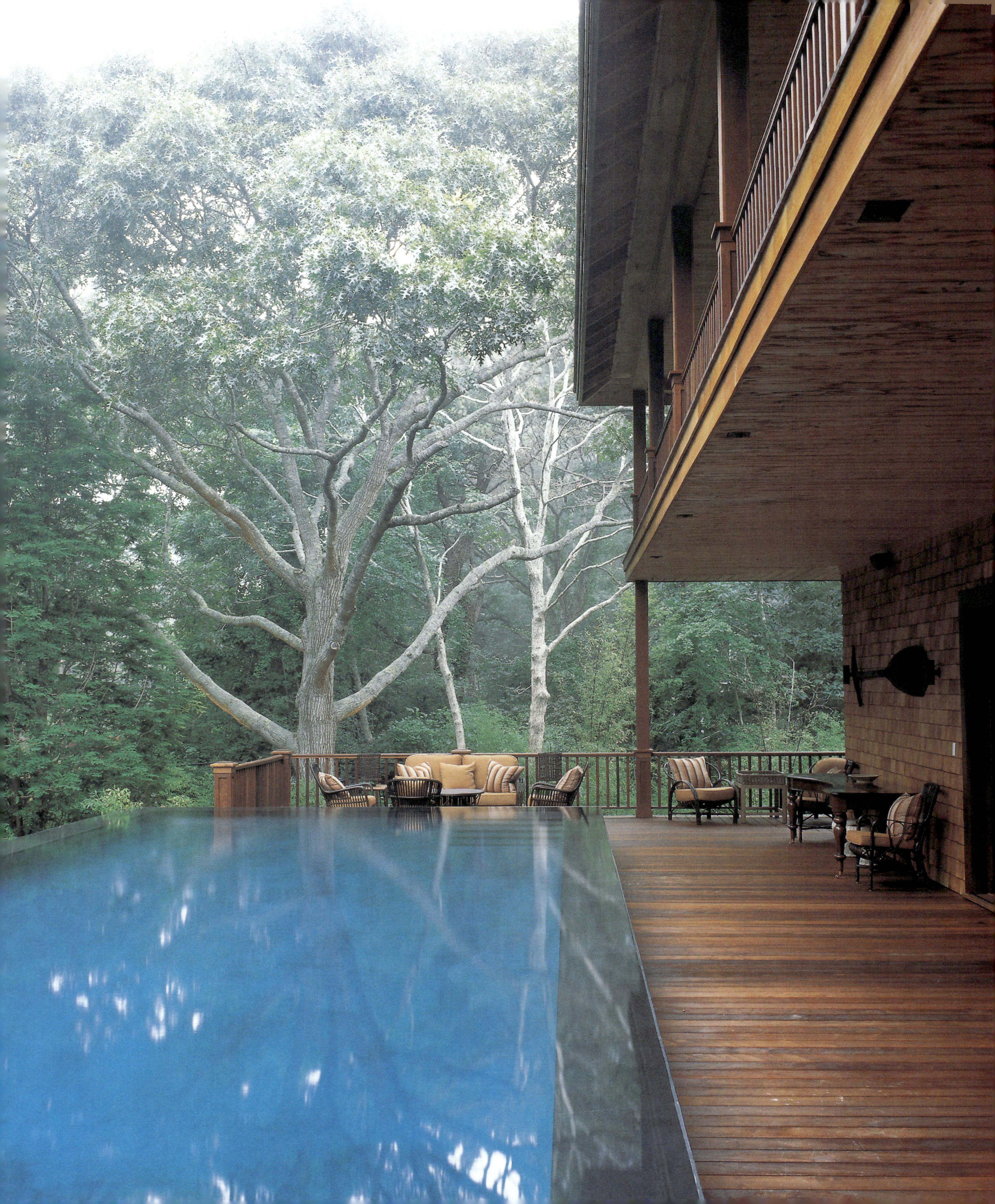

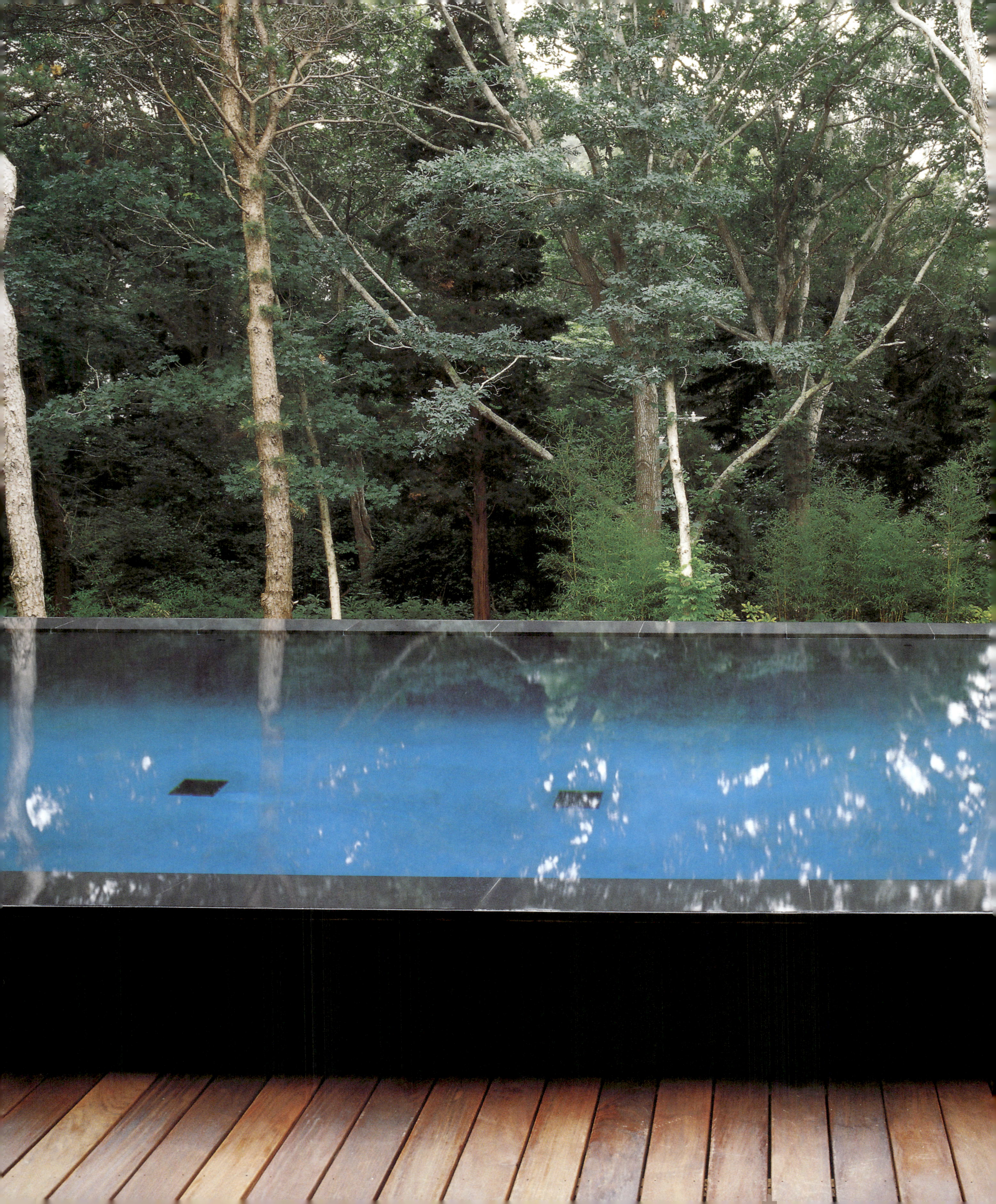

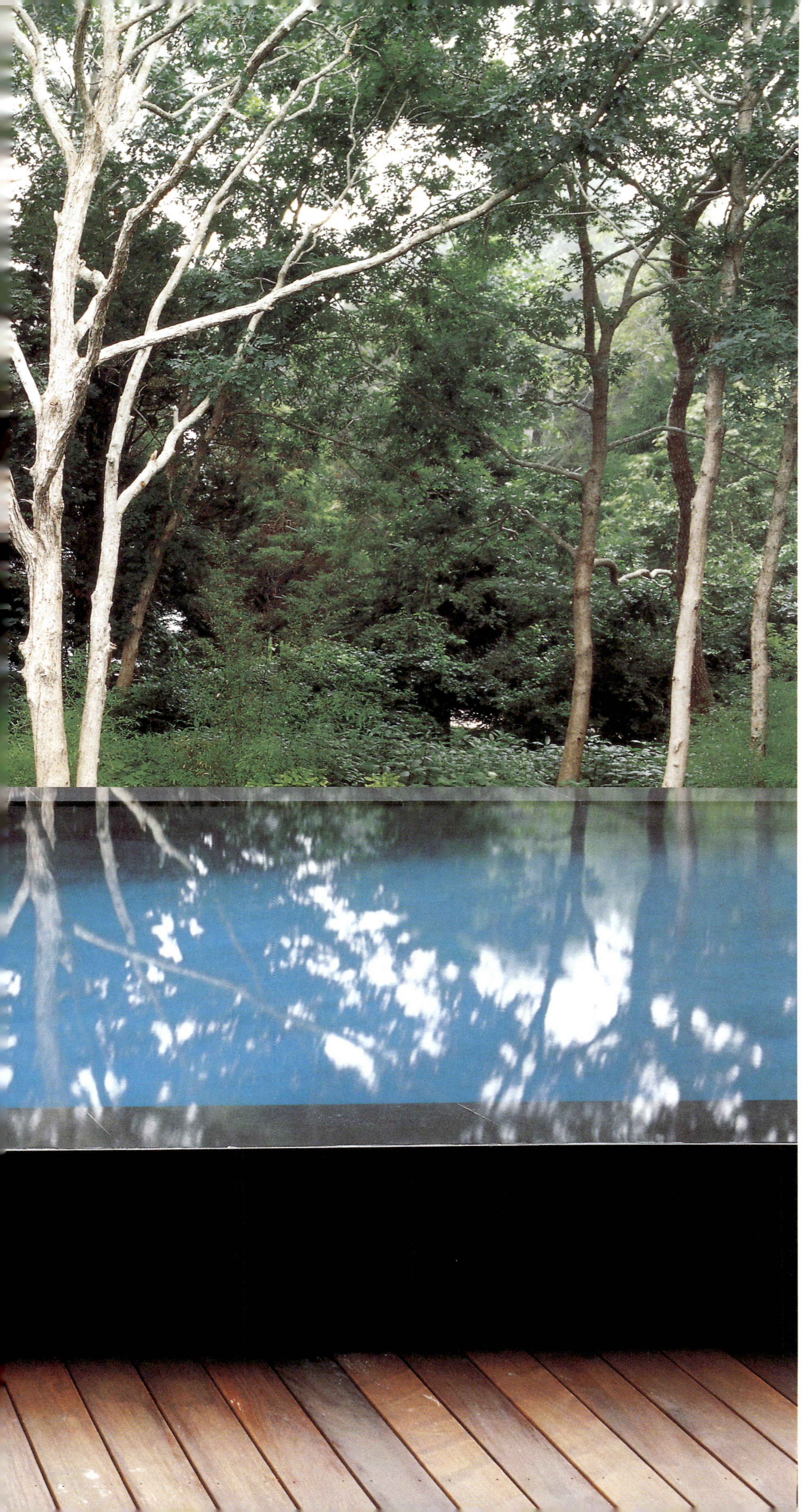

"I believe a house should be comfortable with beautiful accoutrements, but at the same time, it should have an inviting and cozy appeal that is pleasing to the eye. It should be a home that is easy to maintain and that allows for entertaining. With all these elements in mind, it should, at the heart of everything, generate a sense of serenity."

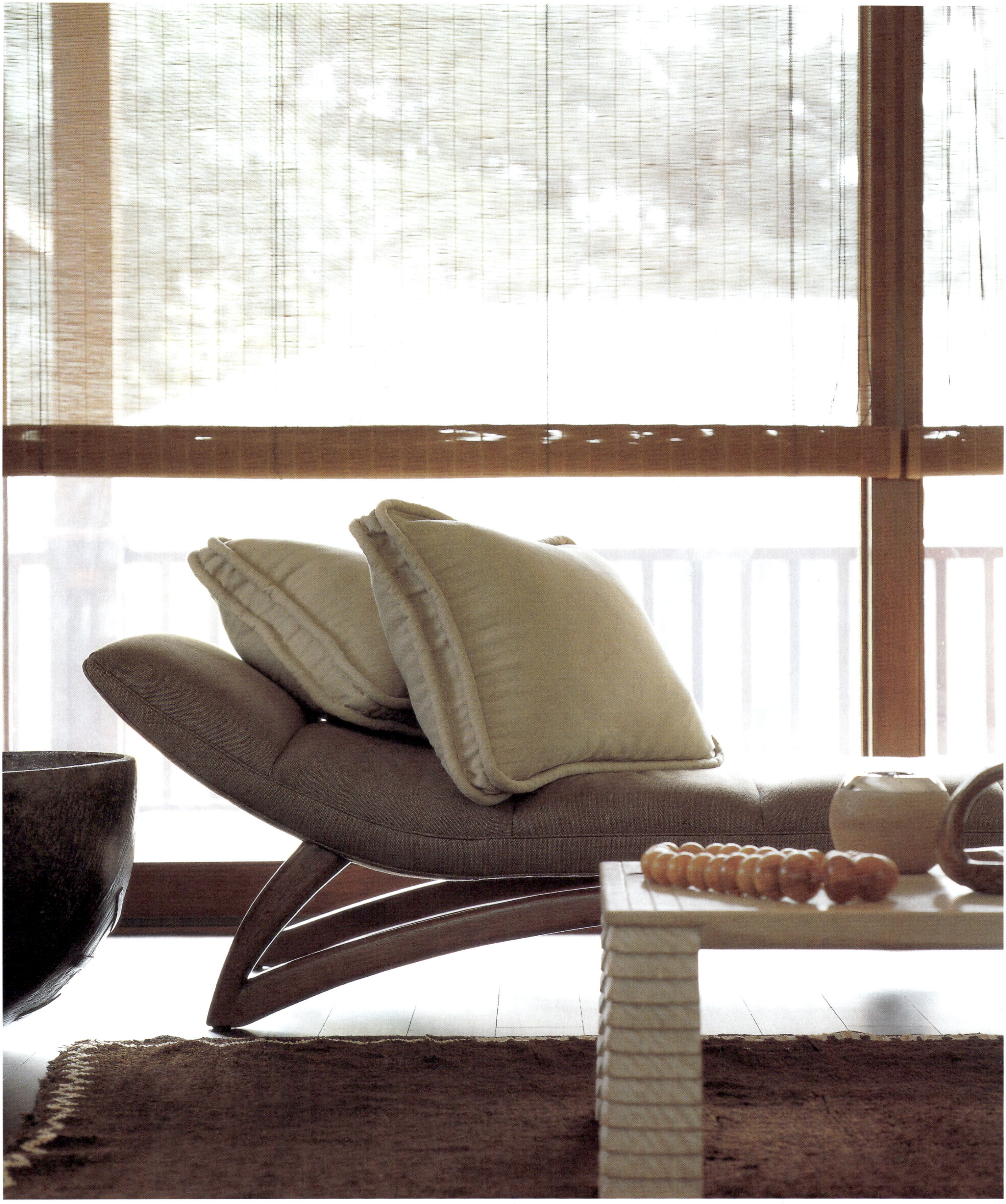

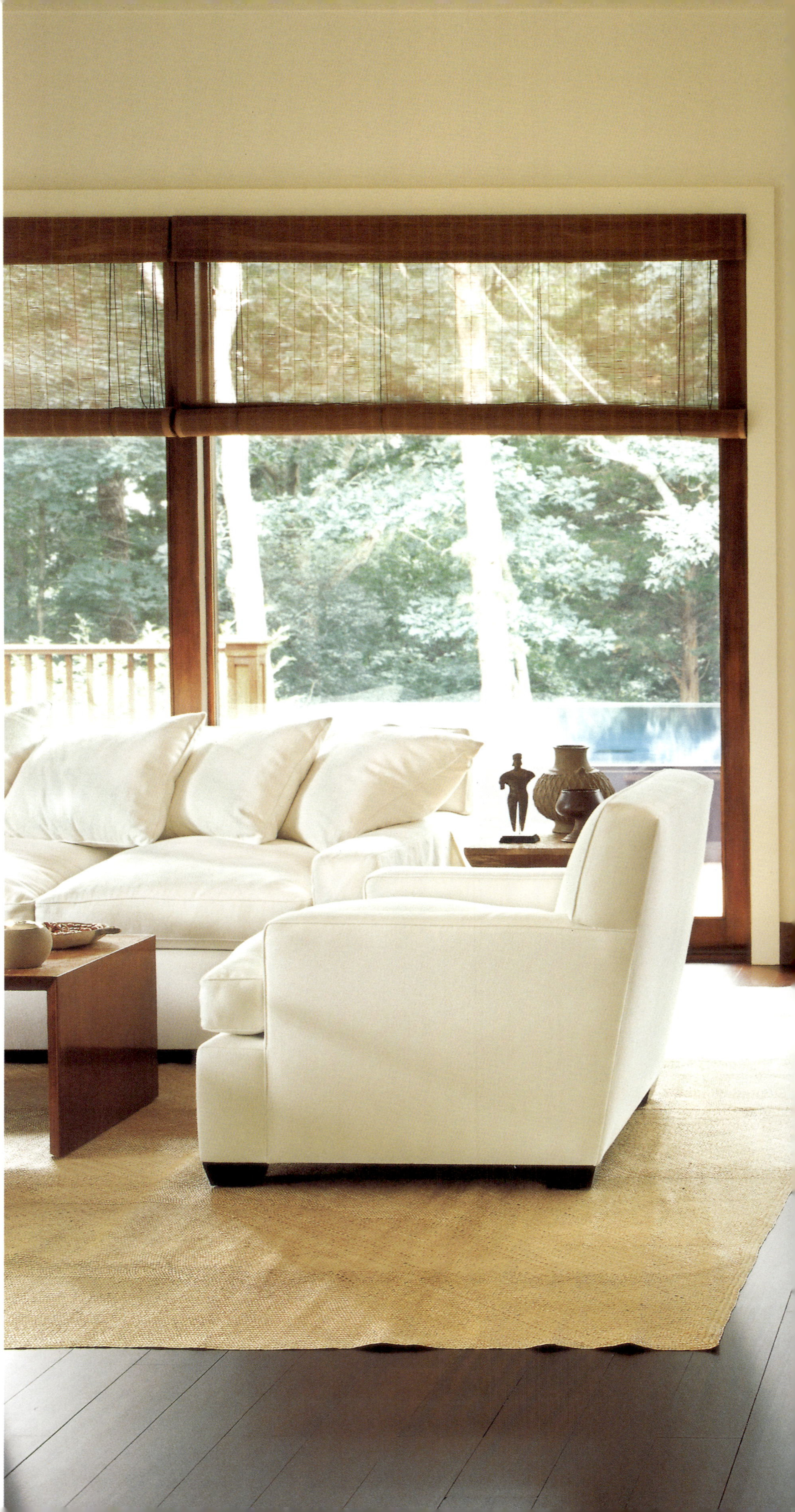

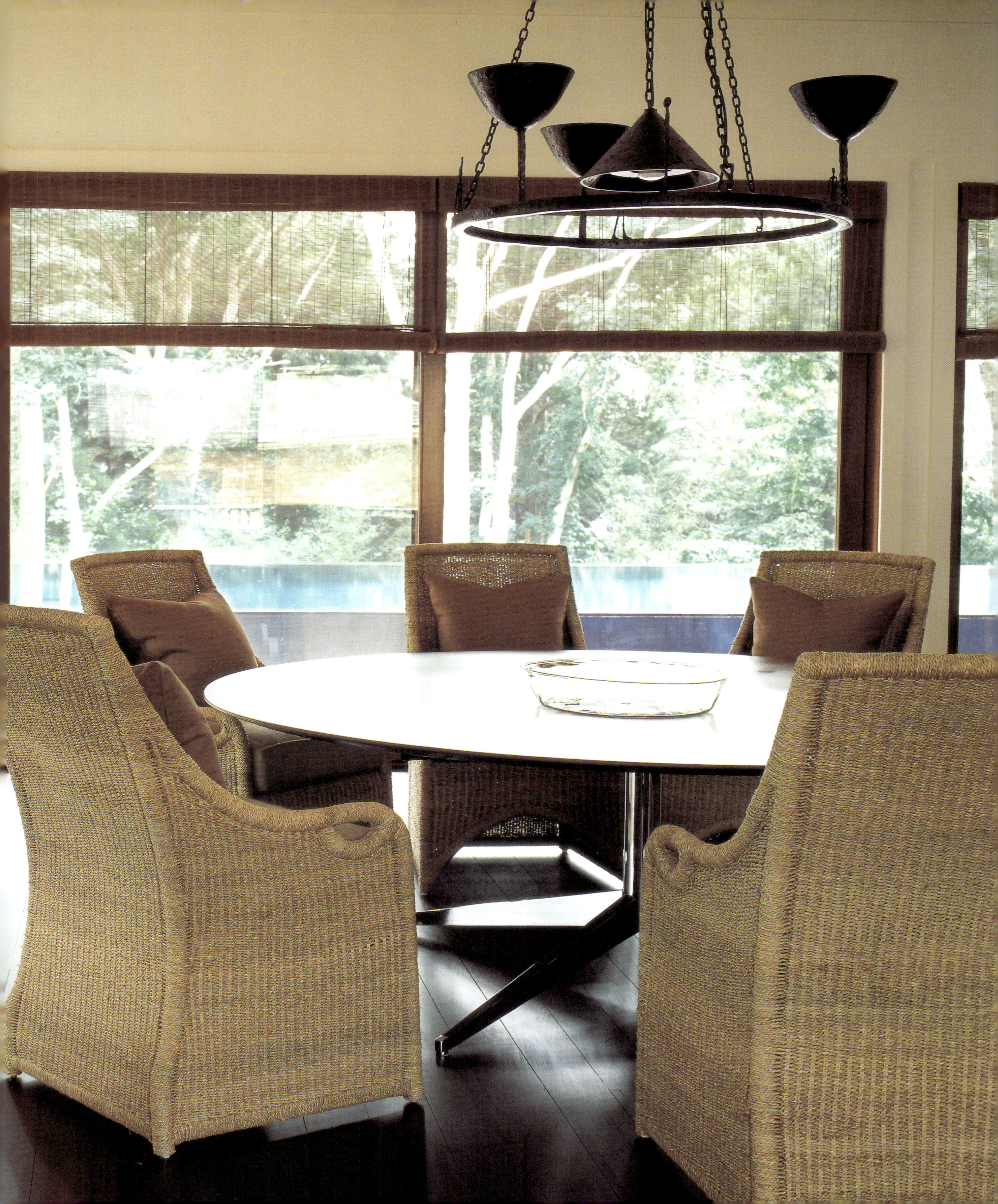

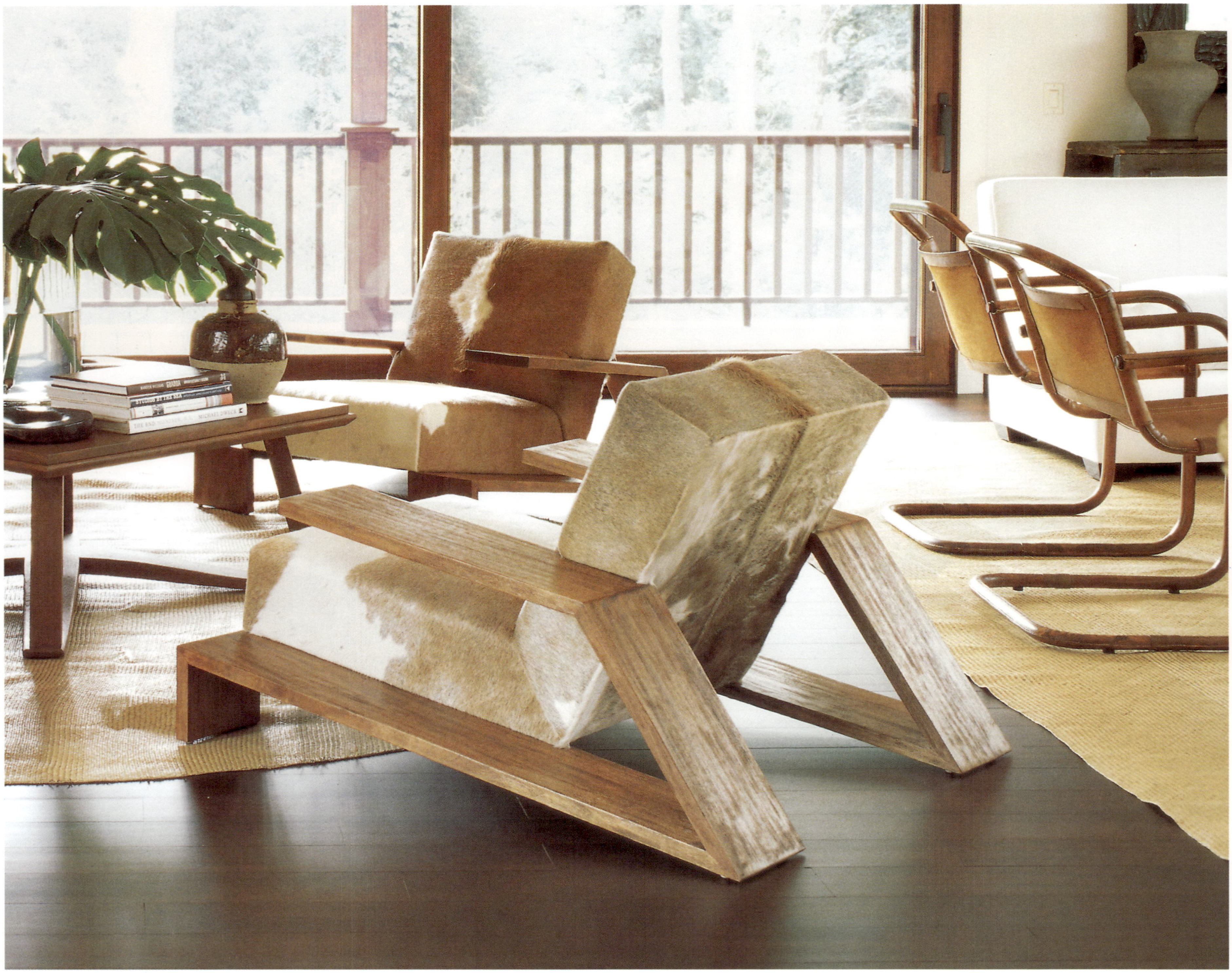

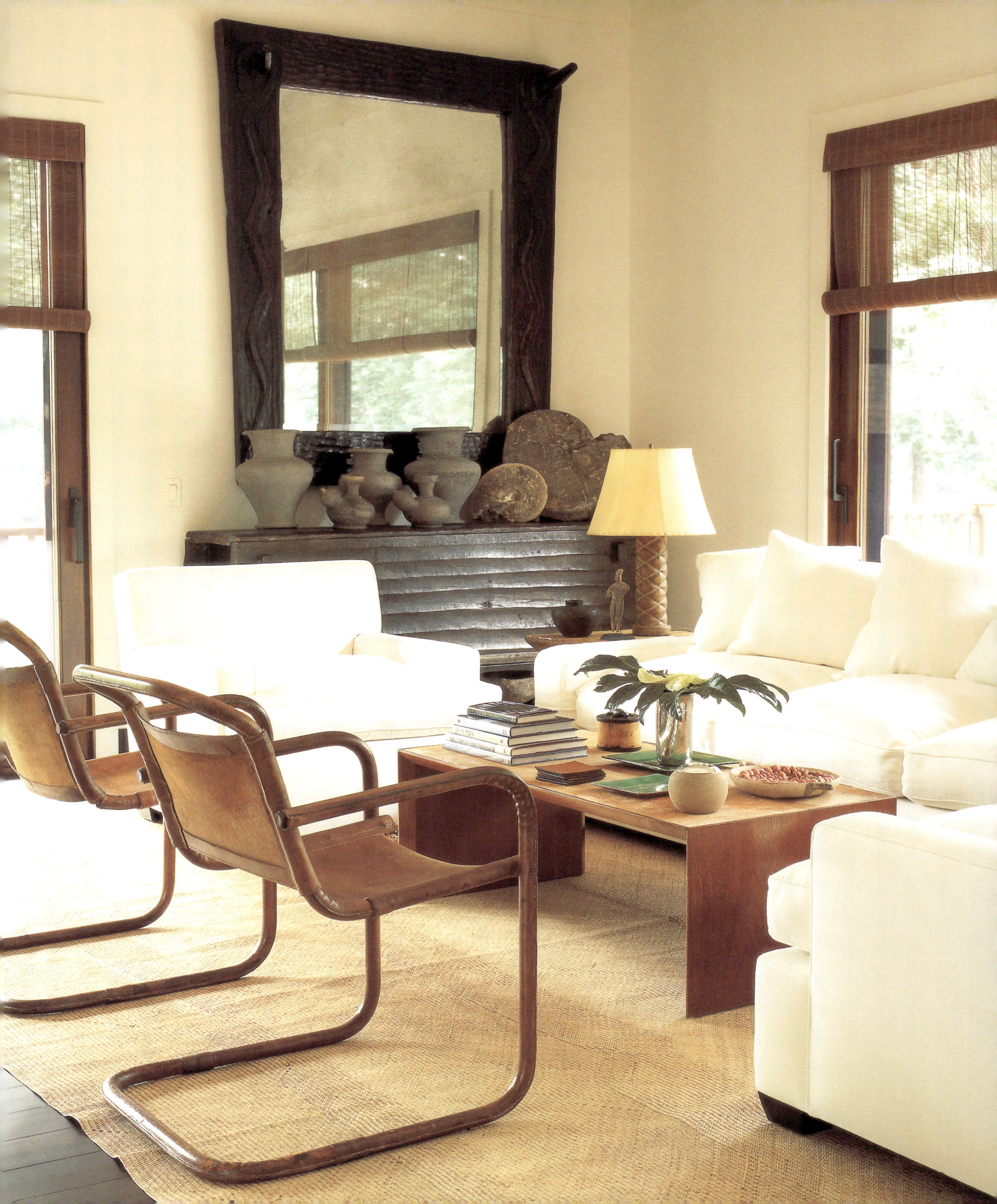

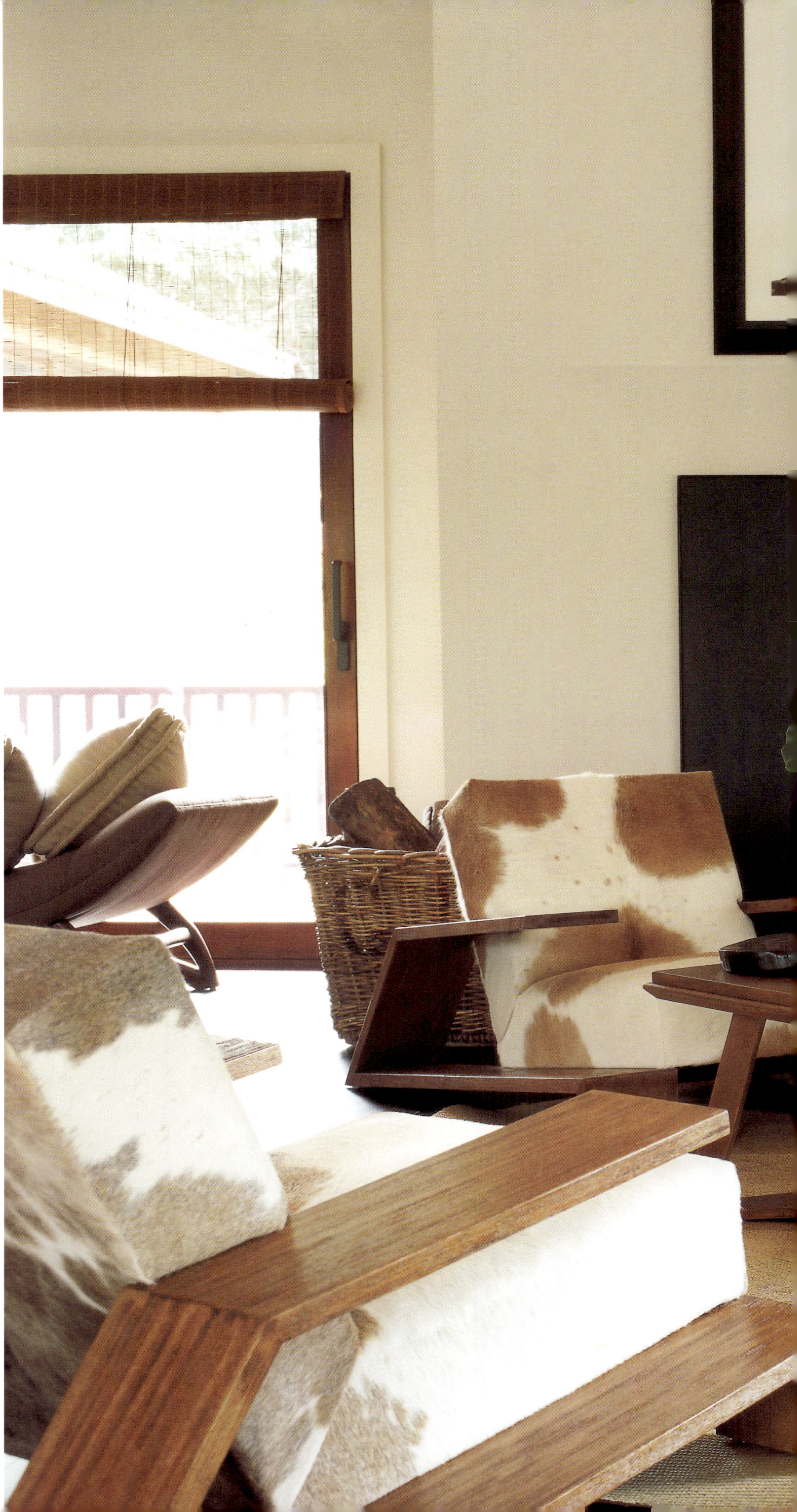

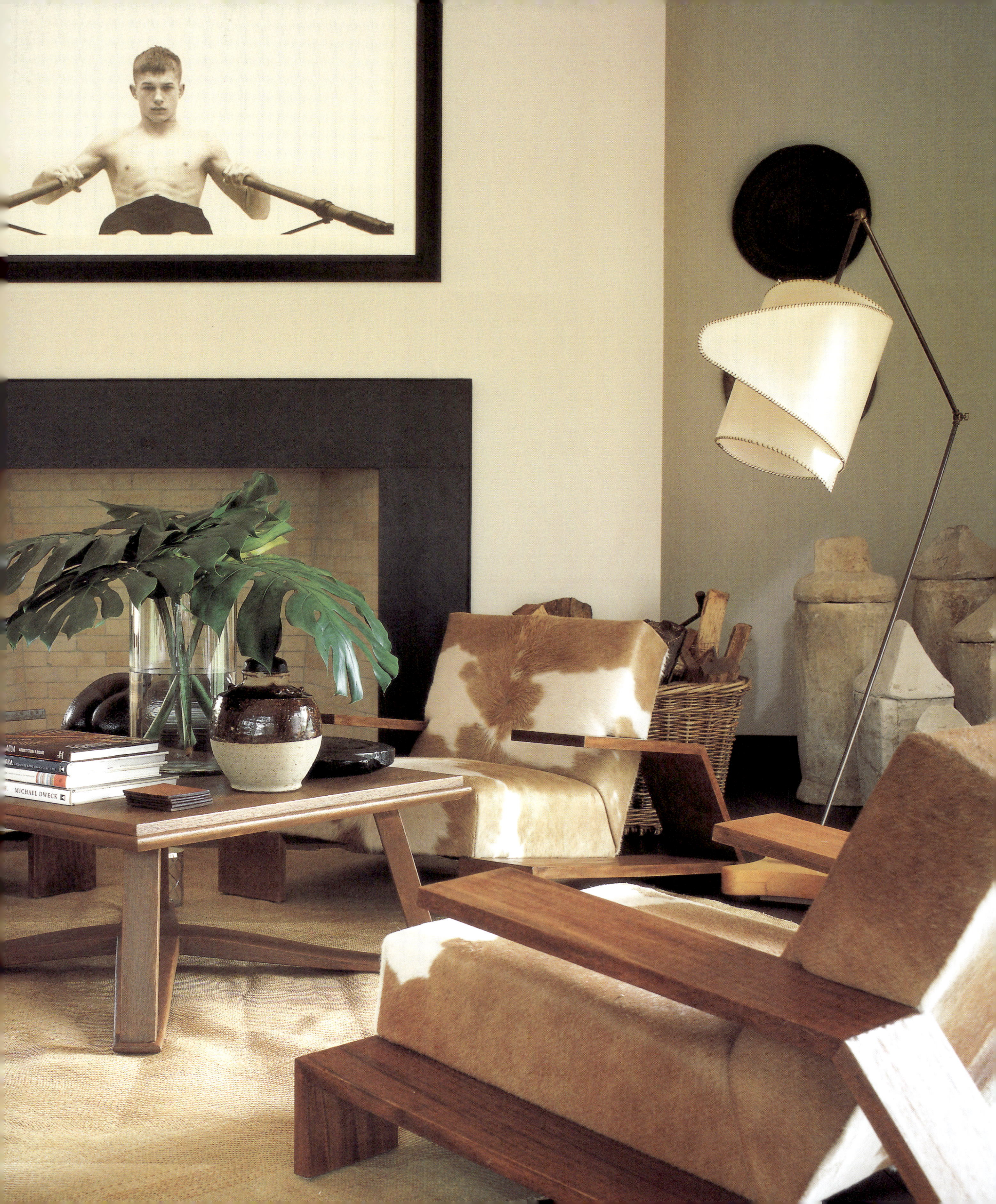
MICHAEL DWECK

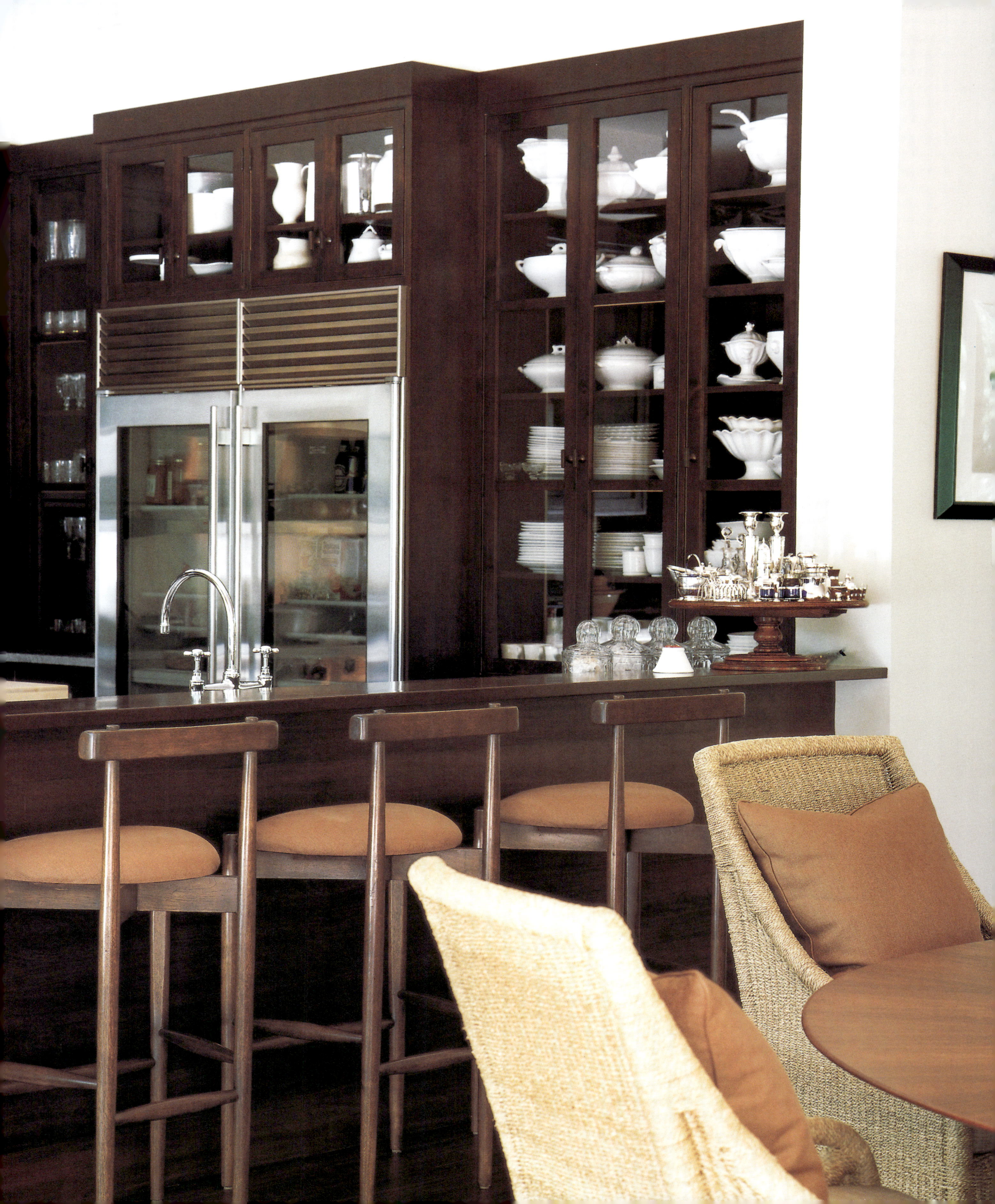

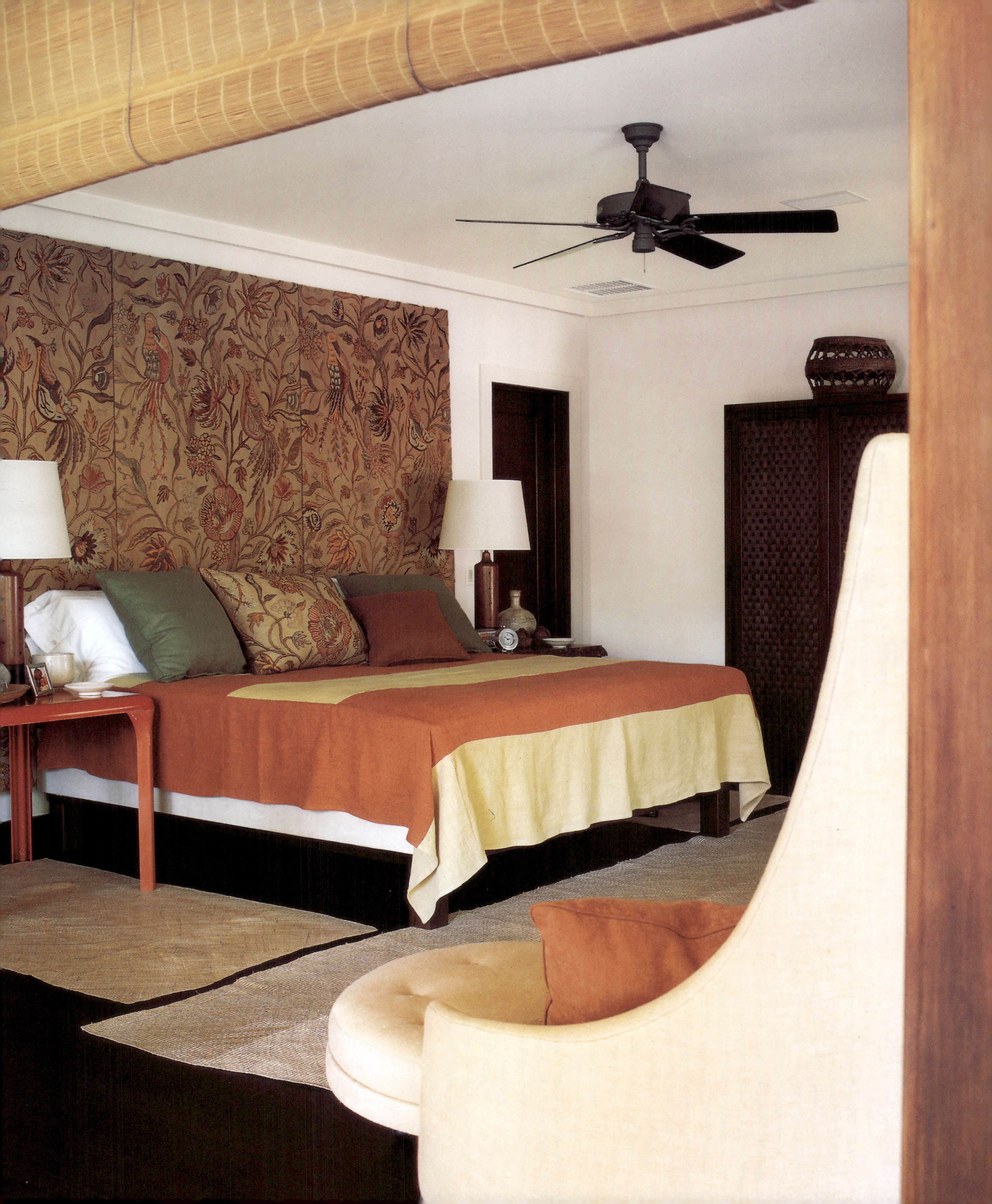

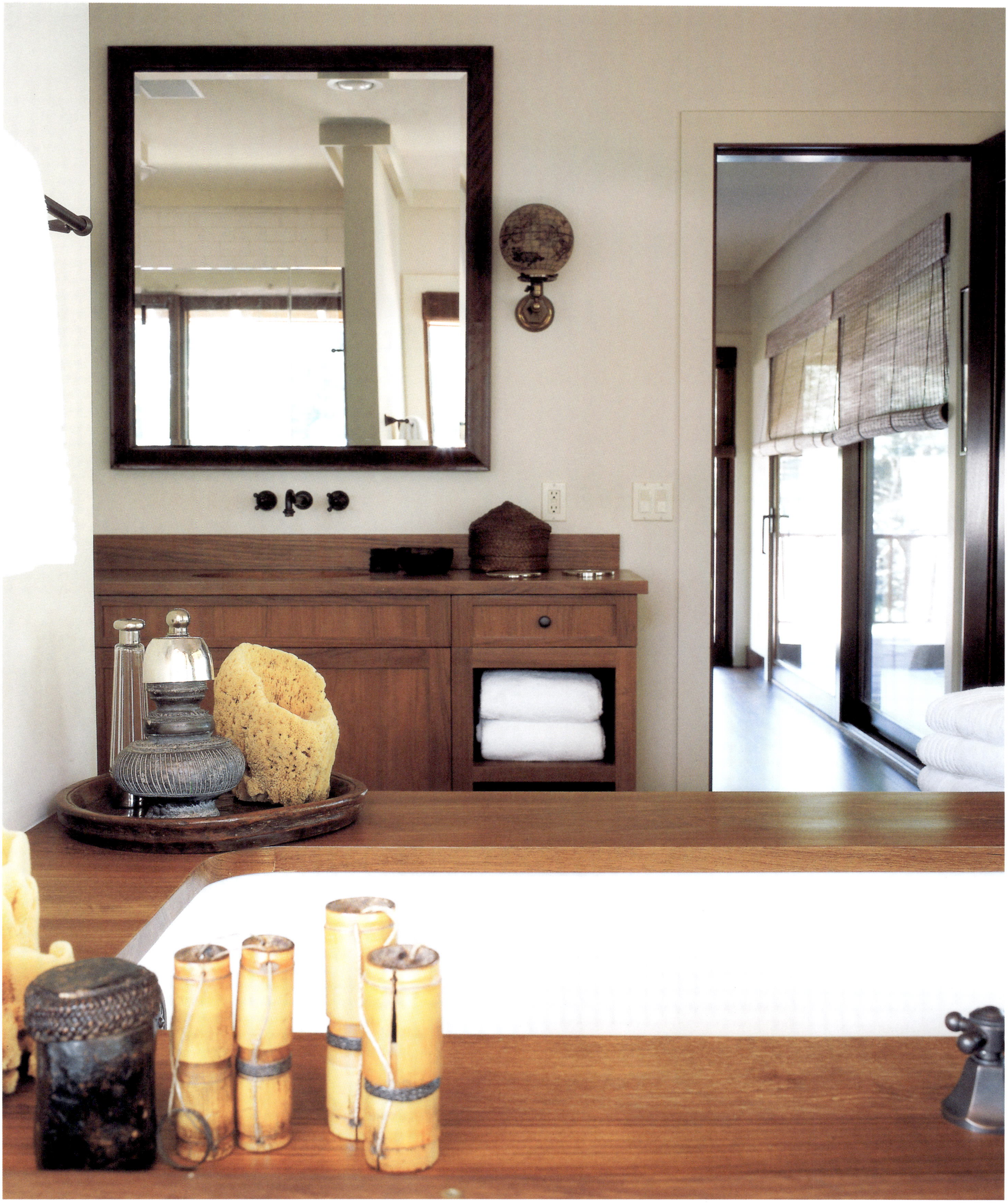

mark ZEFF

"I feel design is the combination of the way we want to live, a style sense, and the willingness to embrace nature and culture. My work is influenced not only by the exquisite light and the proximity to water, but also by the traditional style of the landscaping and mansions—I like to meld it all into a modern style."

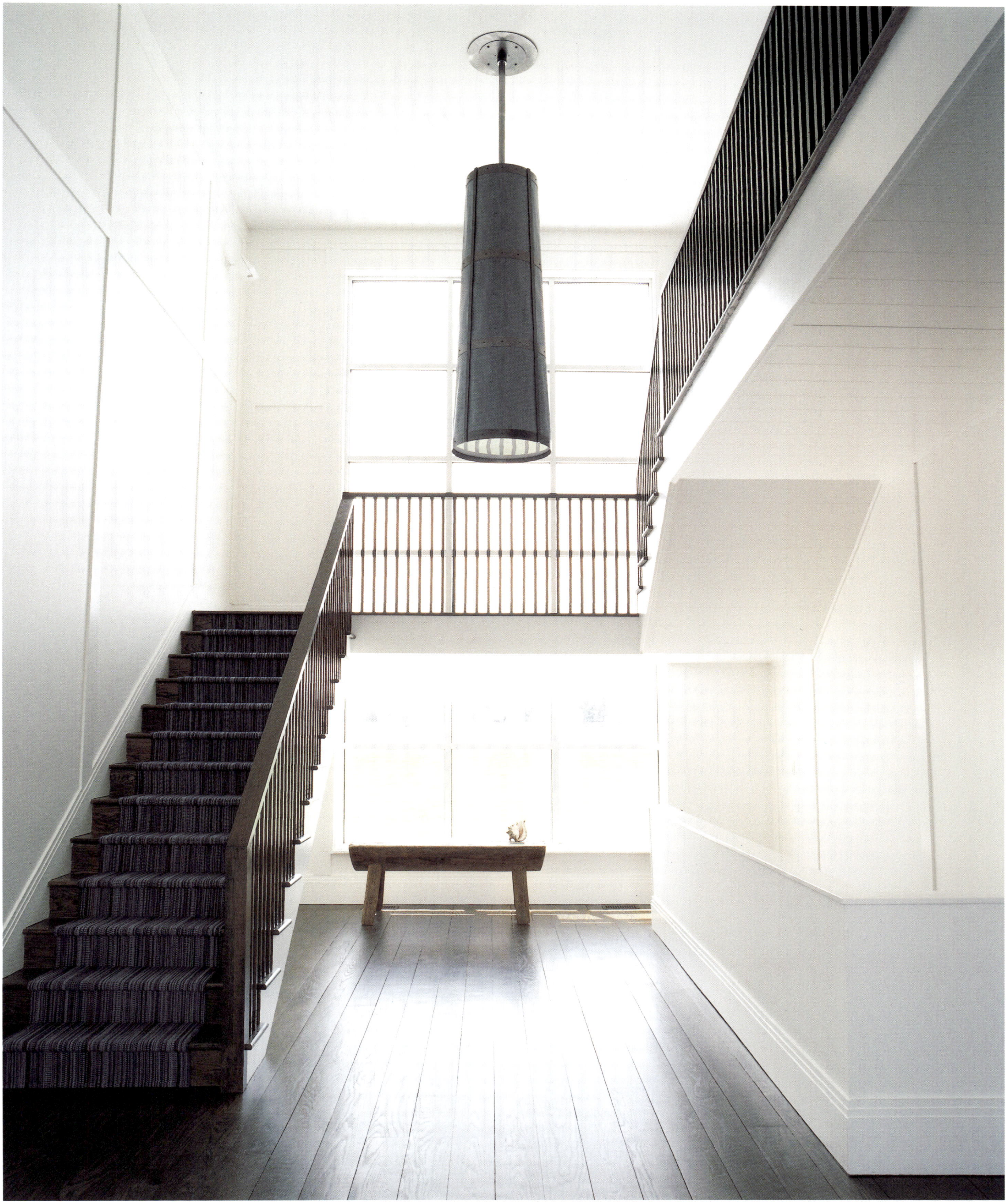

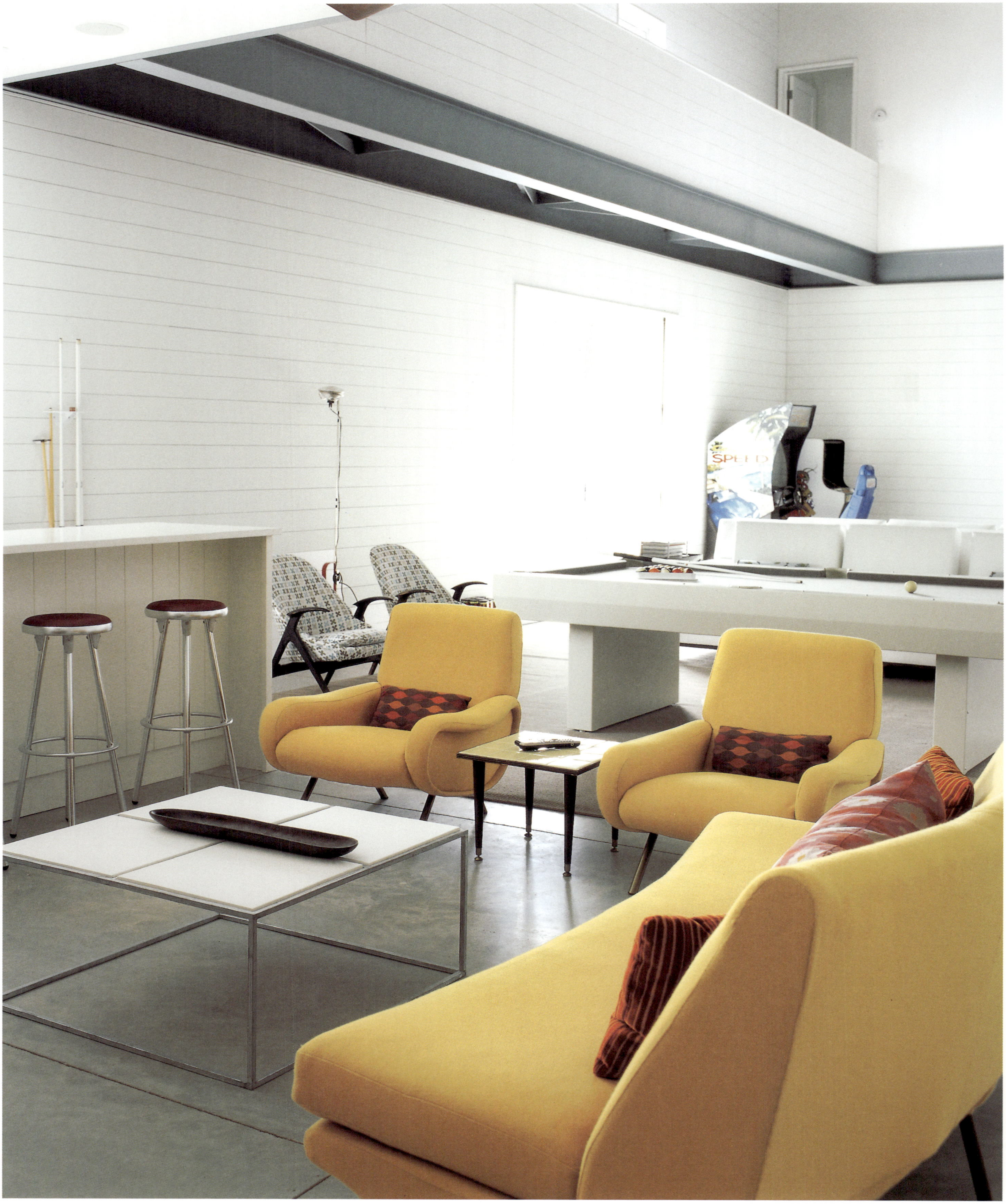
SPEED

the Ray Charles singers
Paradise Islands
PROPAGANDA
Polka Date
with Johnny Bud and his Polka Dots
URANIA
COOL VELVET STAN GETZ AND STRINGS
TONY MOTTOLA
MEXICO/S.A.
Misty
GEORGIE AULD
POINT·BLANK
REVOLVER
CYNDI LAUPER
I JUST CAN'T STOP IT

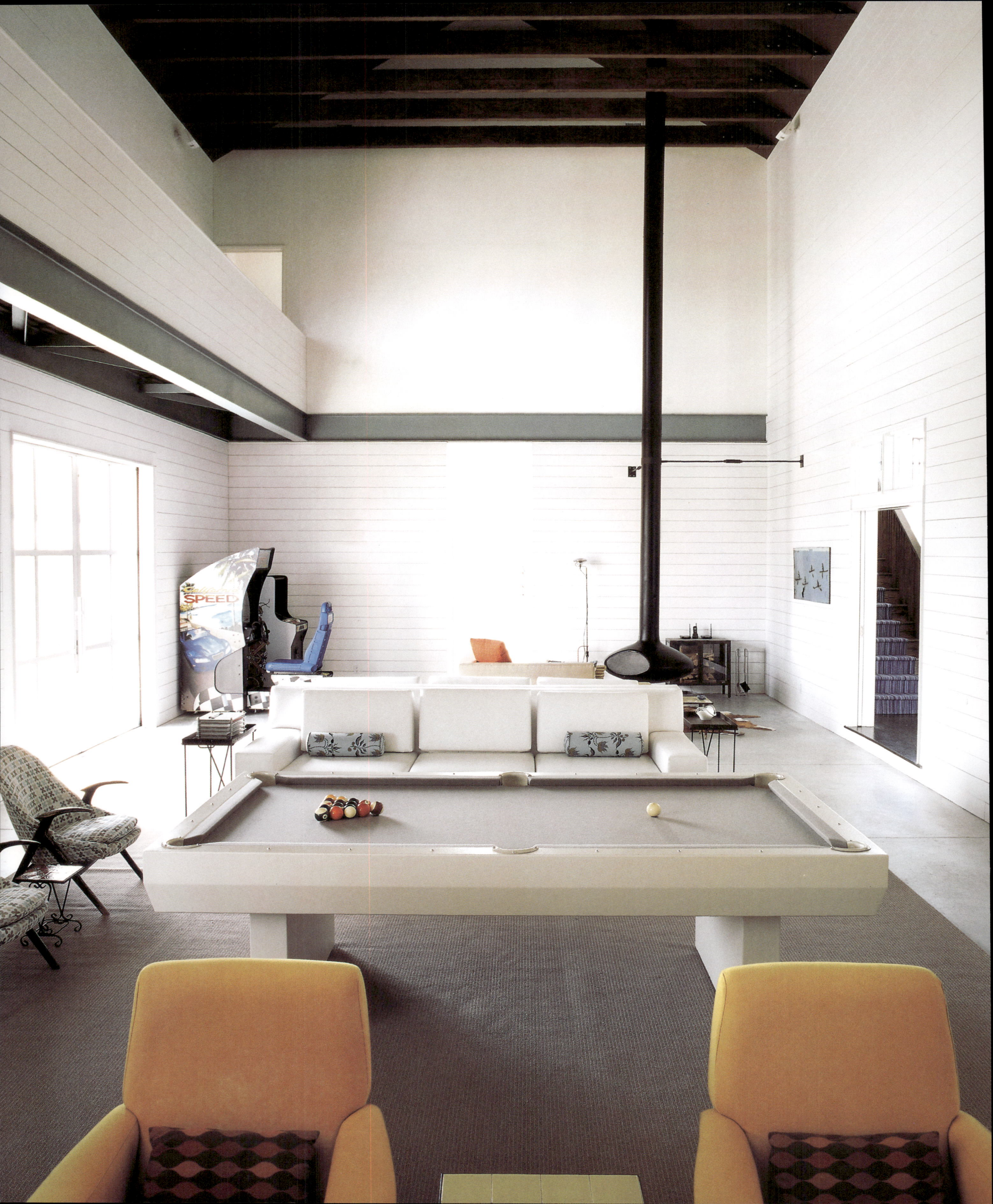
SPEED

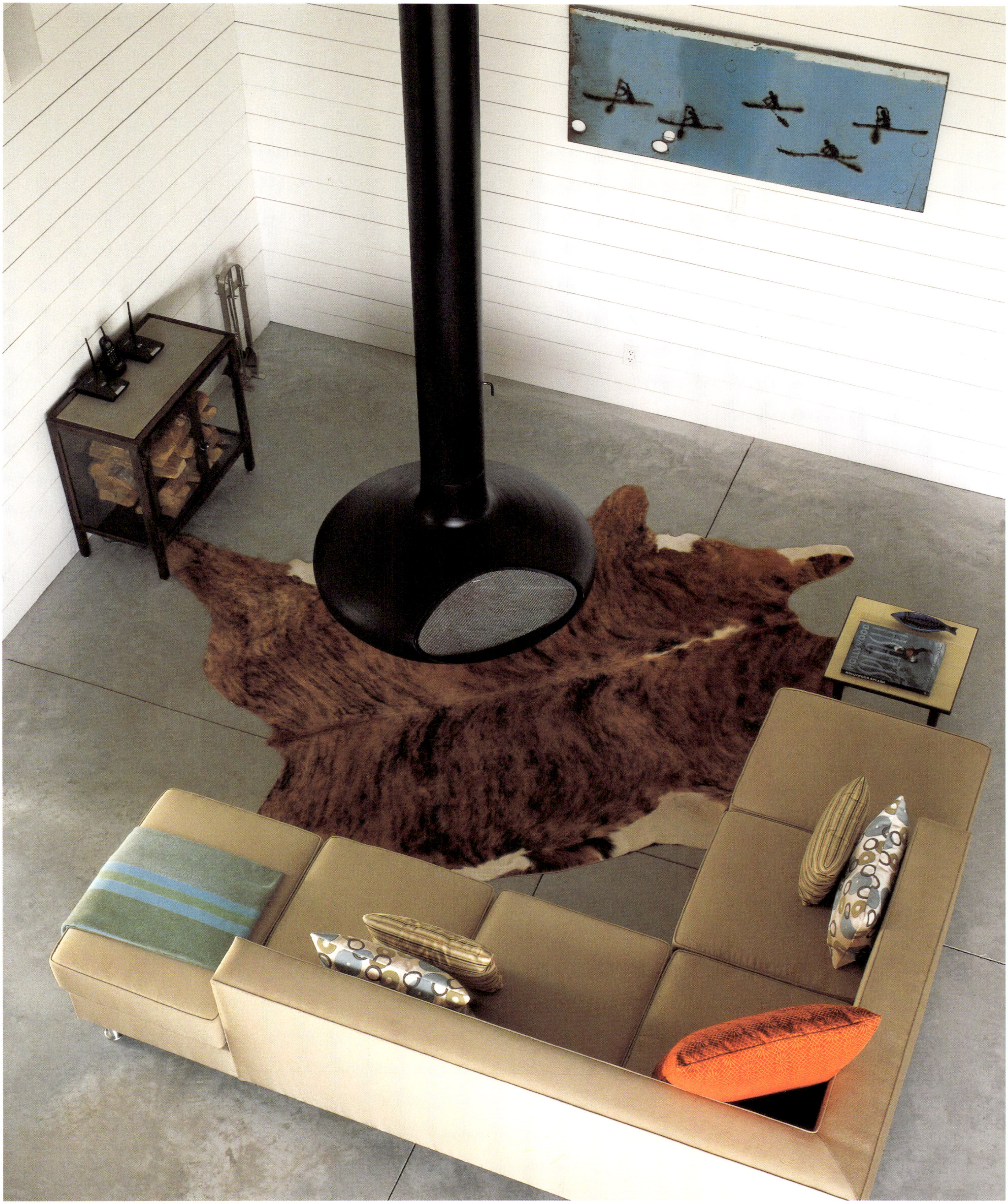

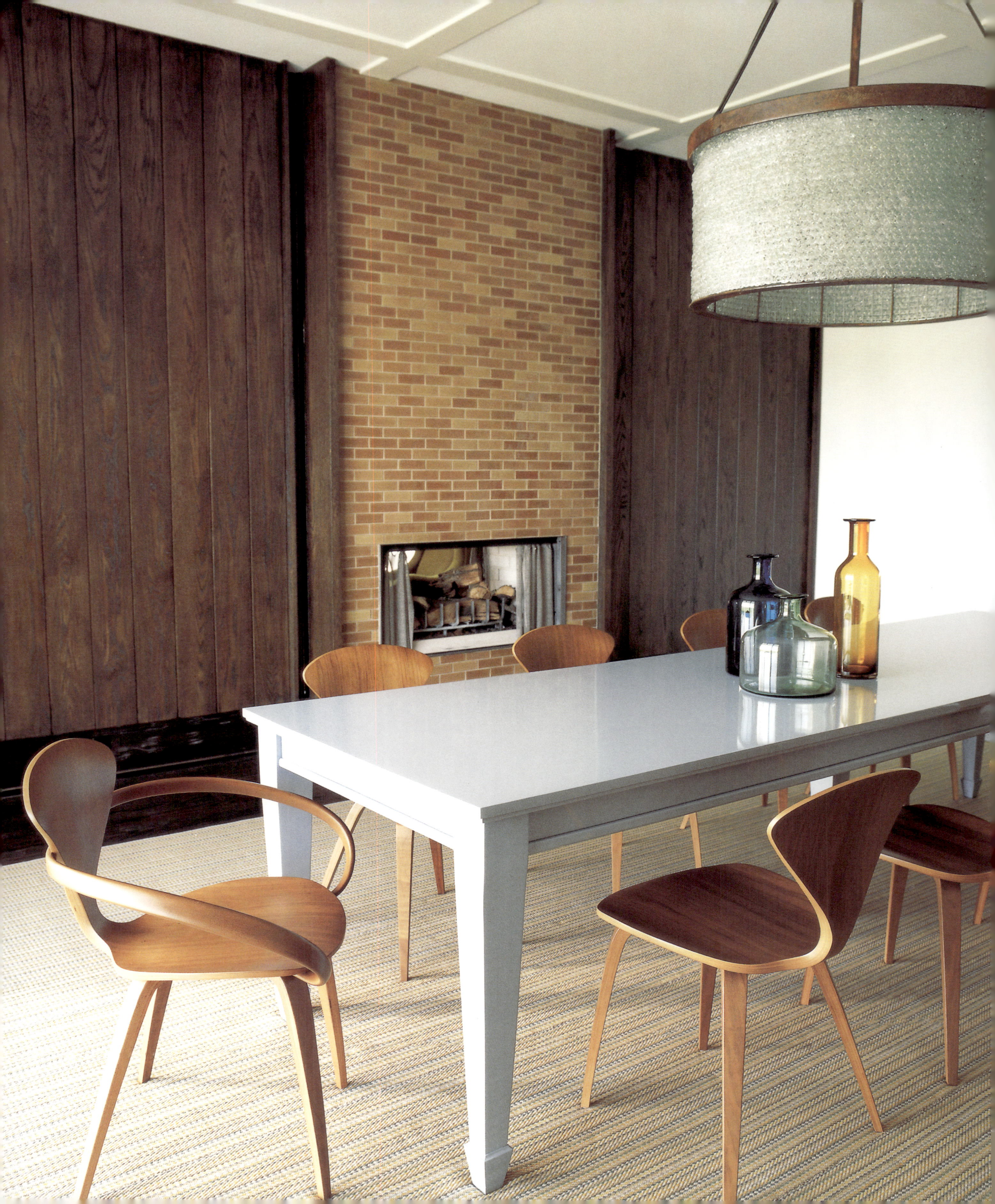

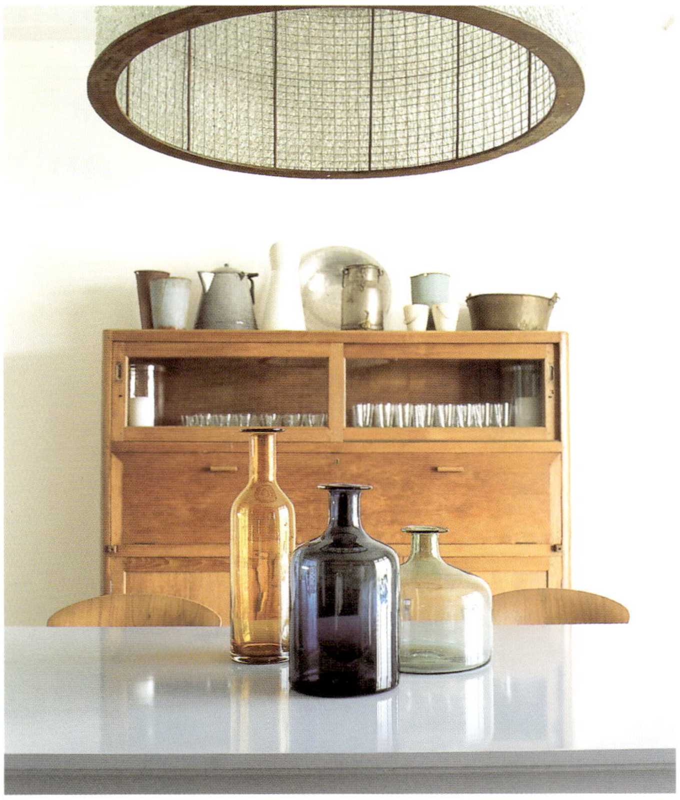

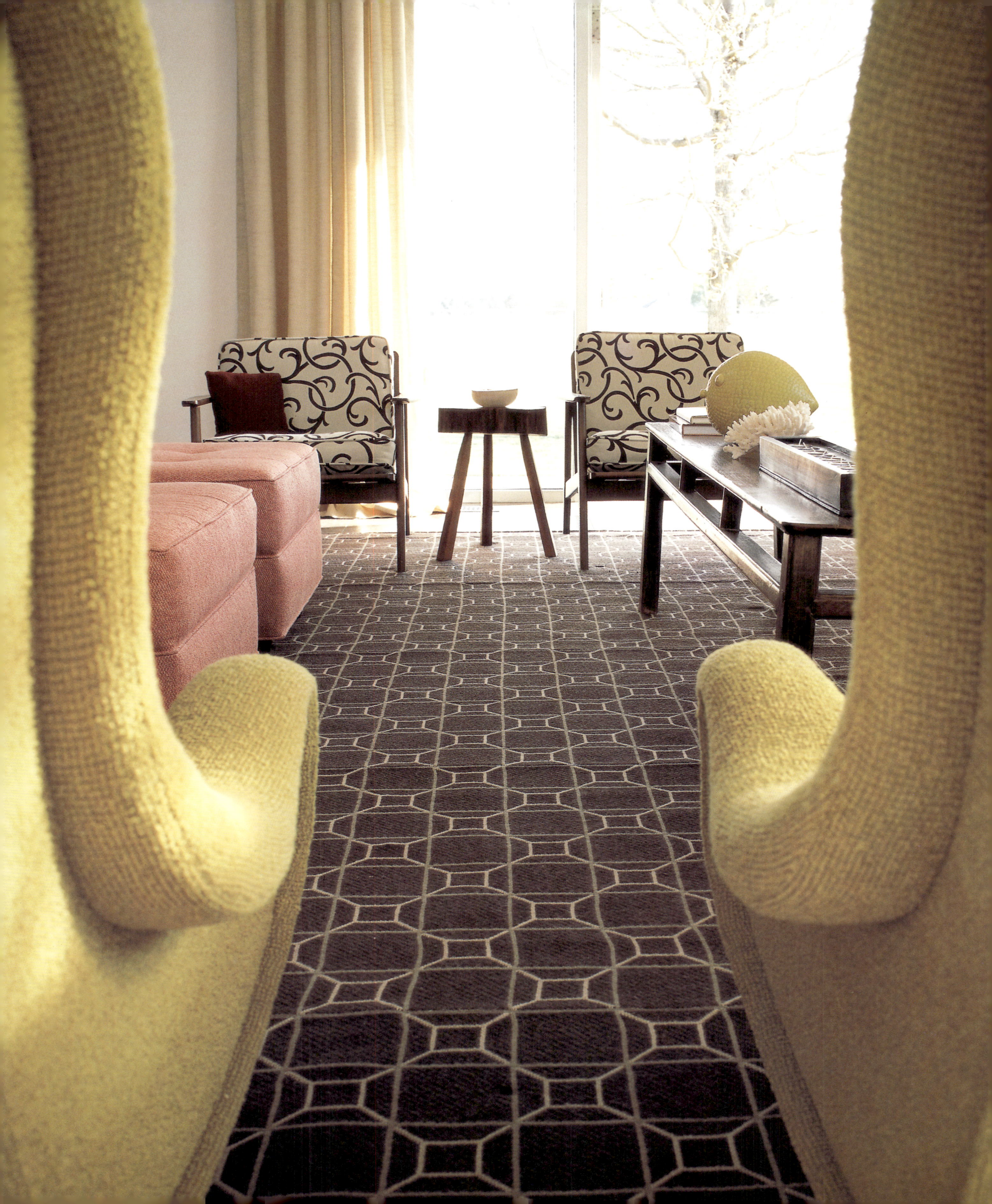

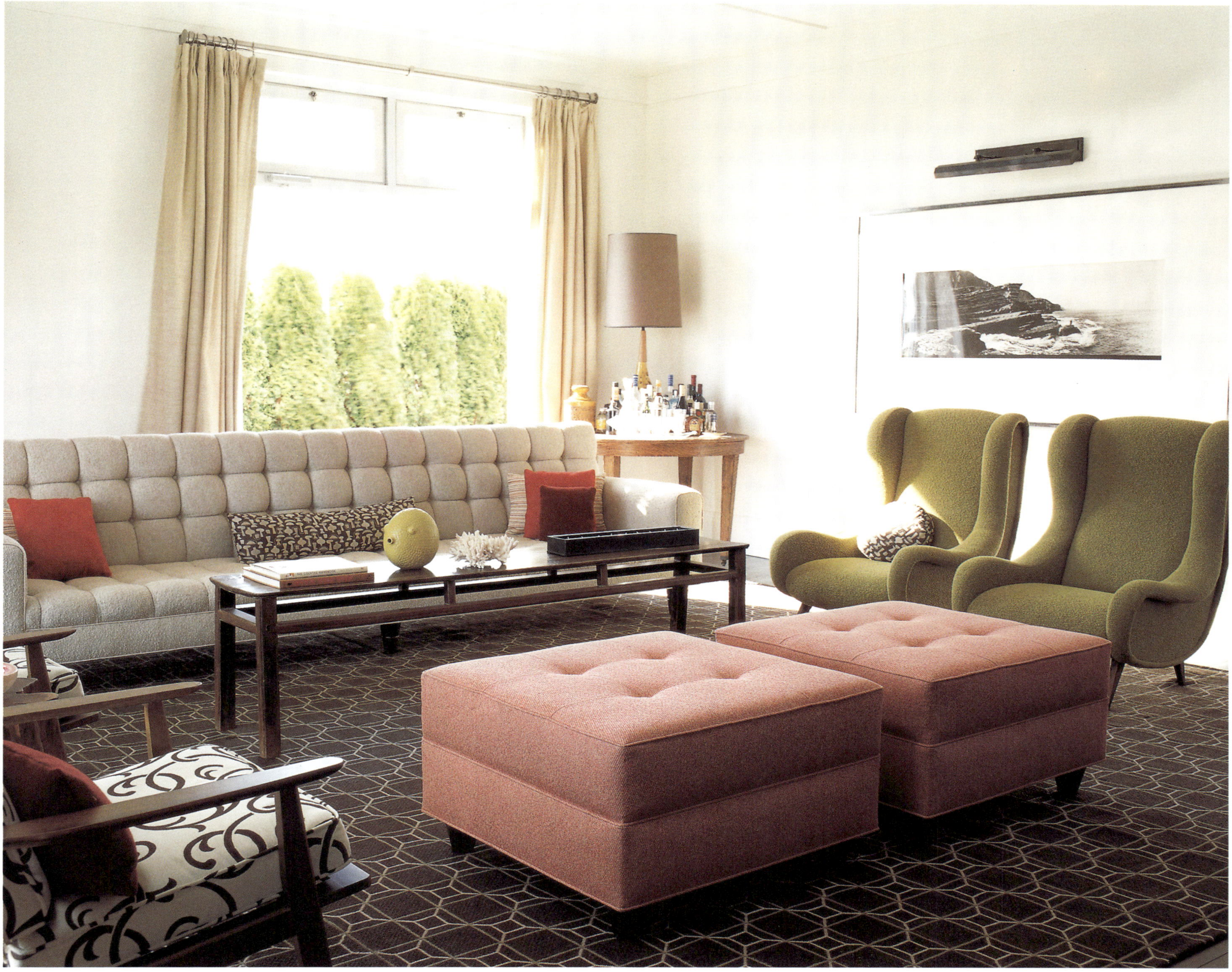

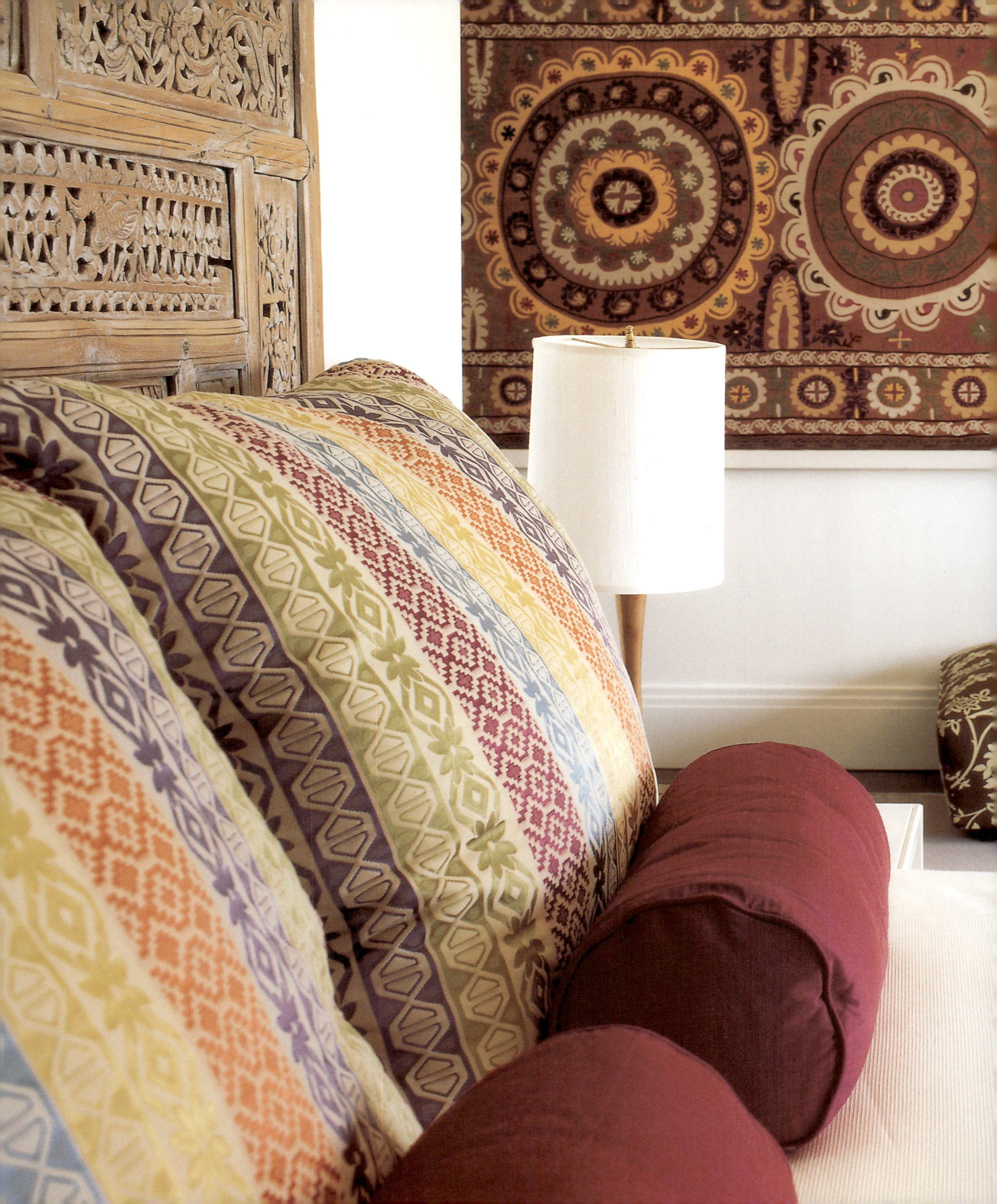

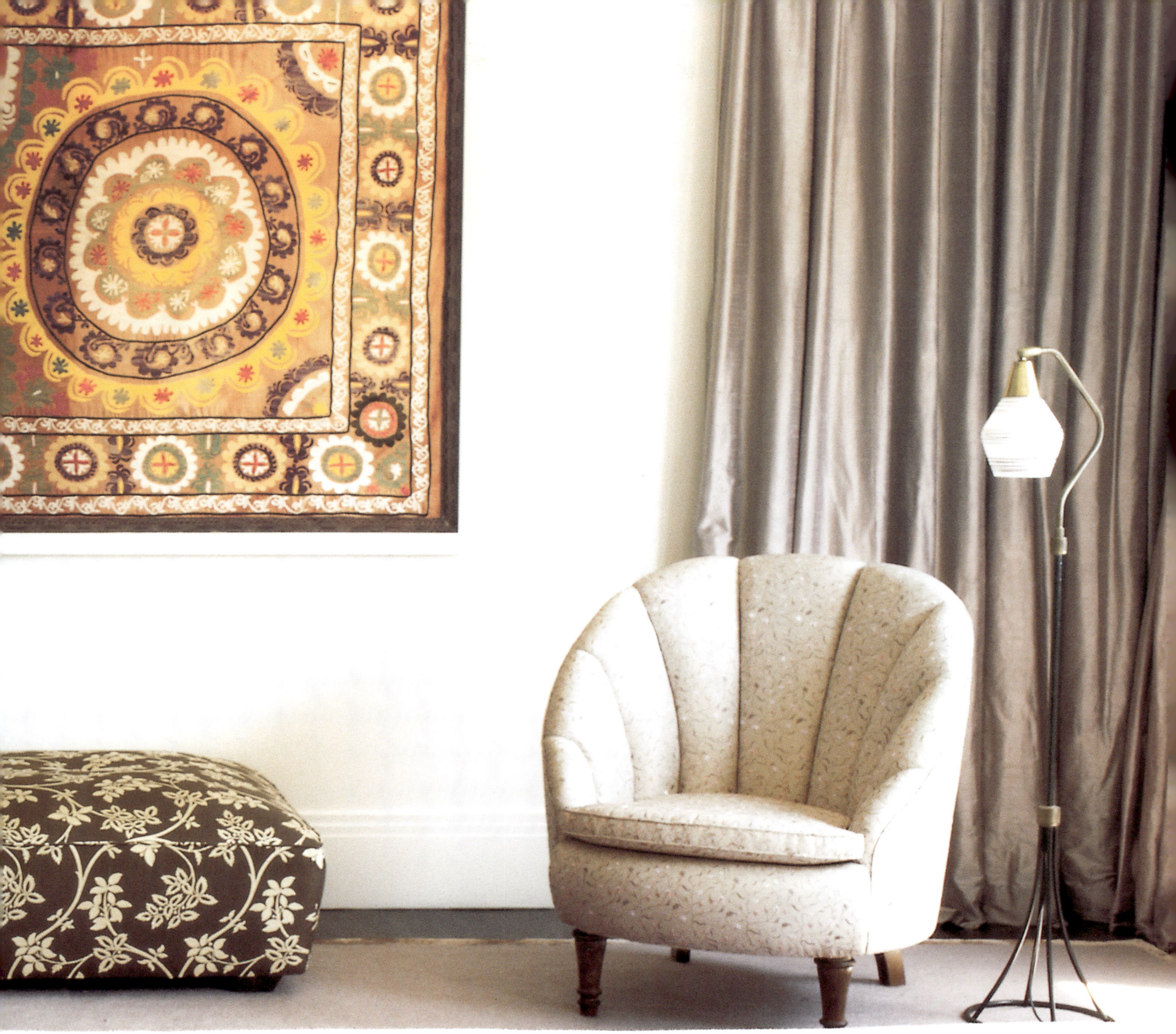

tony INGRAO & randy KEMPER

"We like to keep our work in the Hamptons casual and effortless. Every project seems to develop its own personality—some more classic, some contemporary. For this project, because it is surrounded by reserve and parkland, the house took a decidedly more natural and earthy direction. It's interesting to pay attention to what the essence of a house is, to capture its spirit."

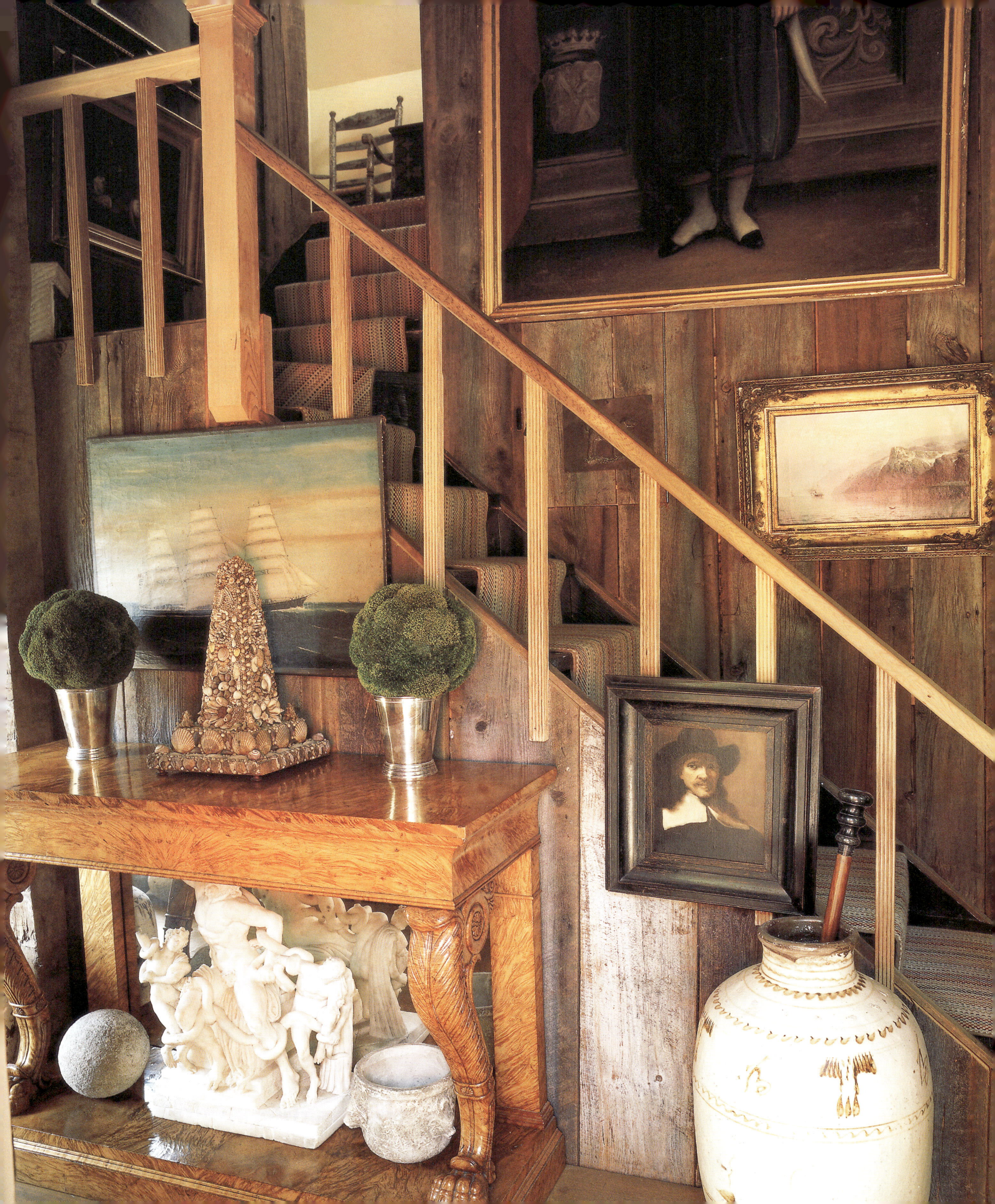

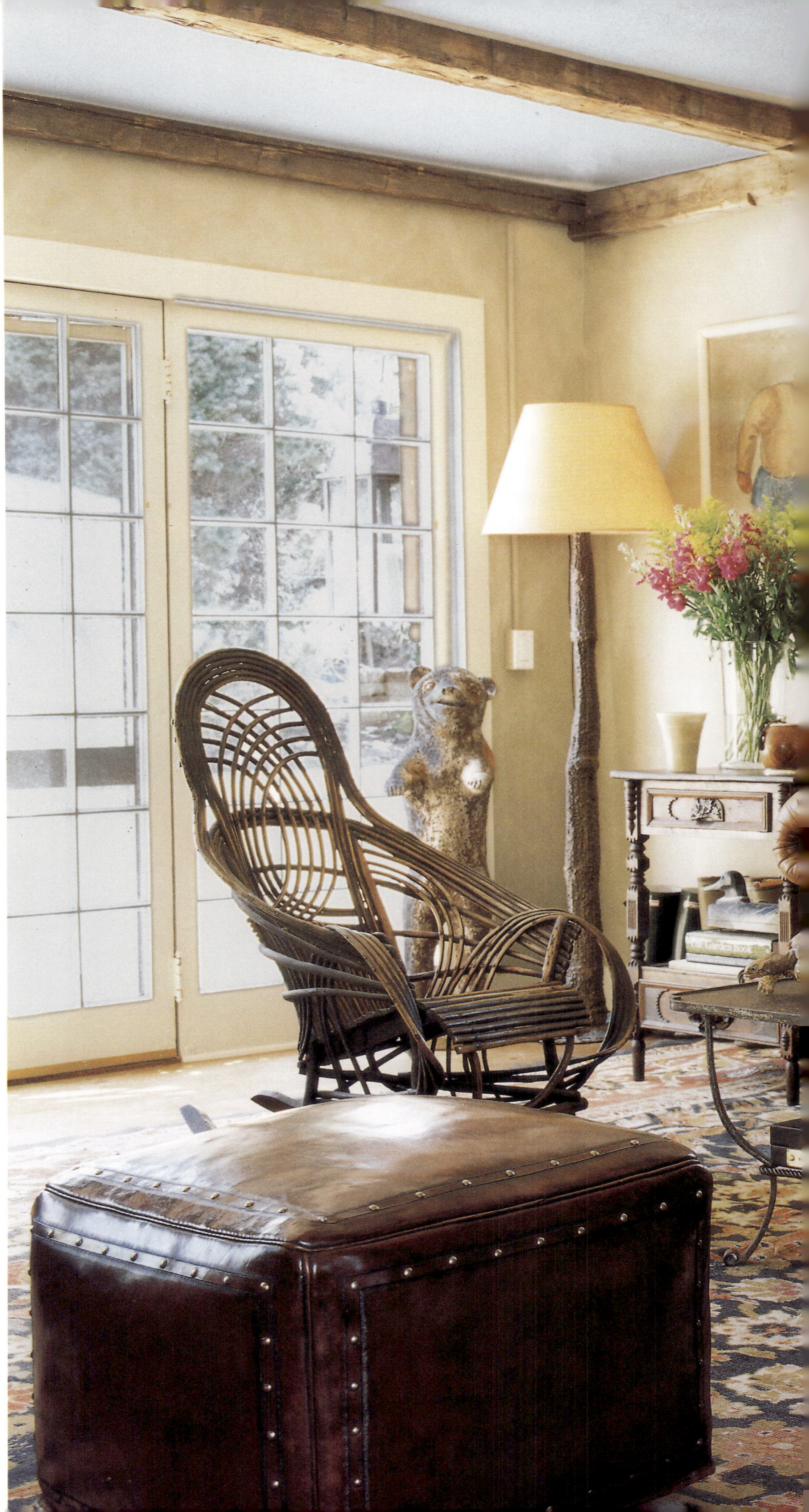

Princely Gardens
ART OF THE FORMAL GARDEN
PRIVATE GARDENS OF PARIS MADISON COX

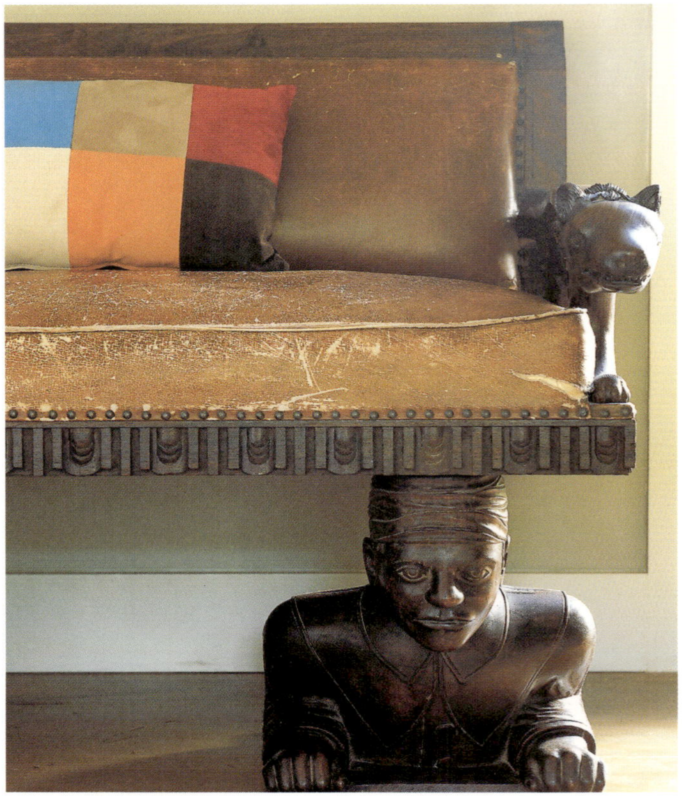

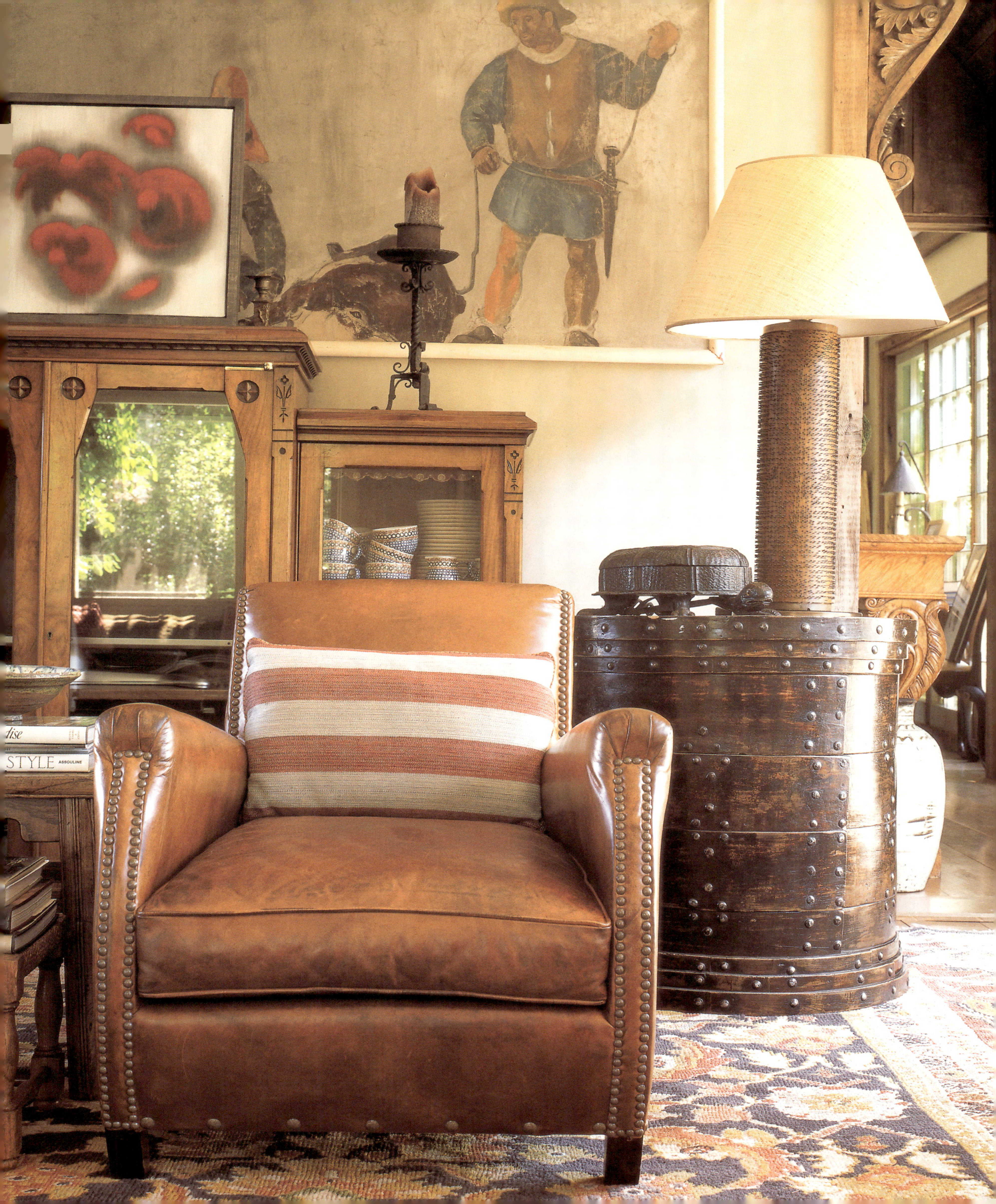
STYLE
ASSOULINE

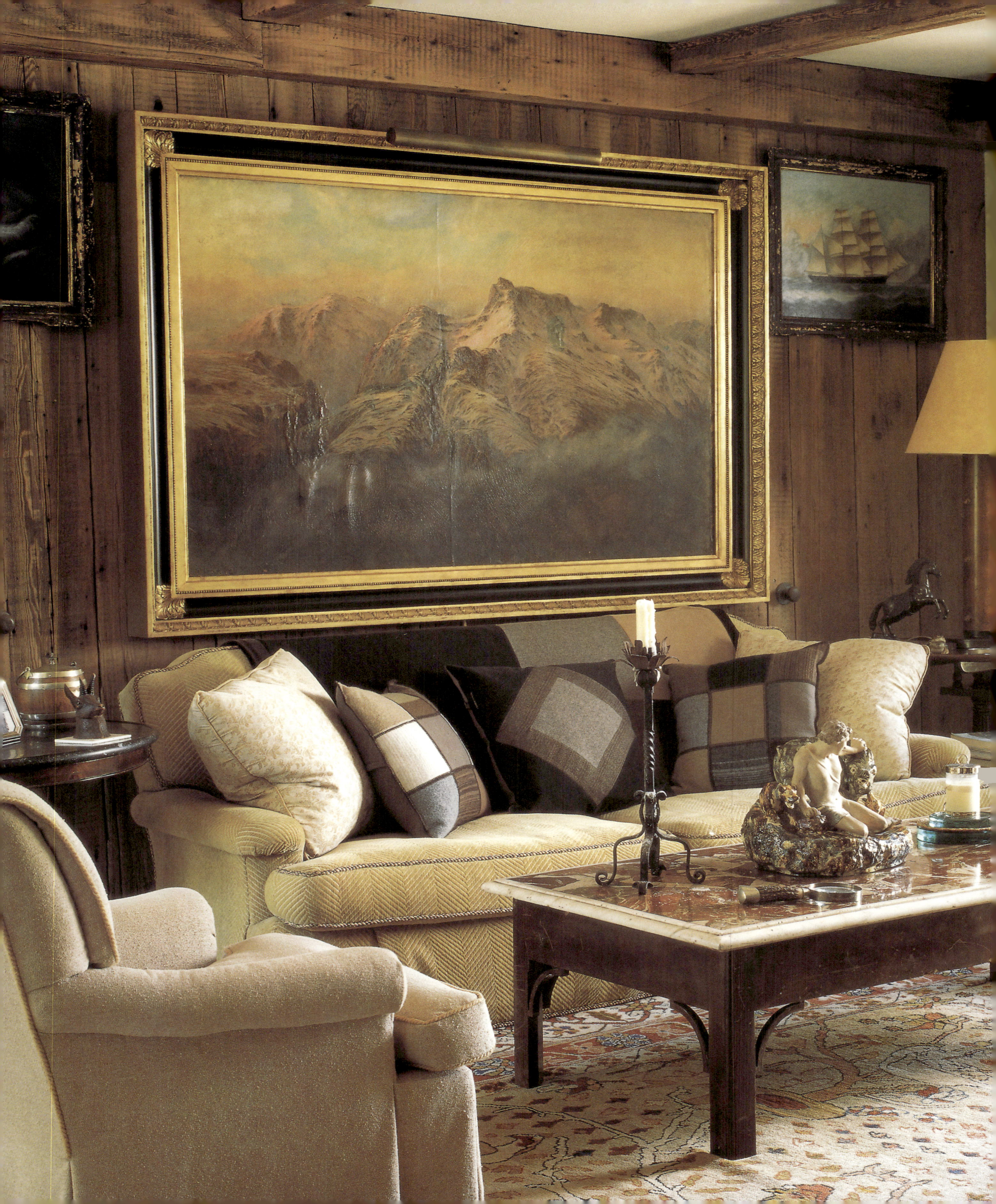

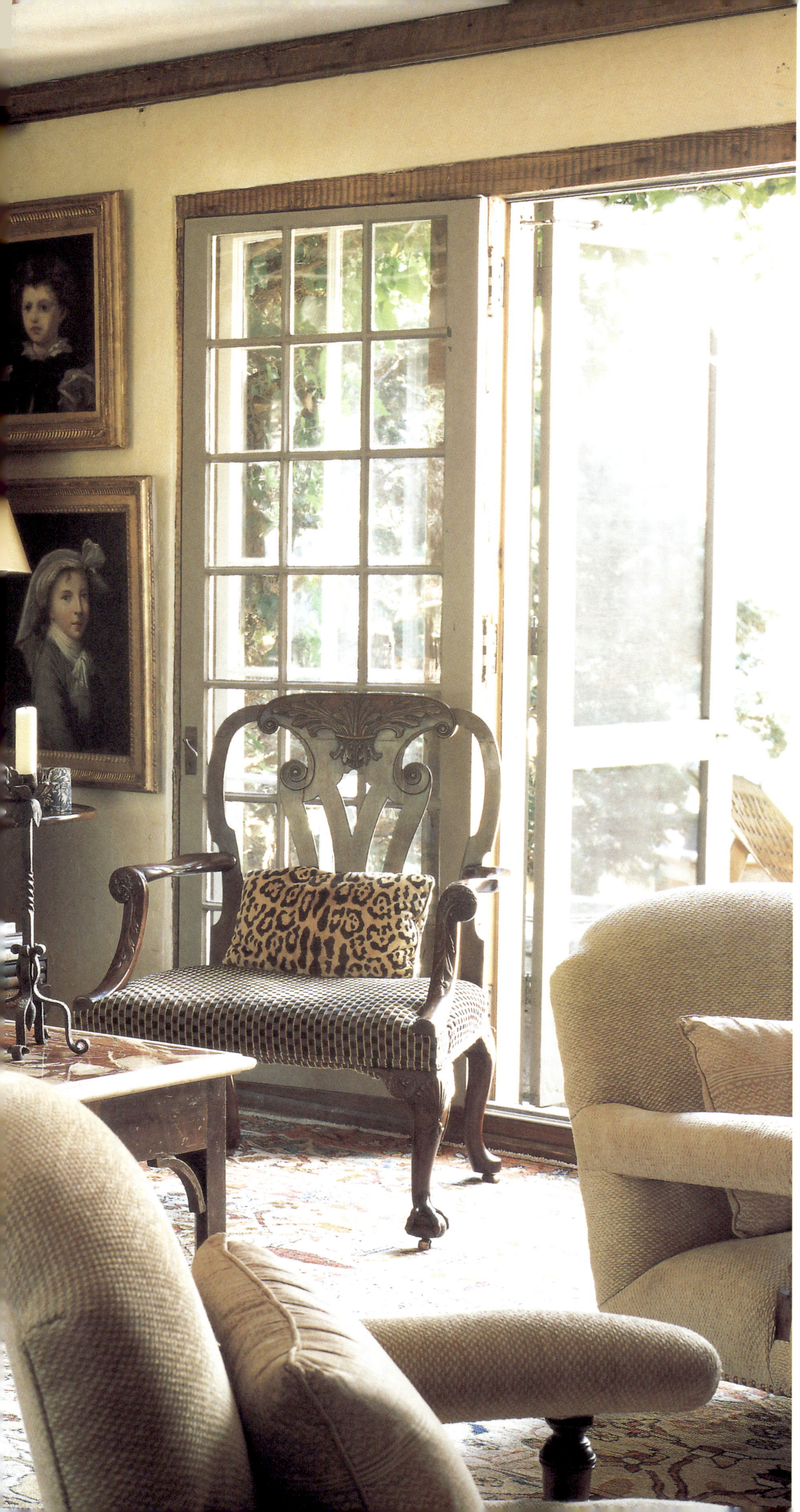

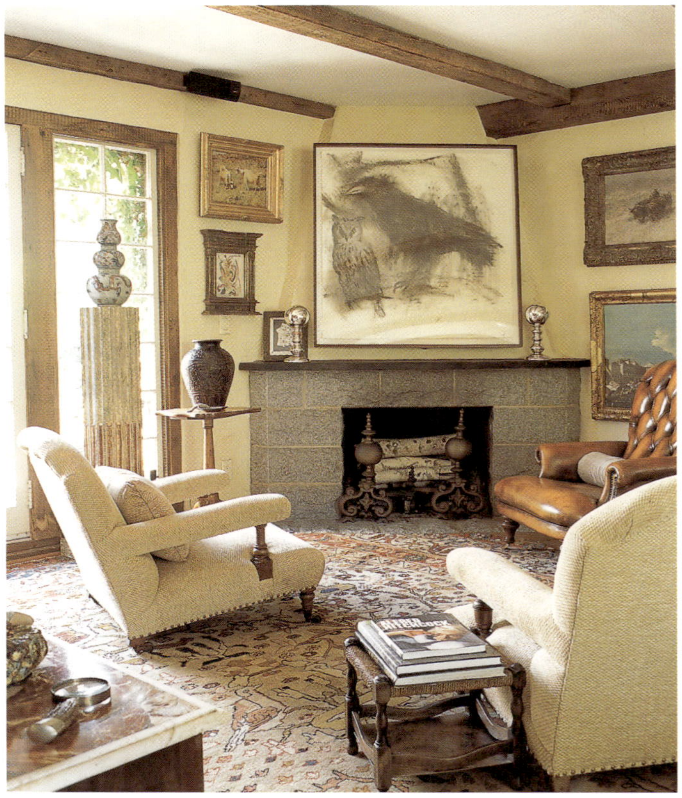

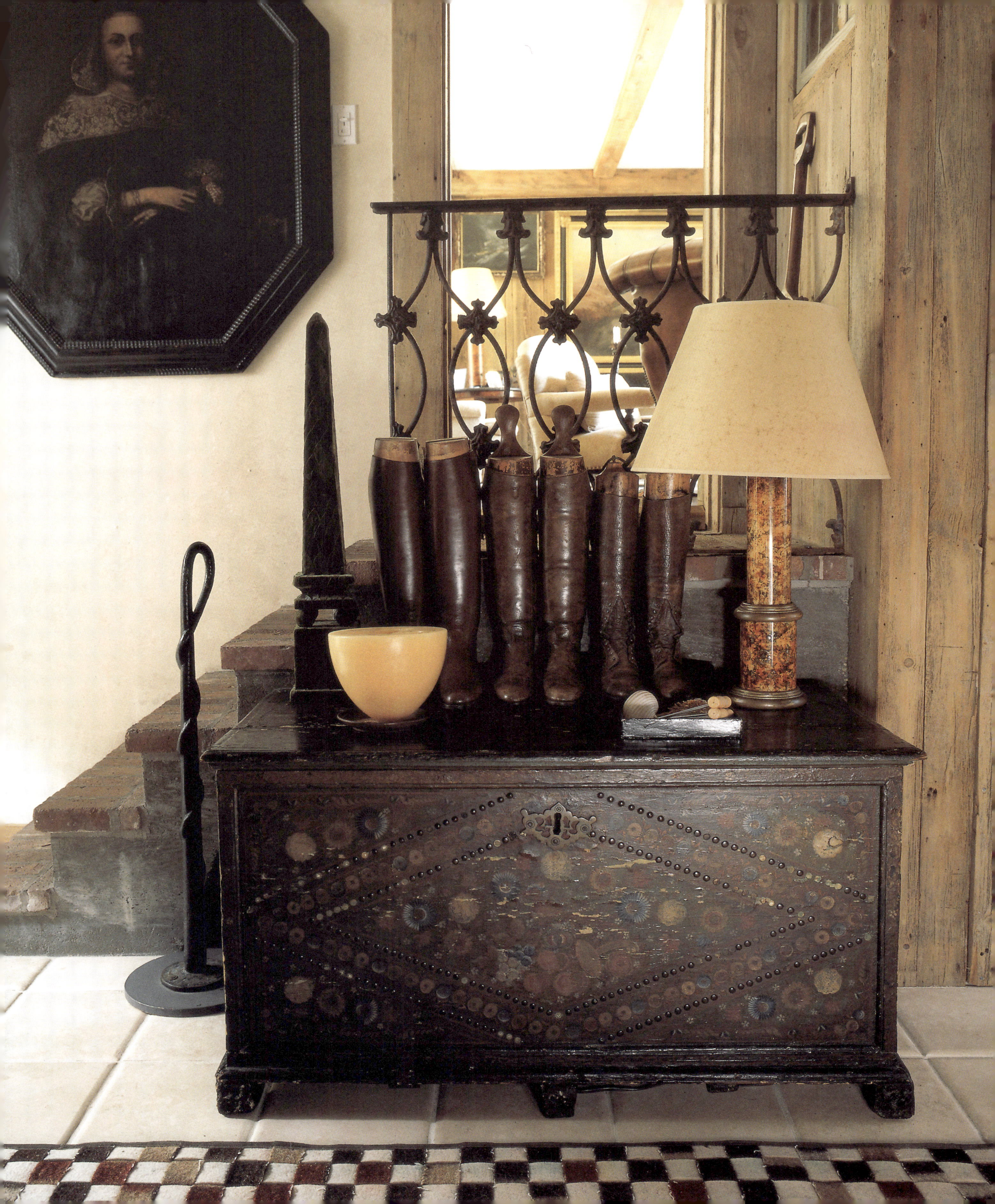

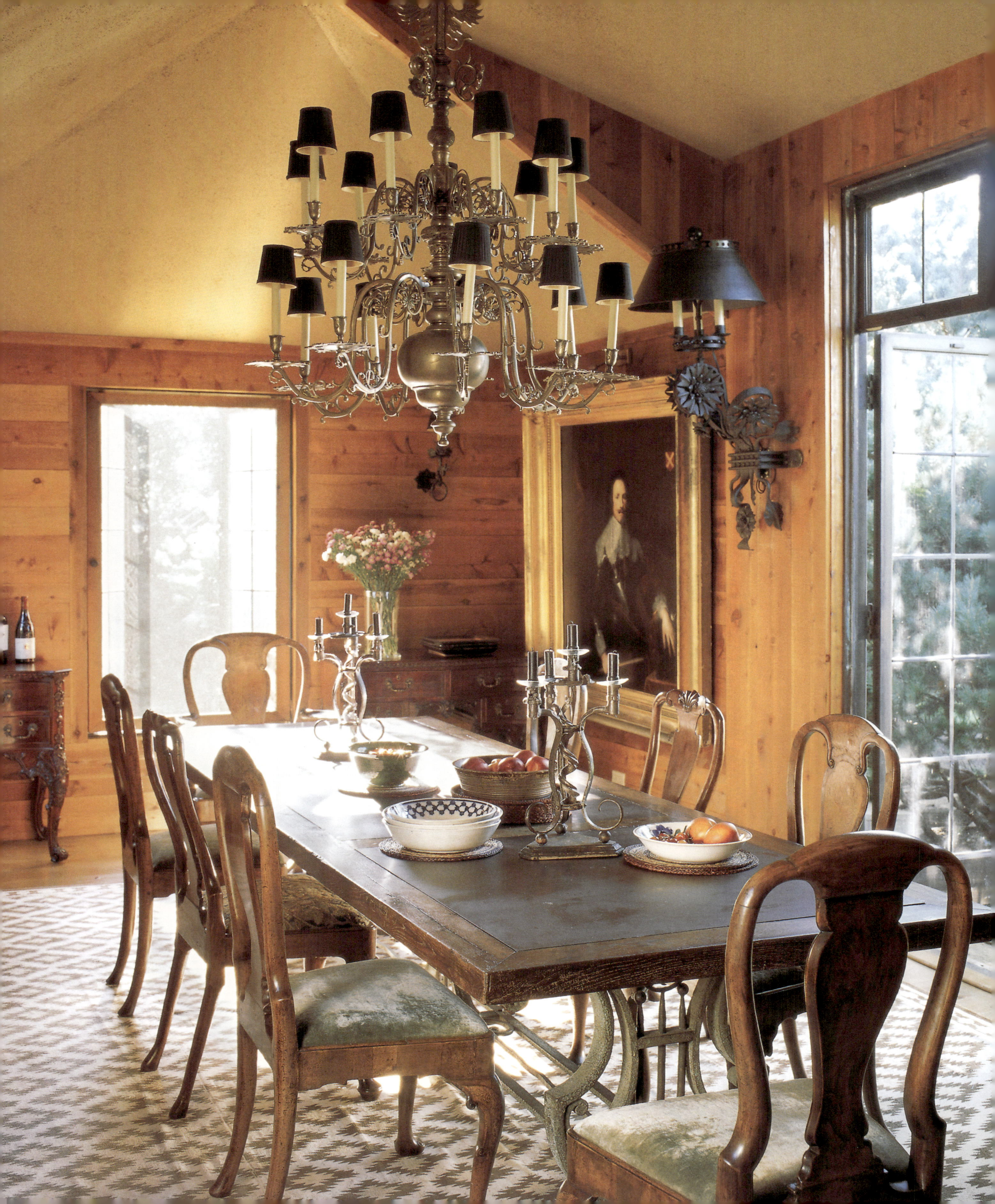

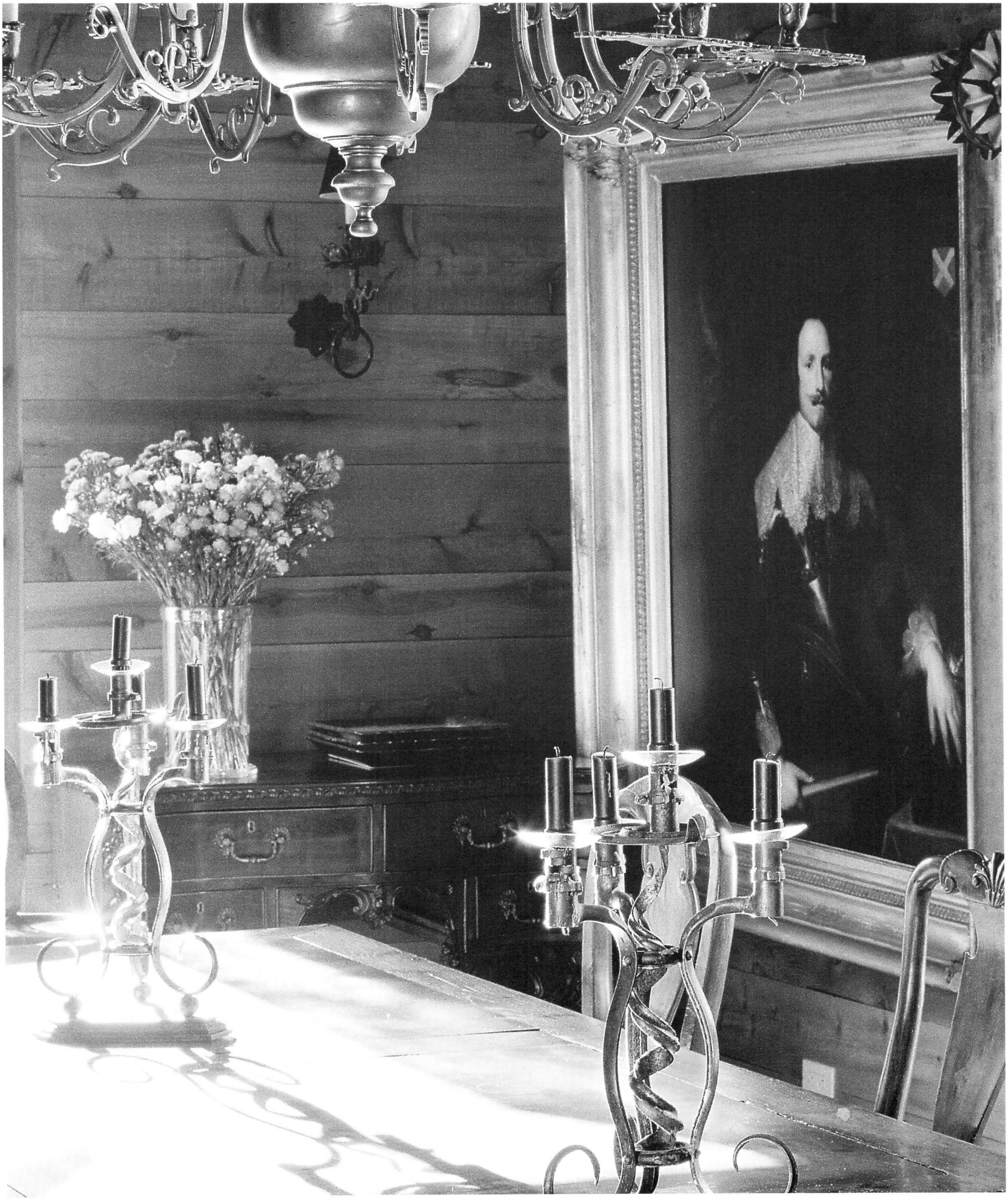

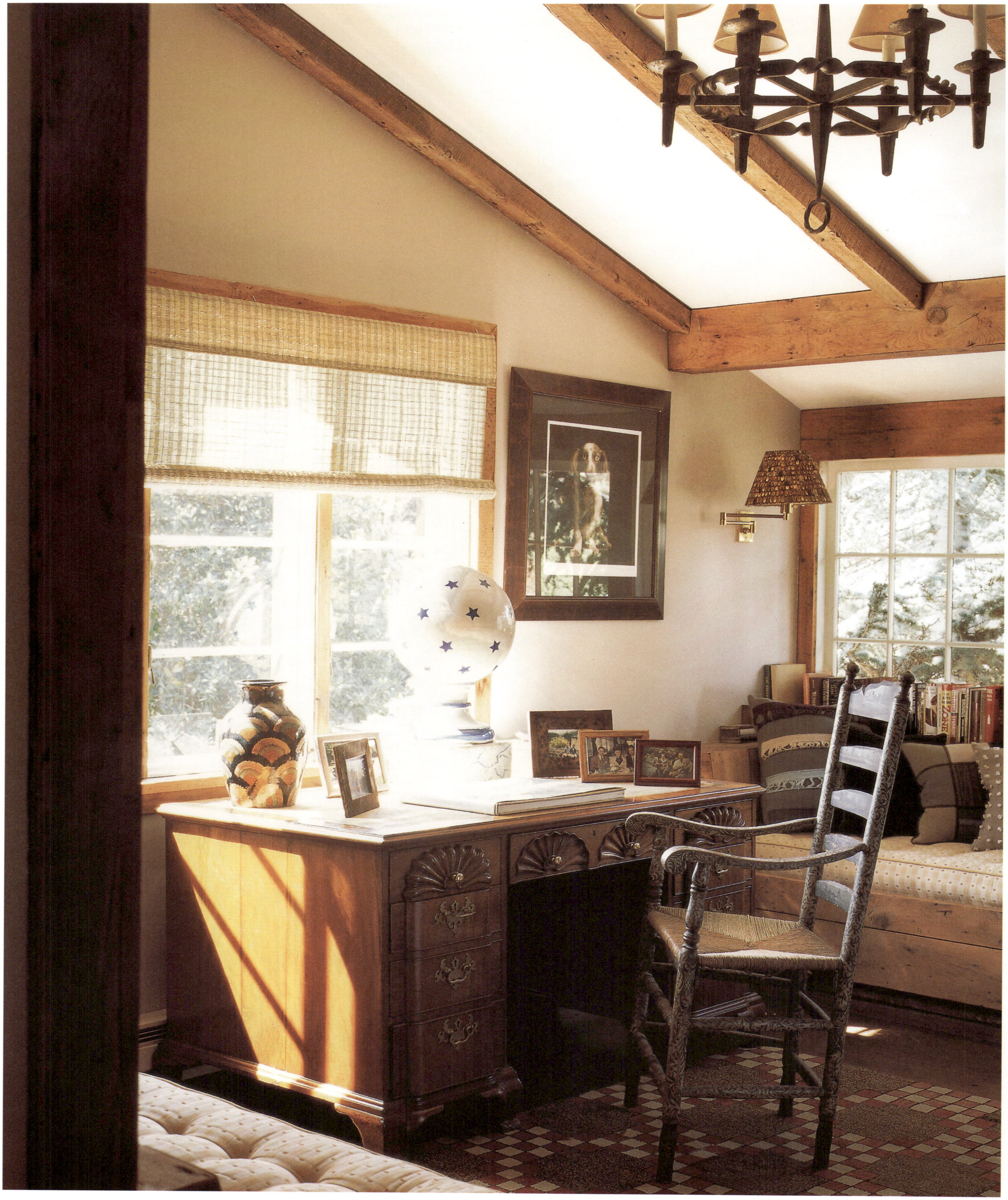

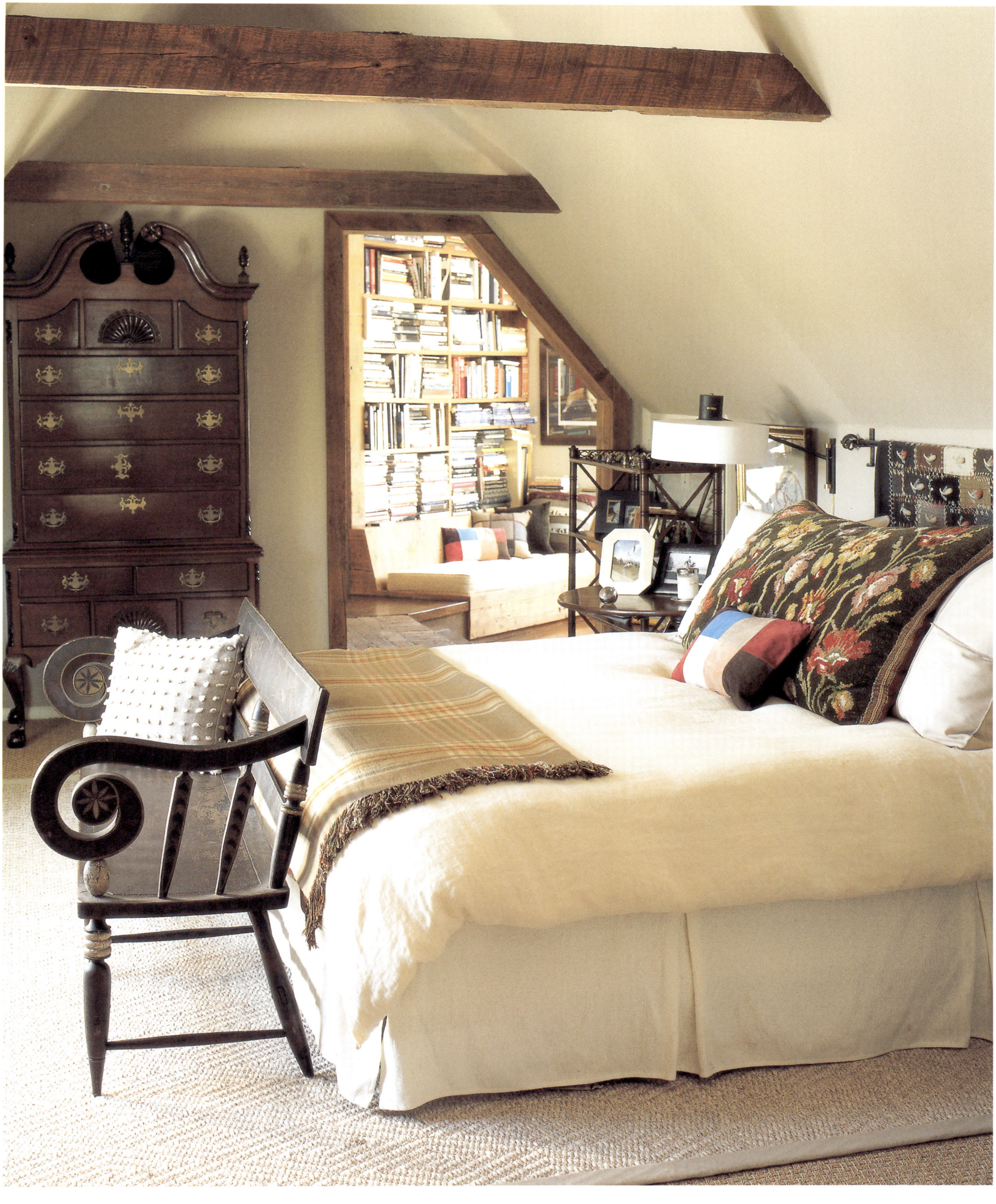

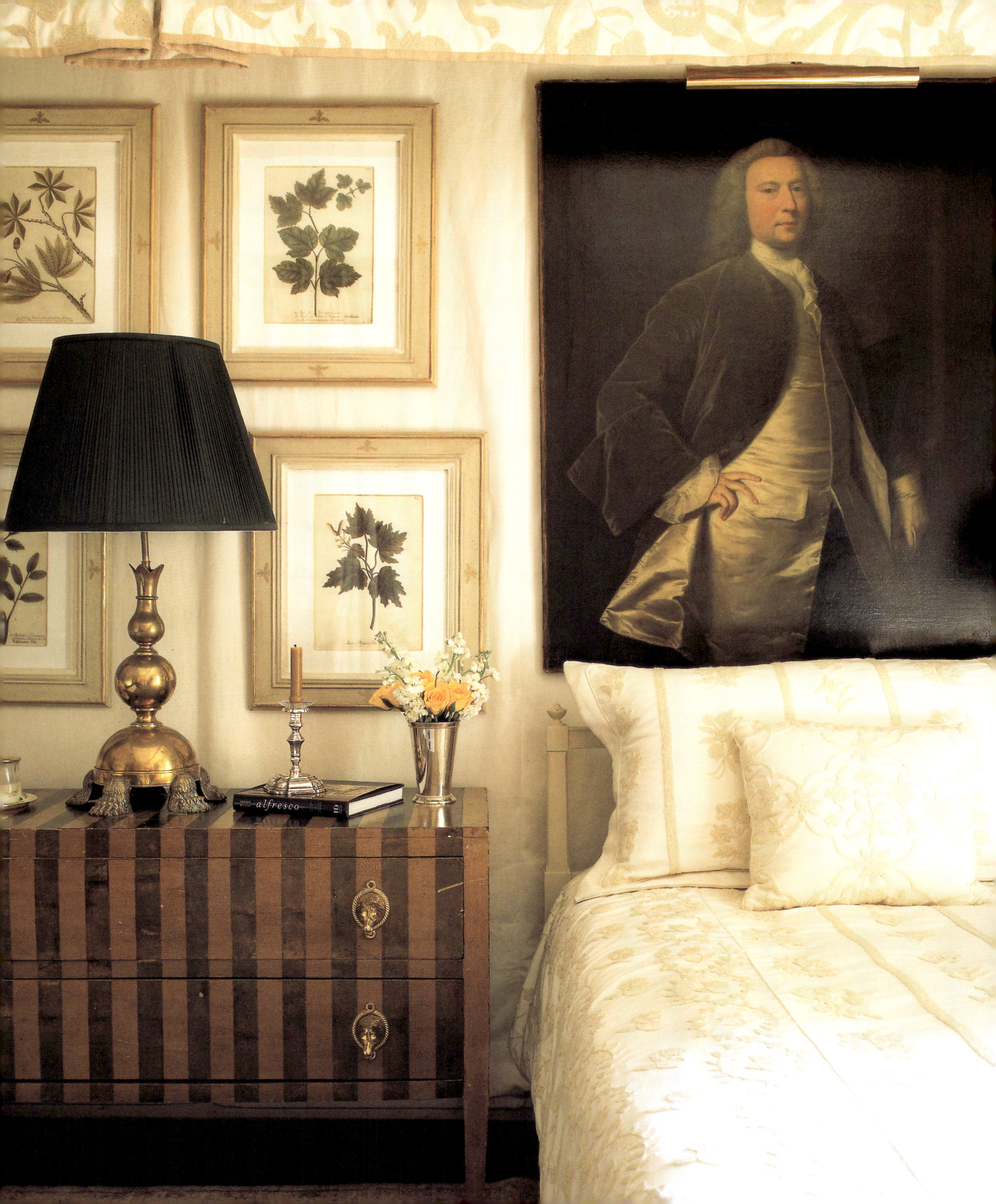
alfresco

tom
FLYNN

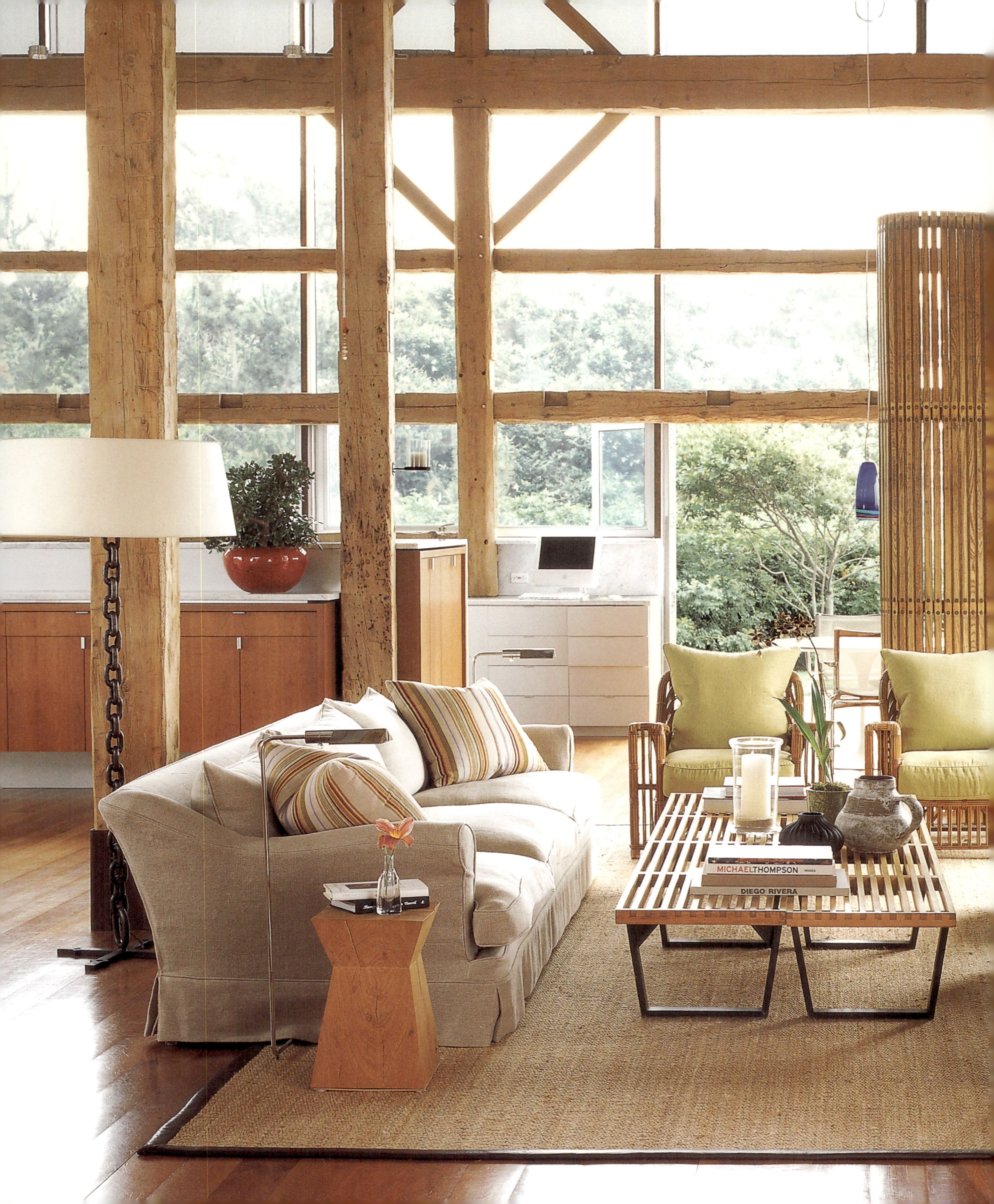
MICHAELTHOMPSON
DIEGO RIVERA

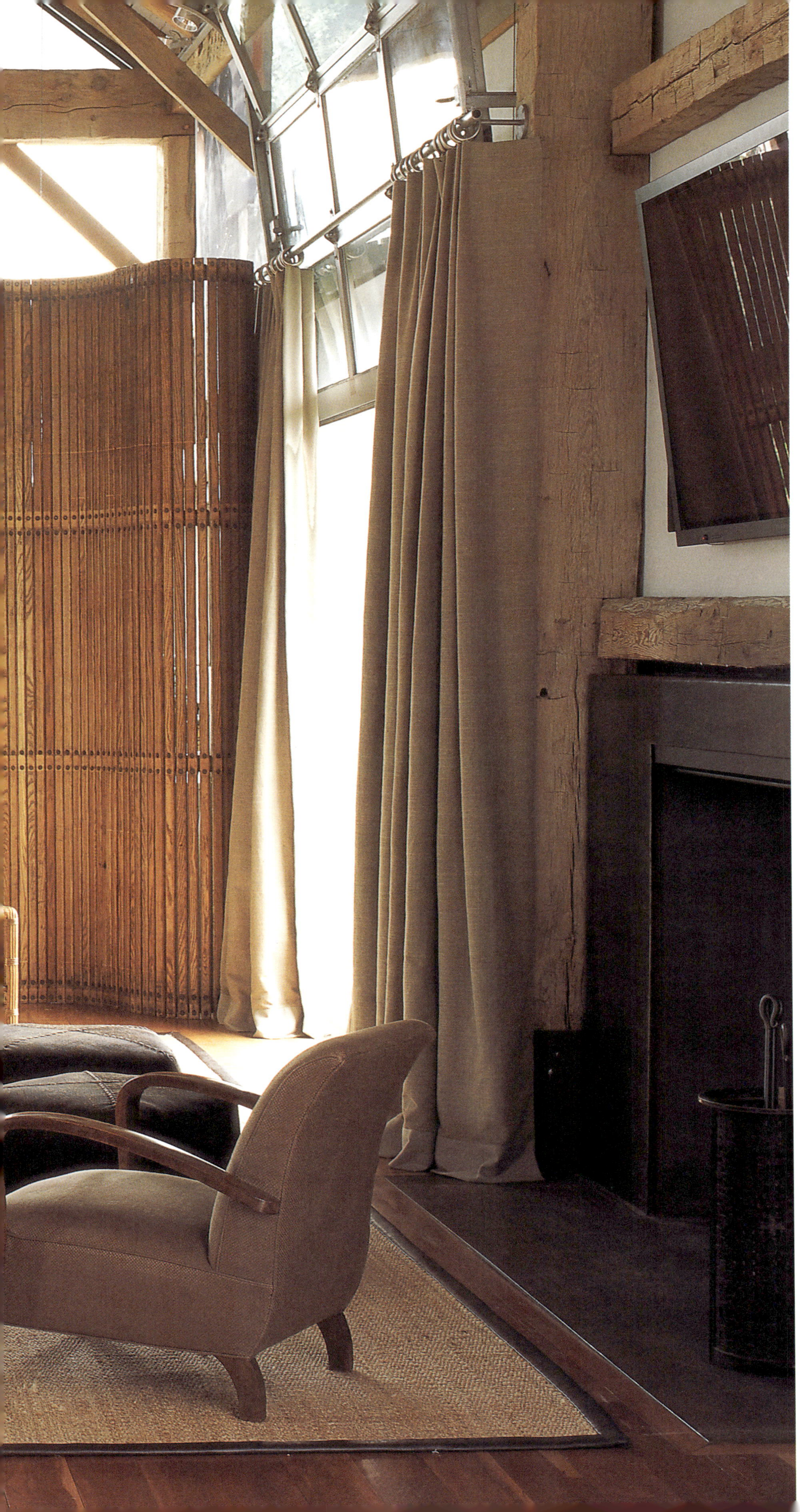

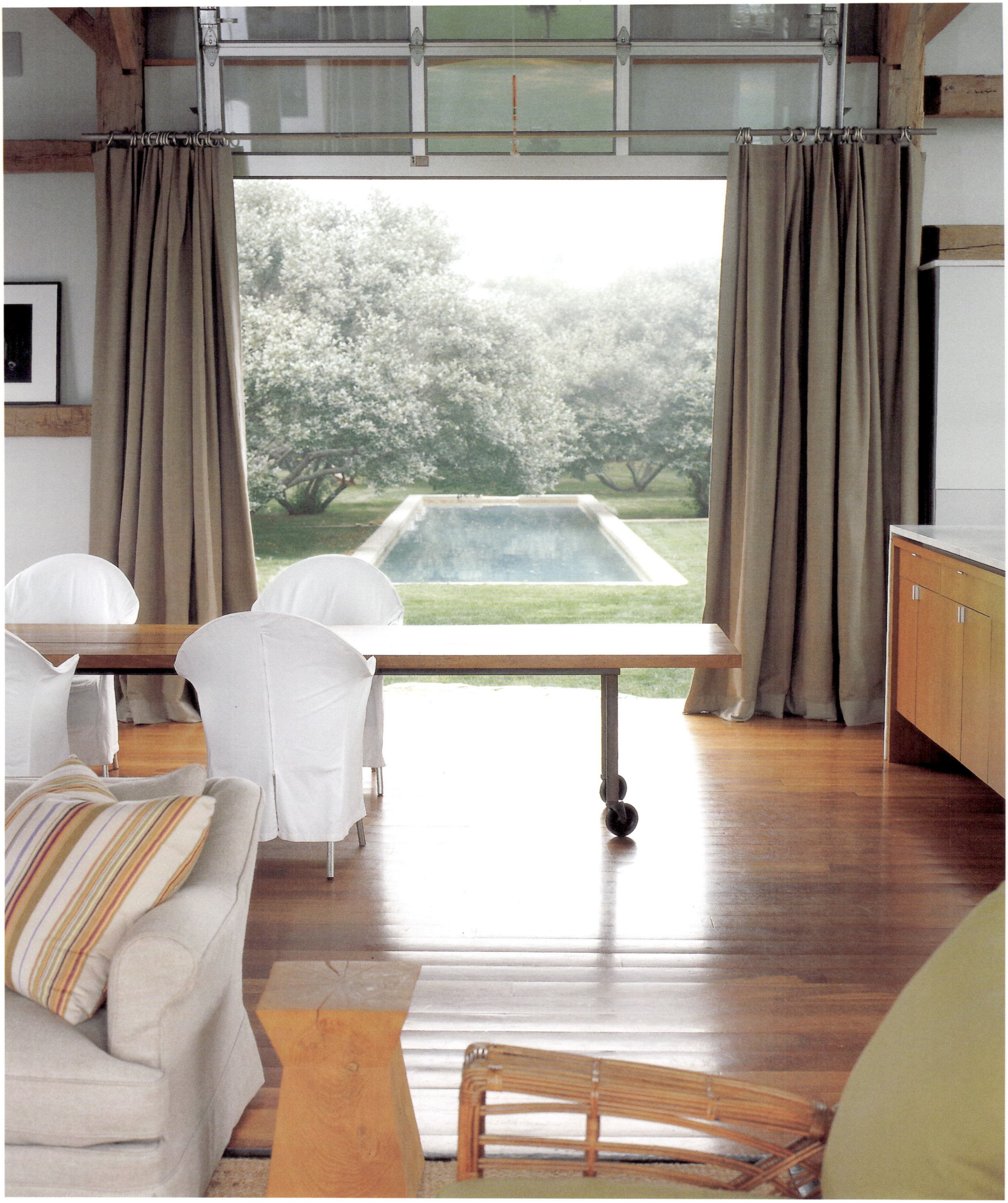

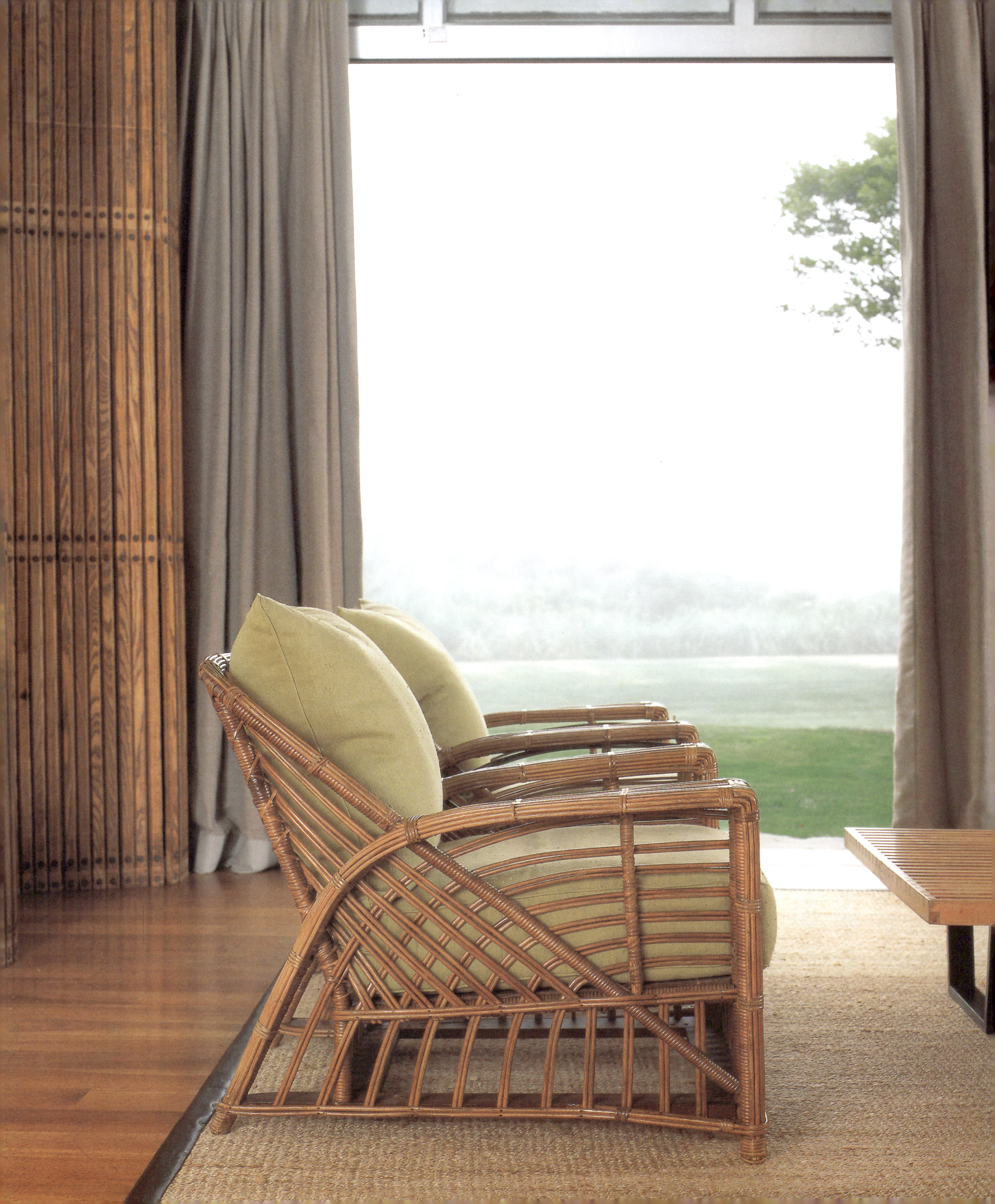

"As an interior designer, it's not my job to impose an aesthetic on a client, but to discover what will make the client comfortable in his or her own home and create an environment that balances style, uniqueness, sensuality, and functionality in a way that's personal. A home should embrace the people who live in it and their guests. Successful interiors don't attract tons of attention, instead they combine elements that encourage people to relax, stay awhile, and enjoy each other's company."

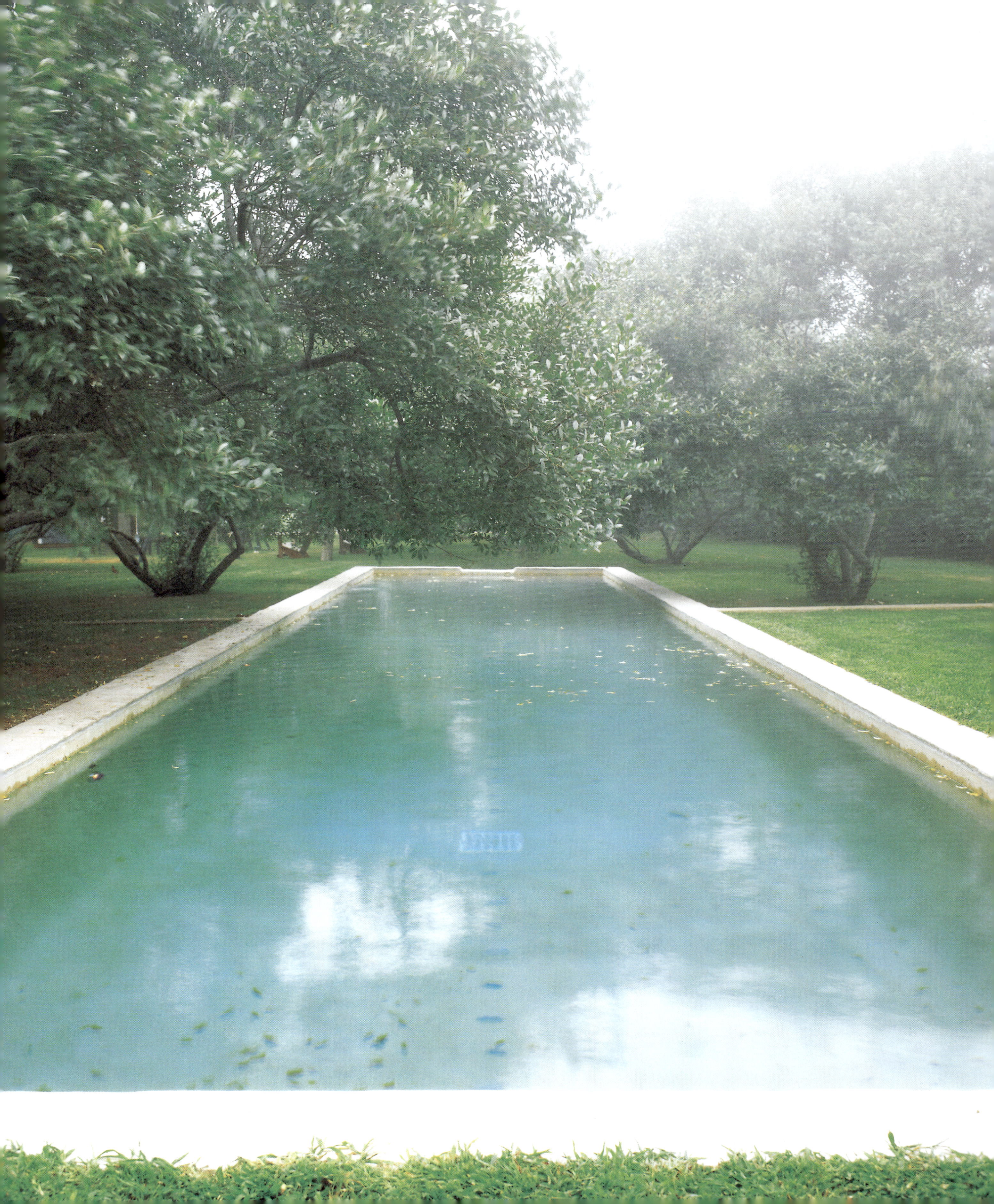

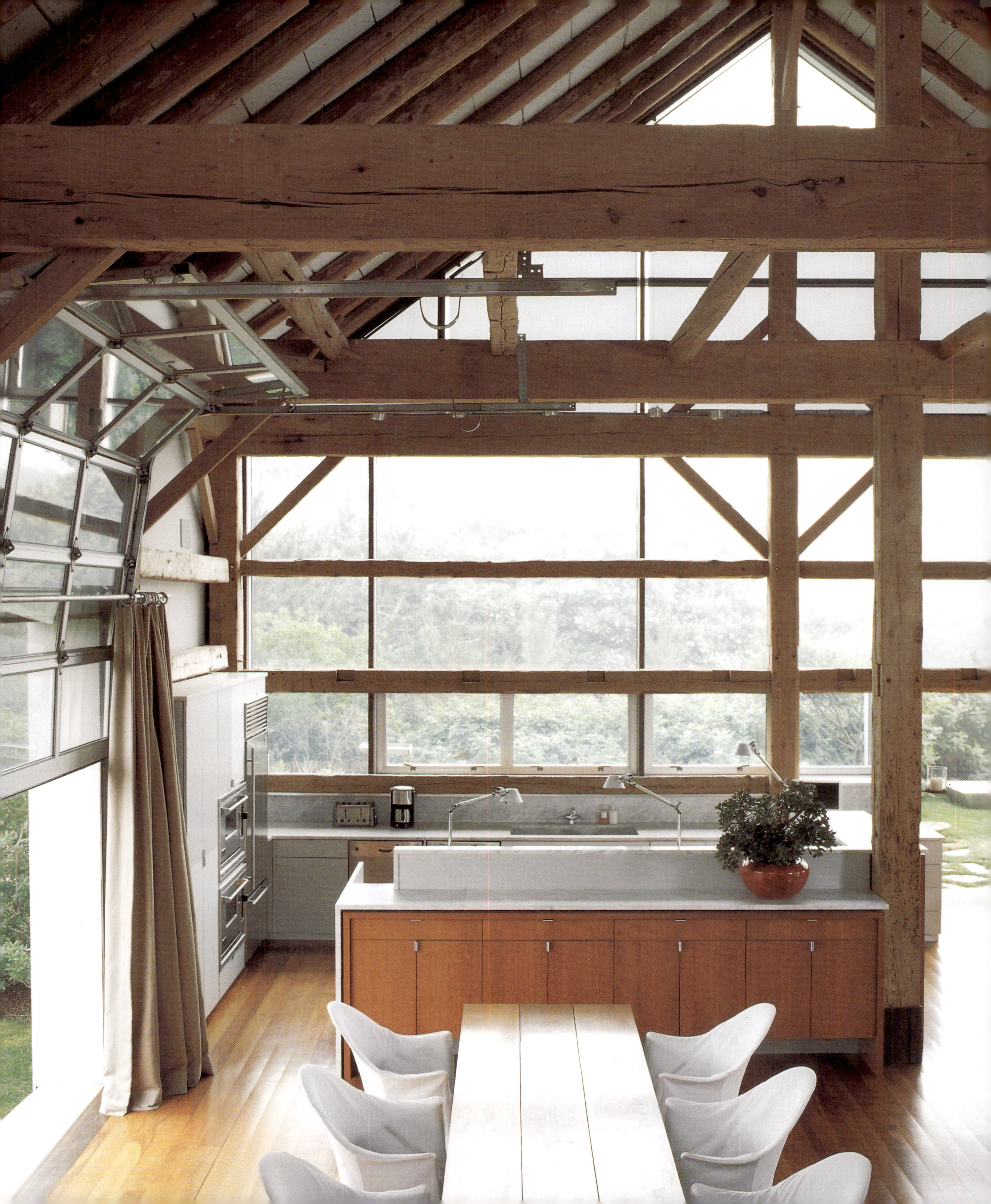

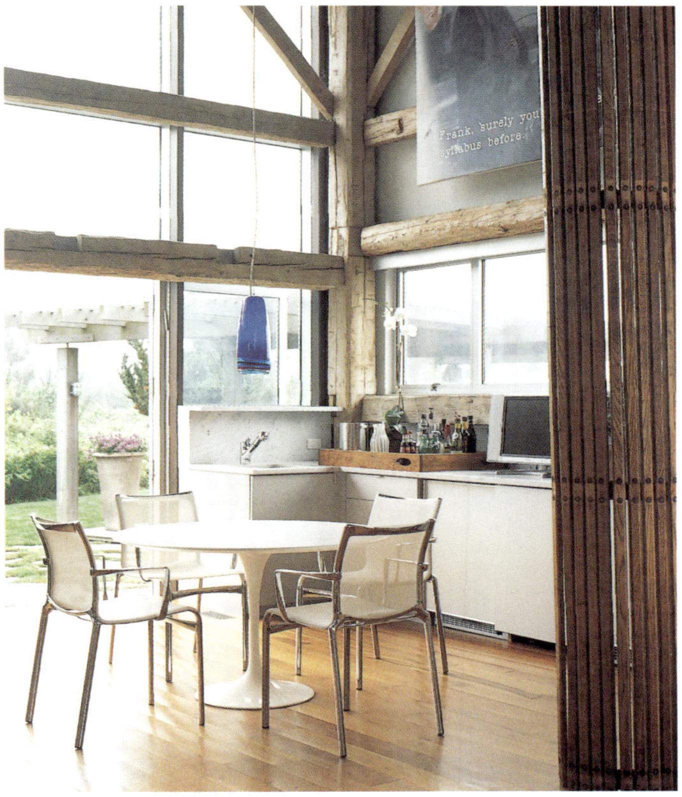

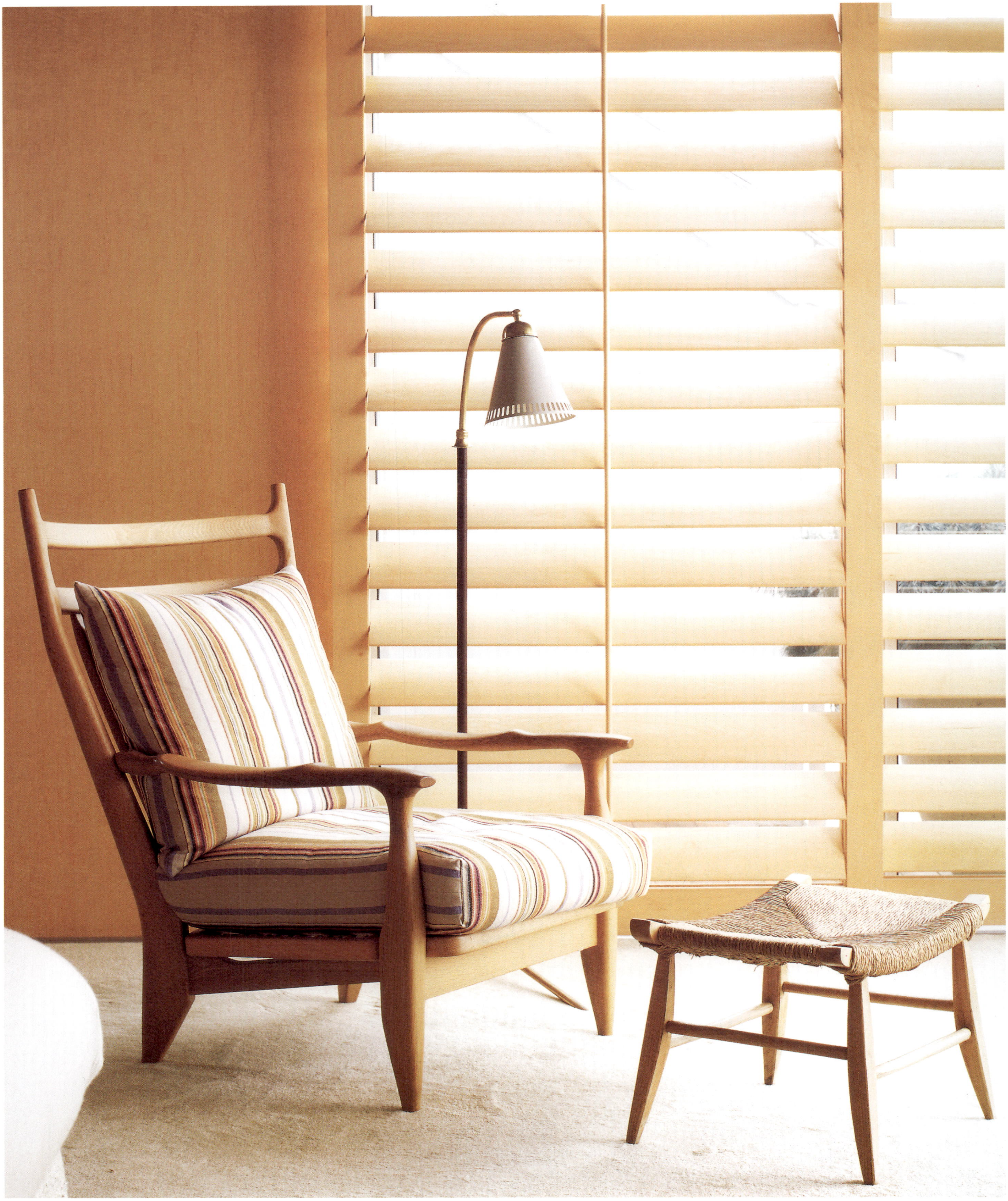

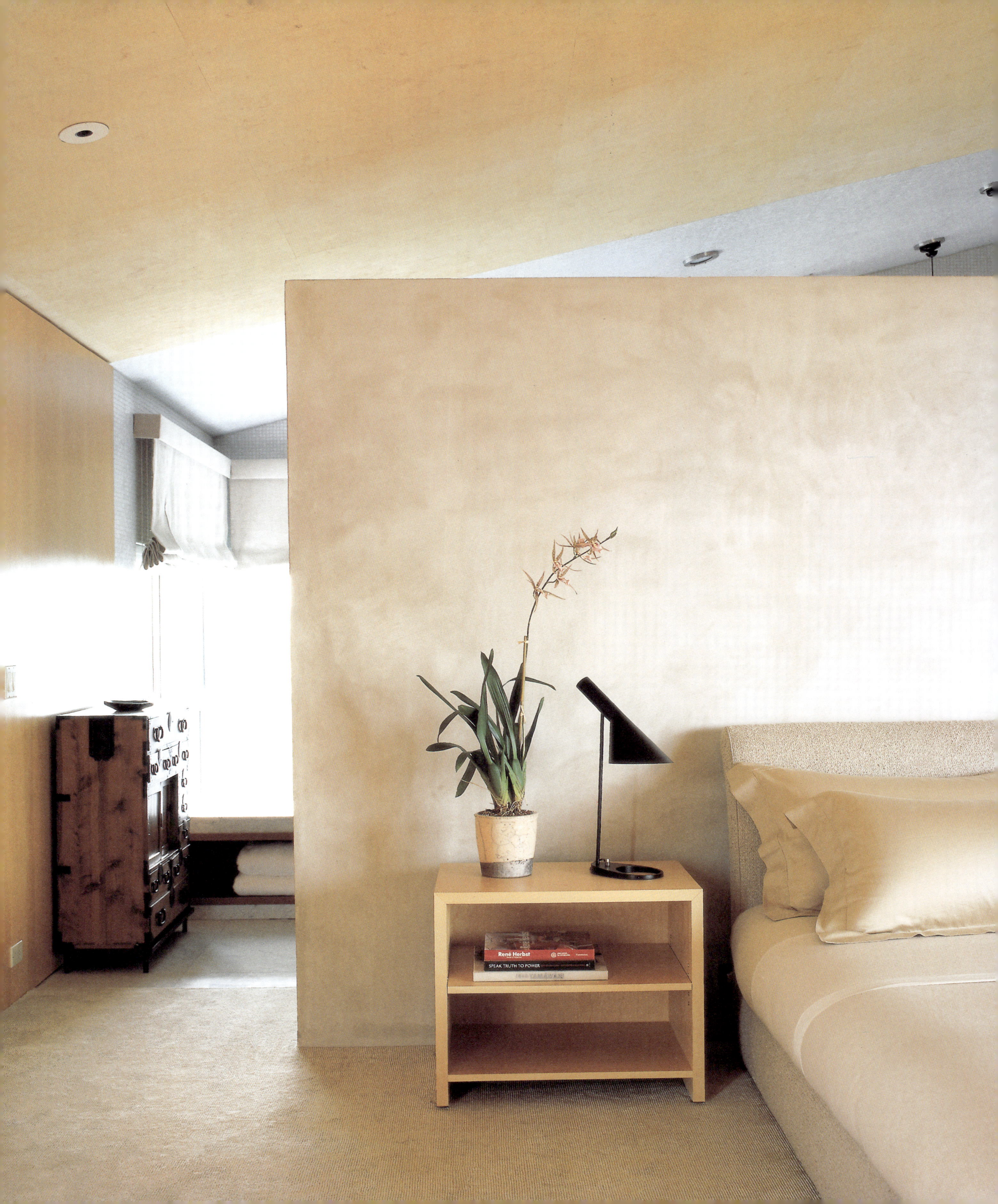
René Herbst
SPEAK TRUTH TO POWER

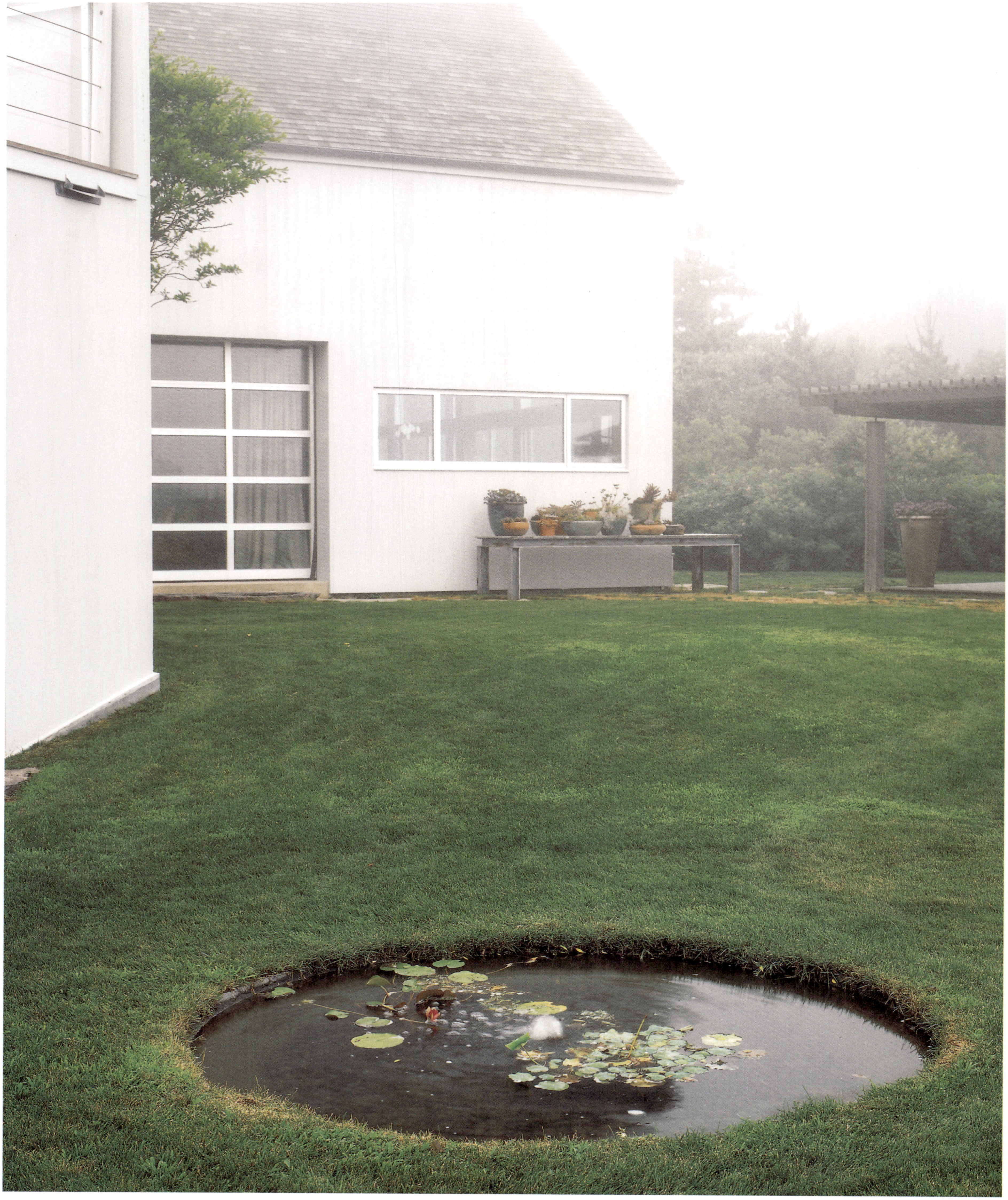

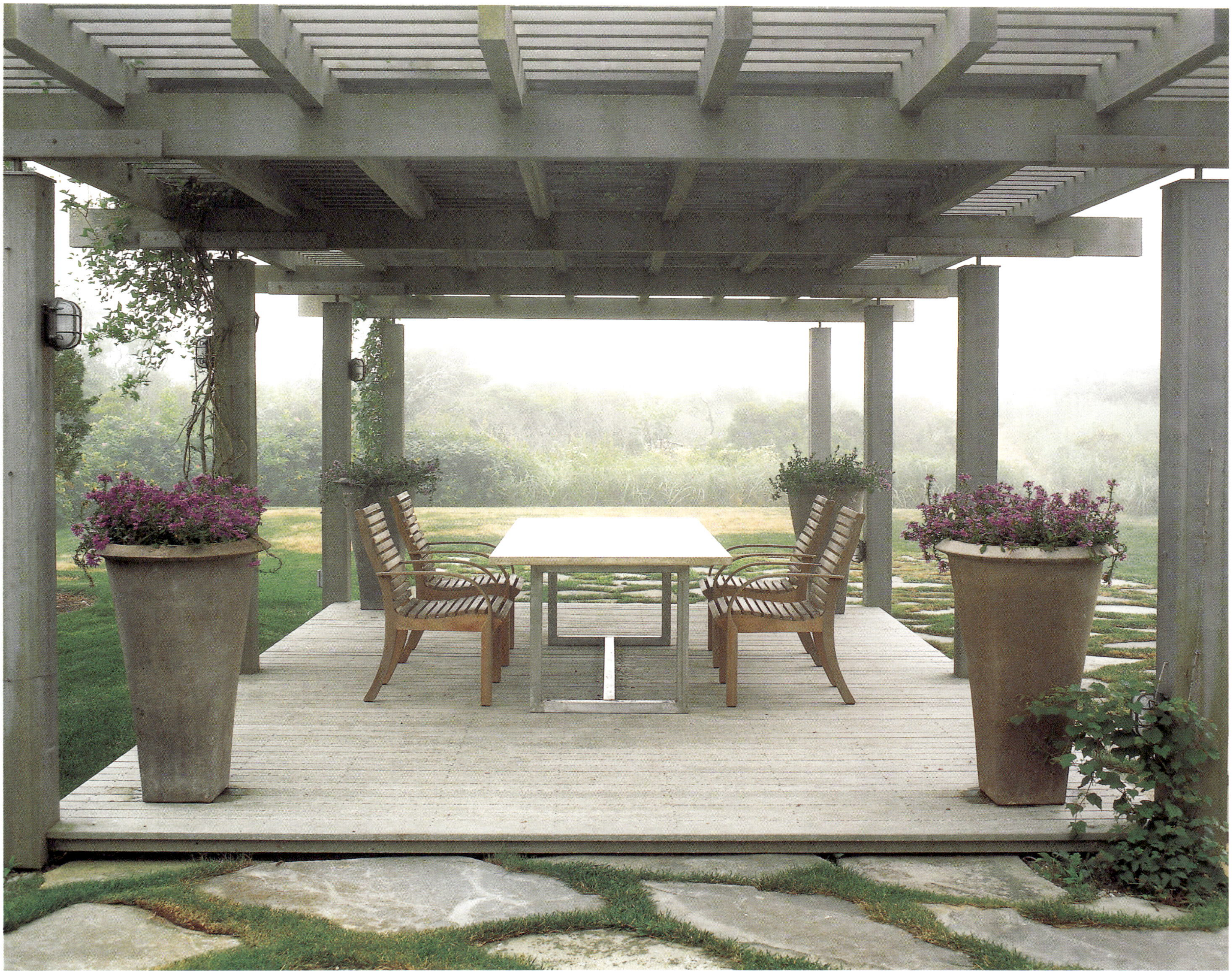

bill SOFIELD &
dennis ANDERSON

"There's nothing precious about the decor. The reality here is three dogs, wet bathing suits, and gardening dirt. Everything has to be user-friendly."

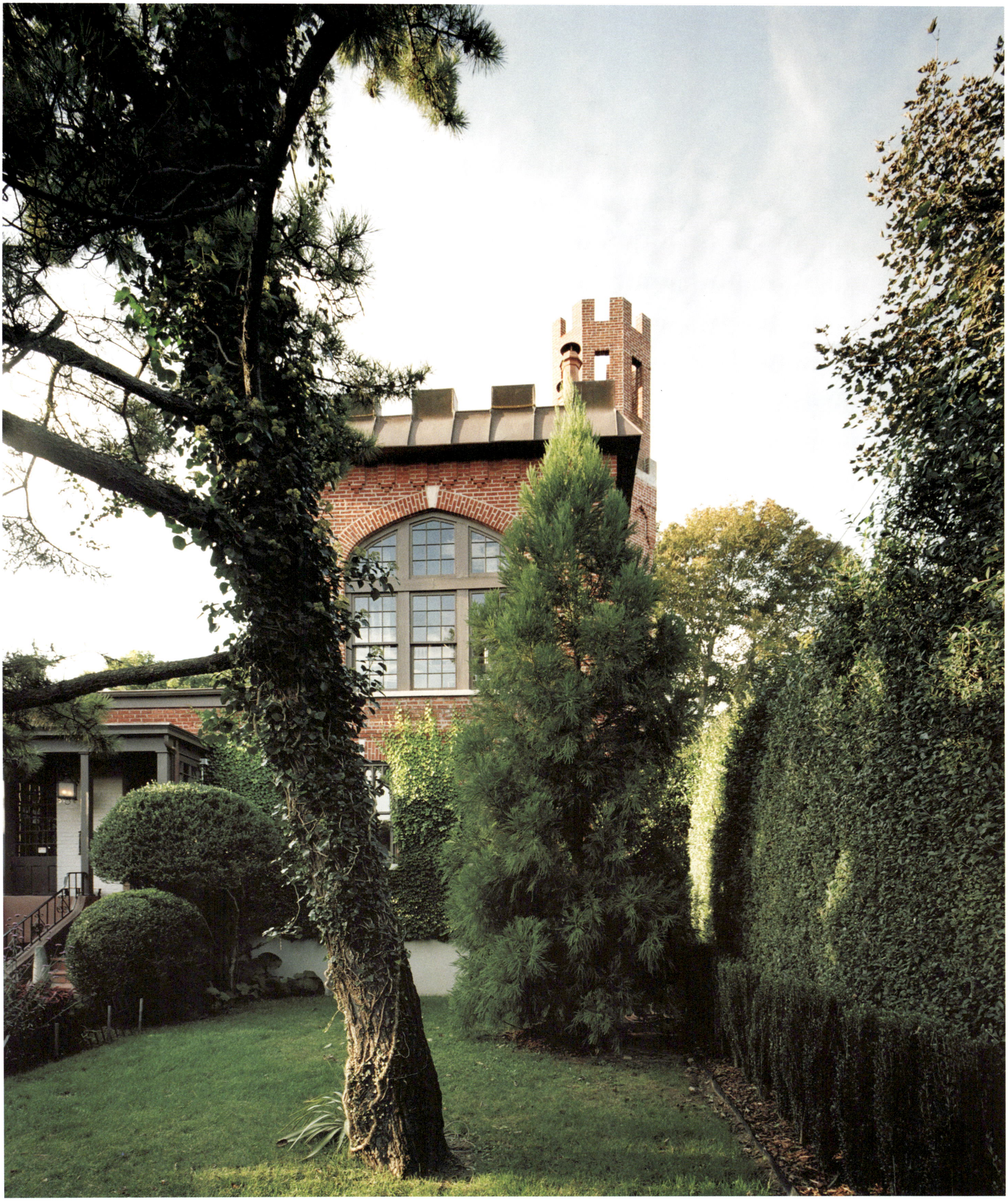

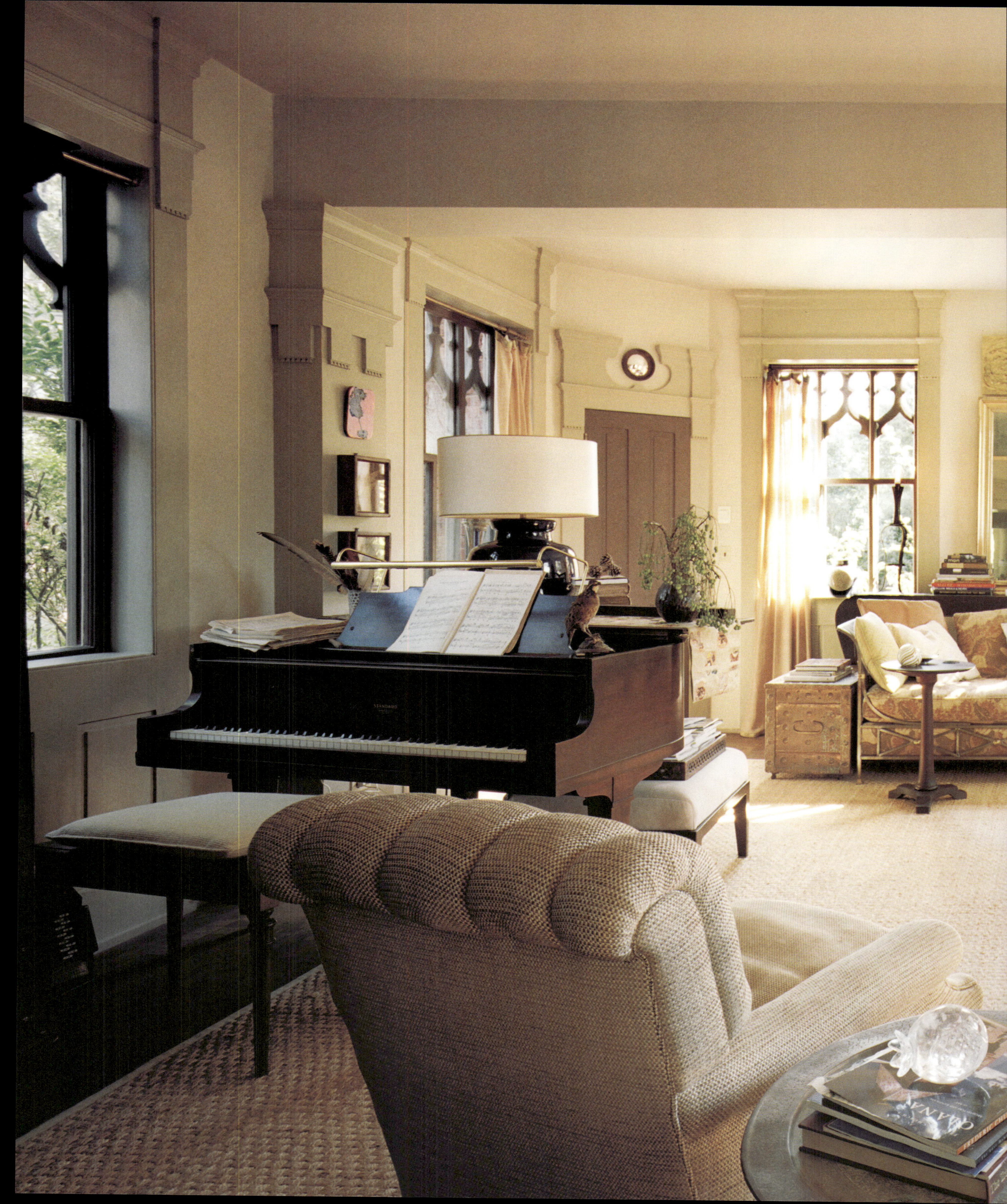

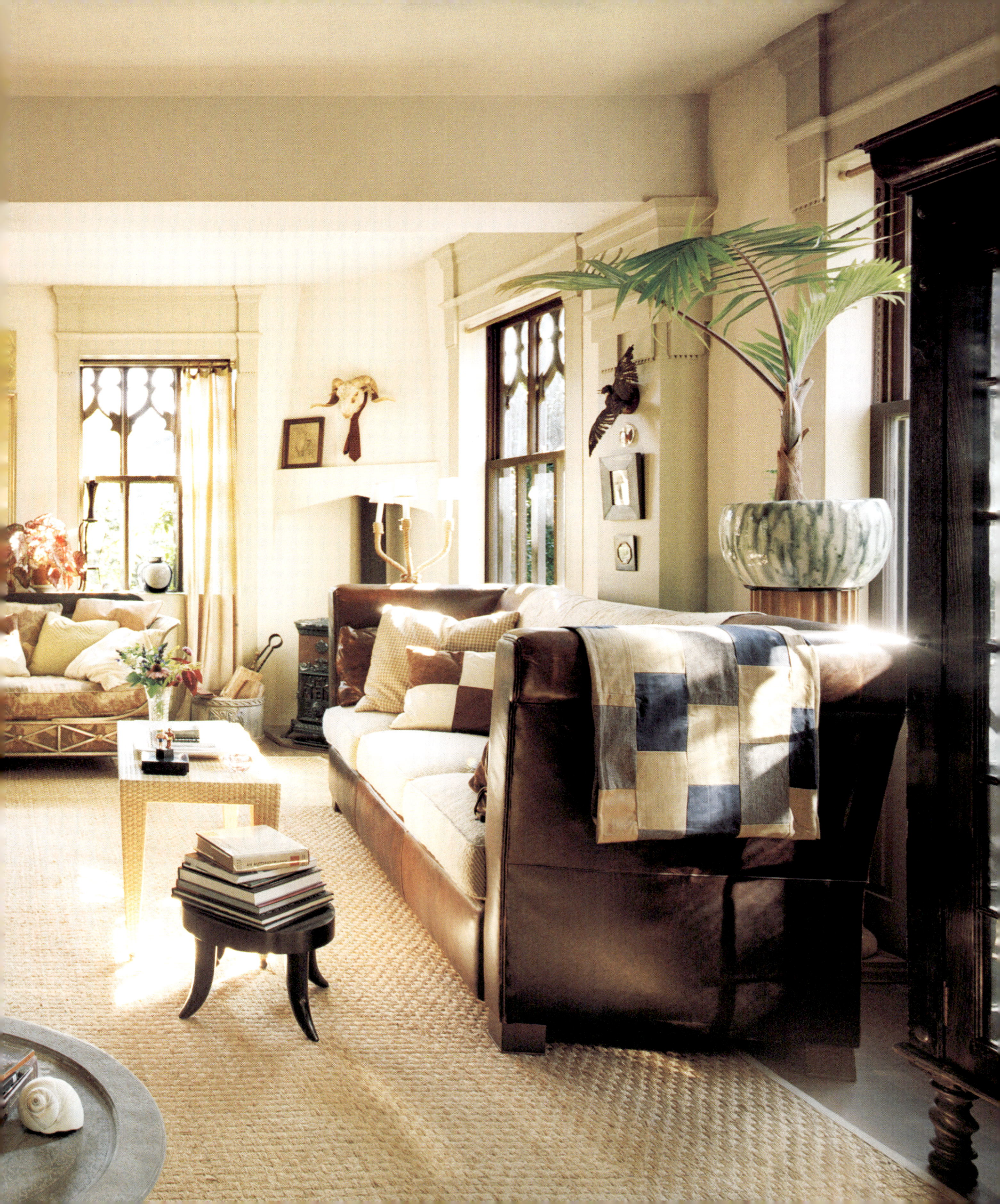

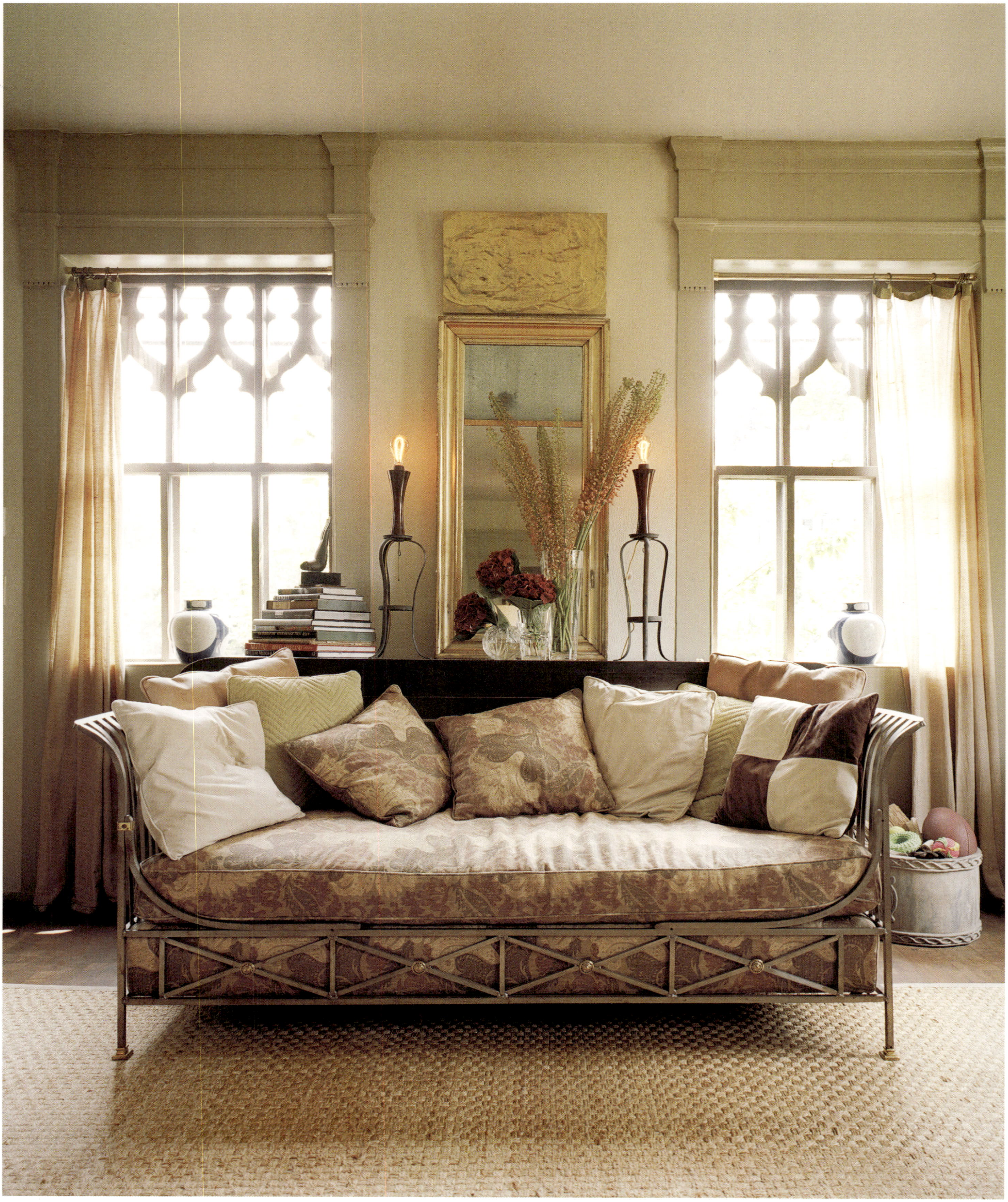

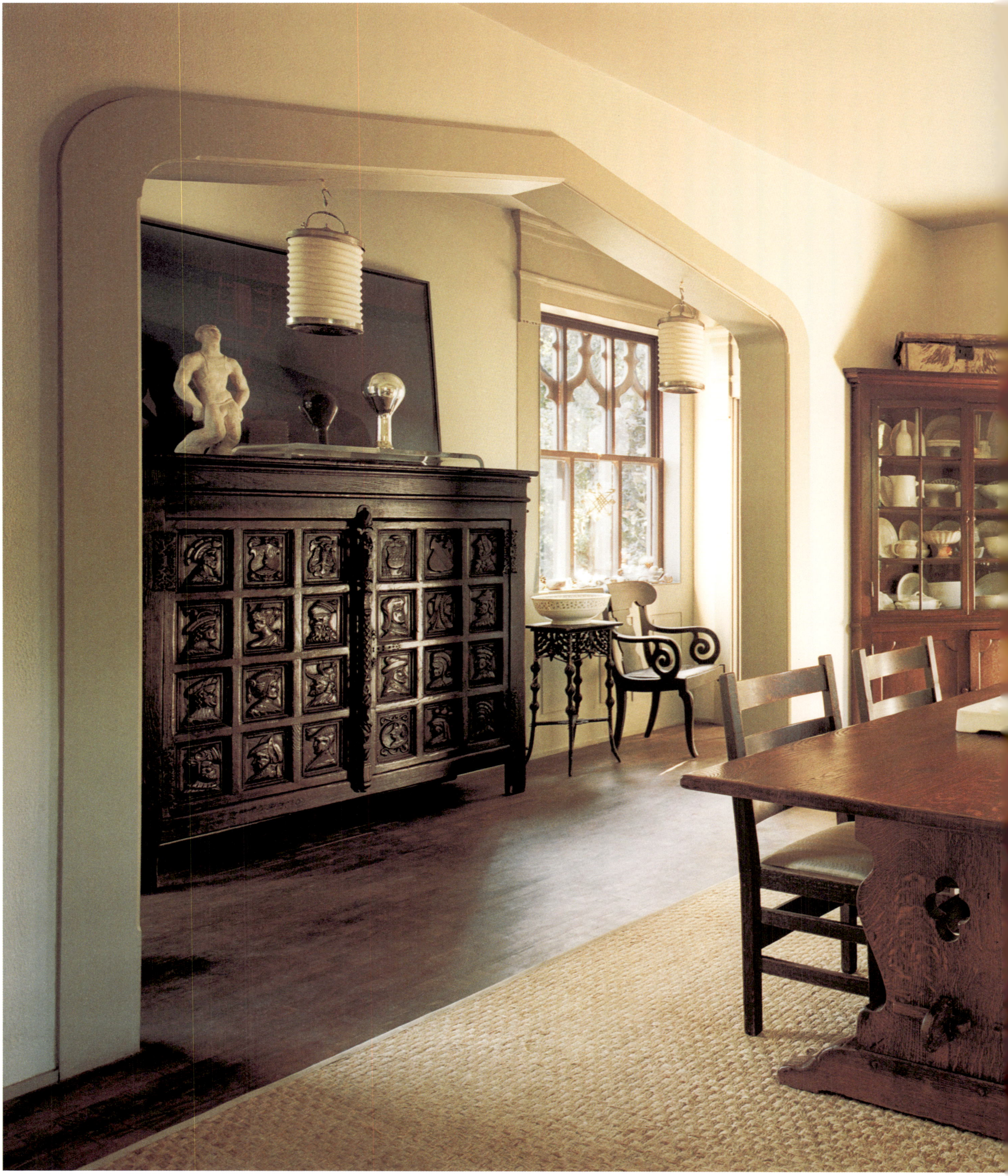

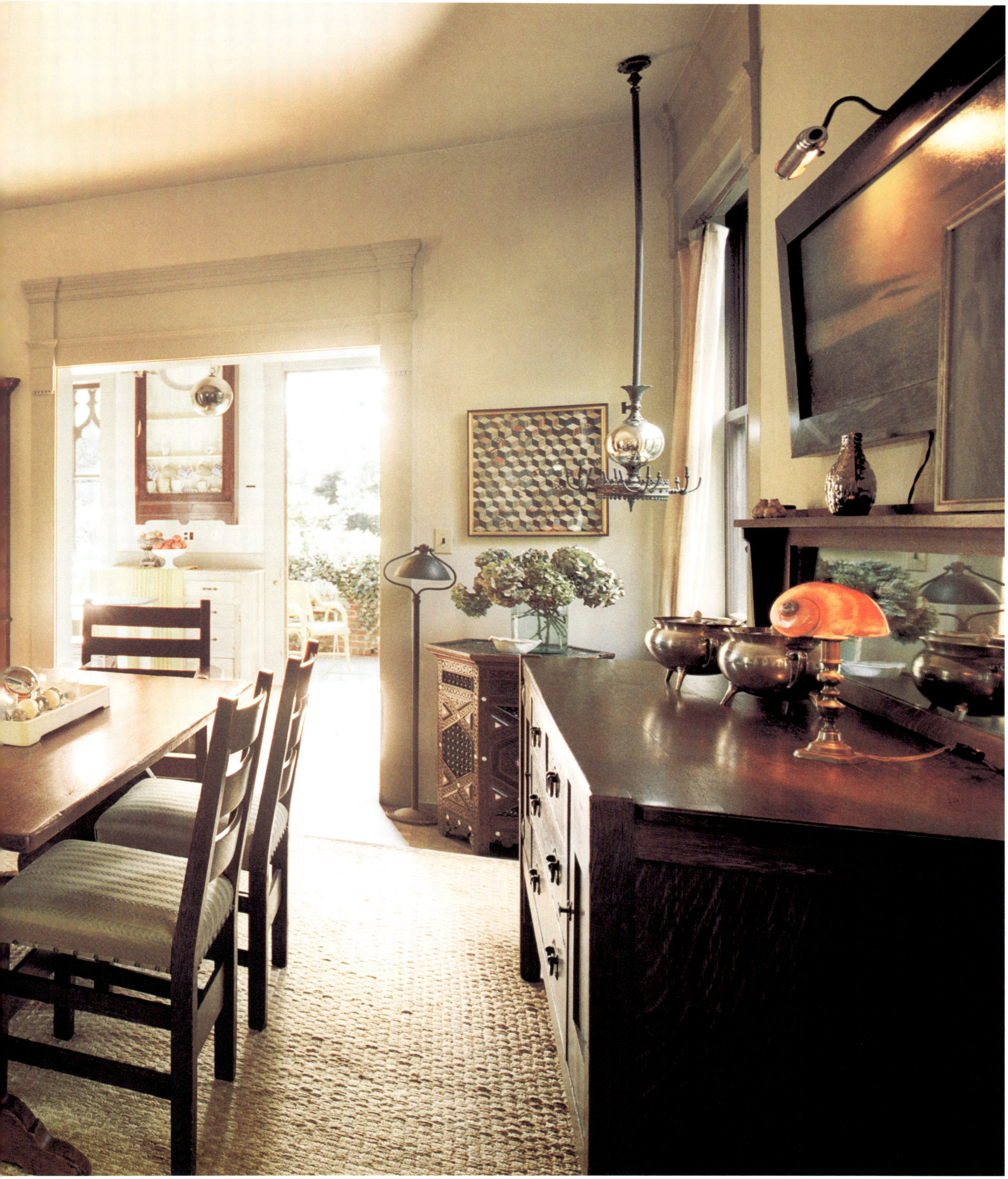

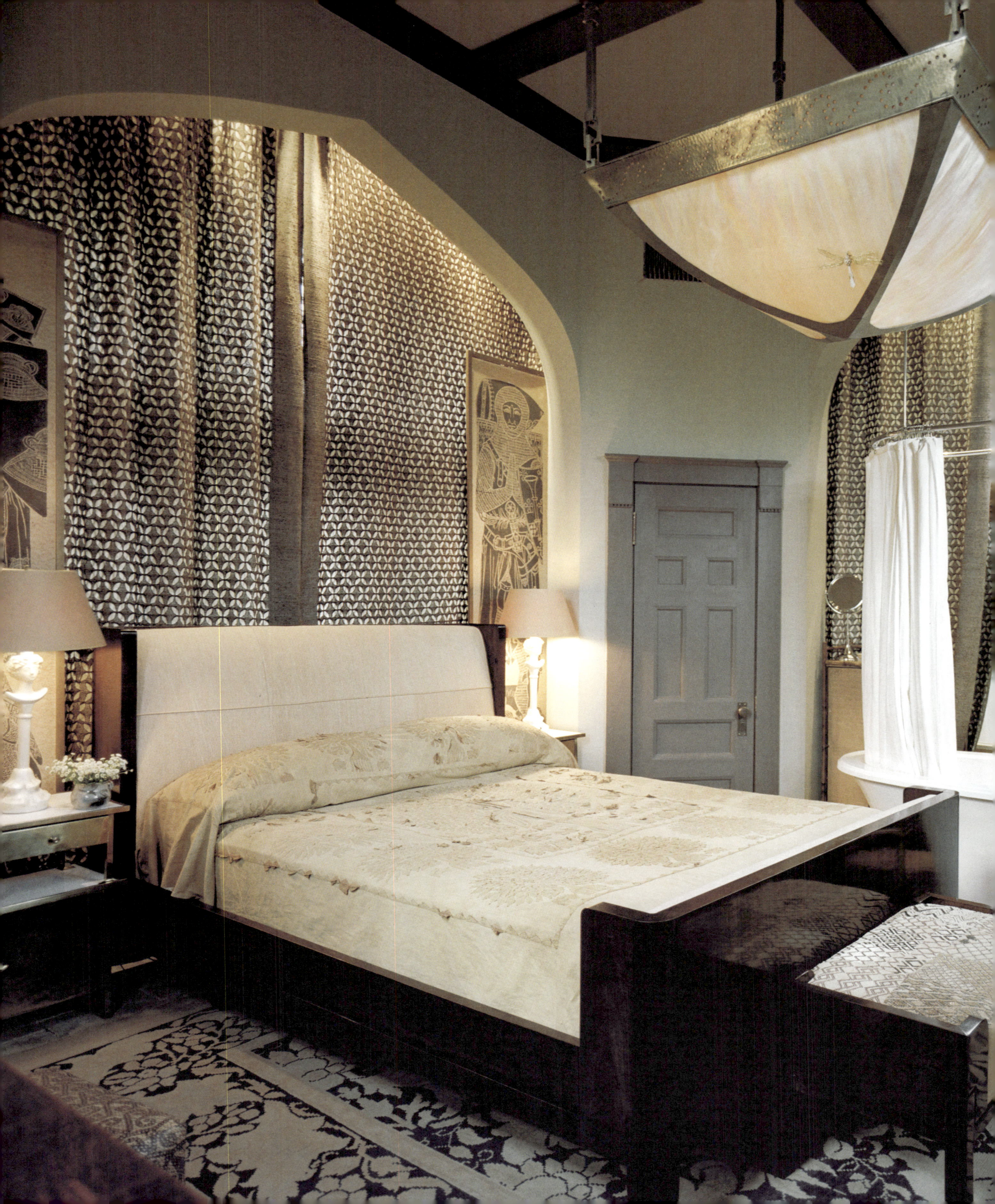

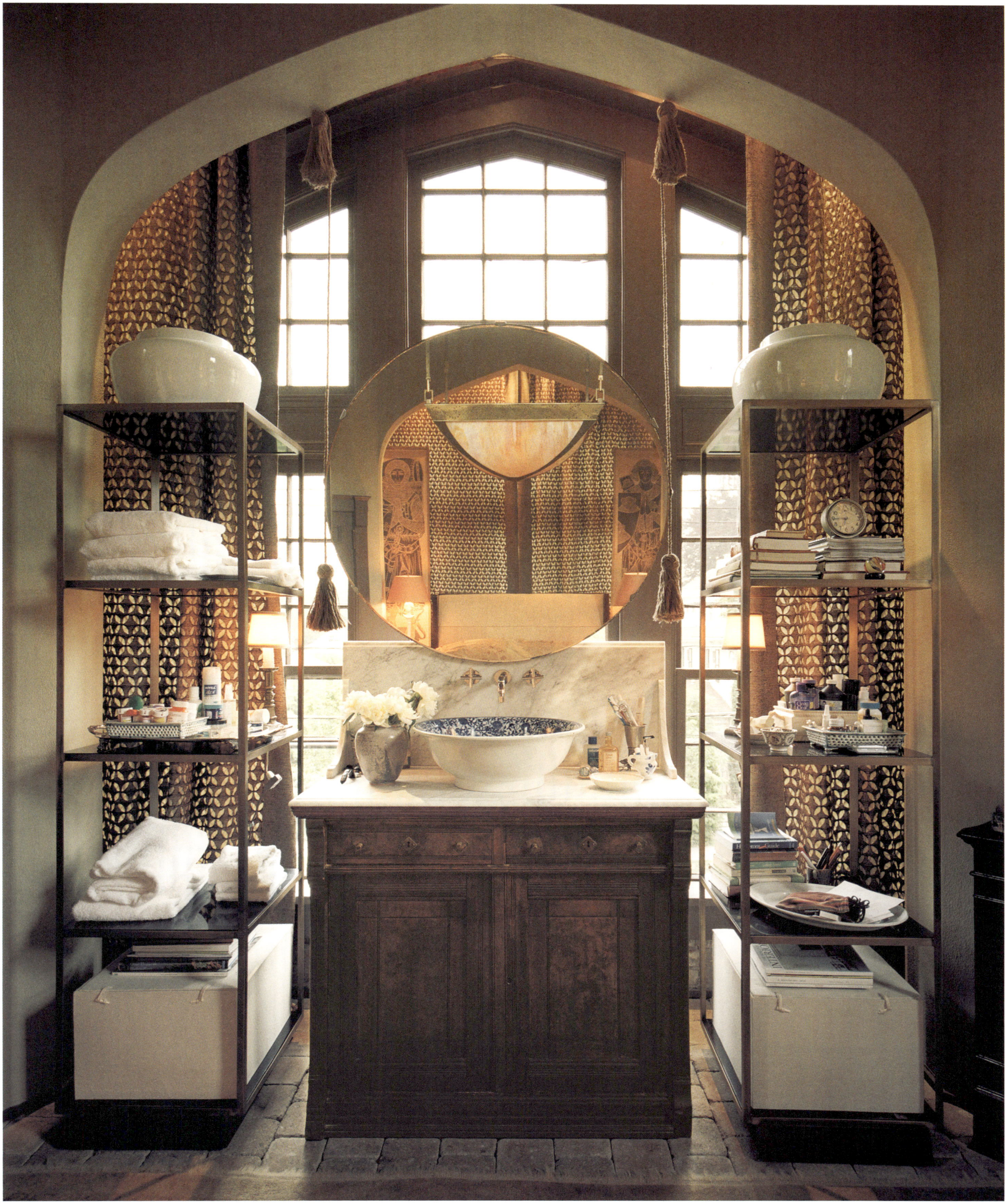

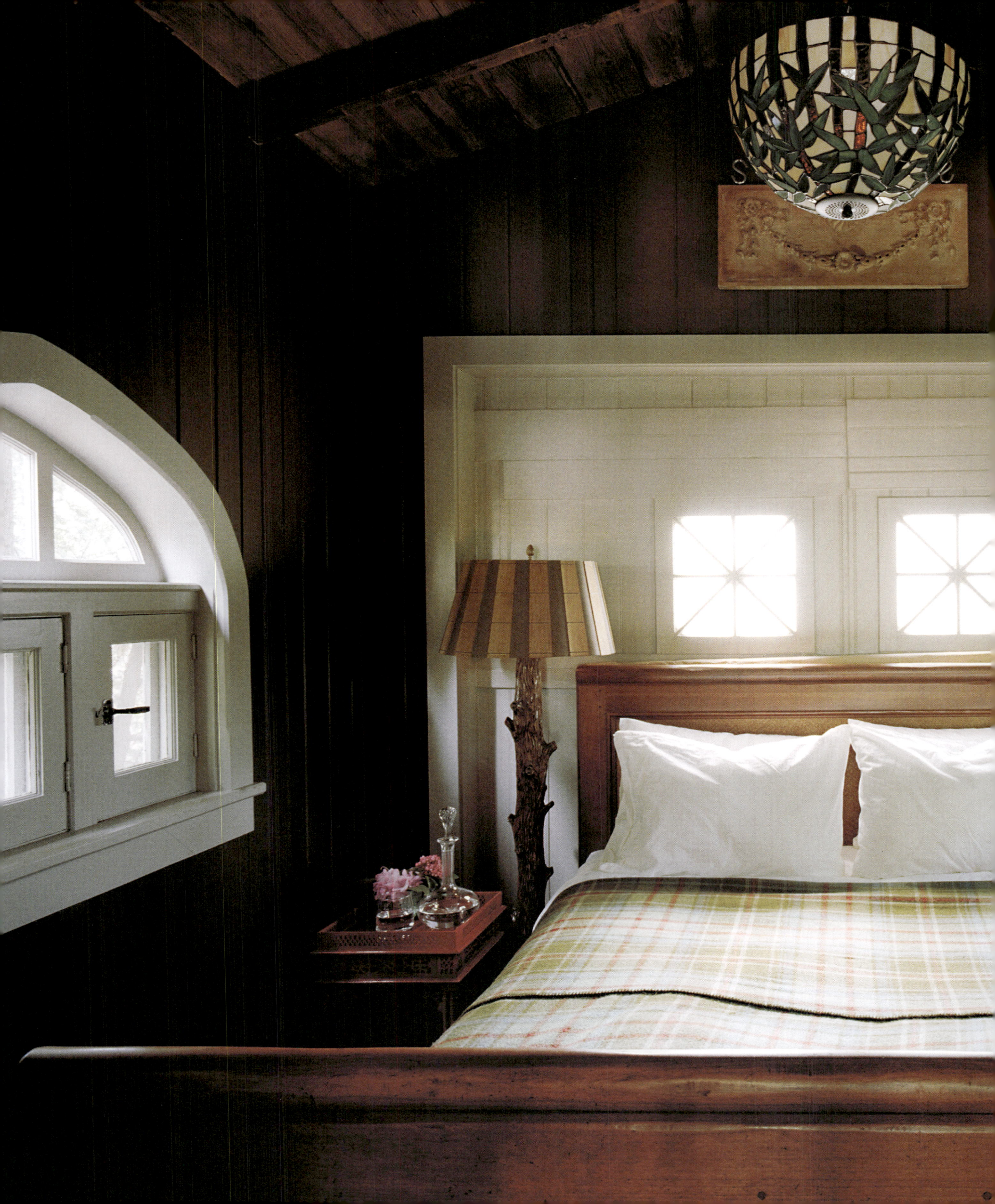

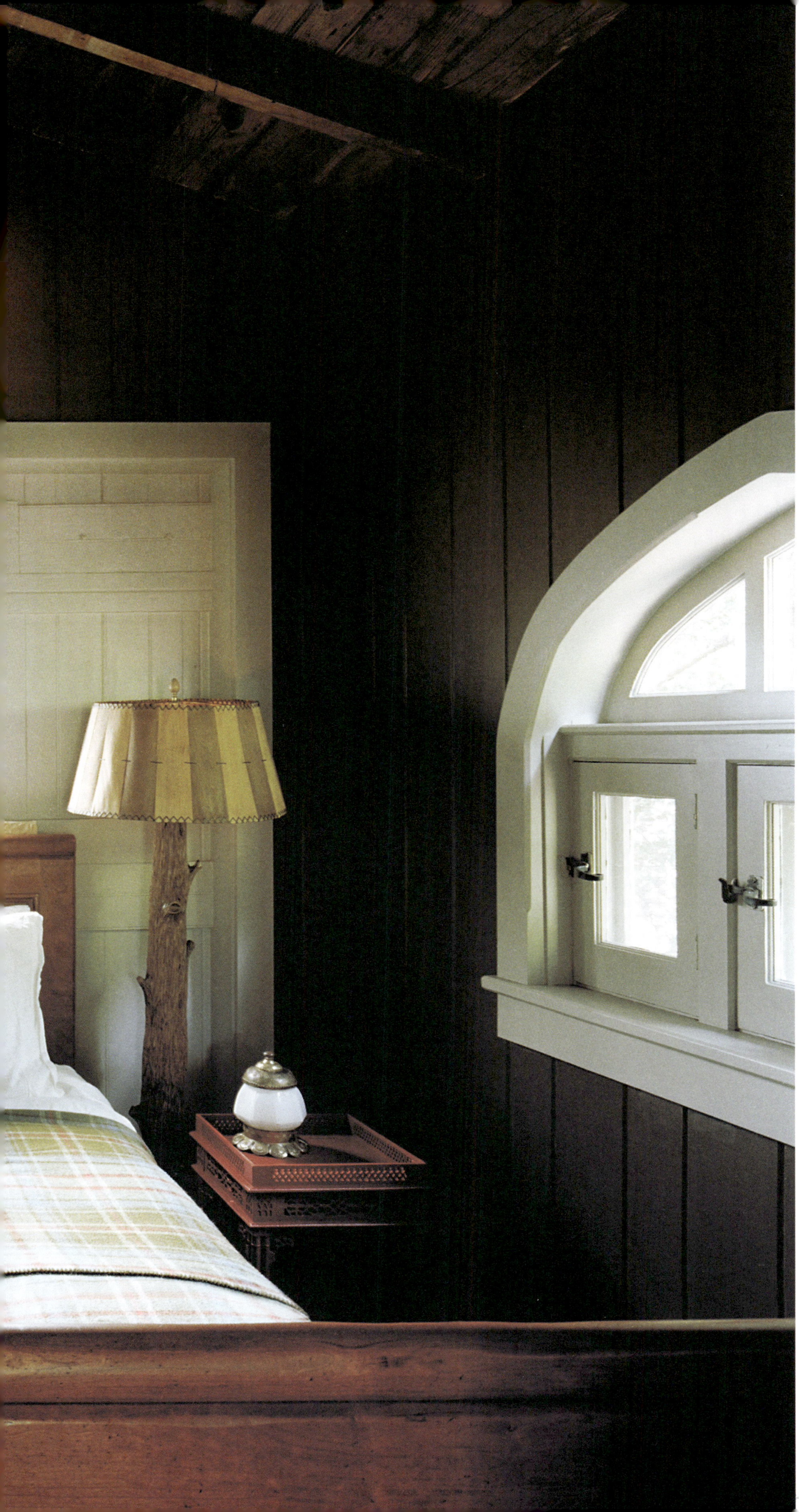

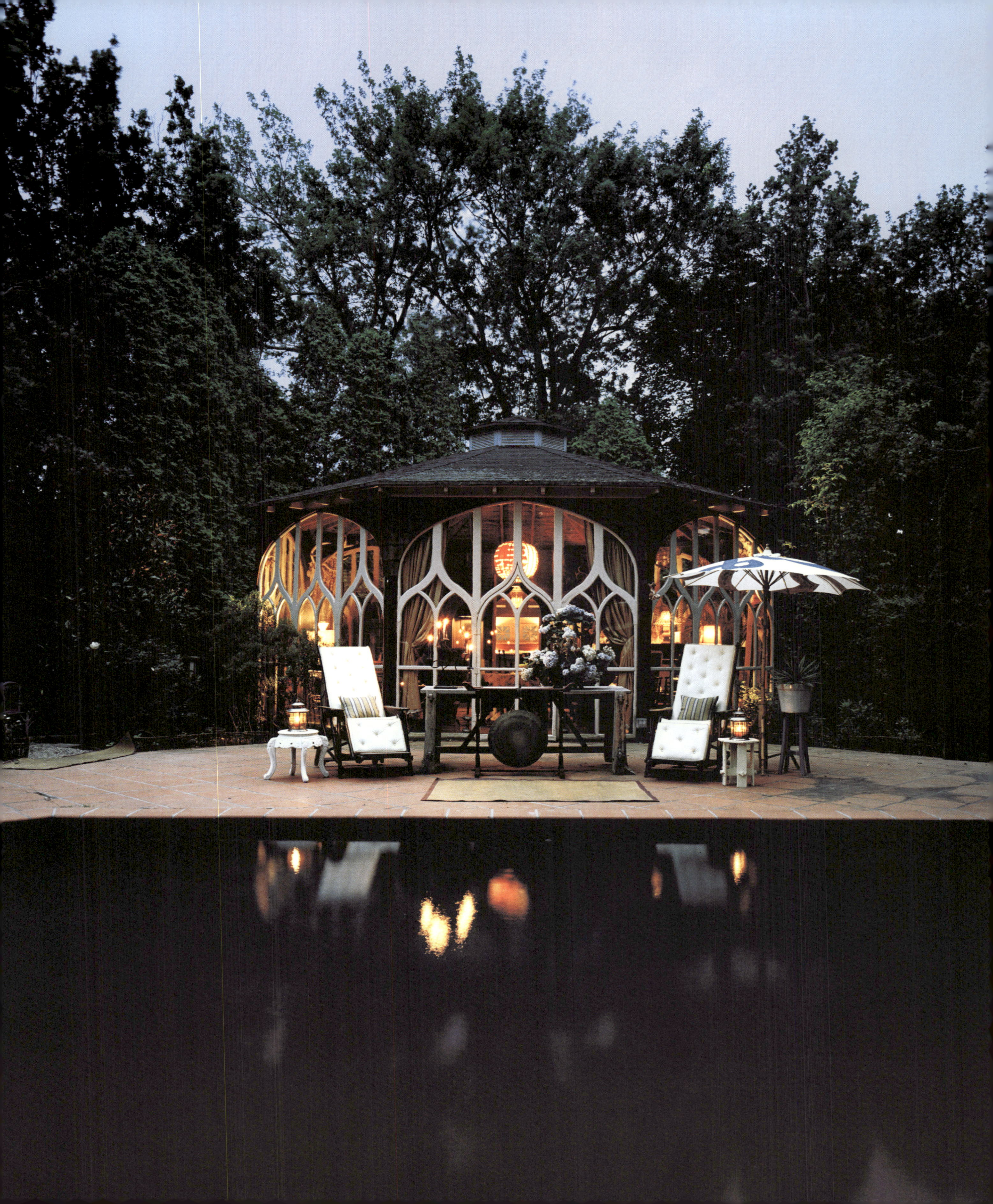

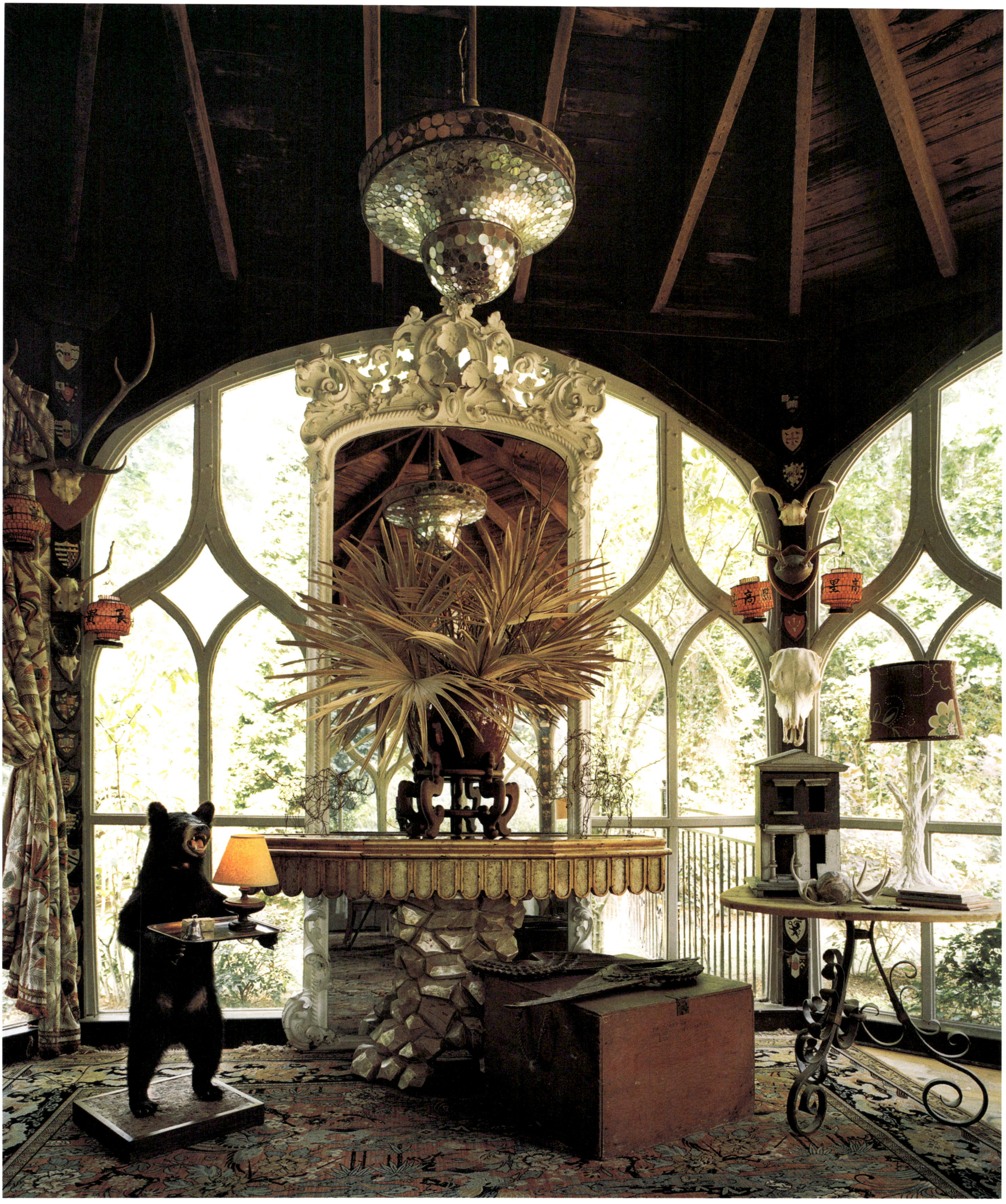

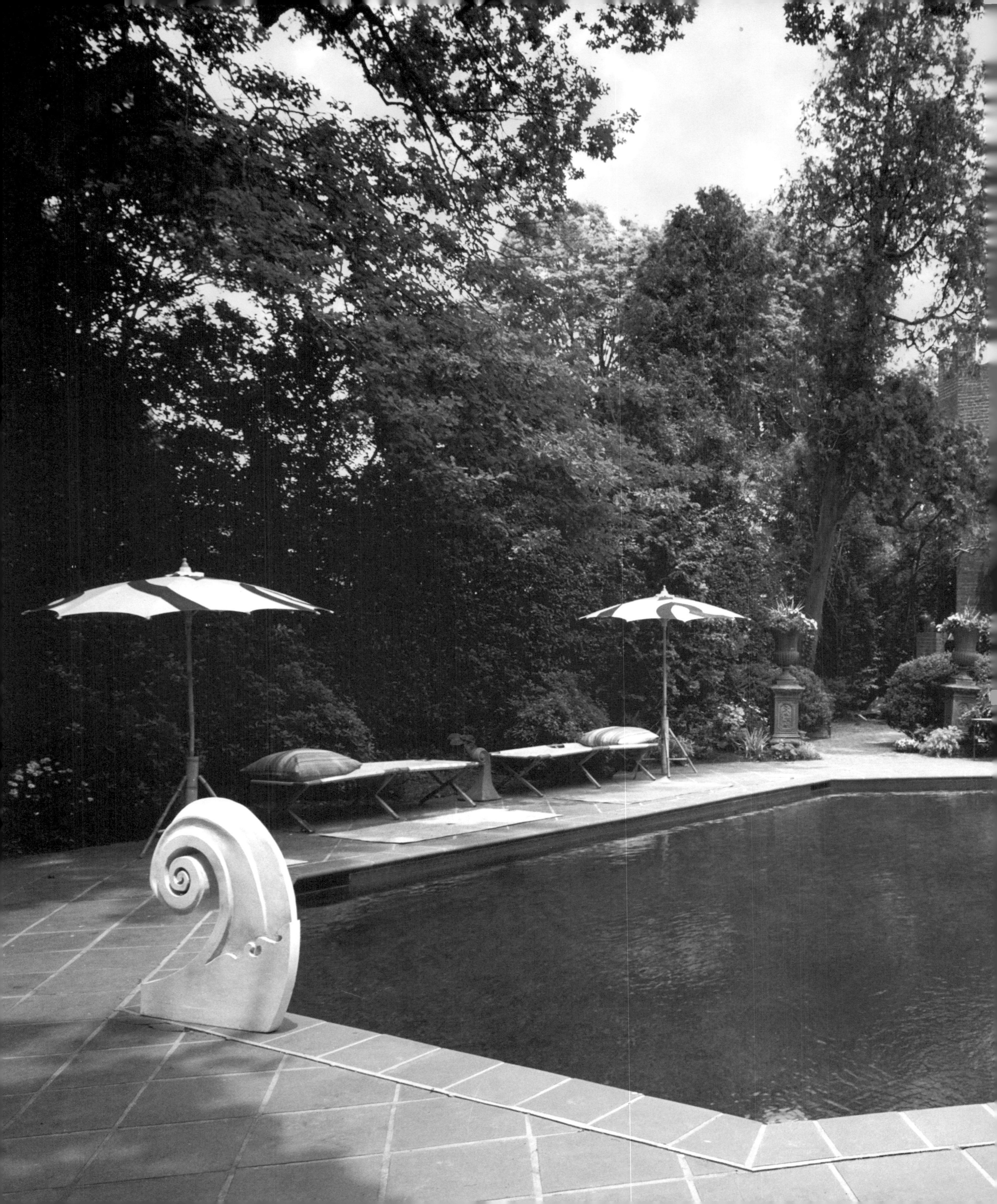

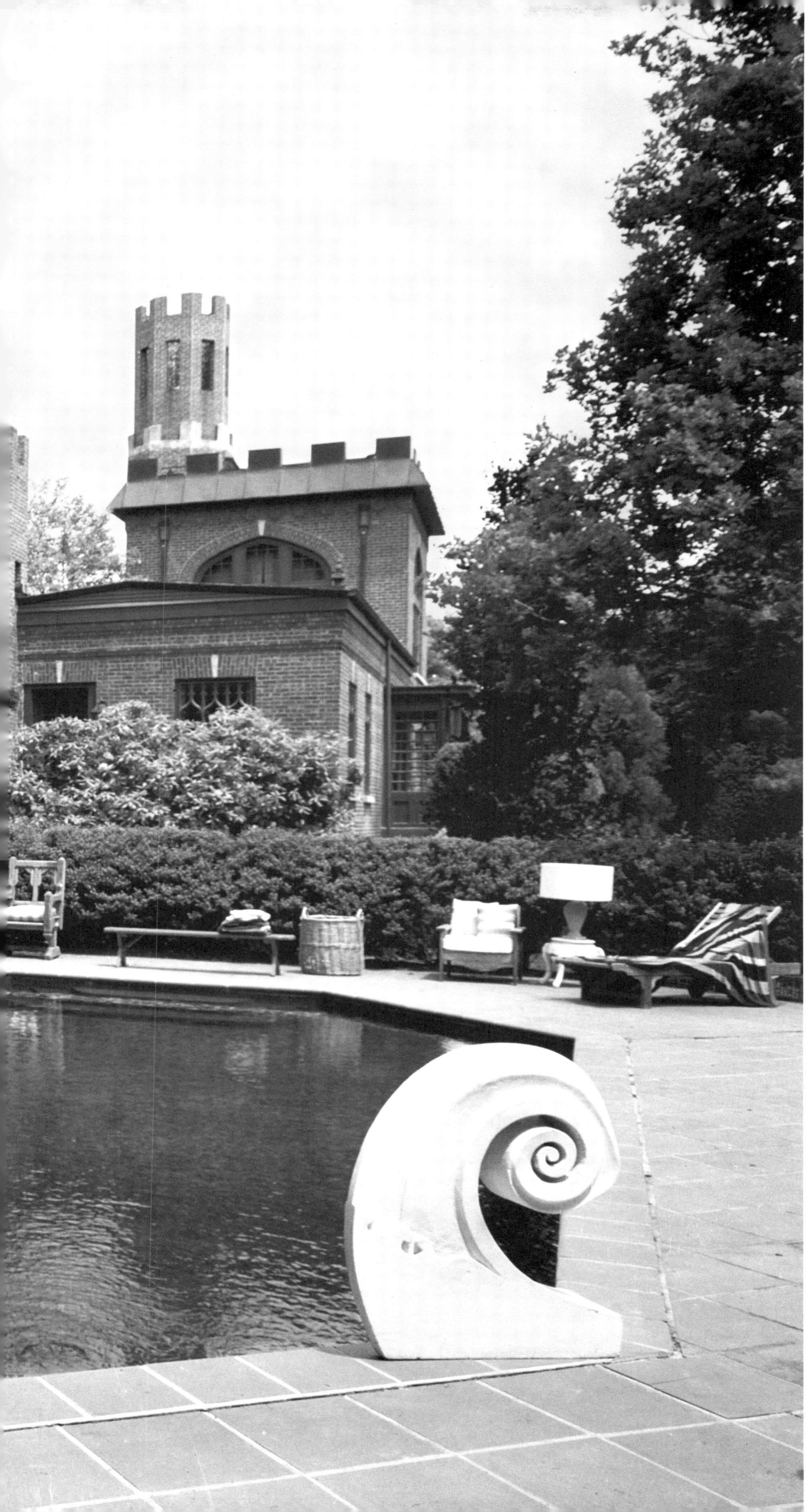

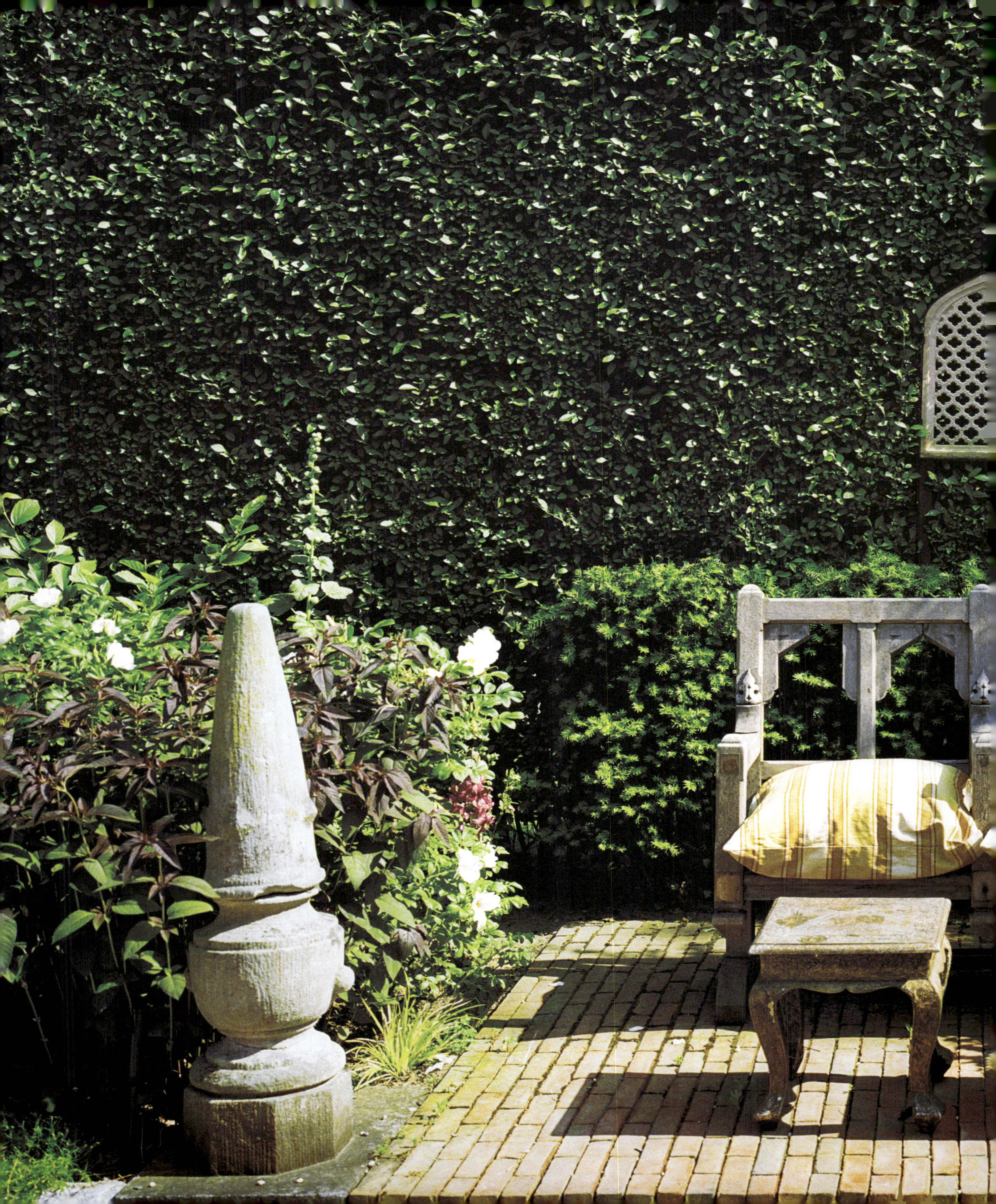

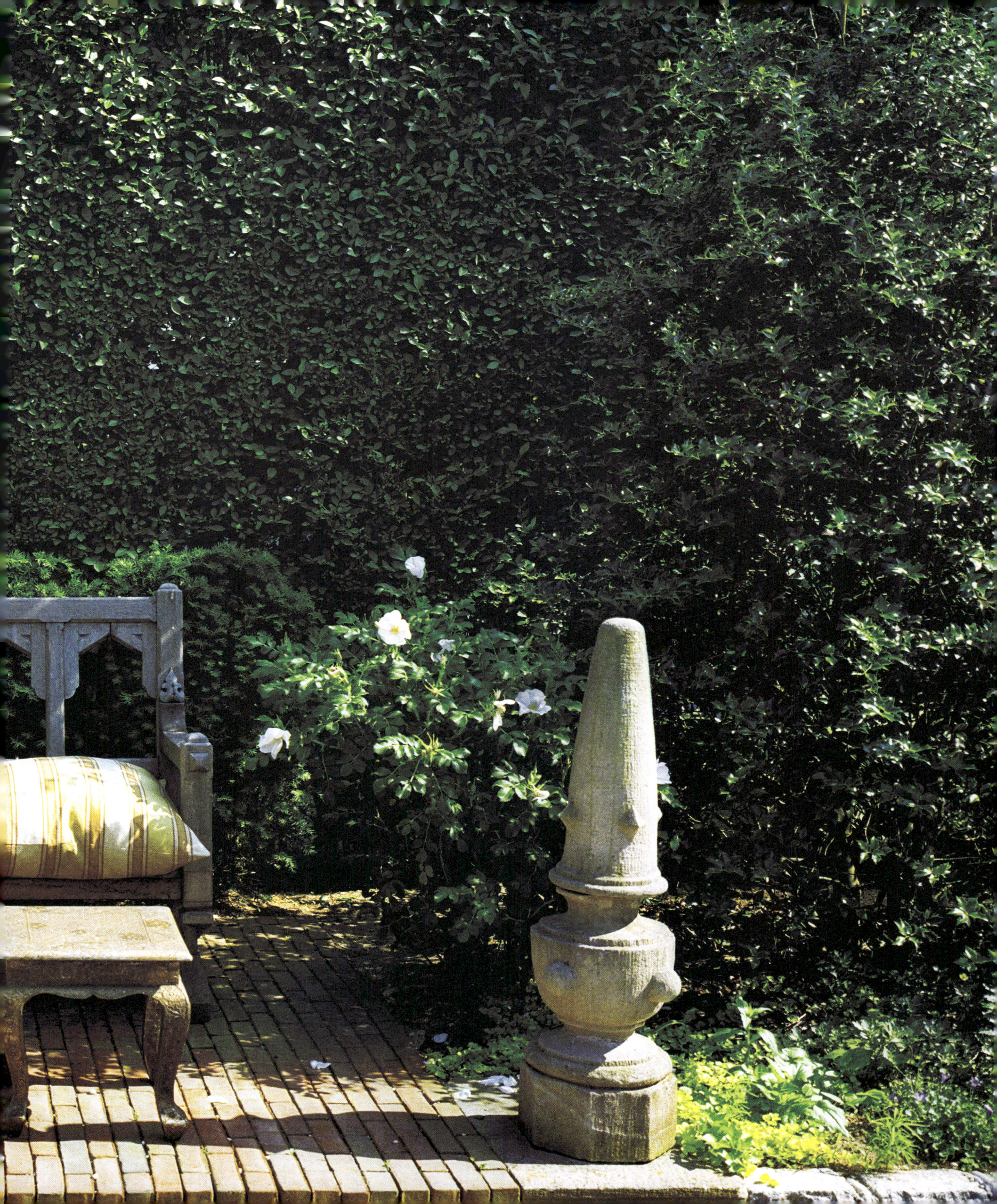

robert
STILIN

"All my work is site-specific, so for this house in the Hamptons, it's a modern take on the local style. The house is loosely based on a potato barn, a traditional American farmhouse. I used local materials and elements such as wainscoting, but I gave it all a new twist. Someone called it "modern rustic"—it's casual but attractive. It's a style that reflects the Hamptons where people are inspired by the past, but live today."

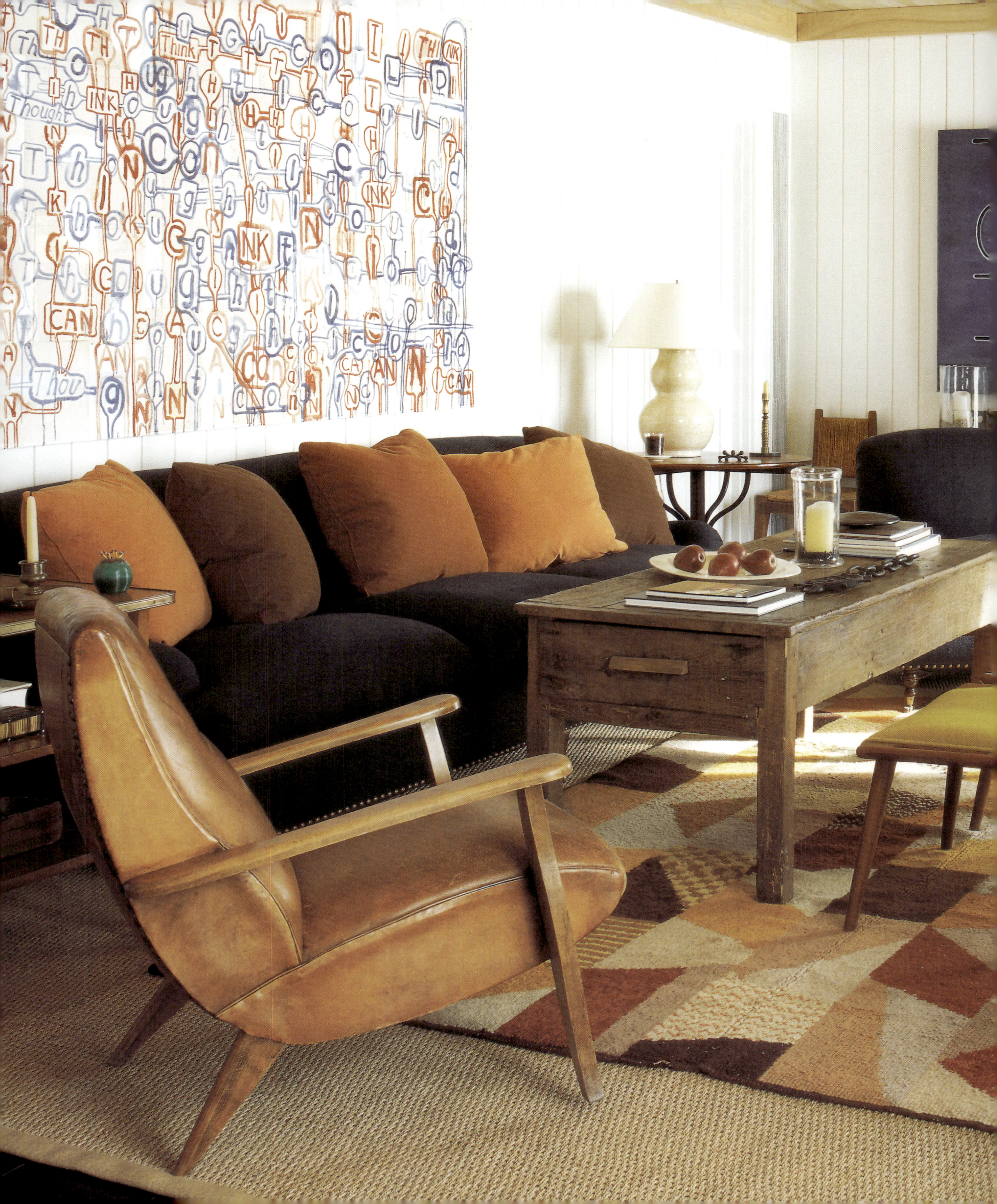

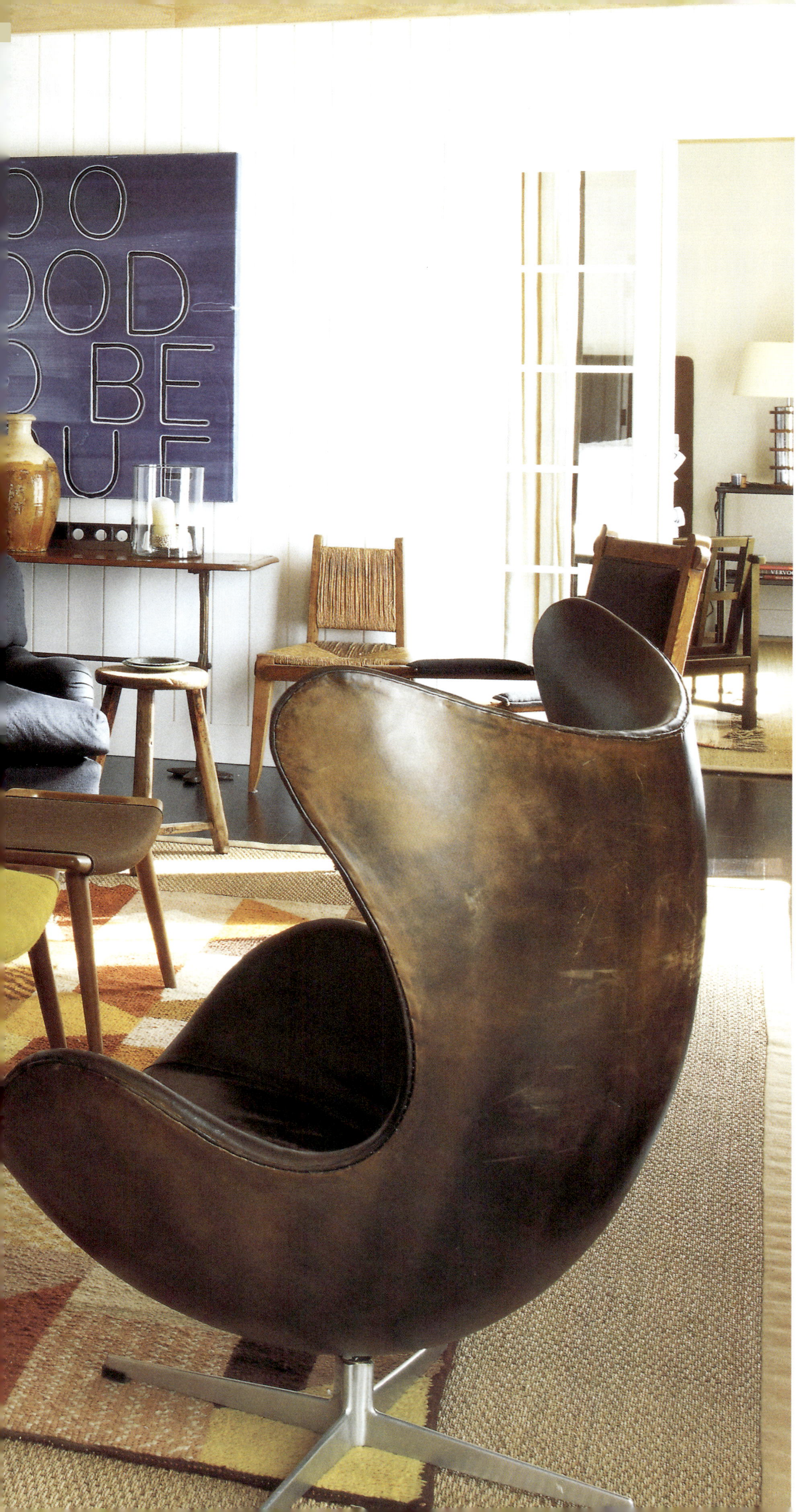

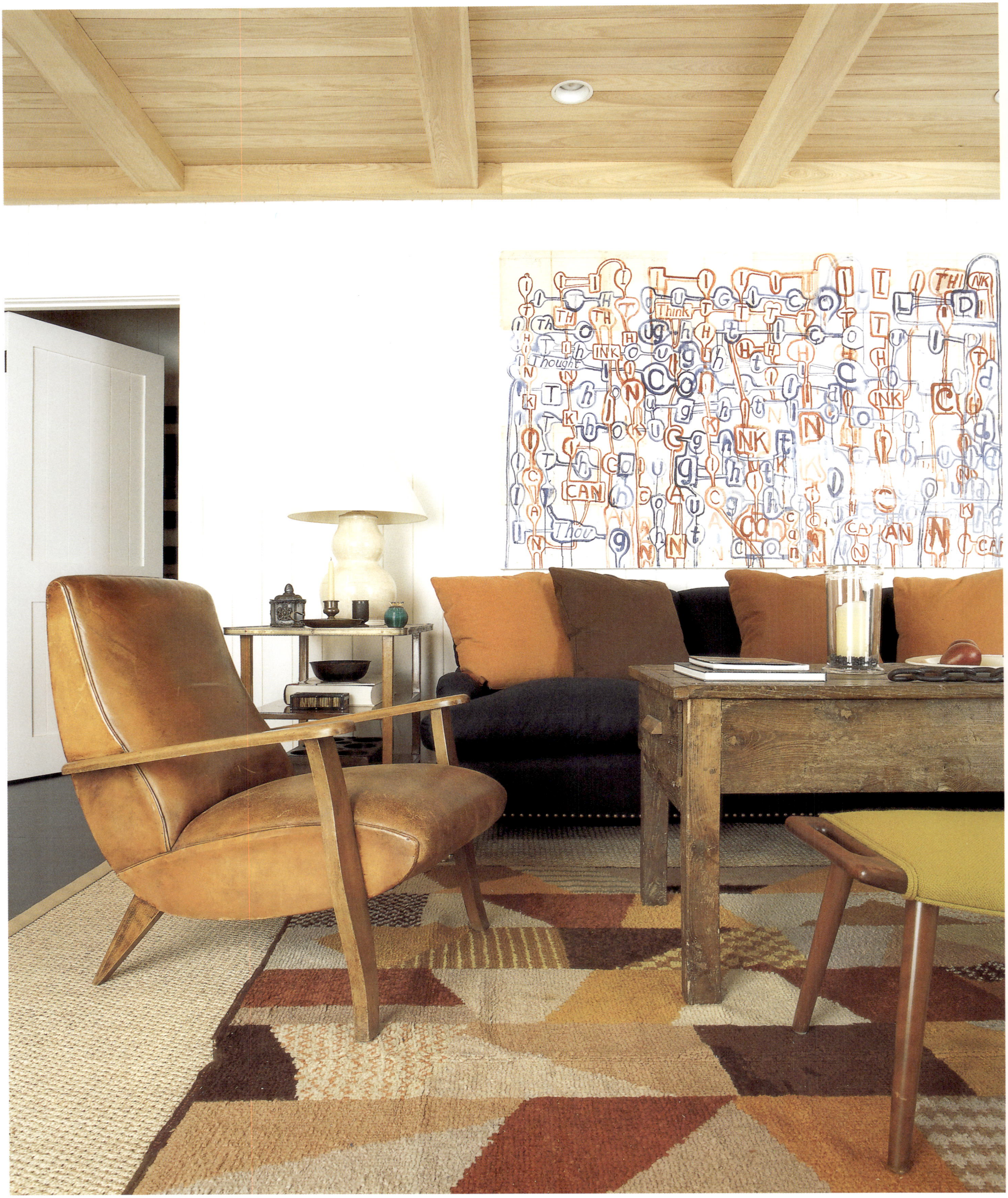

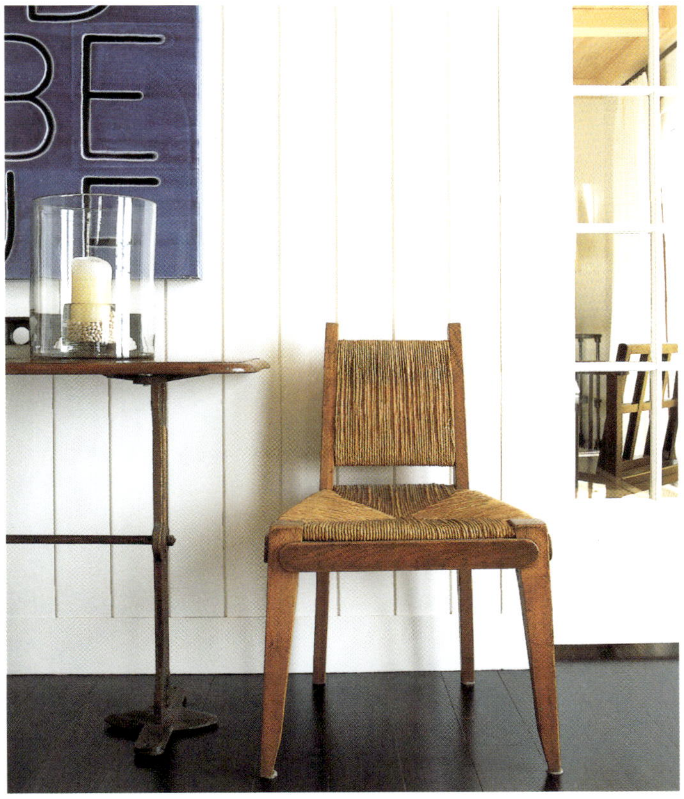

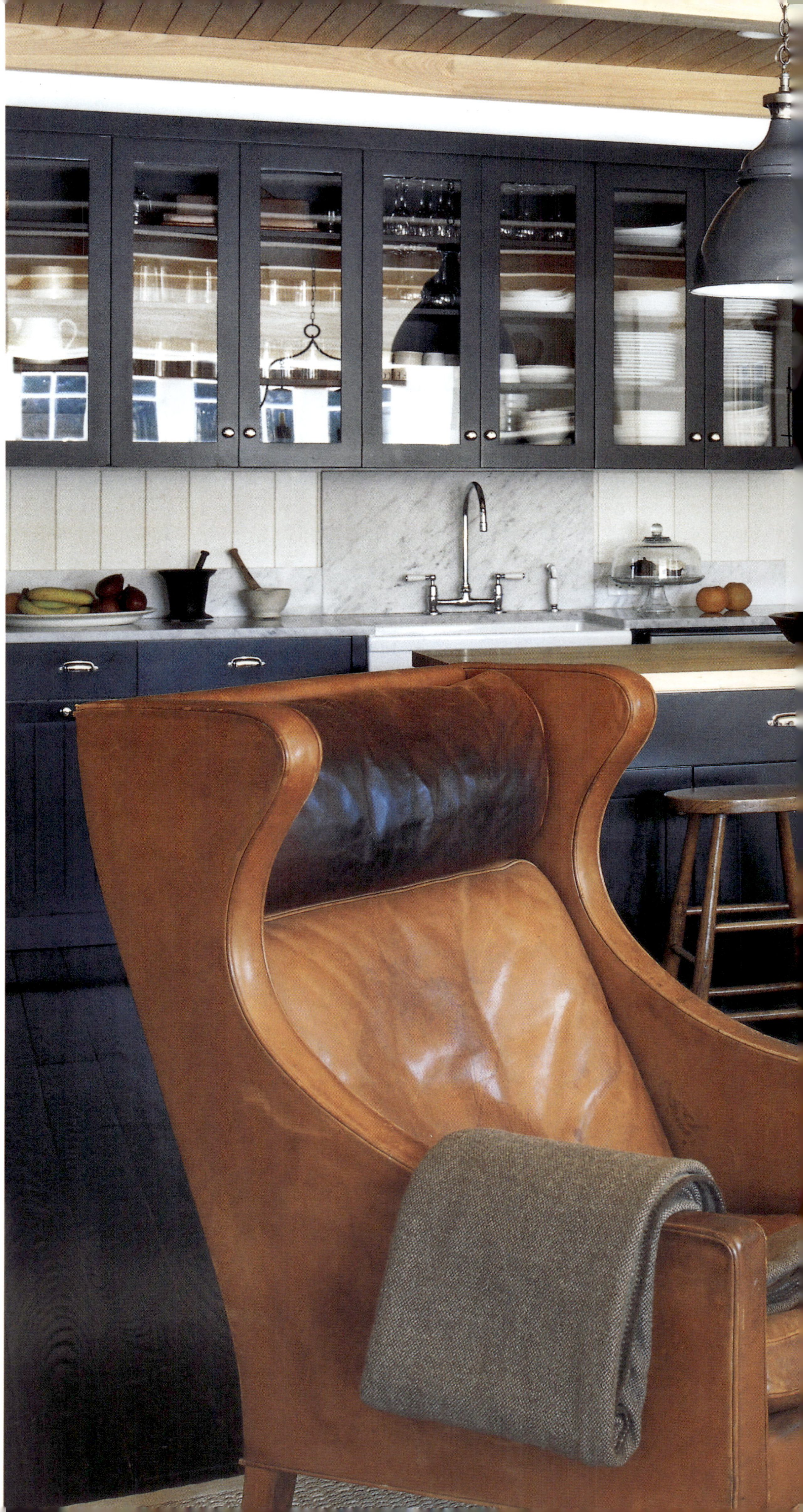

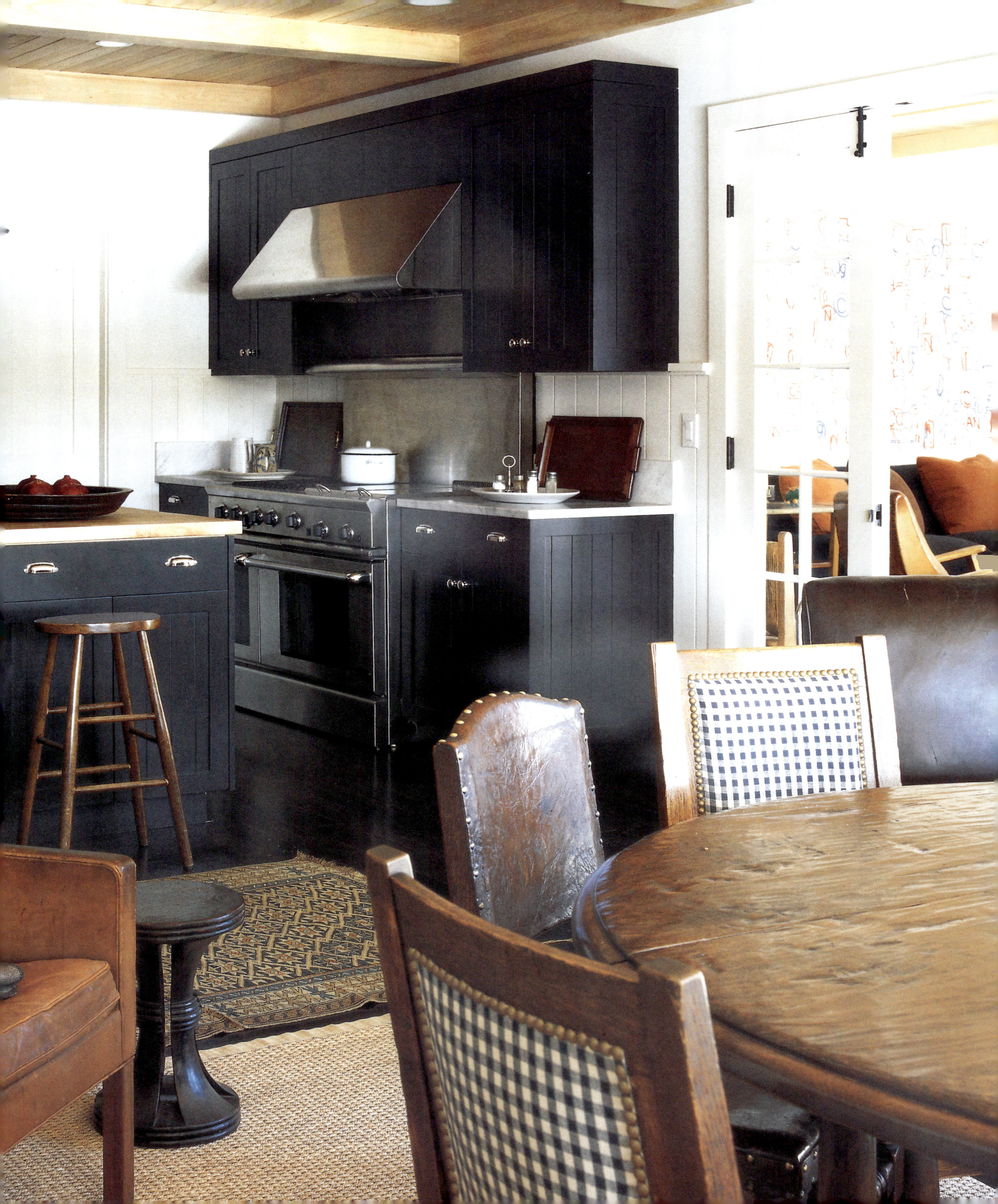

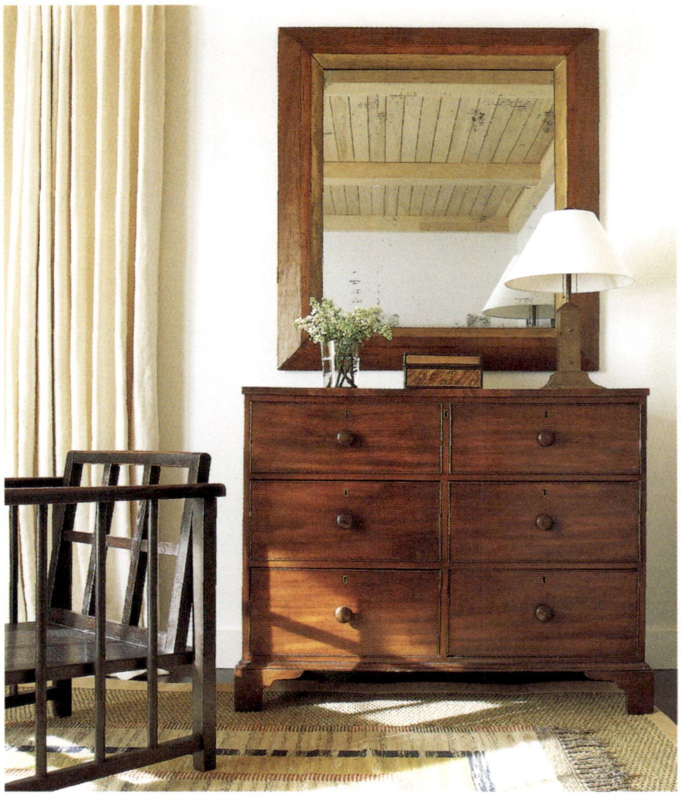

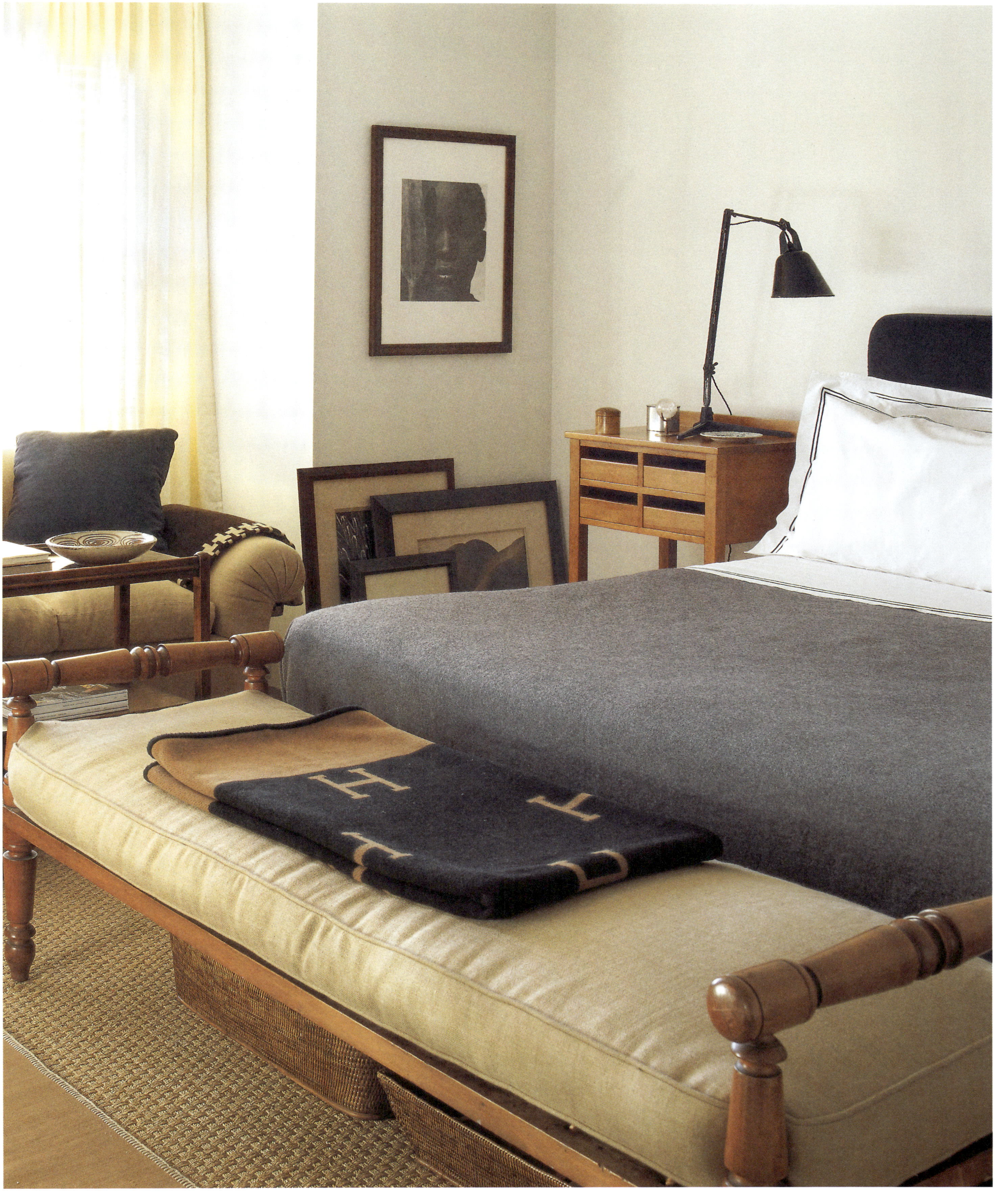

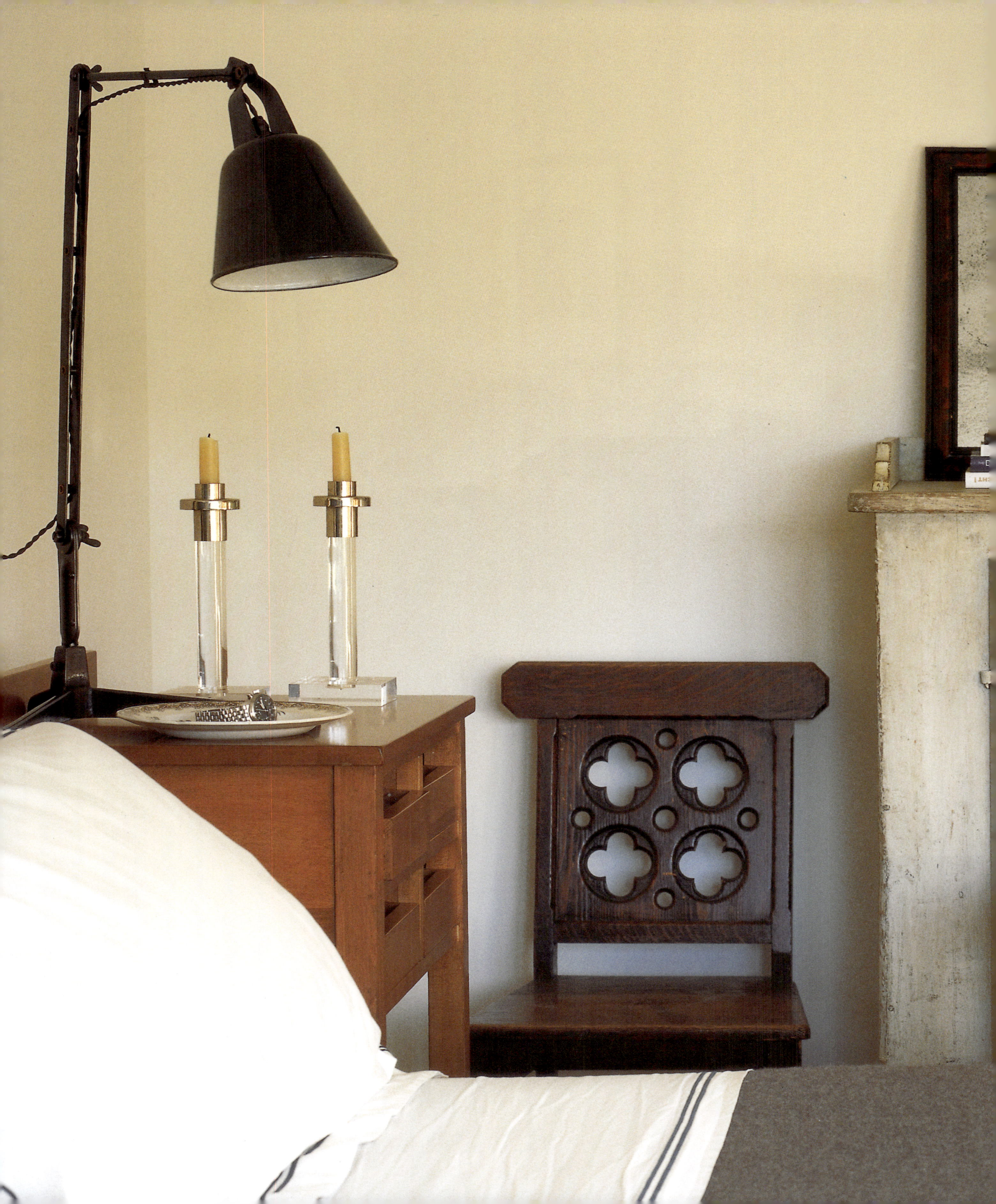

THE ART
IN THE AGE
OF REPRO
DWELLINGS
OUTSIDE ARCHITECTURE
ZEVON
olson sundberg kundig allen
Senses of living
PREFAB
apartment
ALAN POWERS
Country modern
TERENCE CONRAN KITCHENS THE HUB OF THE HOME
JACK FINNEY
Around the House and in the Garden
wright
LUCIAN FREUD DRAWINGS 1940
GEORGE HOWE COLT THE BIG HOUSE
StyleCity PARIS
StyleCity
HILLARY RODHAM CLINTON

enrico BONETTI &
dominic KOZERSKI

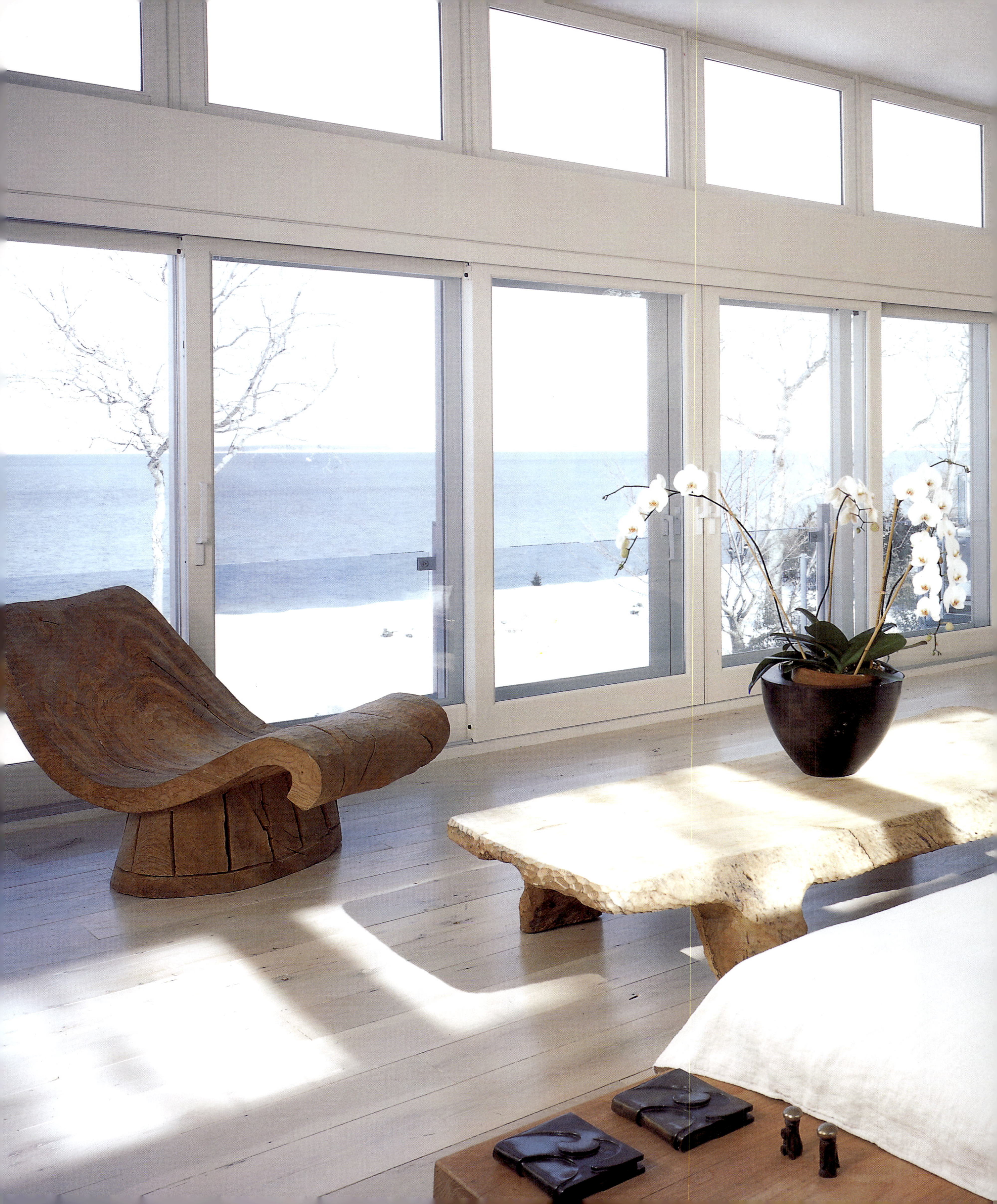

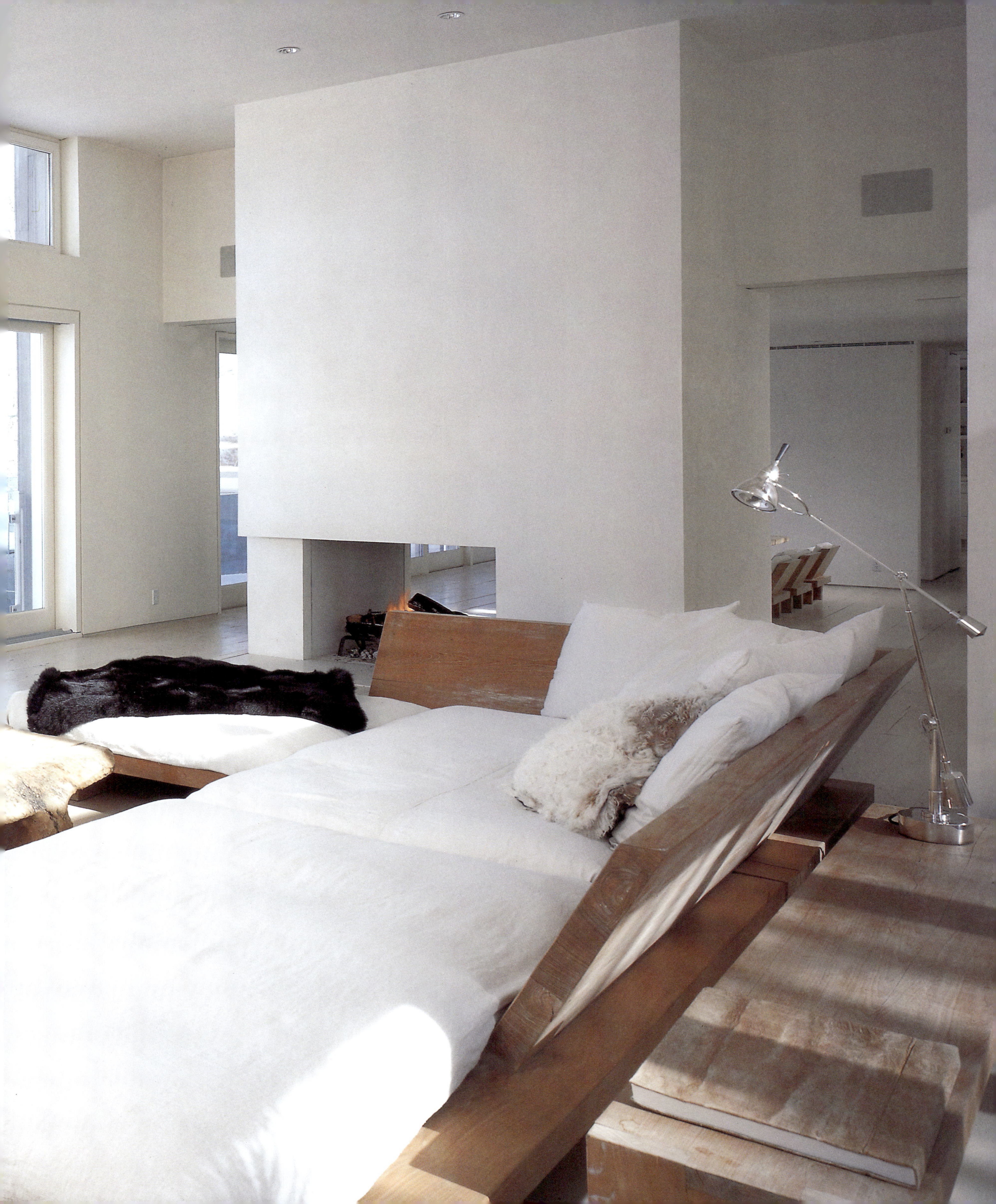

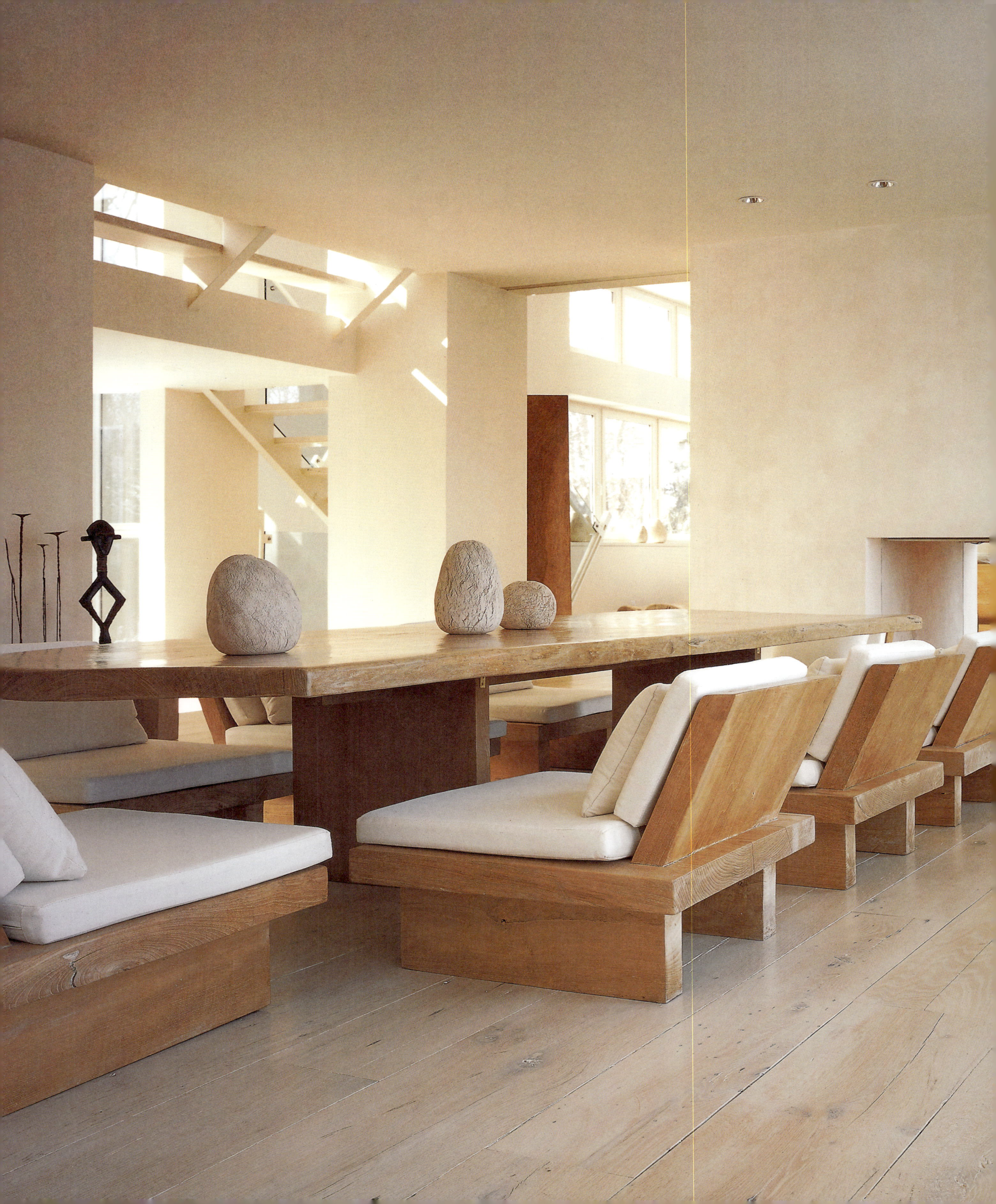

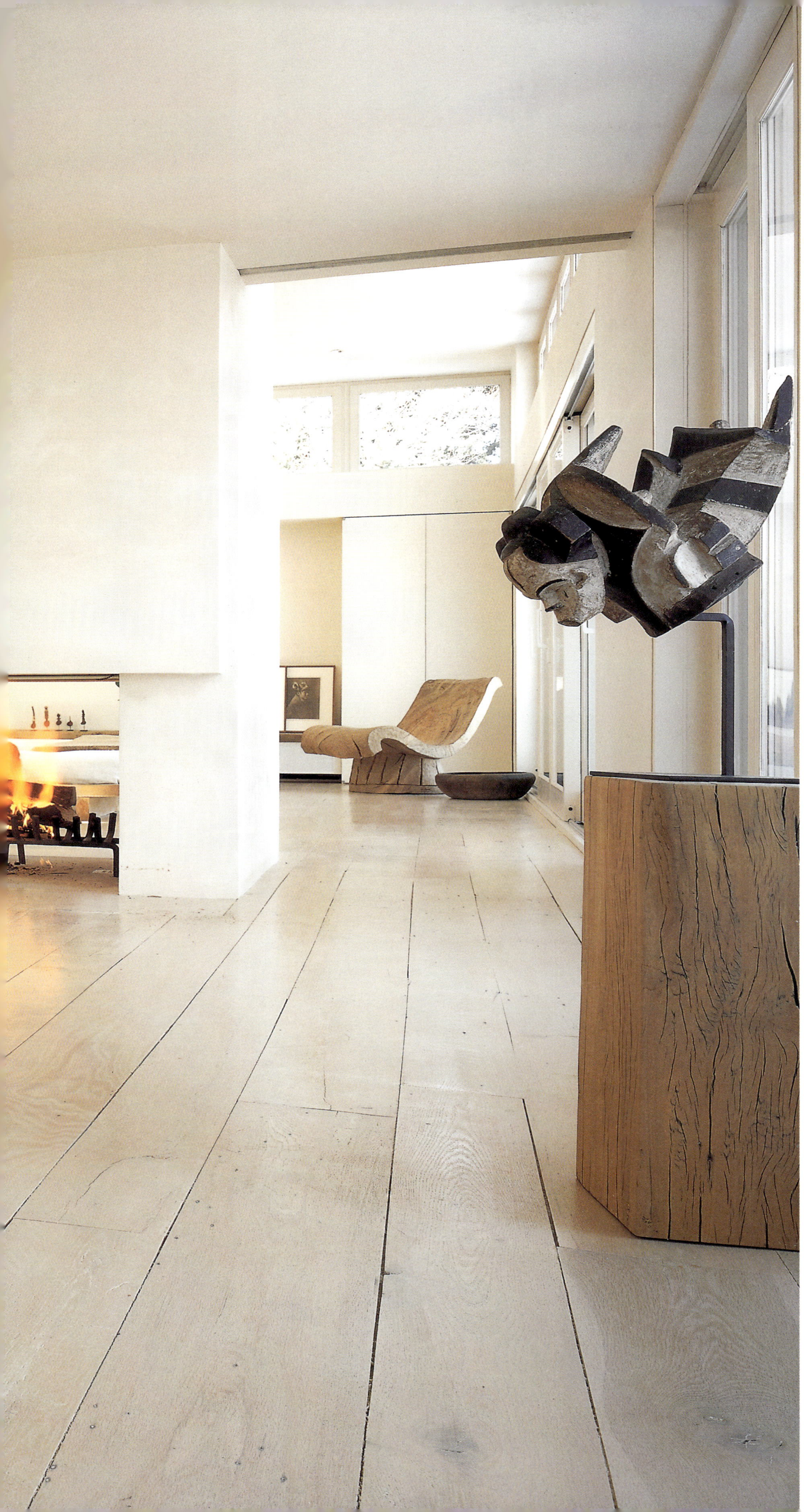

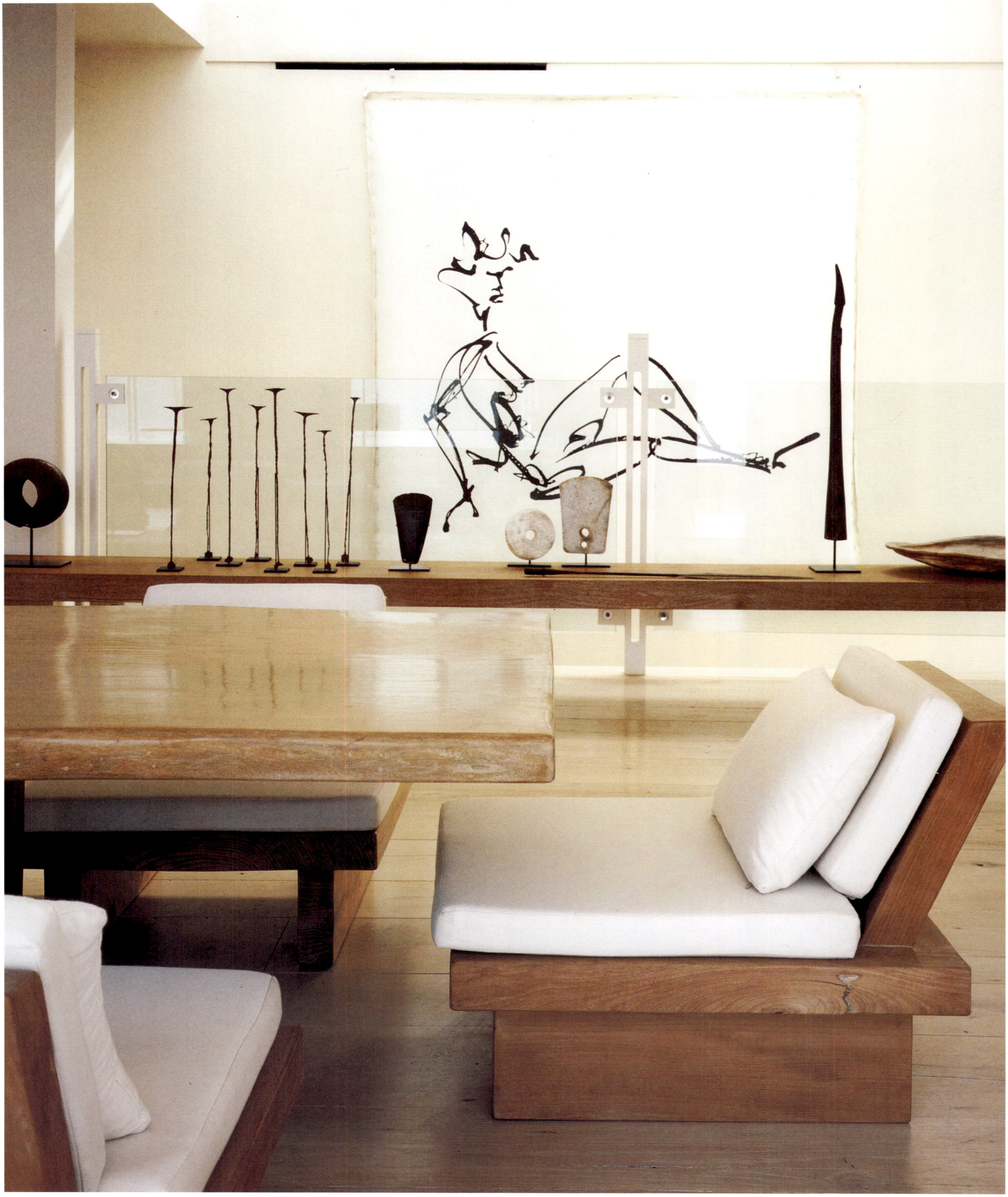

"We conceived of this house as a retreat that was influenced by our client's interest in yoga. We kept the palette neutral and used antique and reclaimed woods to fabricate the low-level furniture and the floors. The result is a space that speaks of relaxation and of connecting with nature—from the spa area to the bedroom."

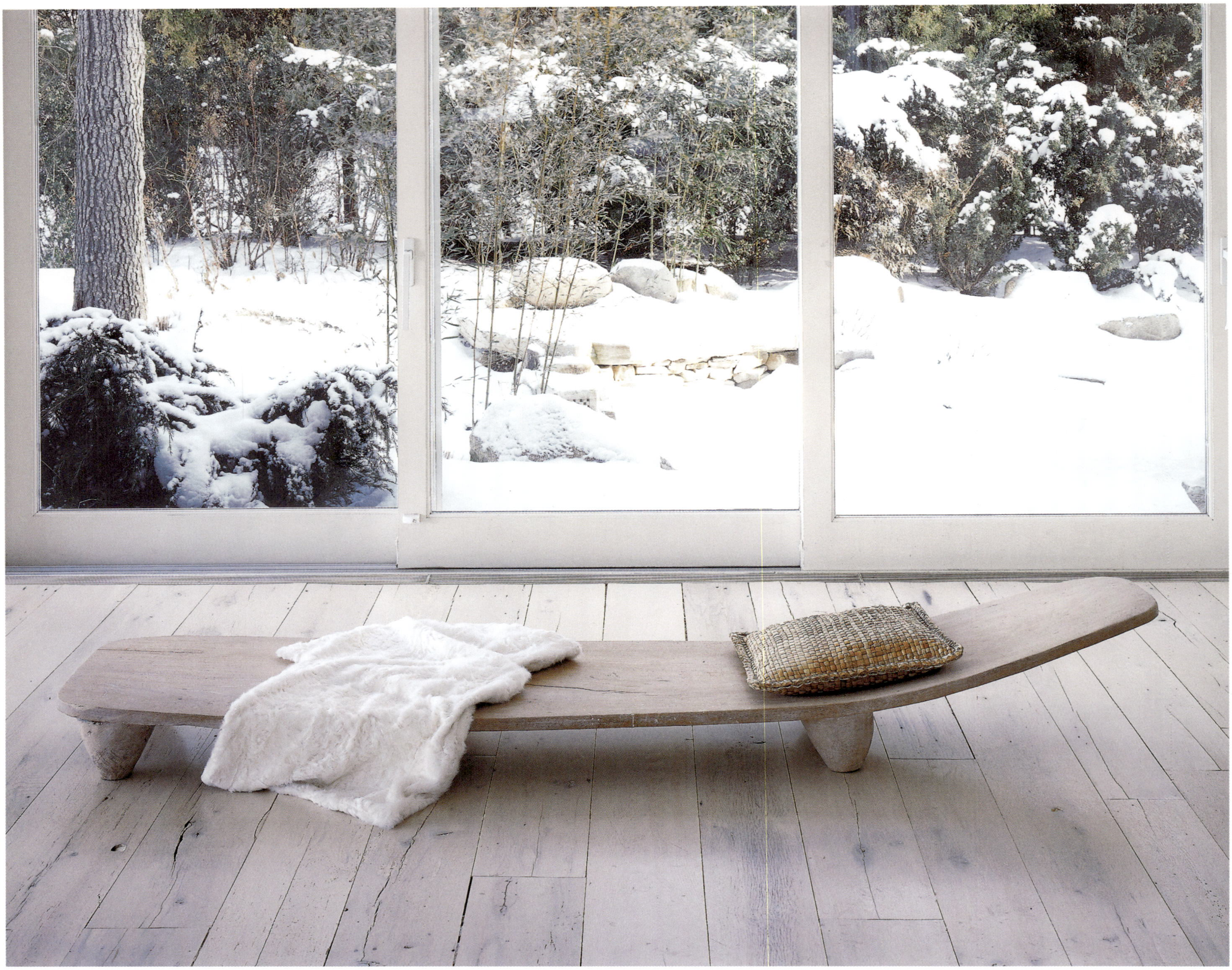

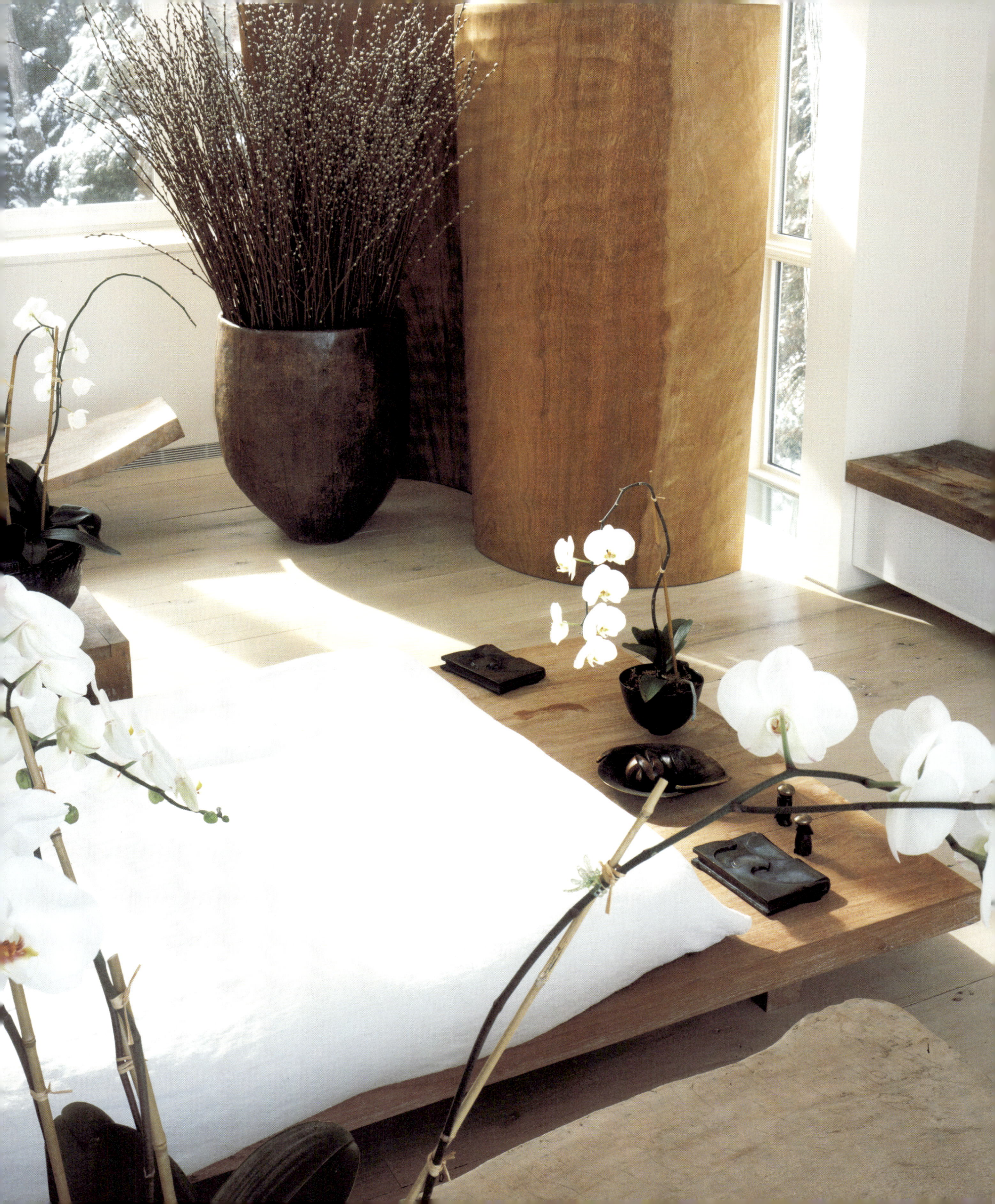

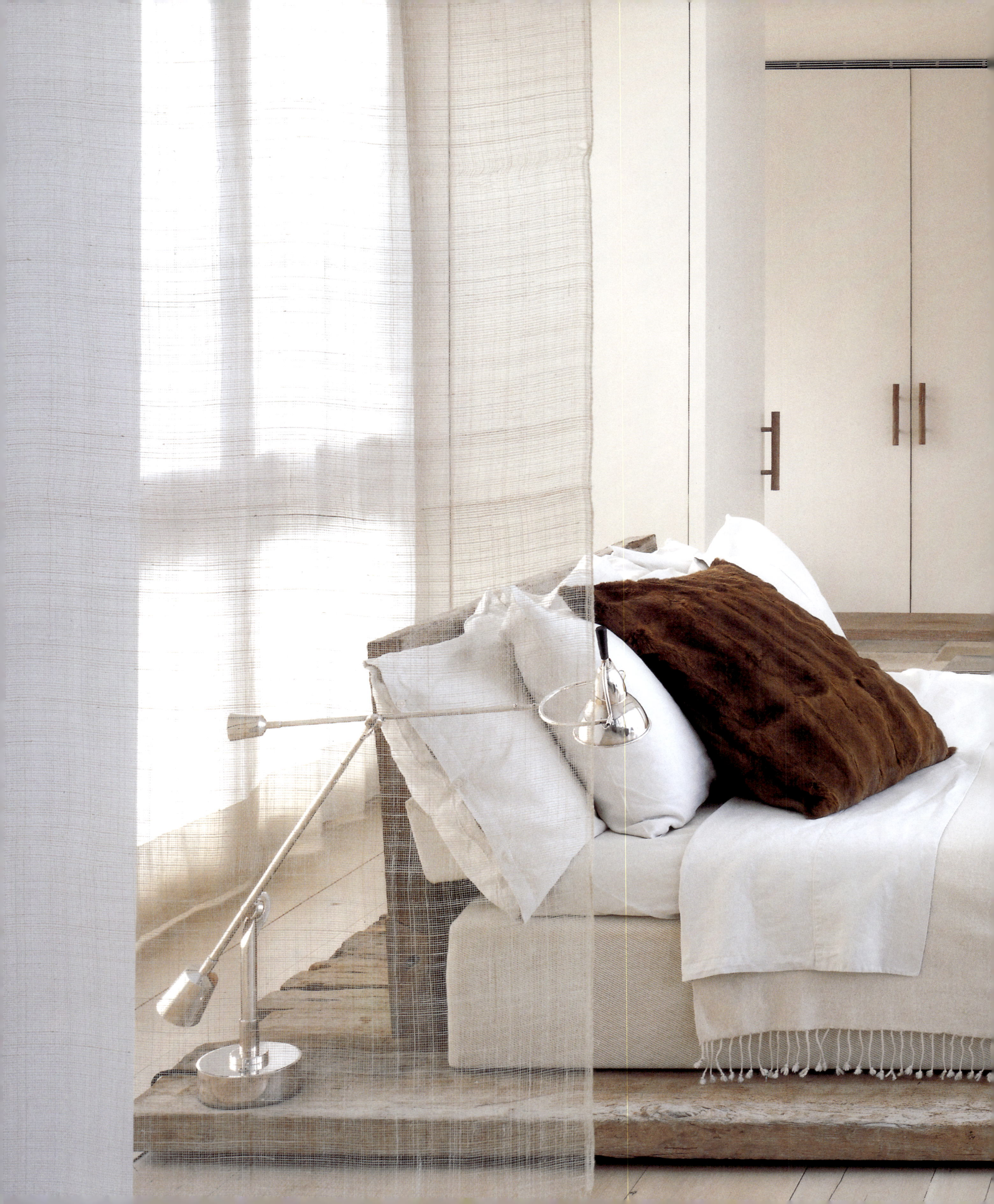

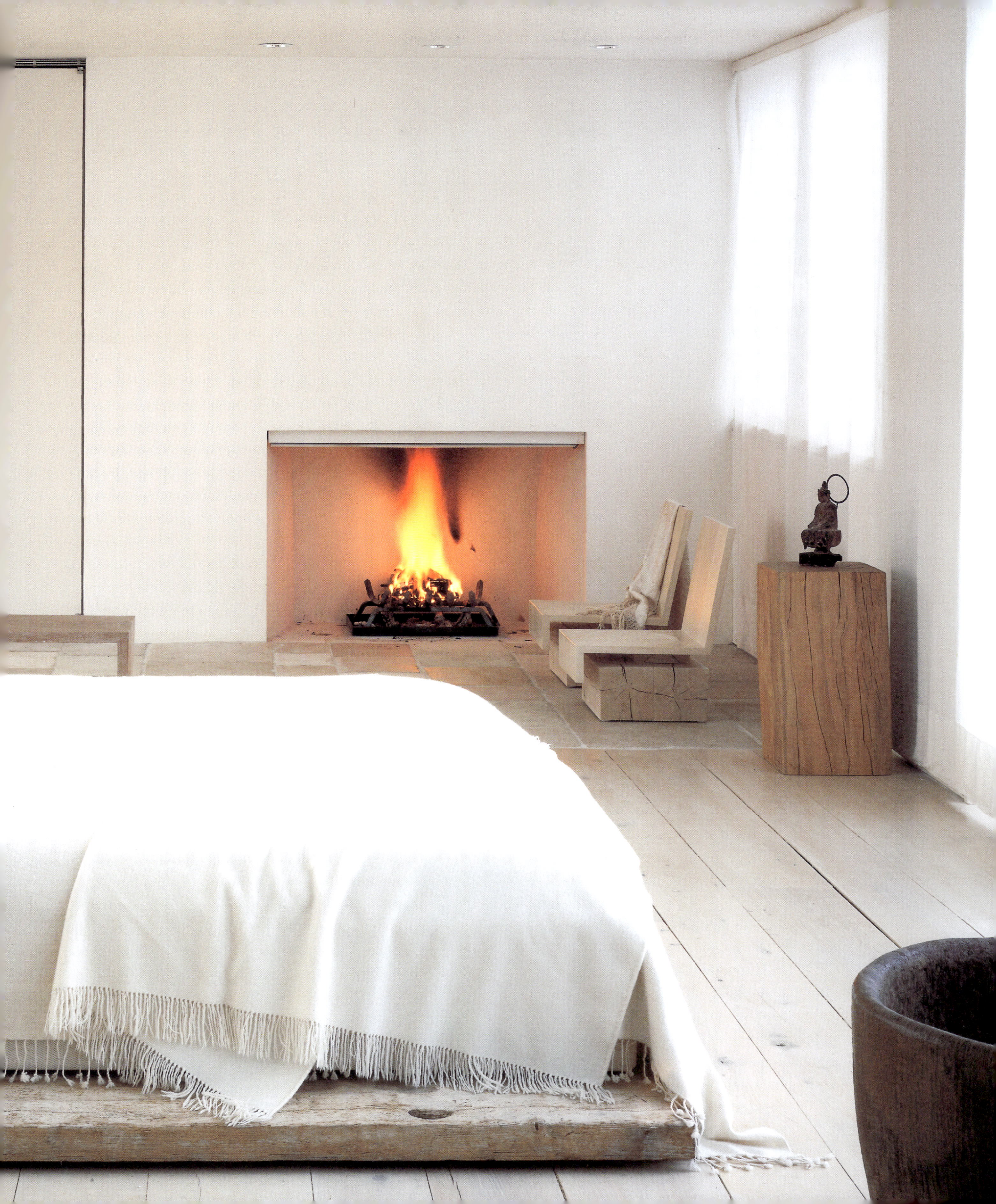

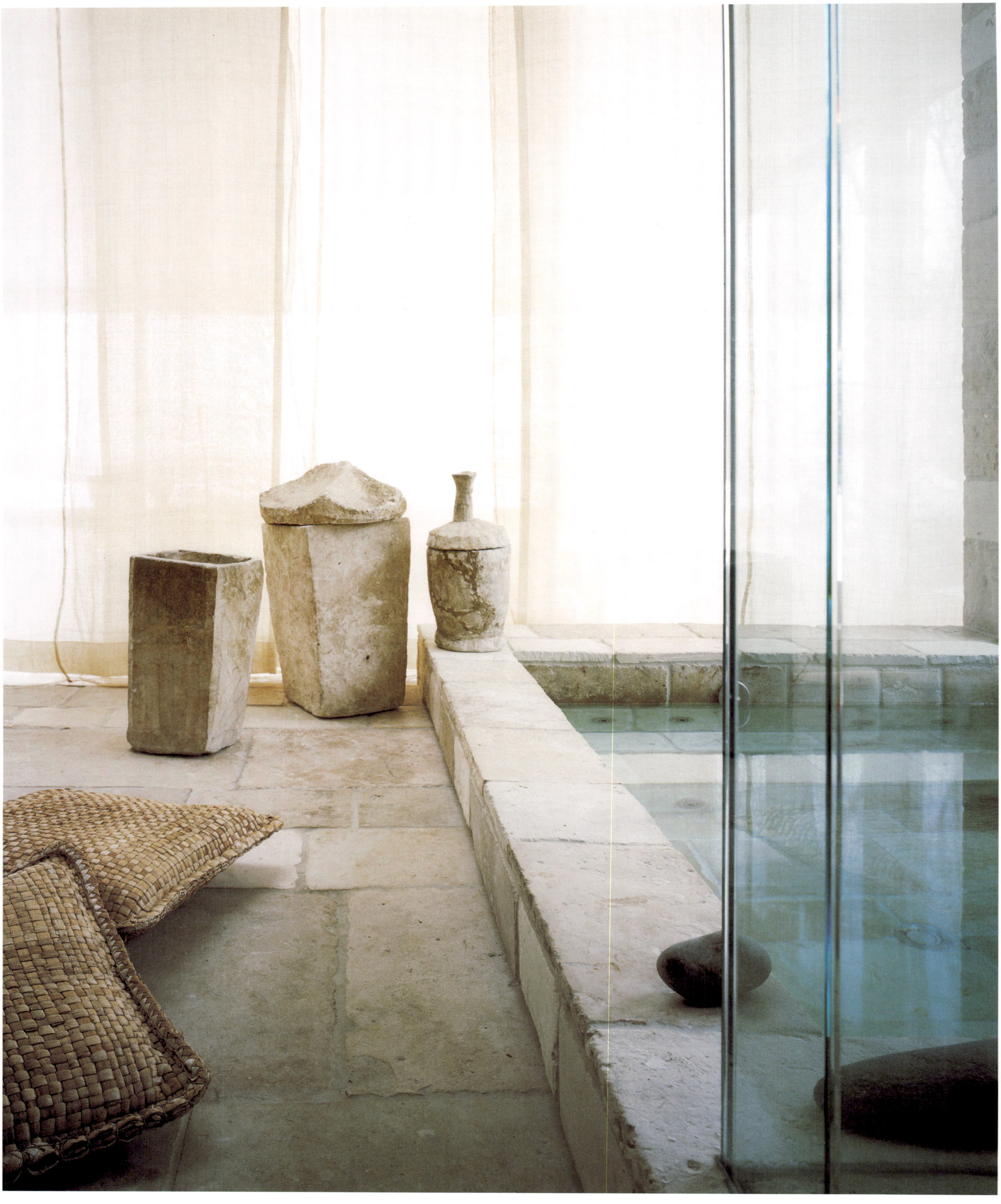

arthur DUNNAM

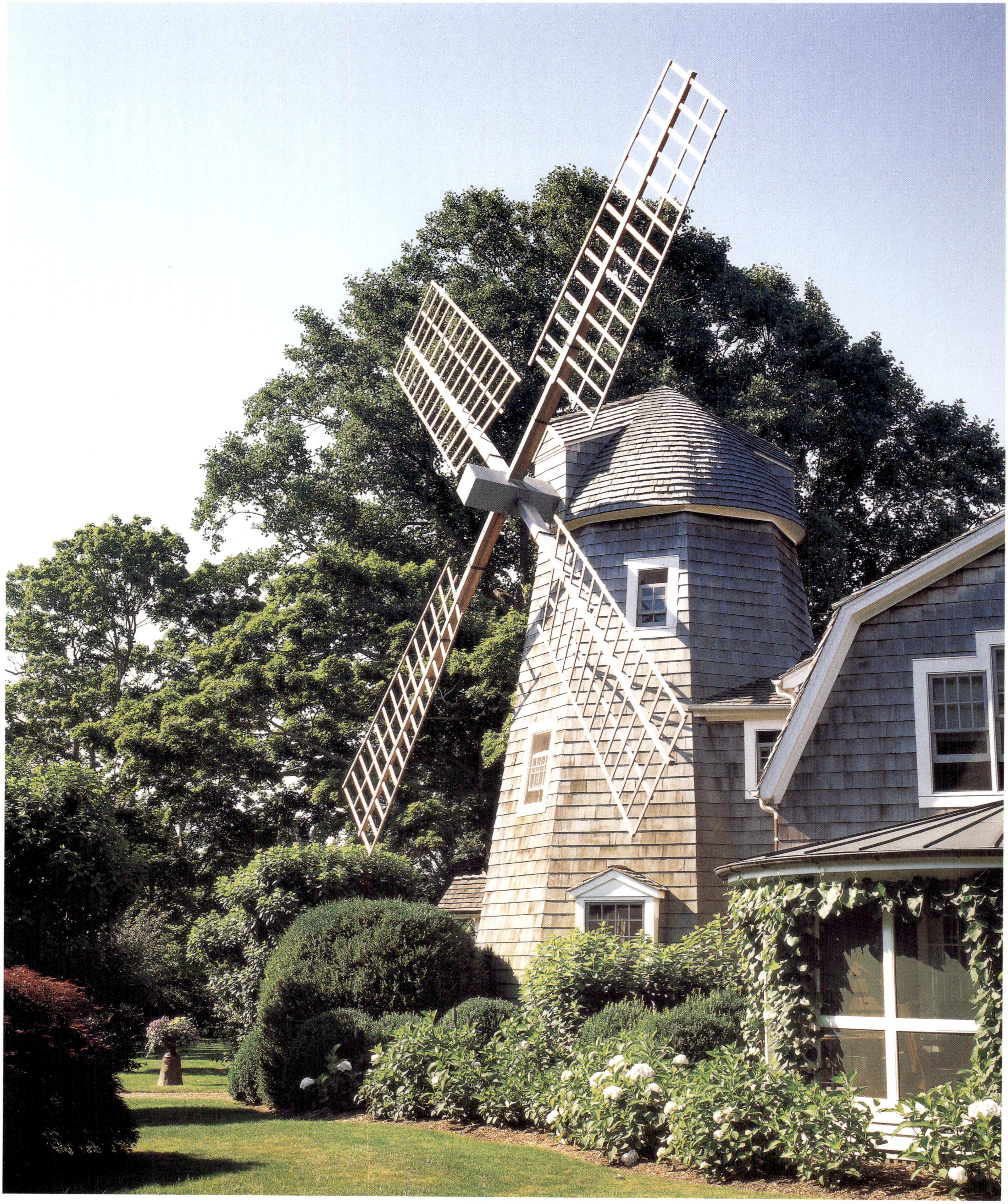

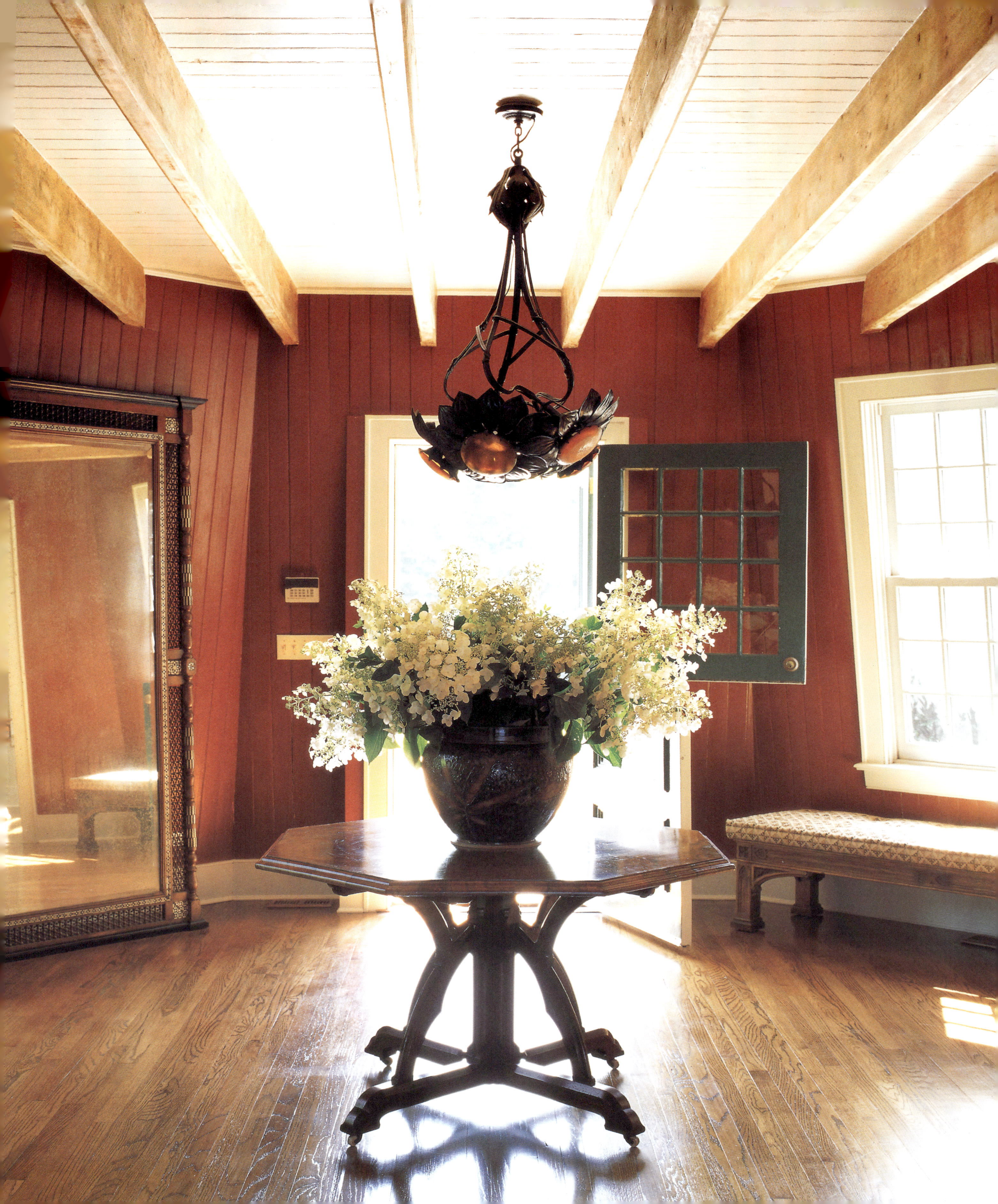

"One constantly marvels at how diverse the Hamptons are: the people, their daily activities, the landscape, the architecture, and the interiors. As a part-time resident for almost twenty years, I have been fortunate to work on an incredible variety of residences and get to know and appreciate the folks who live in them. With each client I try to pick up the vibe, and do what's right for the home and its inhabitants. My goal is to create an environment that feels like it belongs where it is and has a kind of timeless quality."

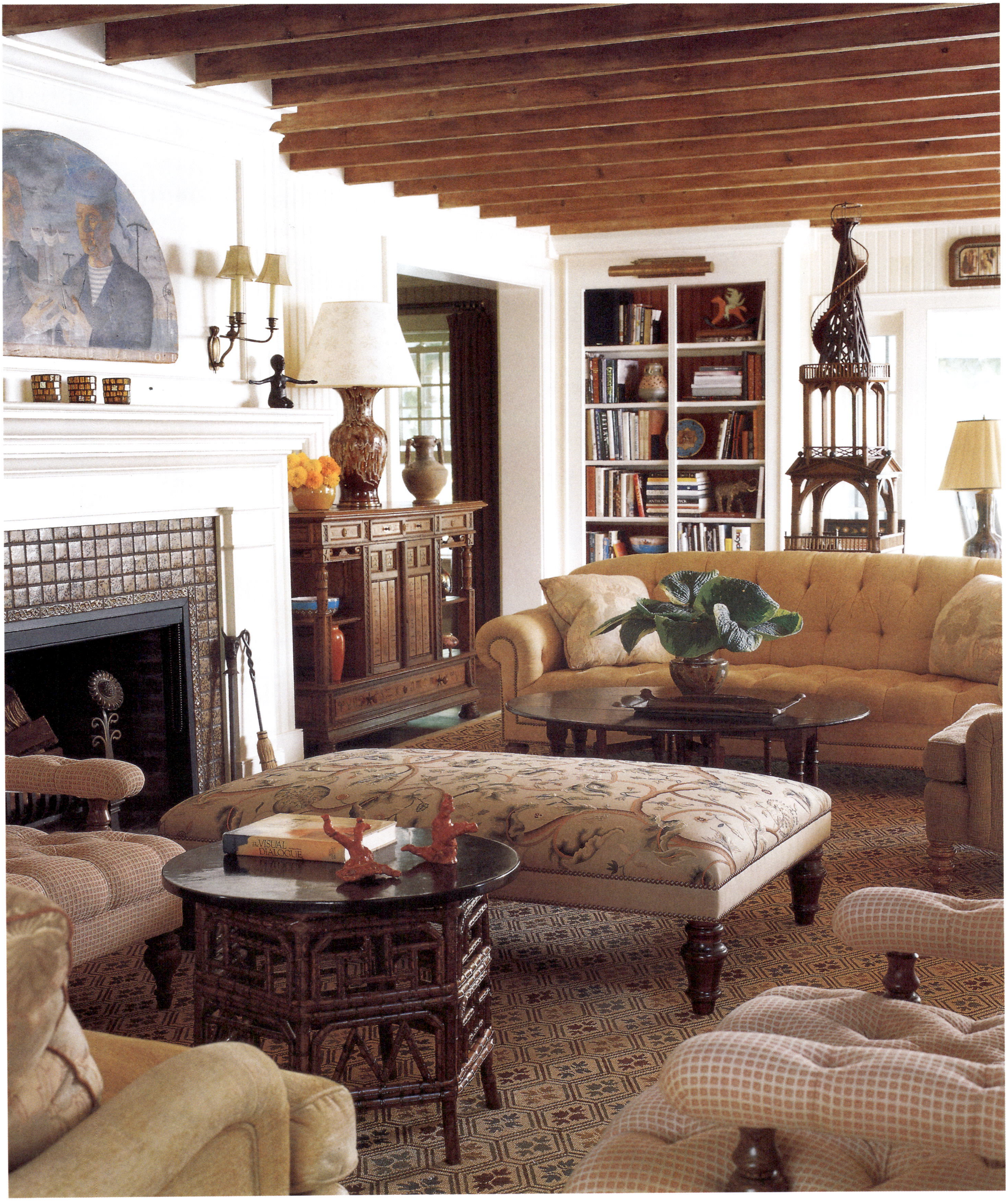
VISUAL
DIALOGUE

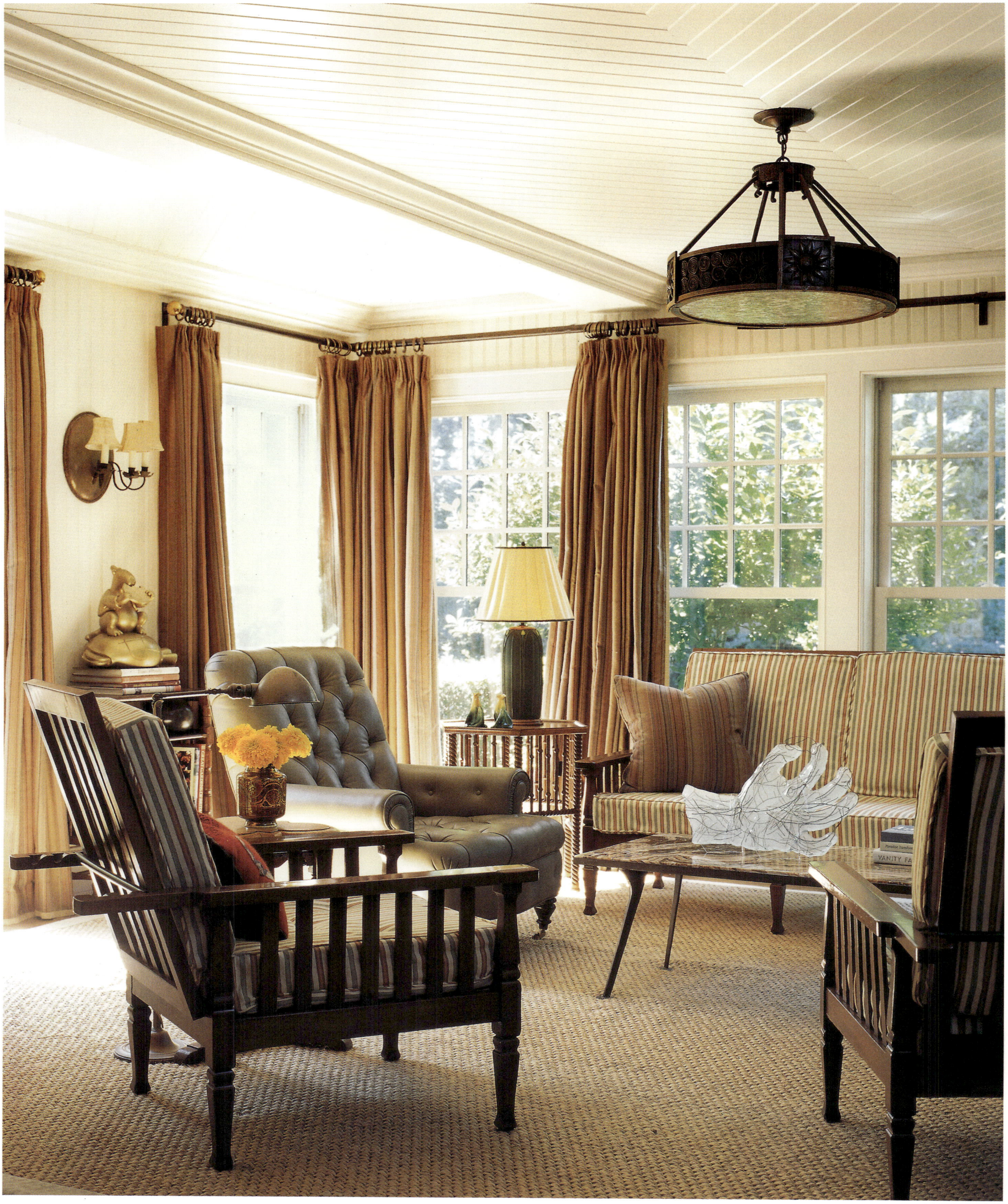

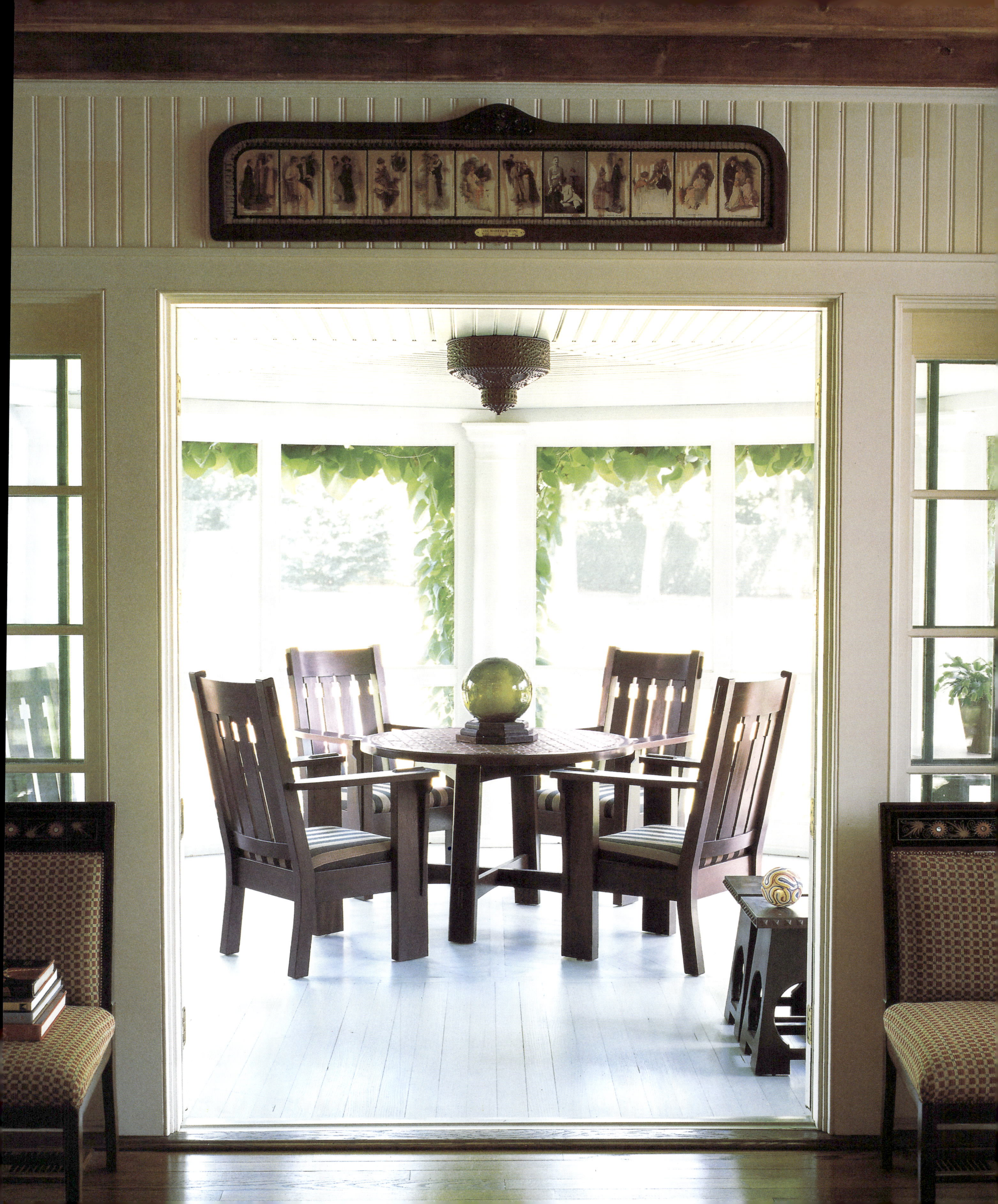

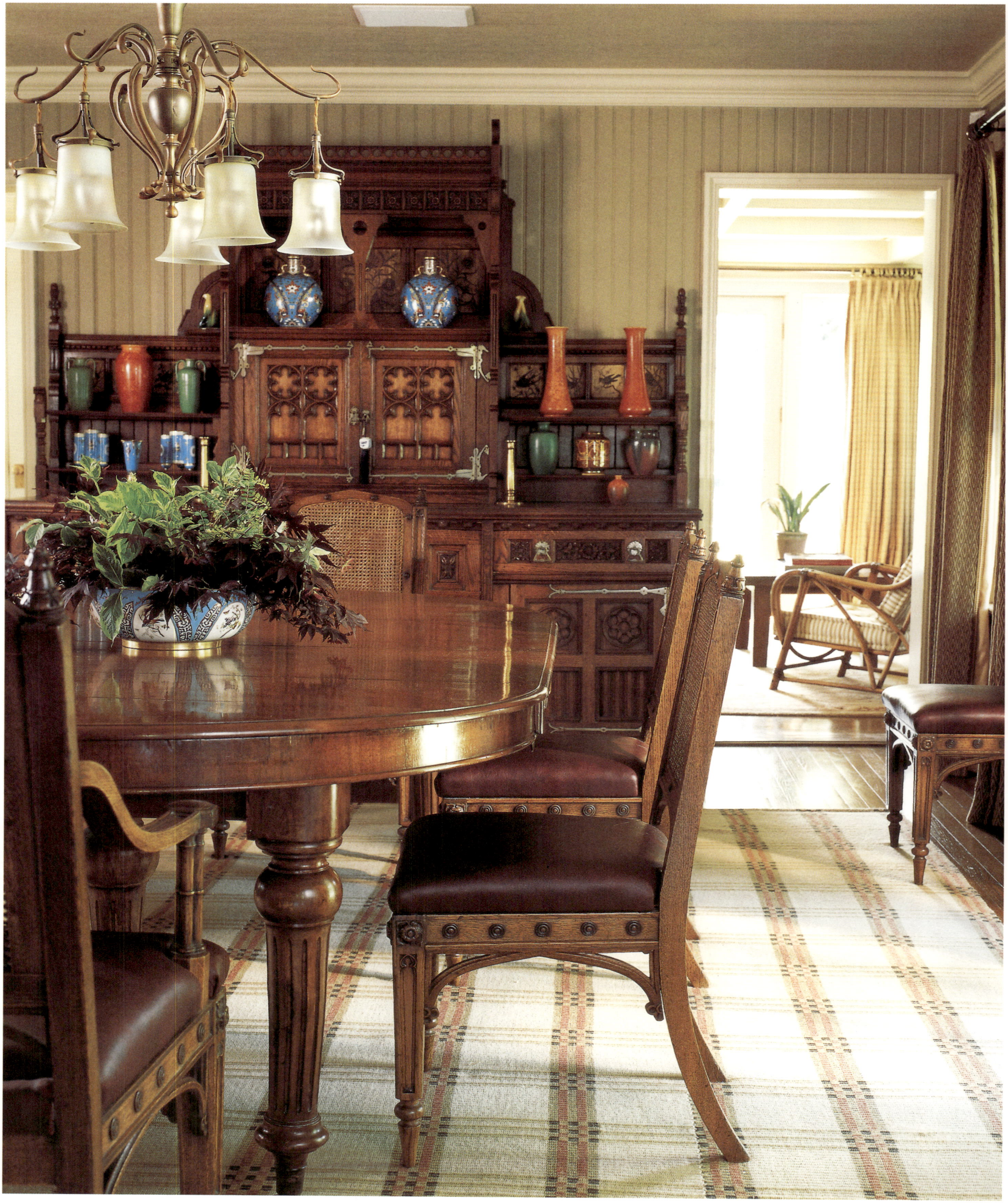

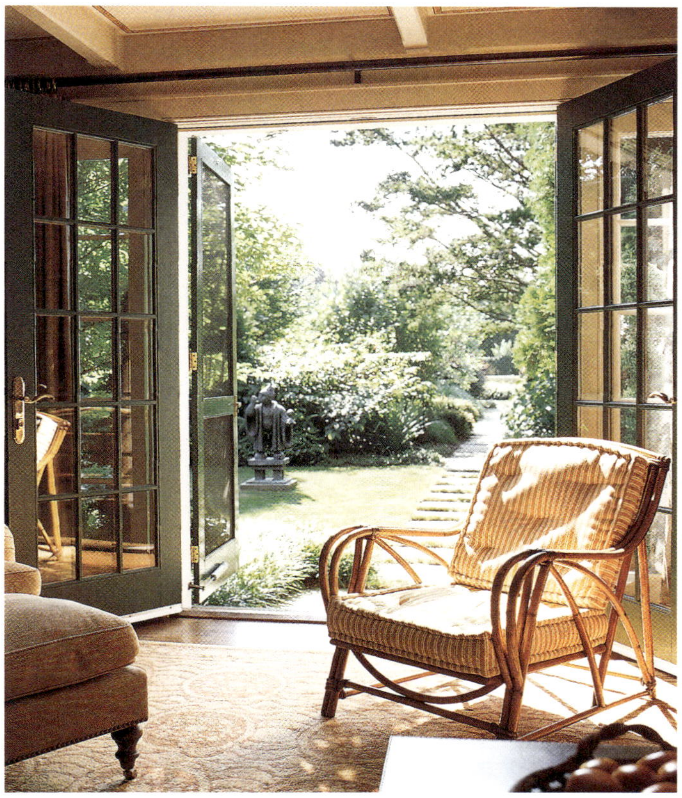

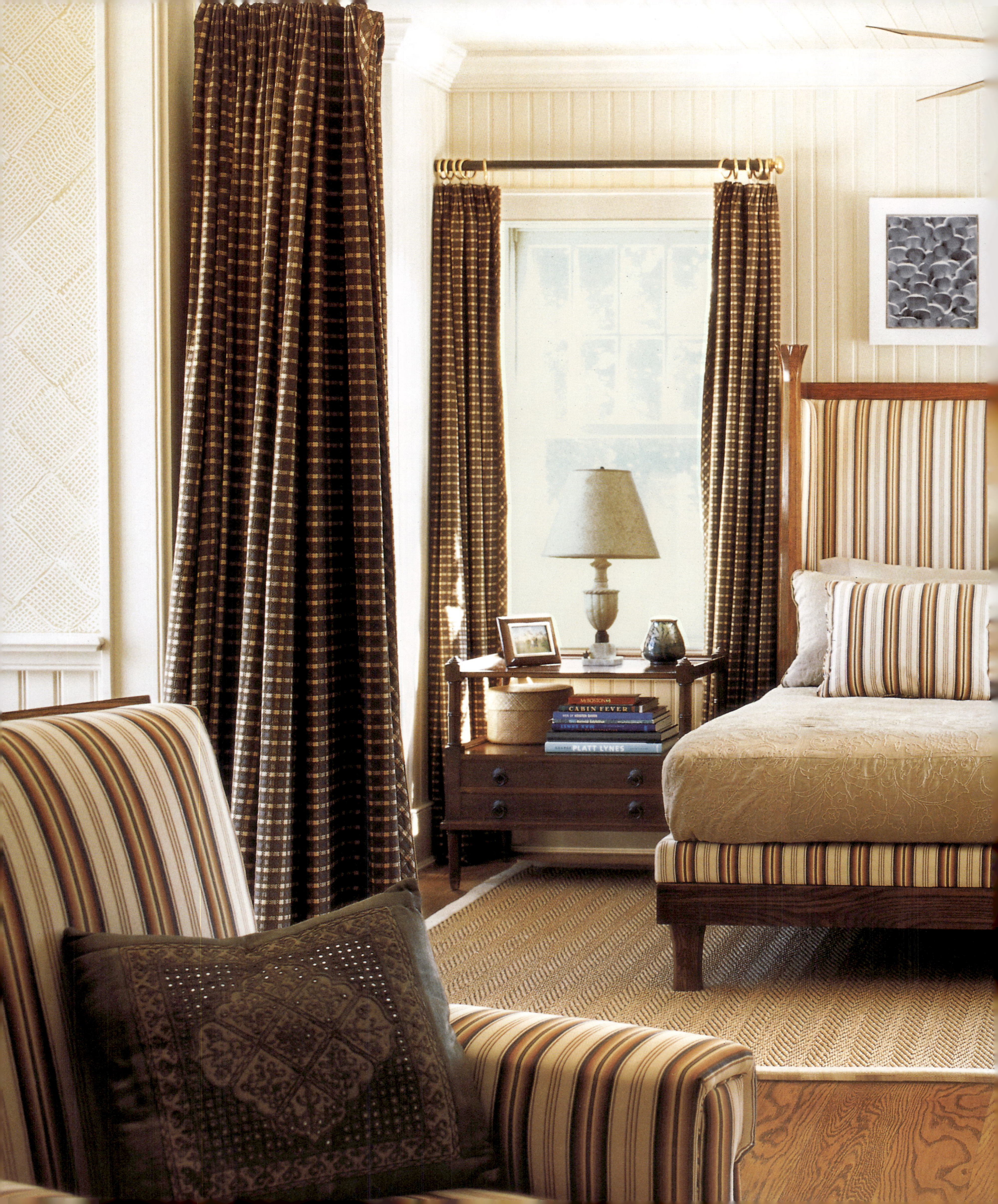
CABIN FEVER
PLATT LYNES

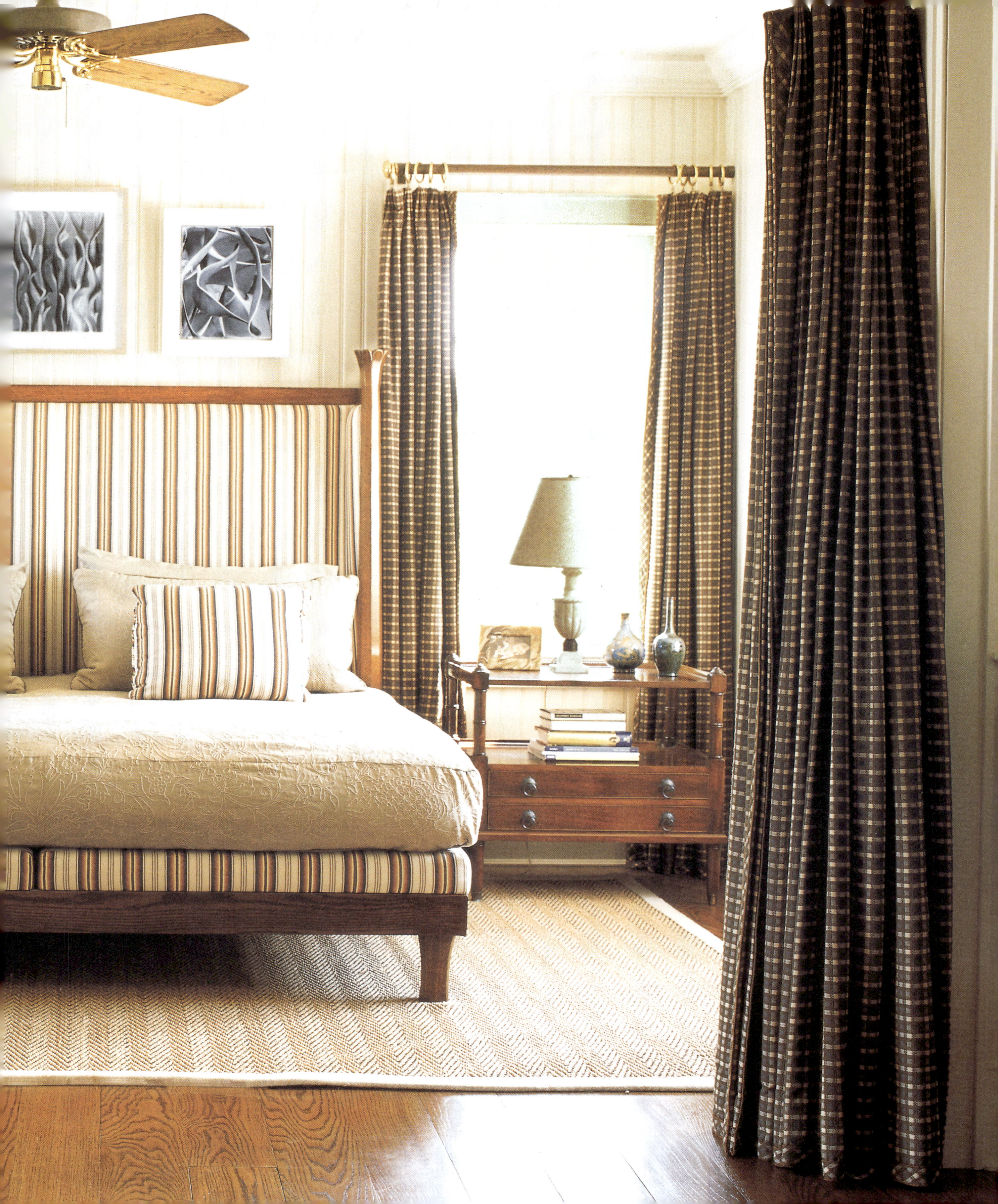

michael HAVERLAND &
philip GALANES

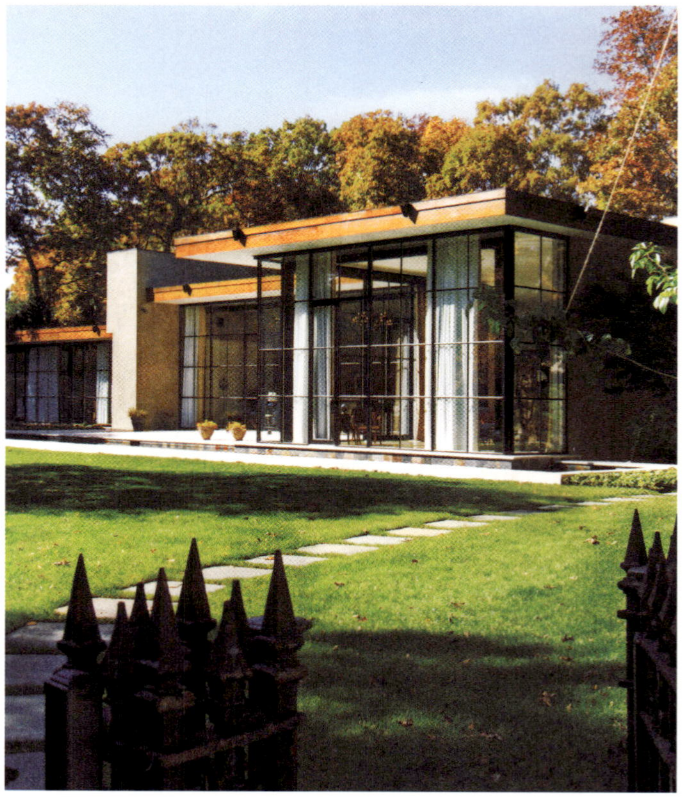

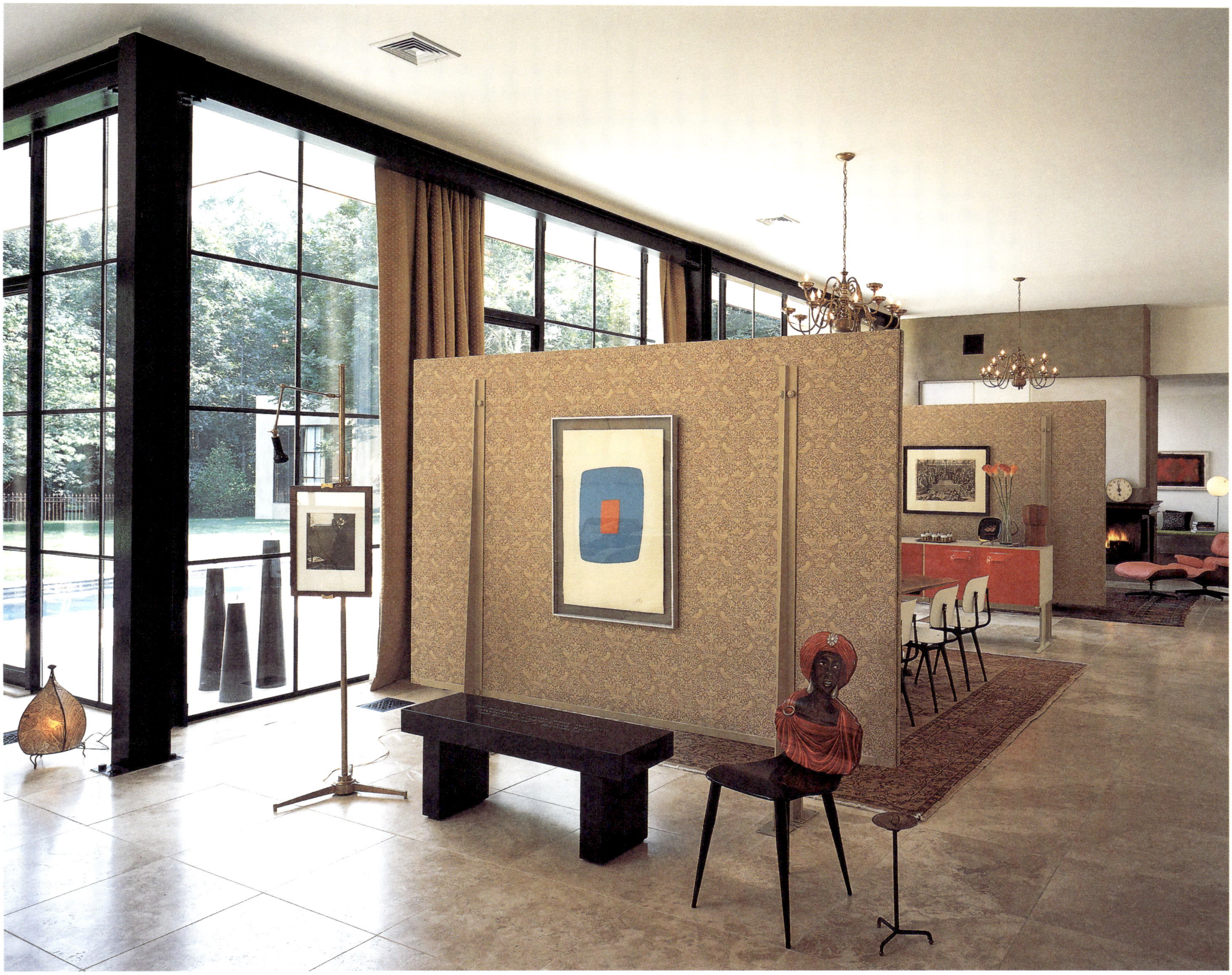

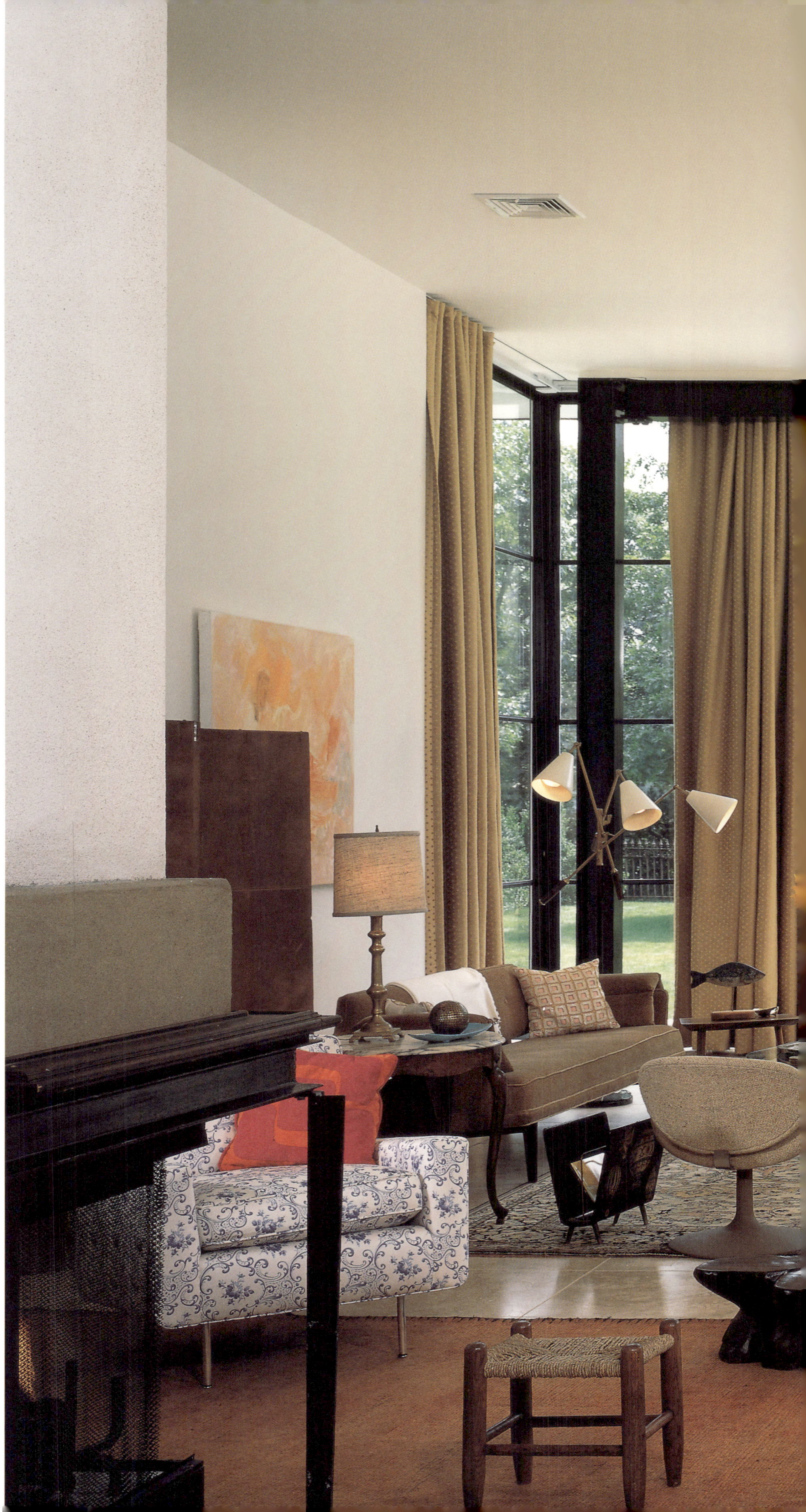

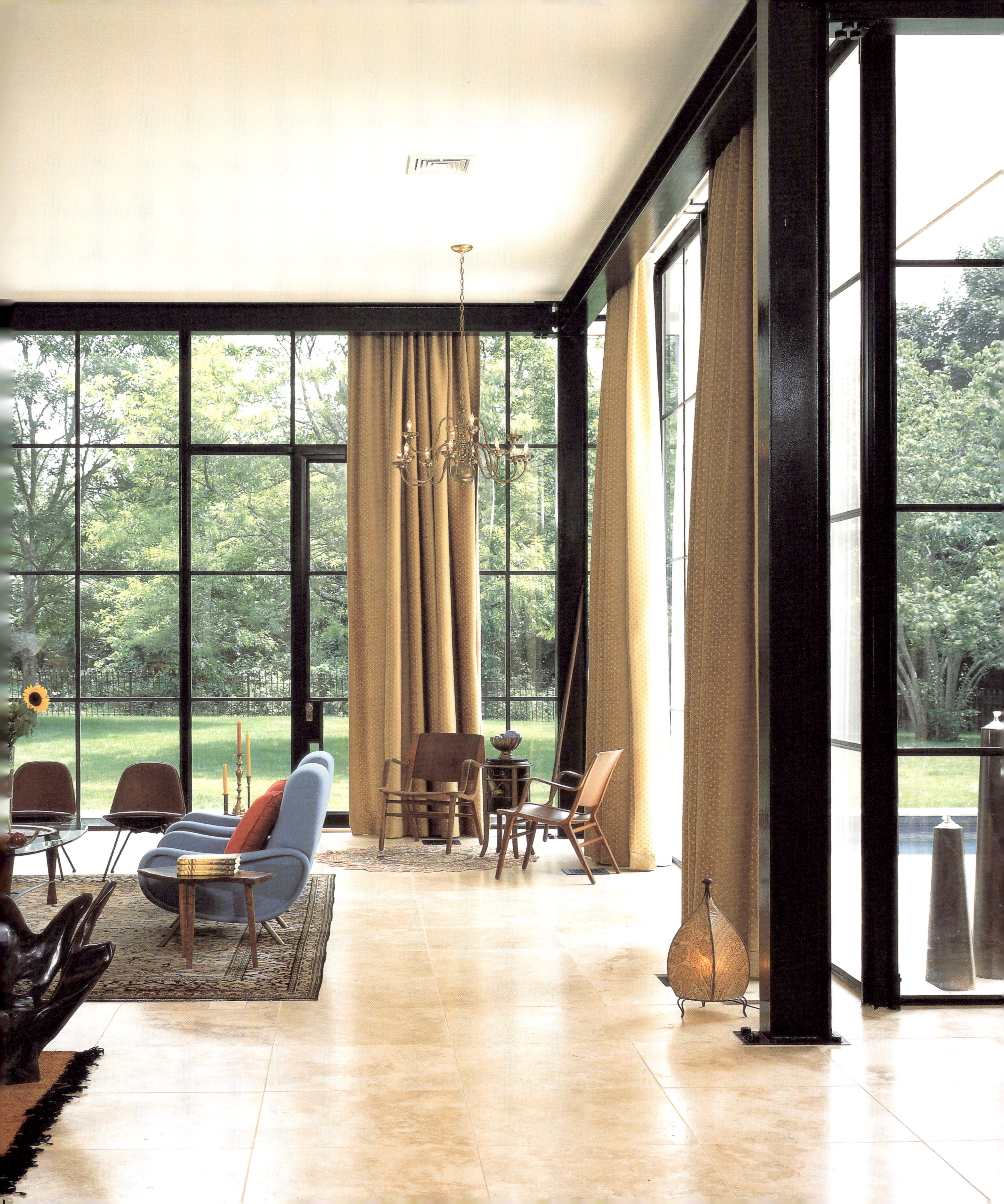

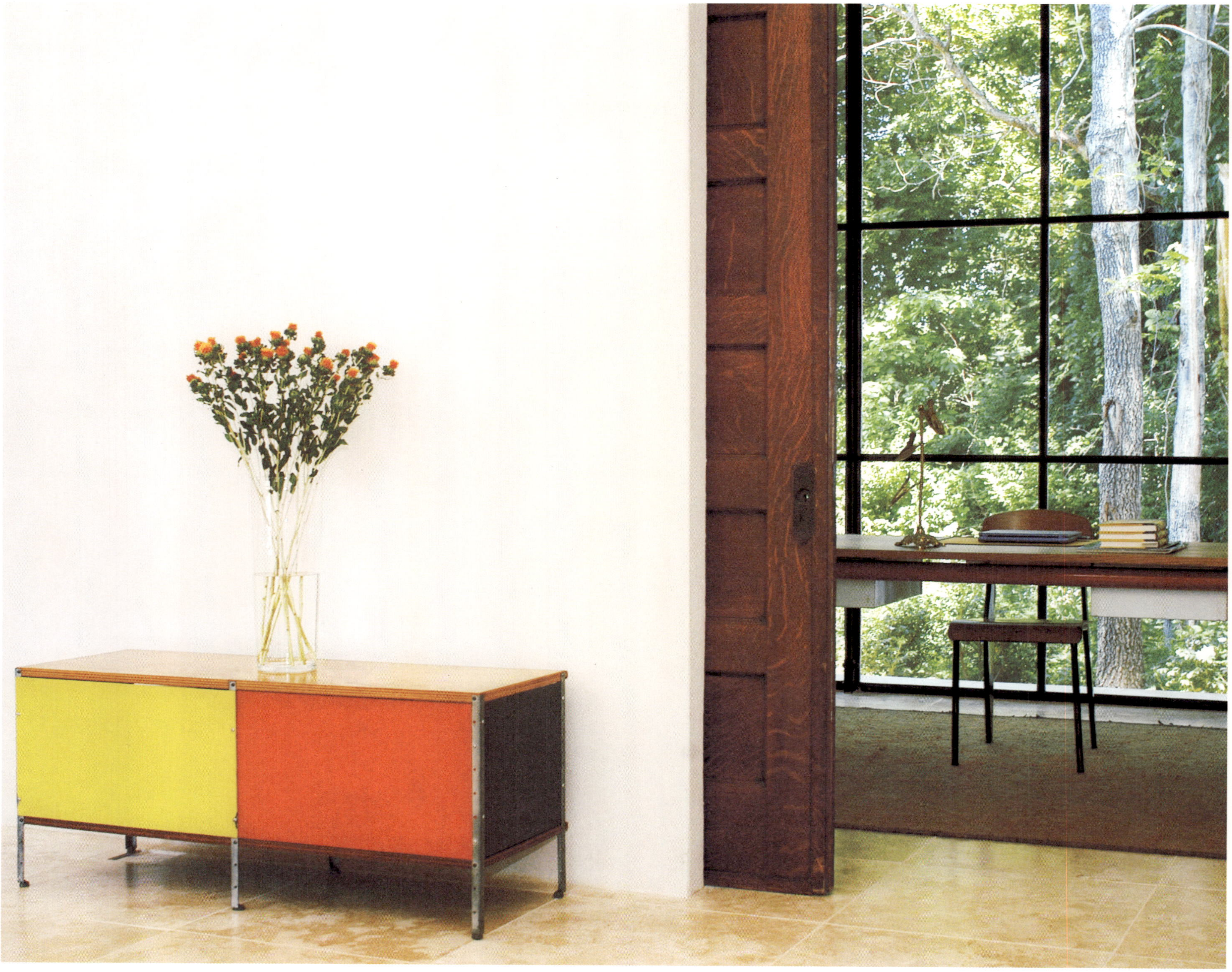

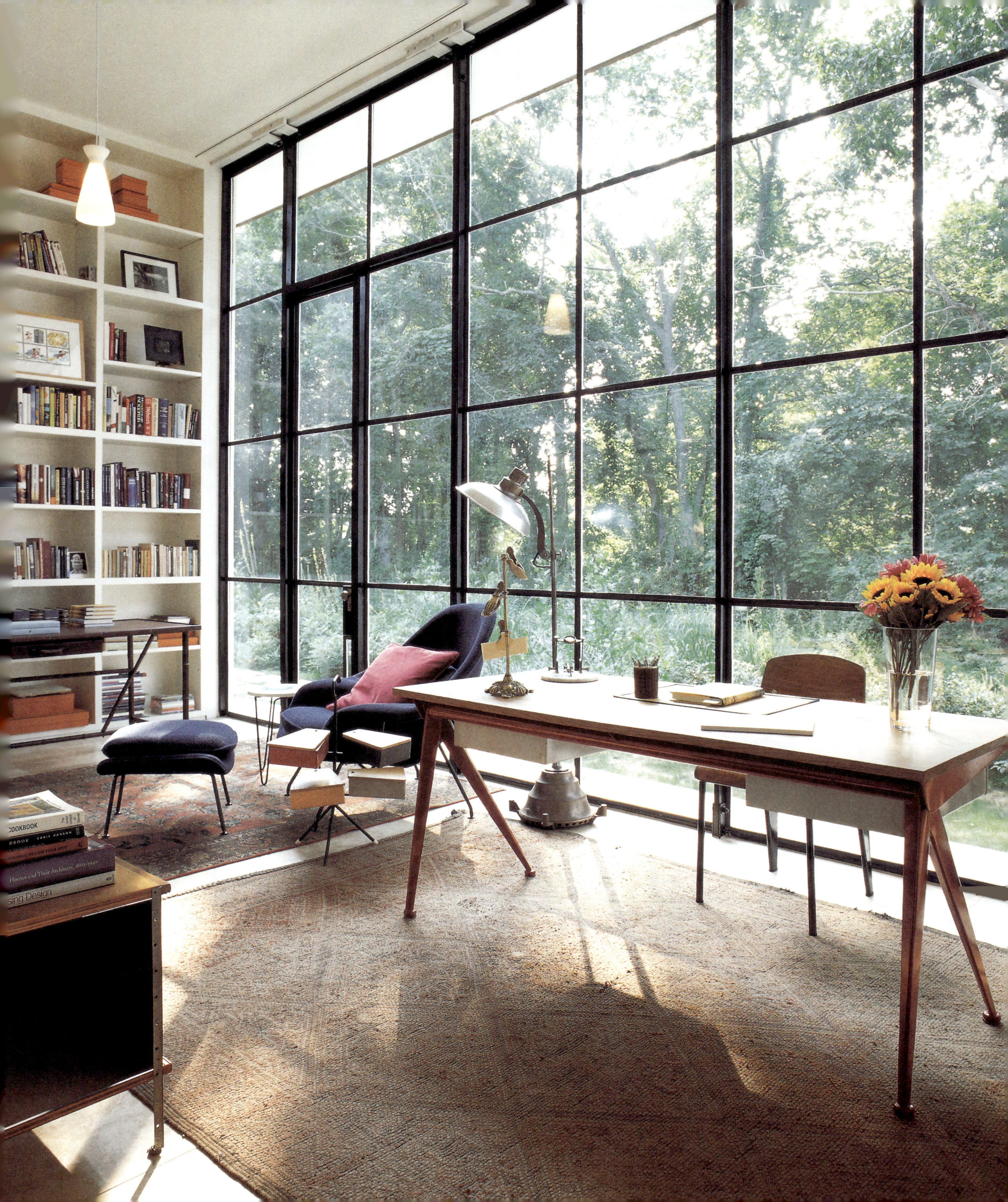
COOKBOOK
sing Design

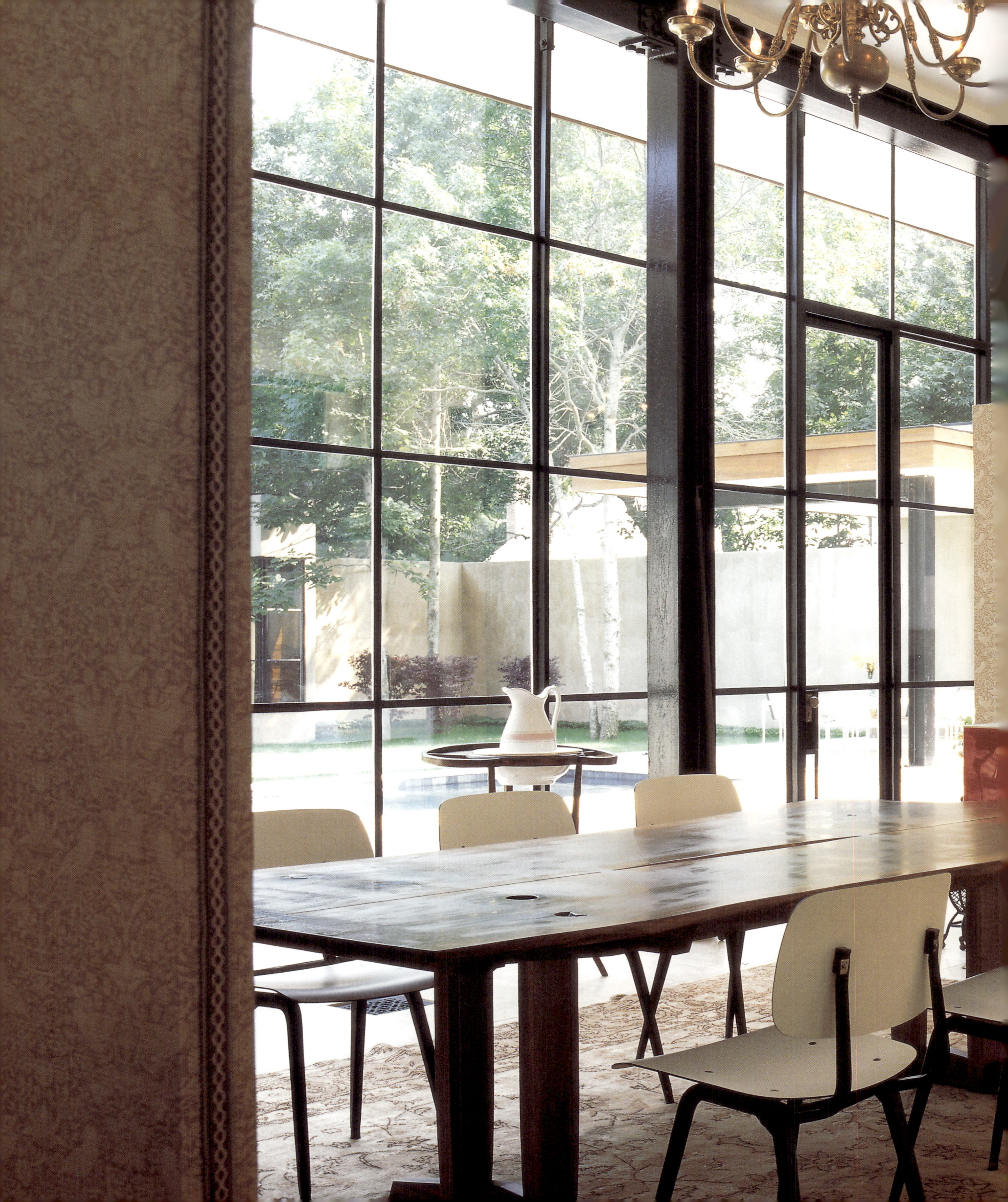

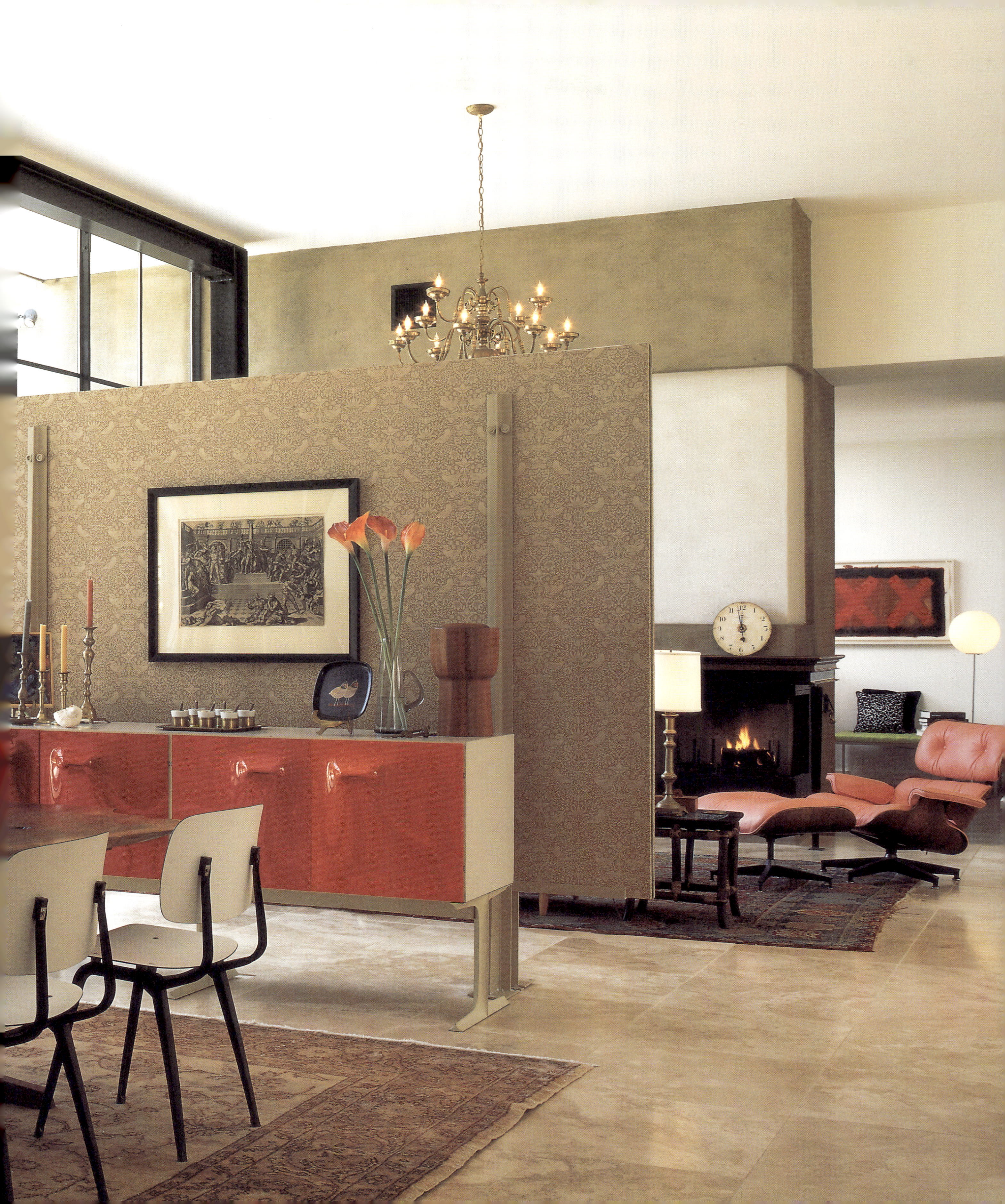

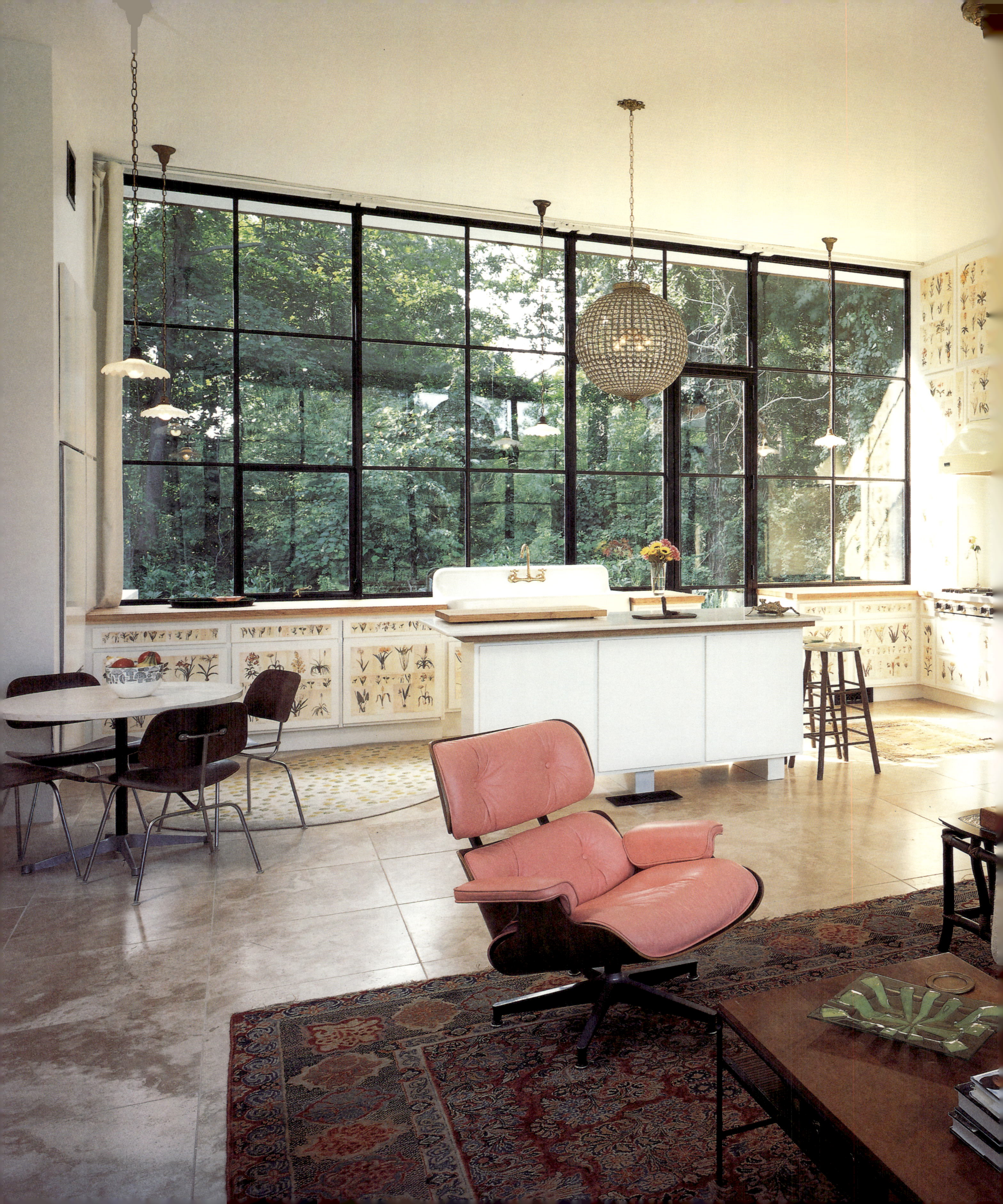

THE ART OF RAISING A PUPPY
THE ART OF RAISING A PUPPY
Bricks and Brownstone
Dirr's Hardy Trees and Shrubs

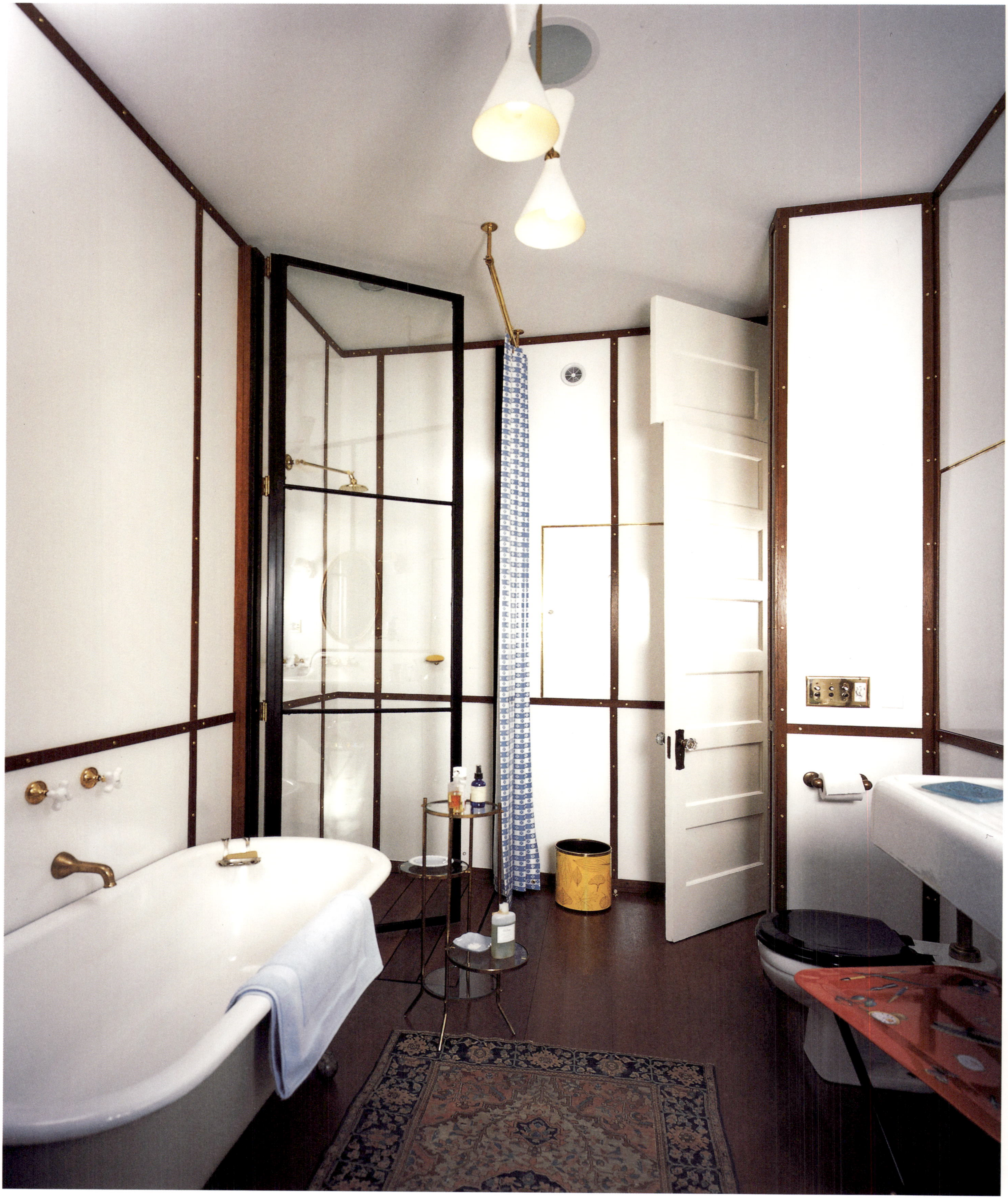

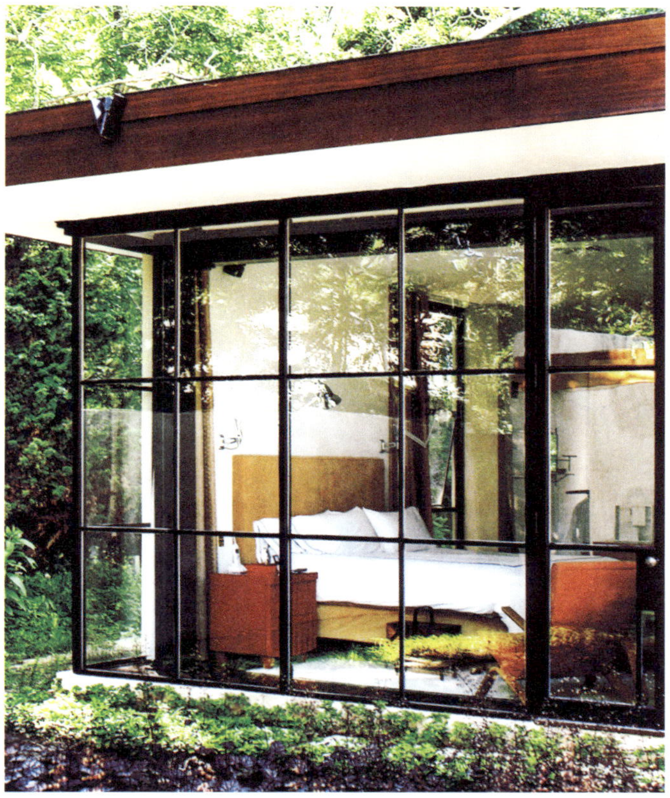

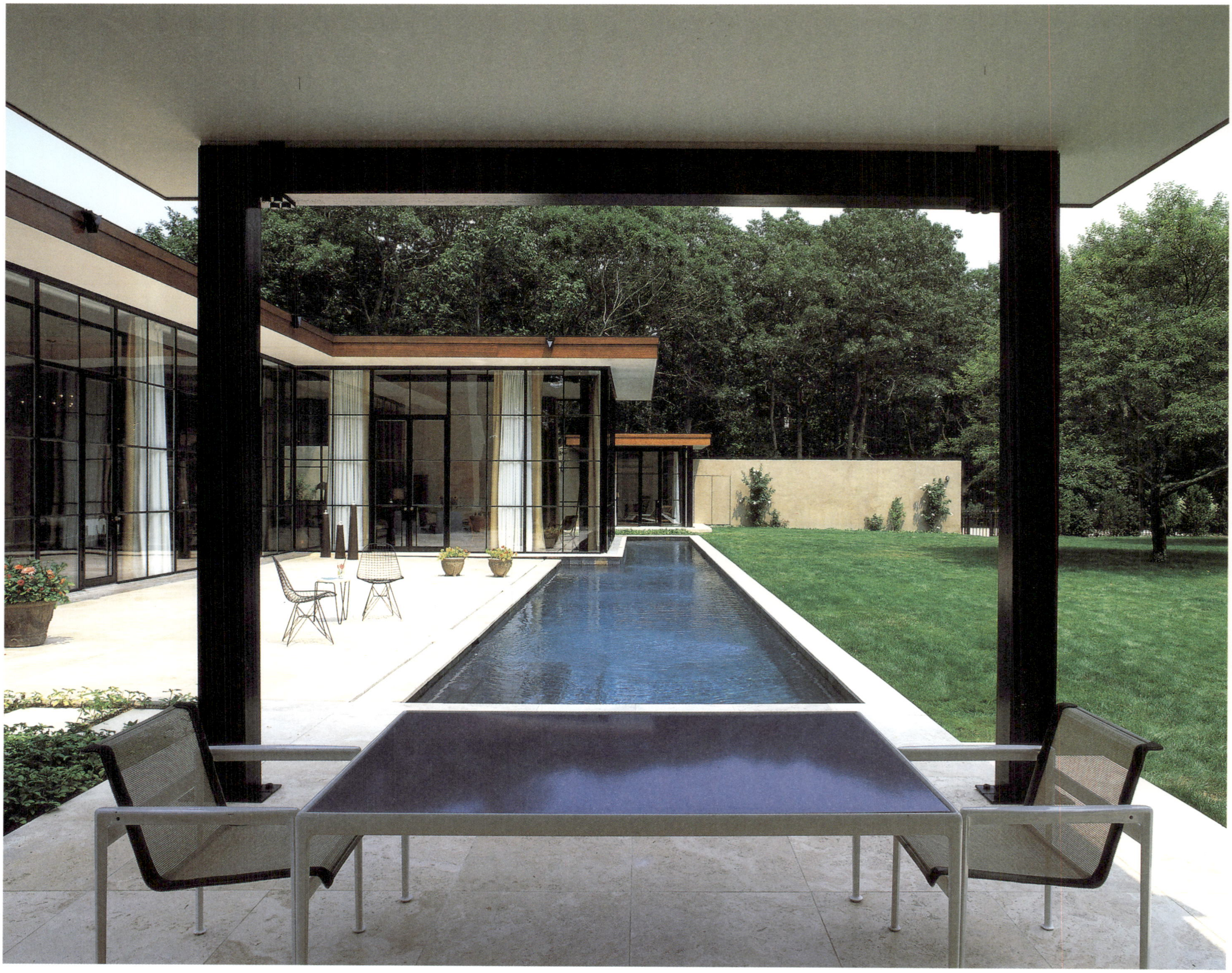

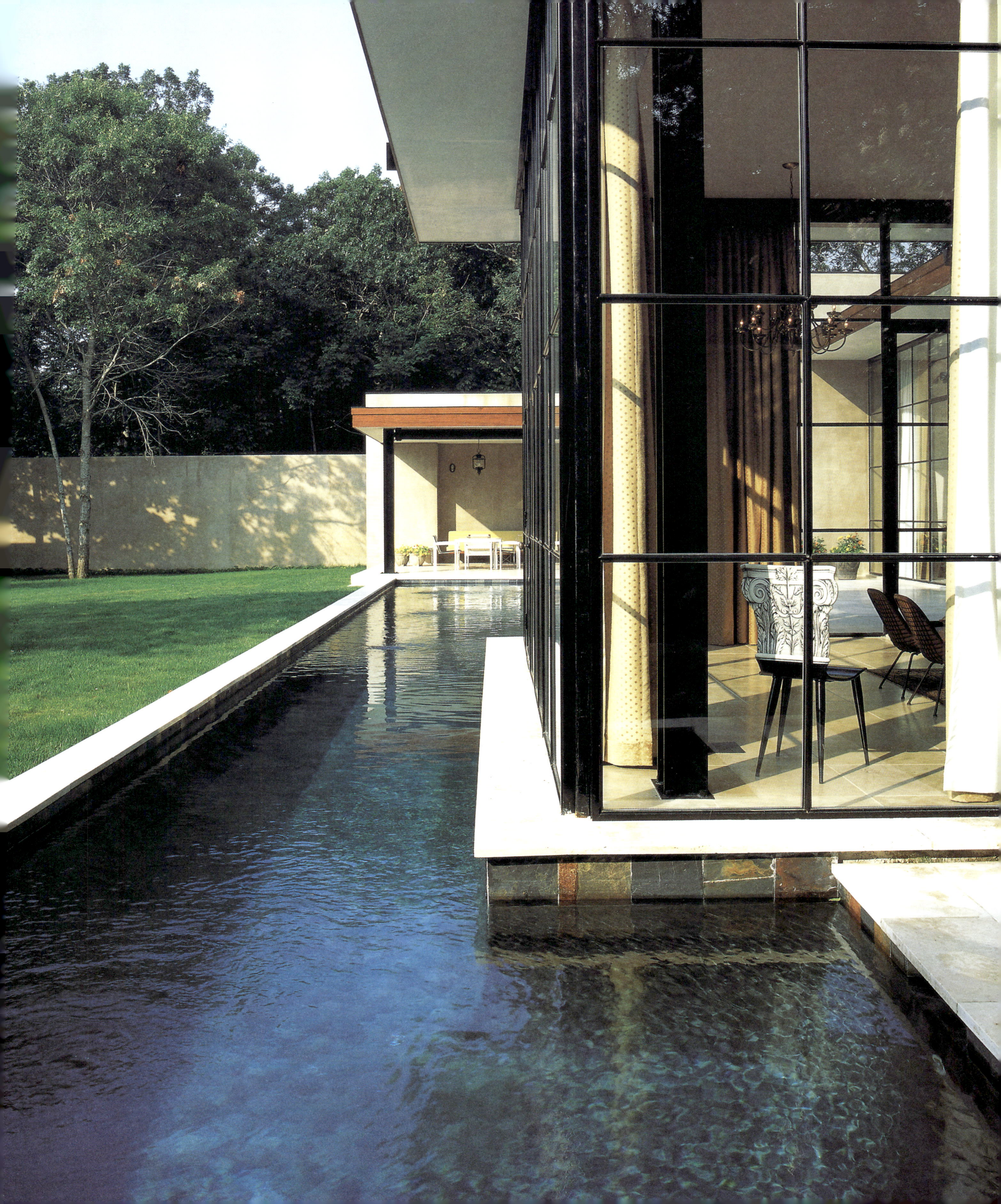

"One of our original ideas for this house was to create a simple glass box that was appropriate for the climate and context of Long Island. We mixed classic furniture with turn-of-the-century antiques, antique brass chandeliers with vintage Morris wallpaper. The result is a house that is modern but warm with patina."

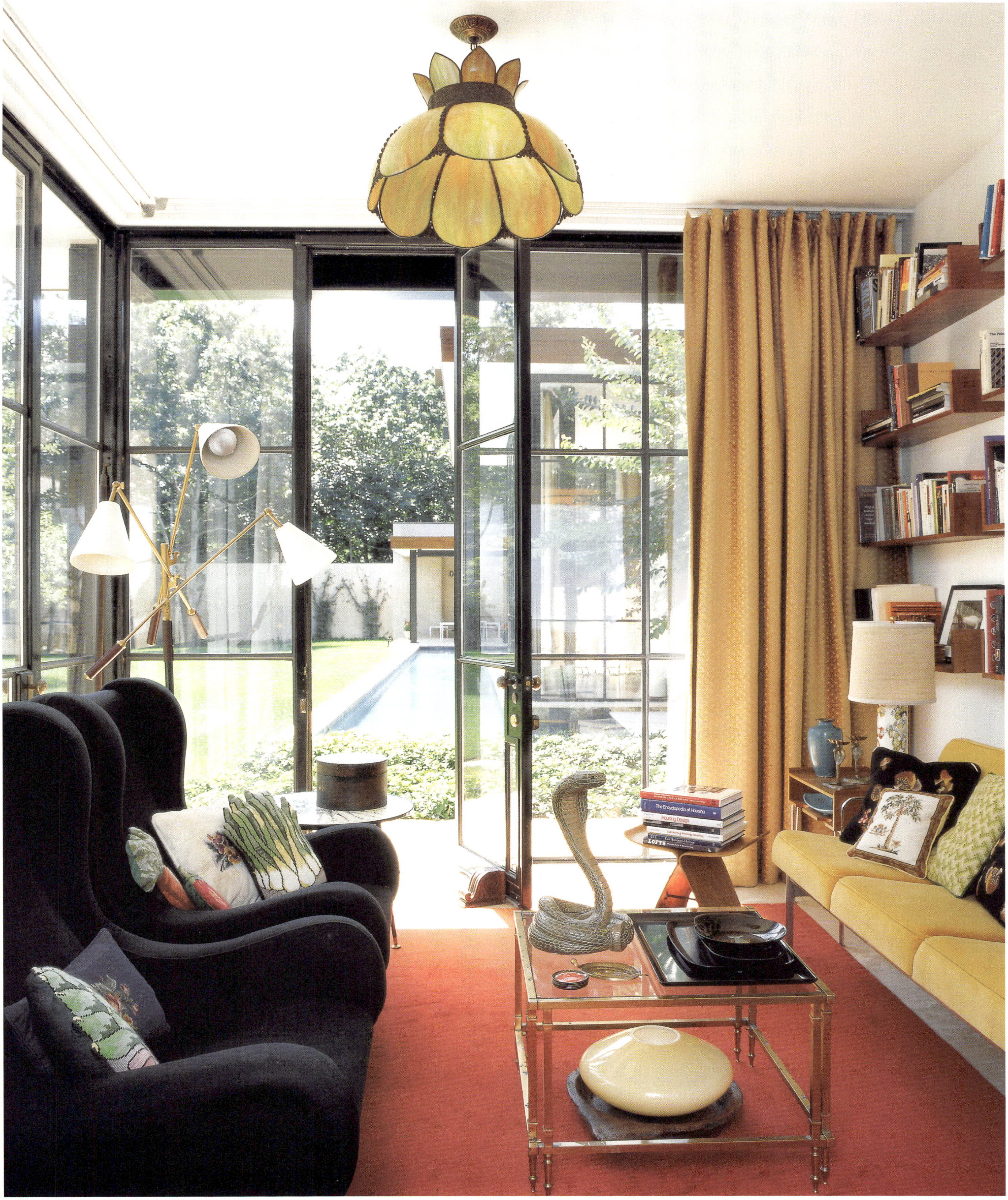
The Encyclopedia of Housing
Housing Design
LOFTS

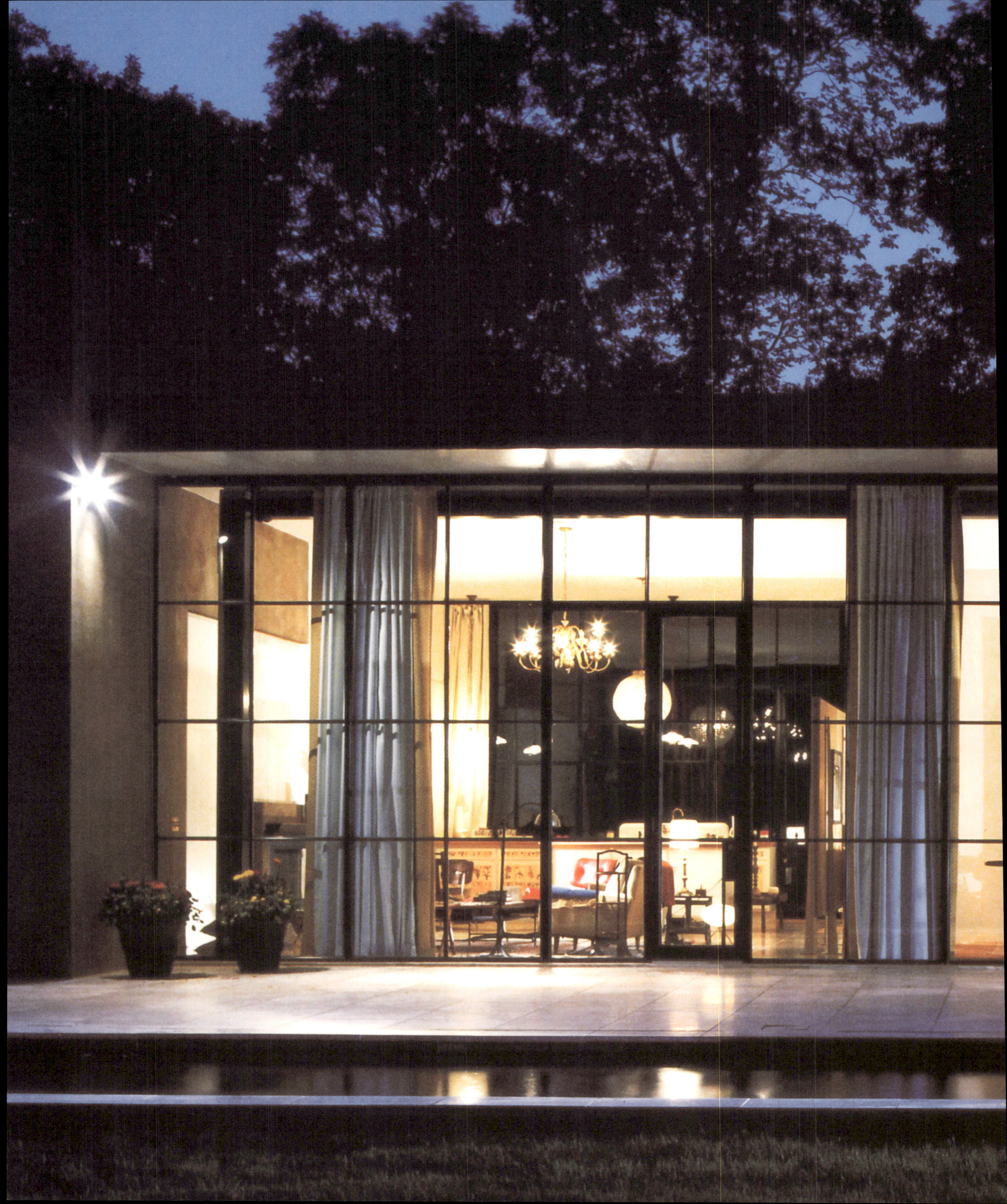

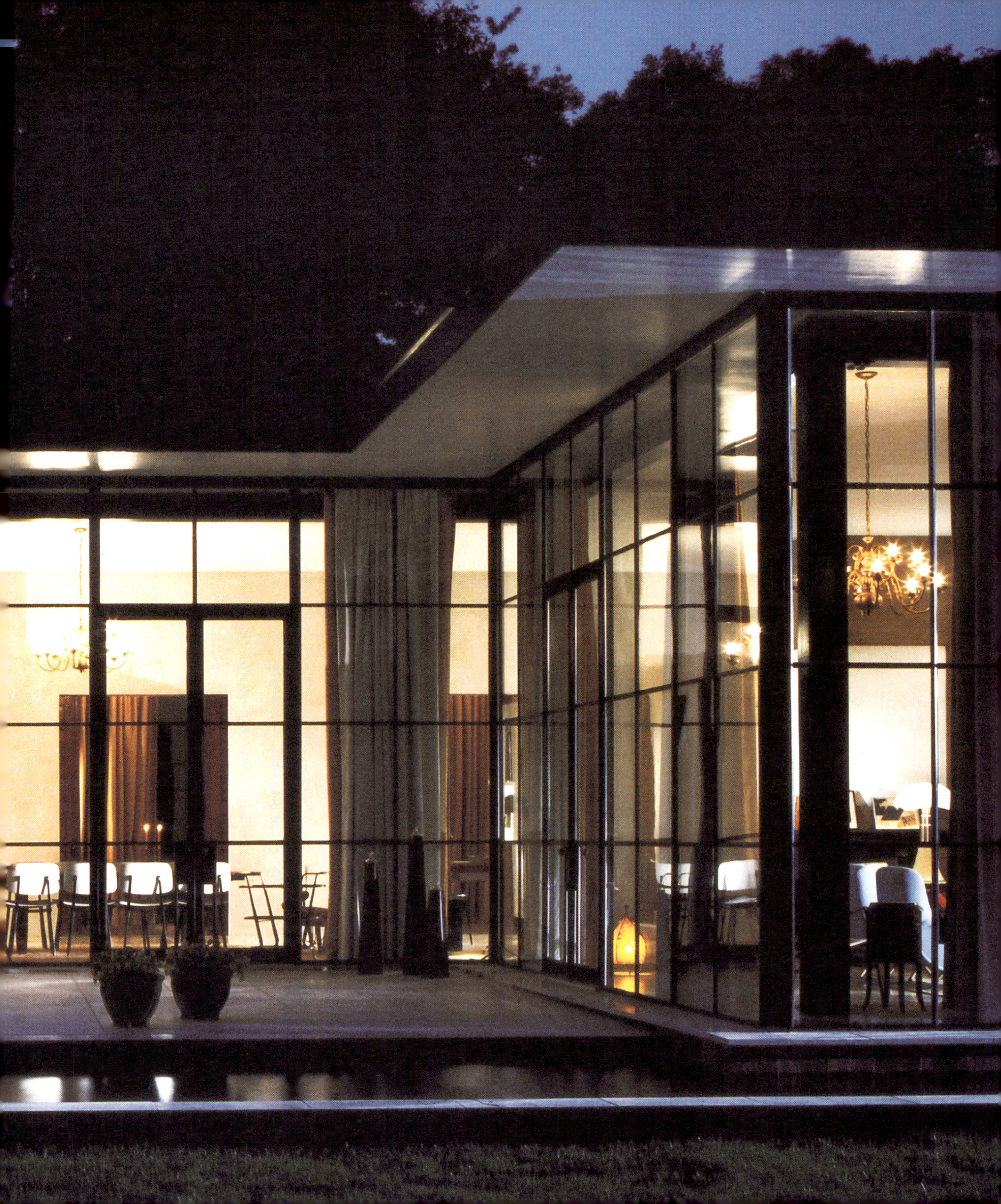

thom
FILICIA

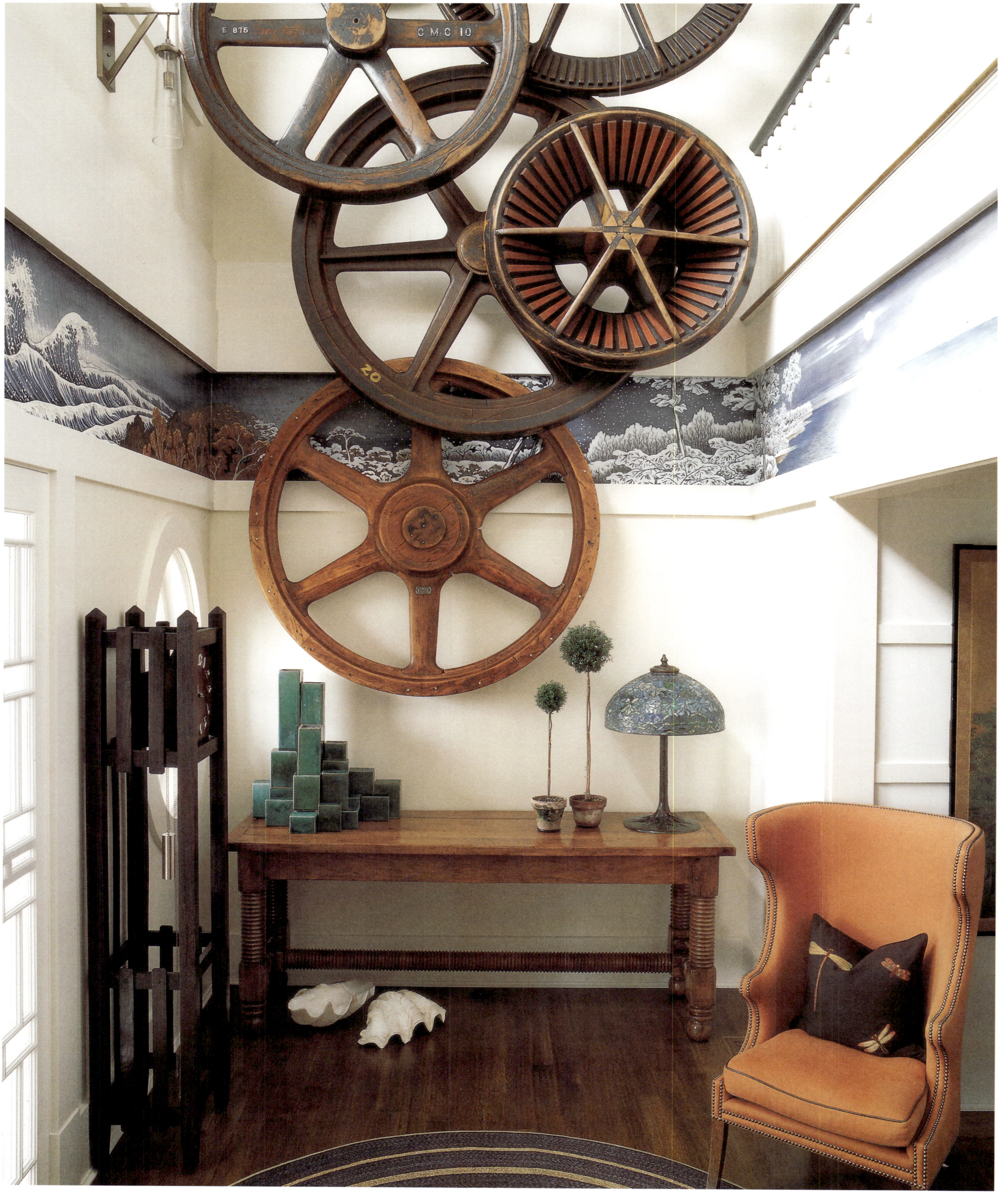
E 875
C M C 10
20

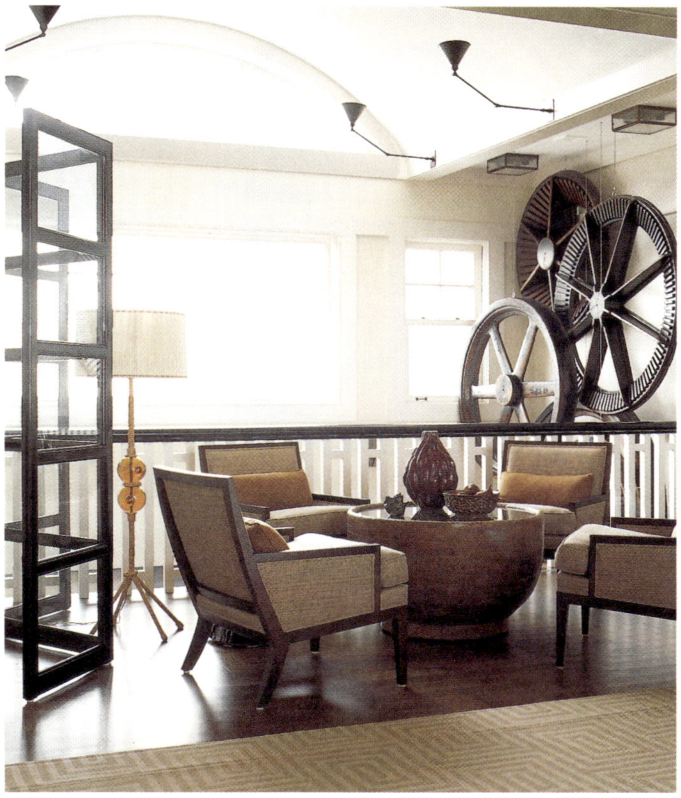

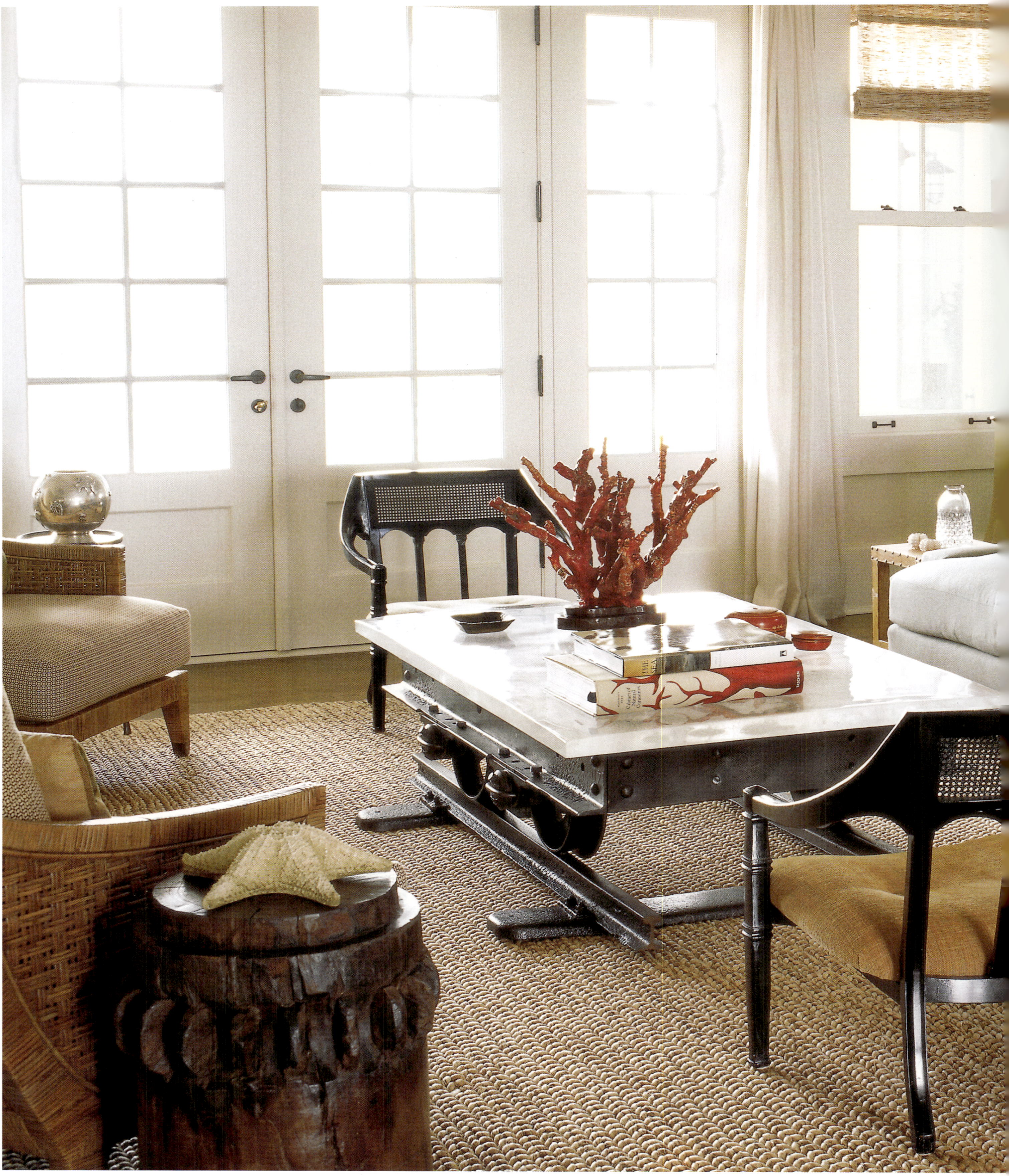
THE SEA
Cabinet of Natural Curiosities
TASCHEN

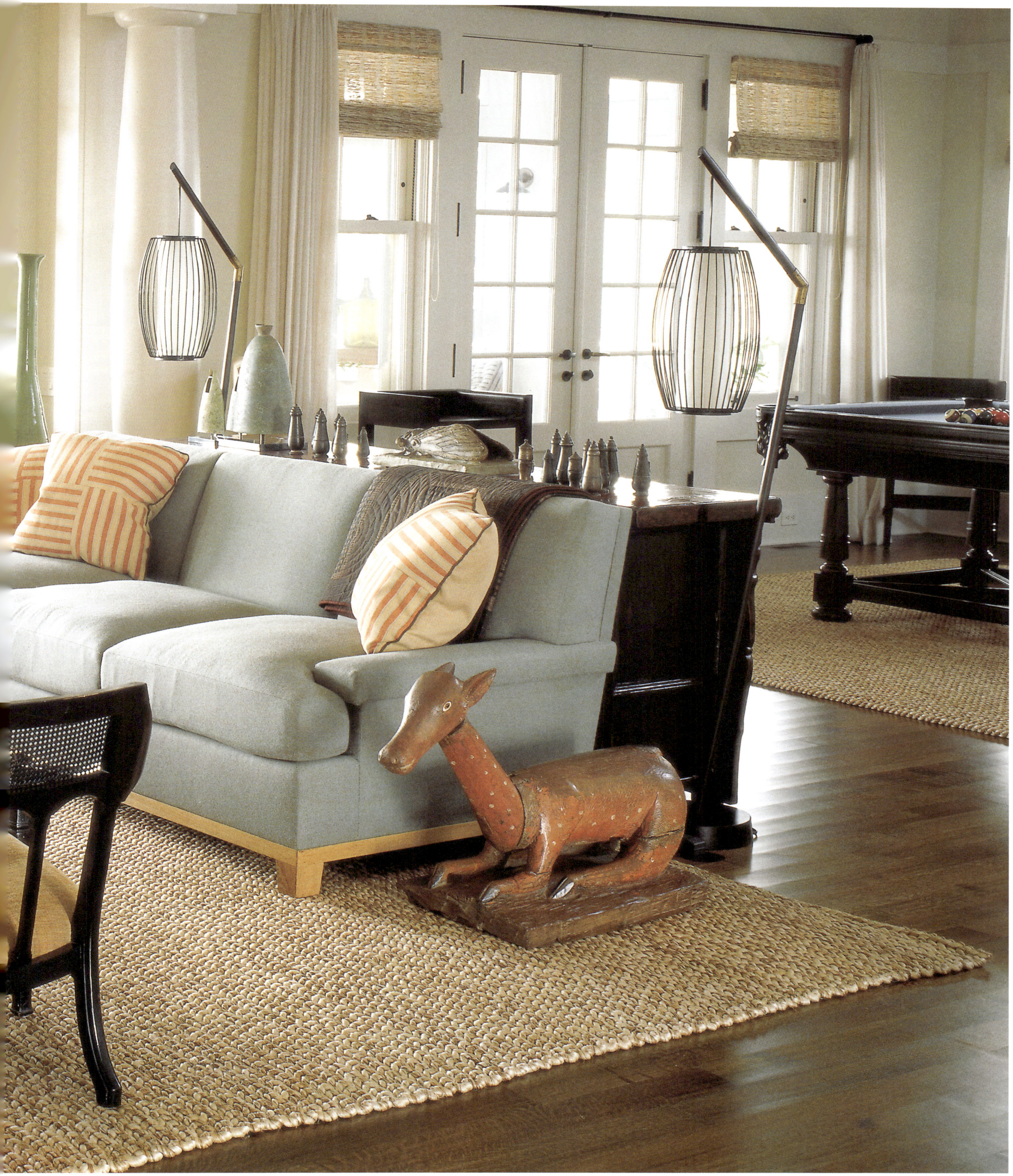

"Most people are coming to the Hamptons from New York, L.A., Boston, and other cities, so it's nice to have a place where everything slows down. First and foremost, a home here needs to be appropriate for the environment—something serene, calm, and clean. The interiors should have a sense of humor, be modern yet traditional, and reflect the personality of each client. What I want my interiors to say is: relax, have a drink, kick your feet up, you don't have to deal with anything until Monday."

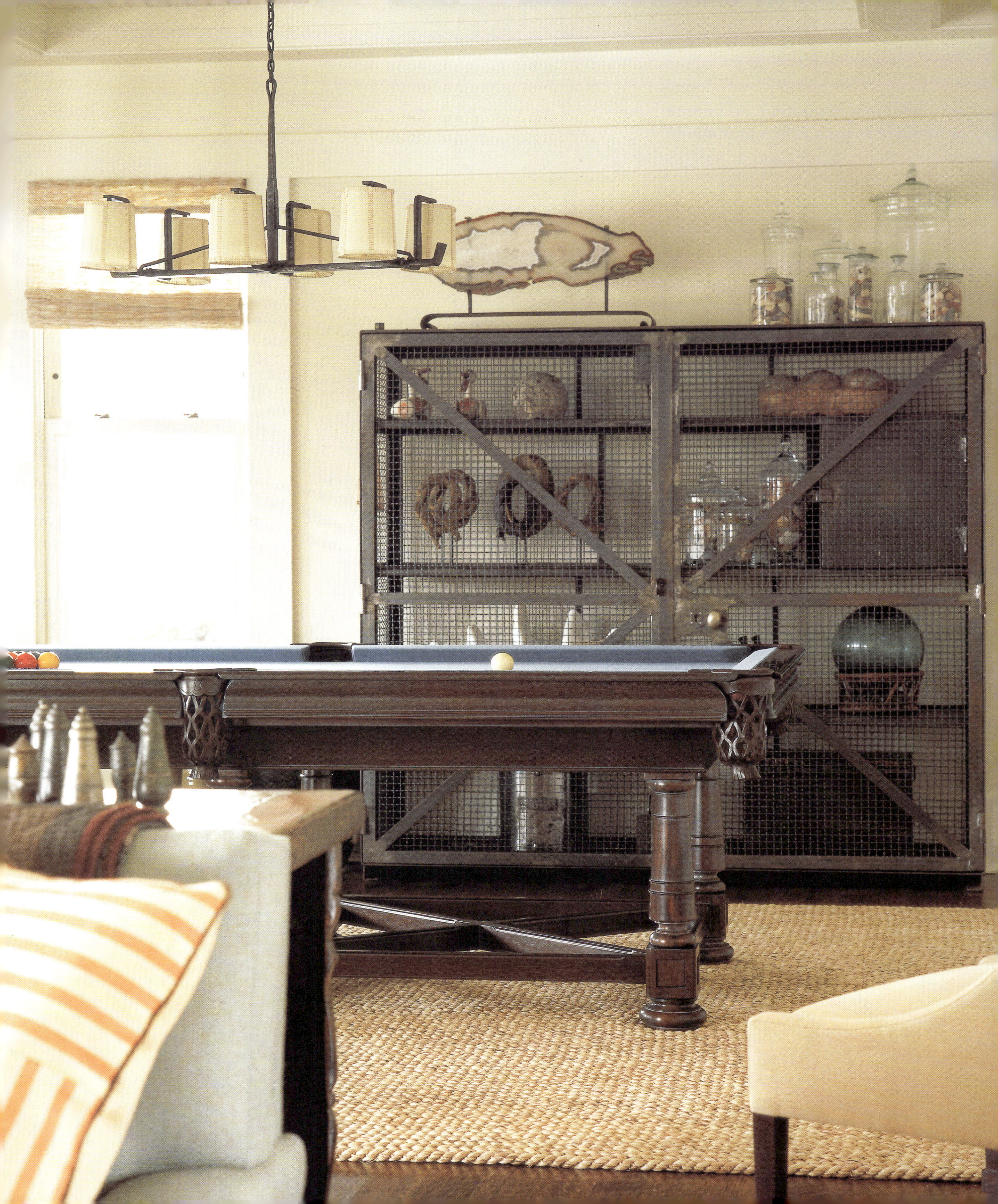

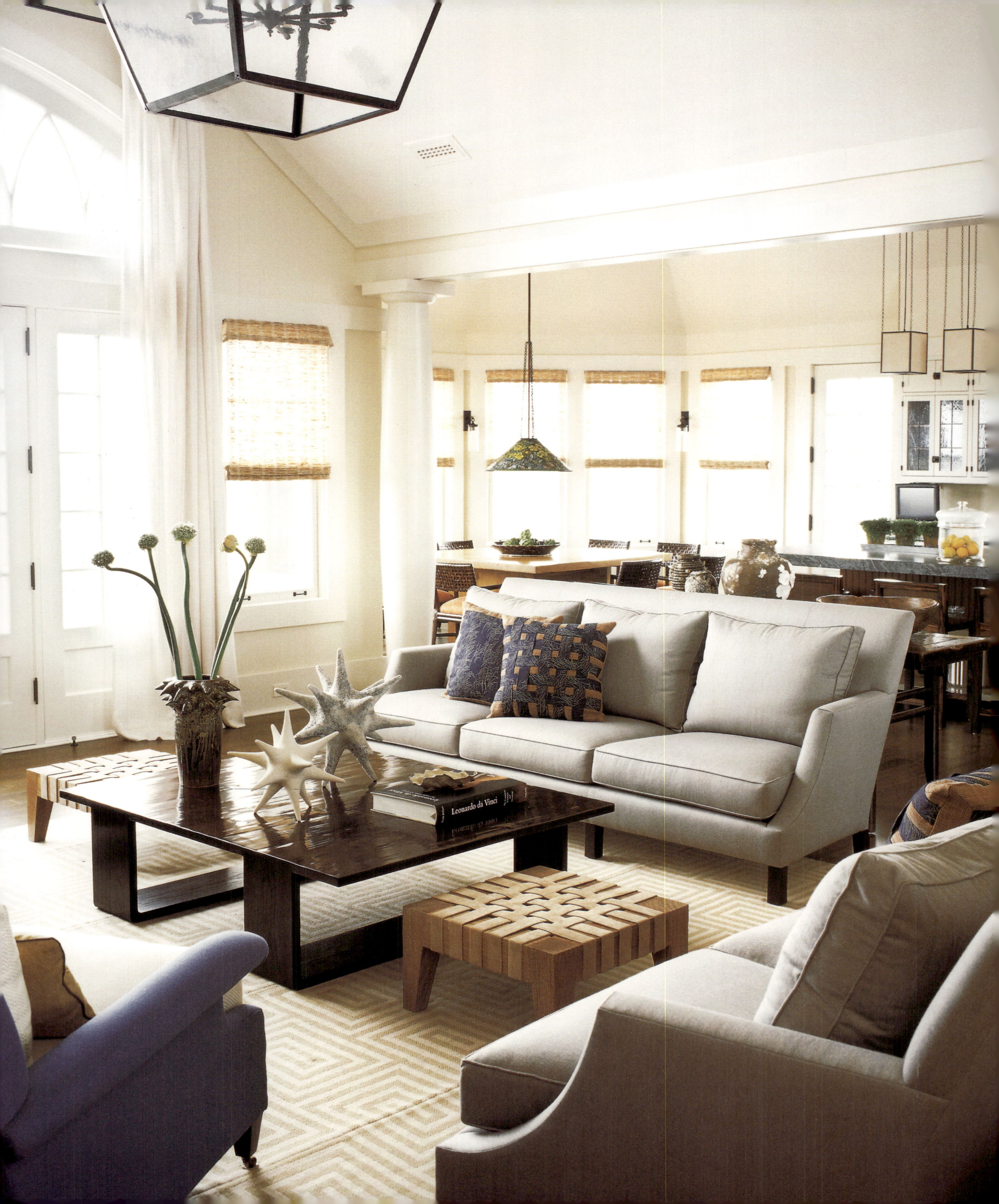
Leonardo da Vinci

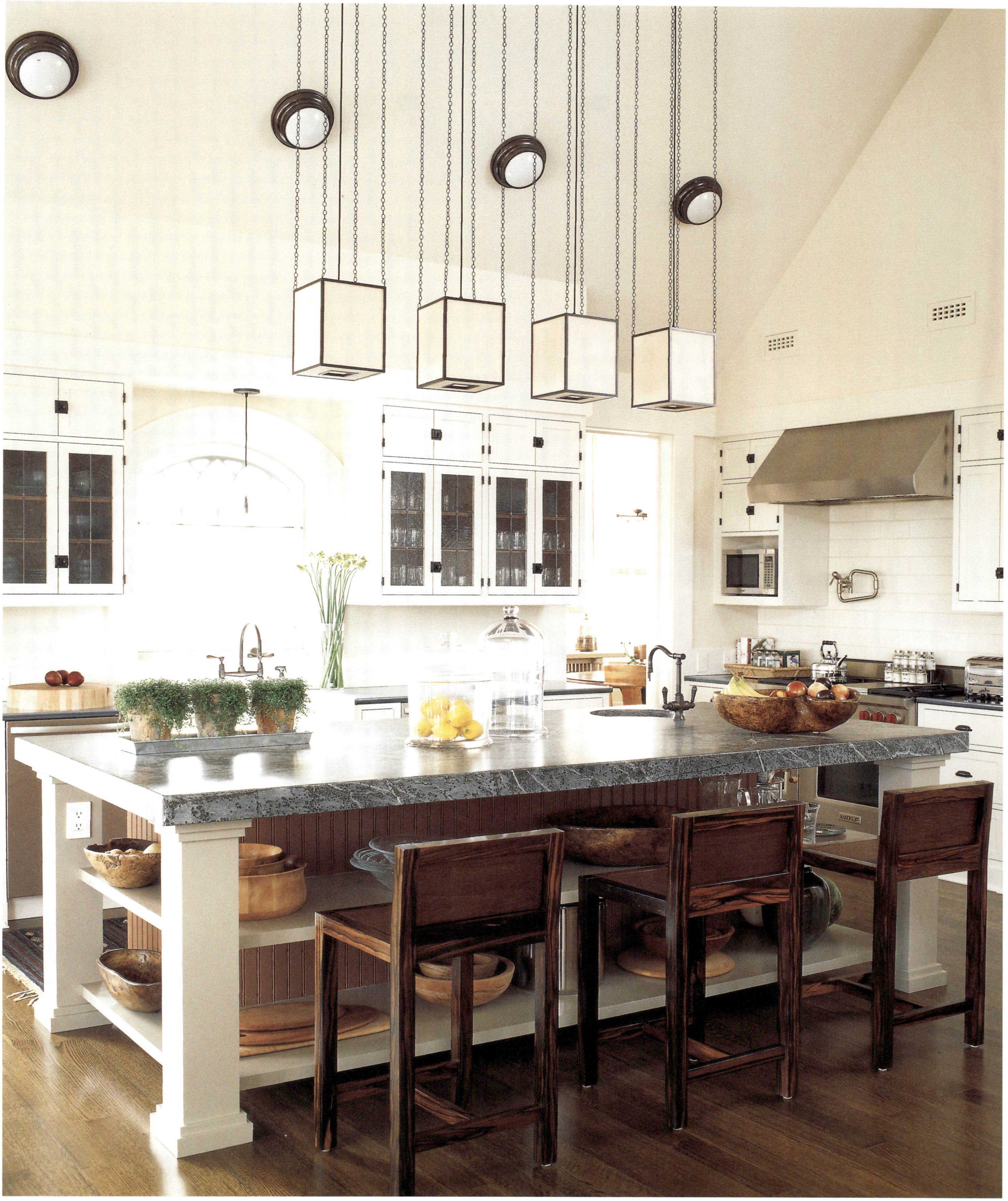

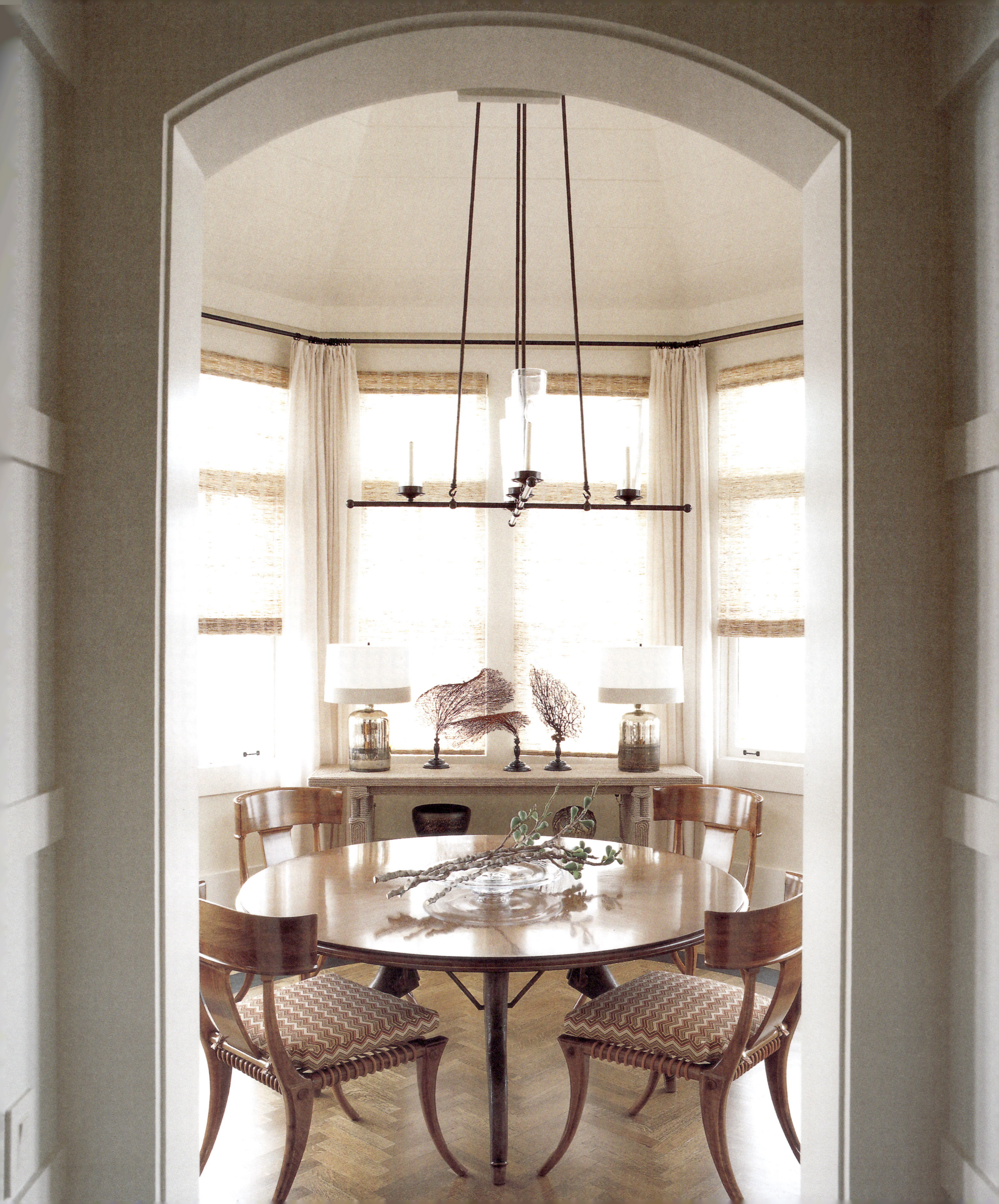

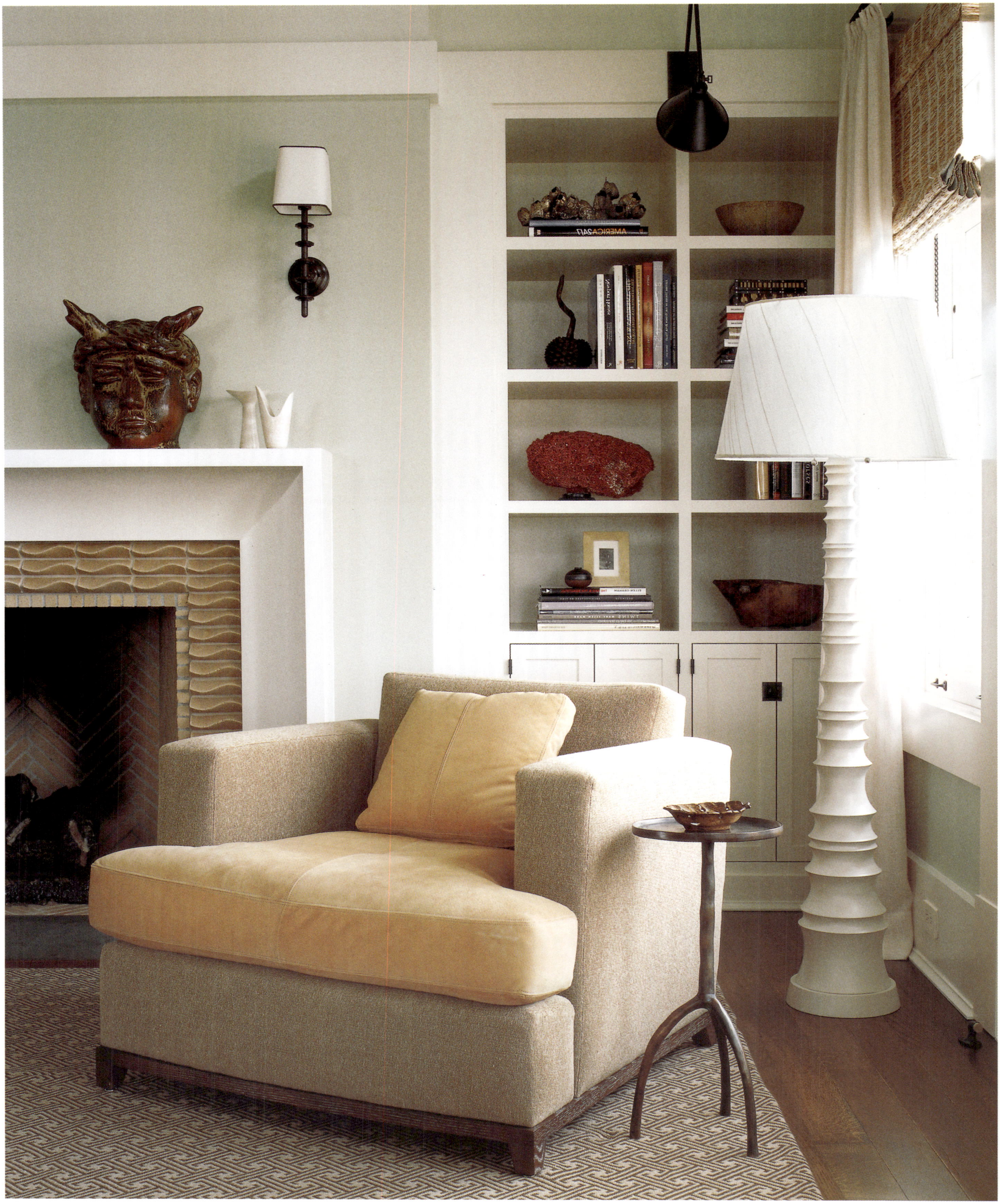

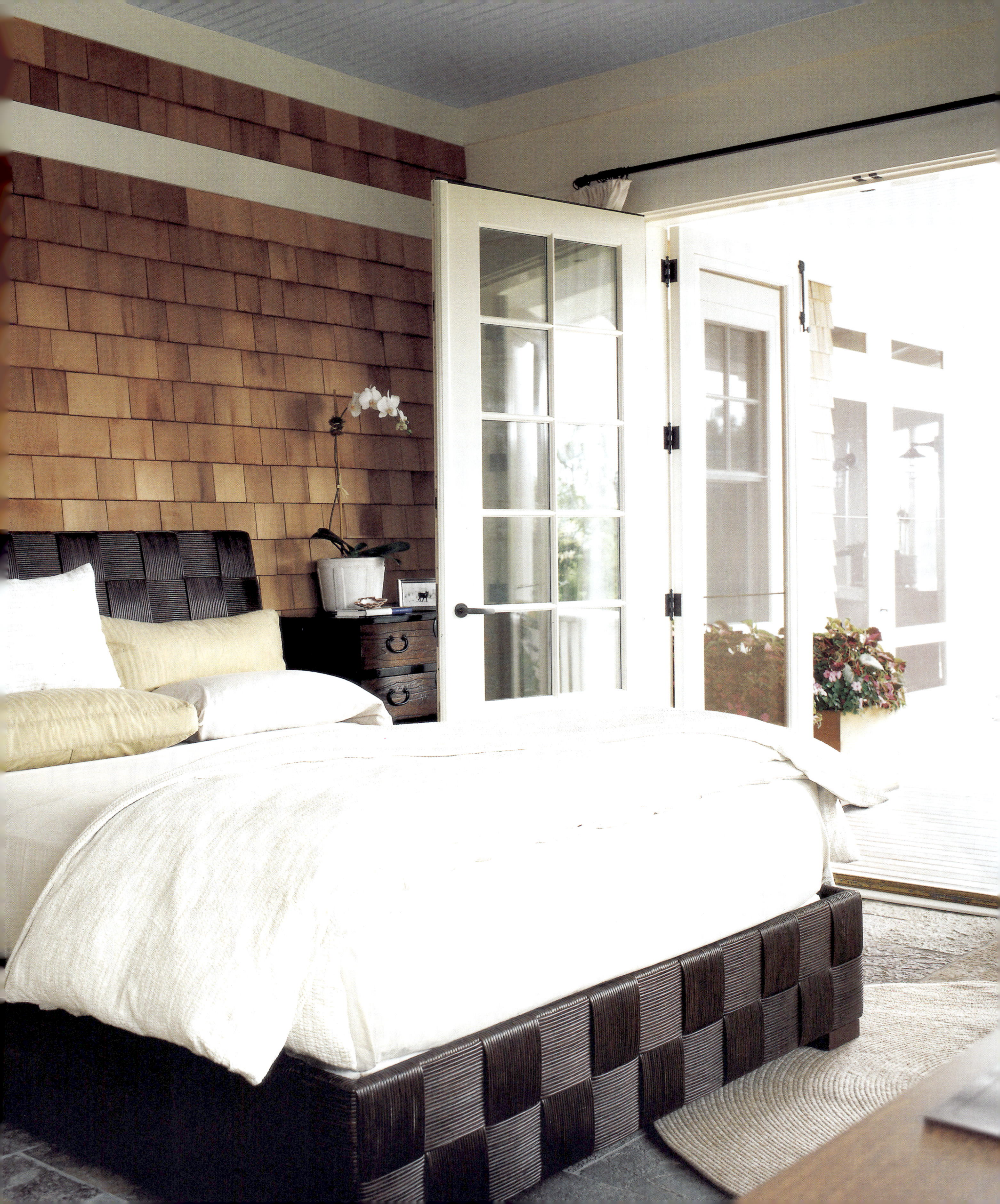

john BARMAN & kelly GRAHAM

"When I started working on this house, situated on farmland with a view of the dunes, it was little more than a cottage with a couple of cozy rooms and lots of charming details.... I transformed the exterior into something I would refer to as 'pure Hamptons' while the interior is more Cote d'Azur. I enjoyed mixing dark wood floors, white walls, and vintage finds from the '40s, '50s, and '60s with a sprinkling of old-world antiques."

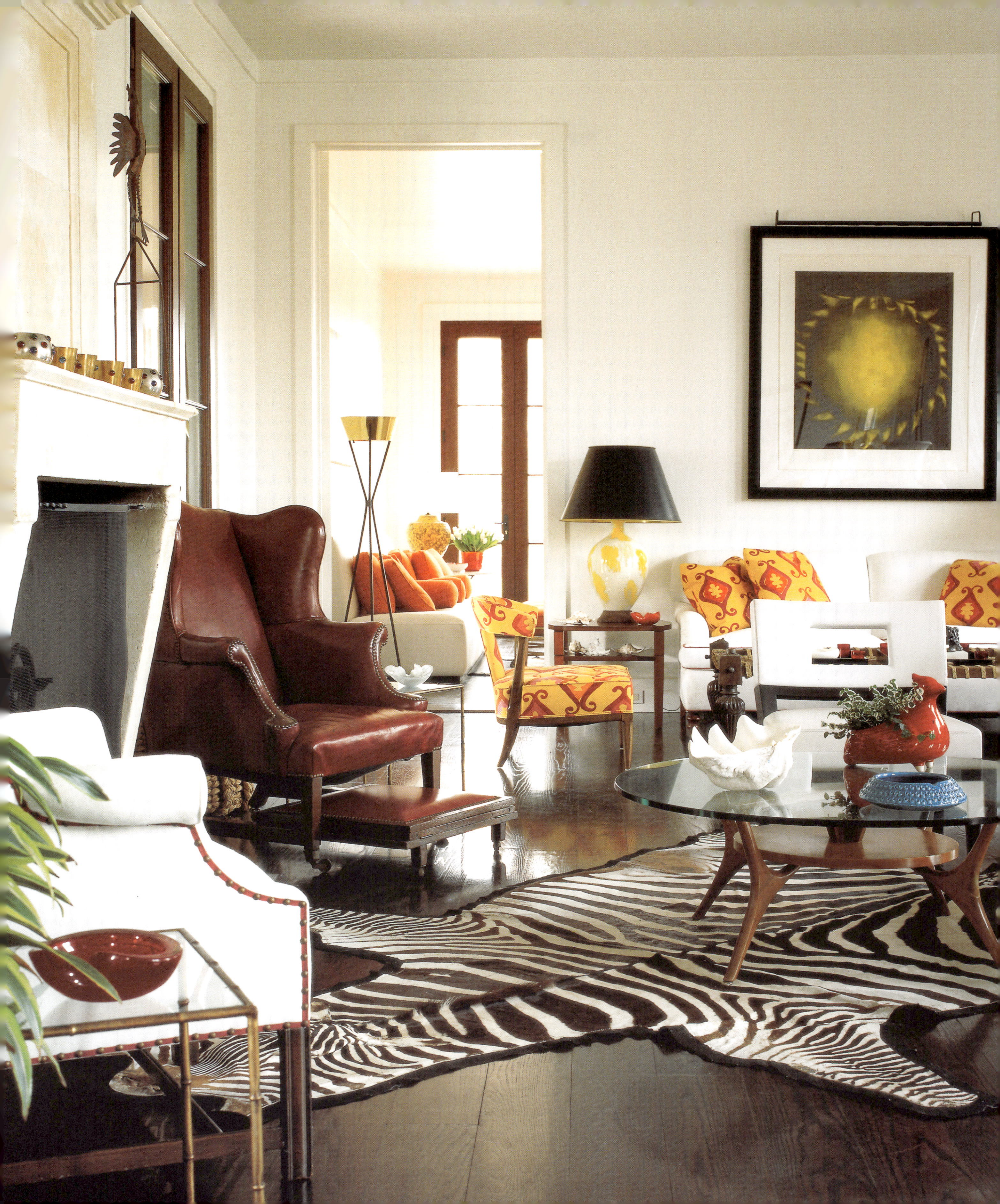

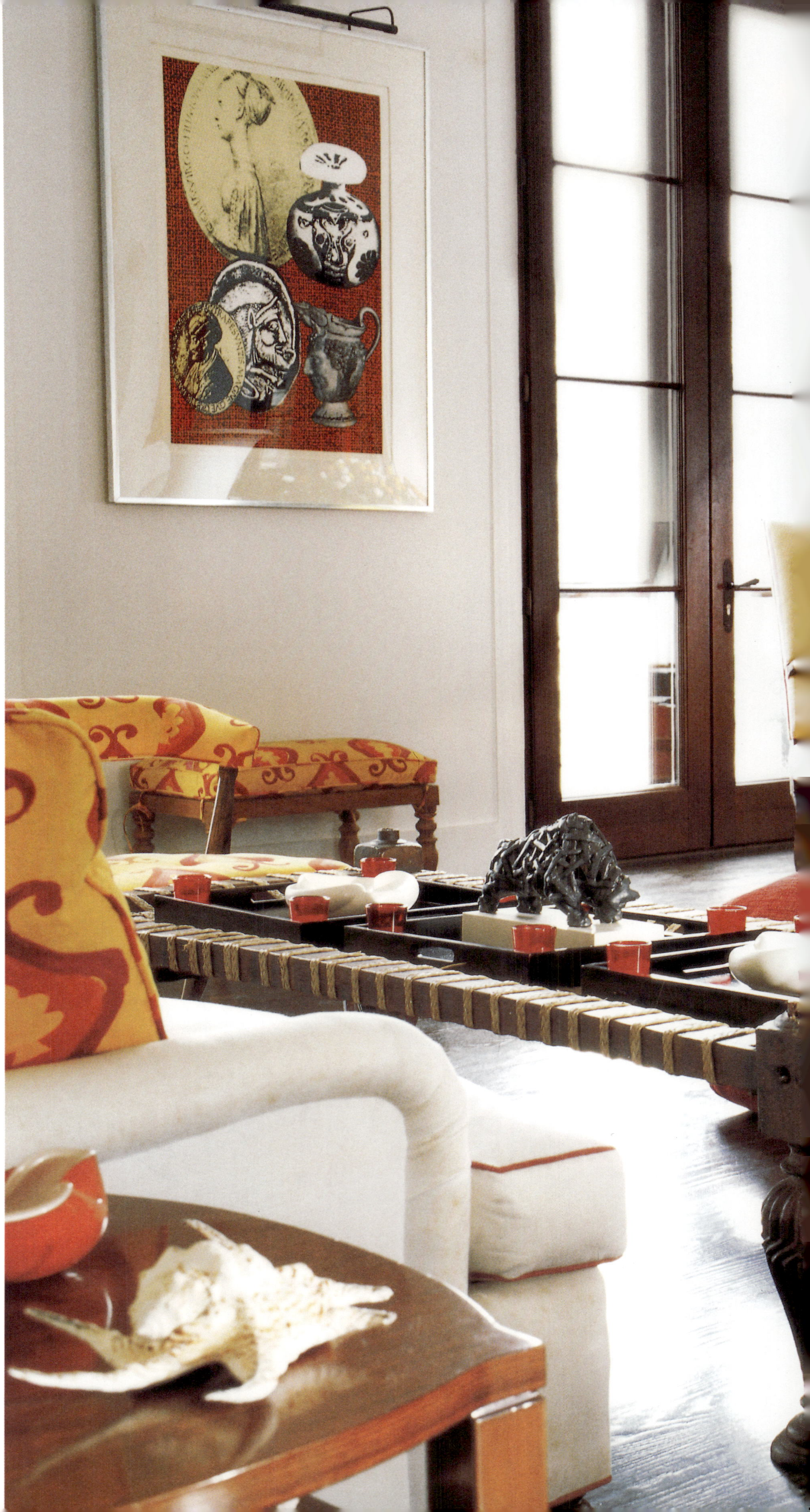

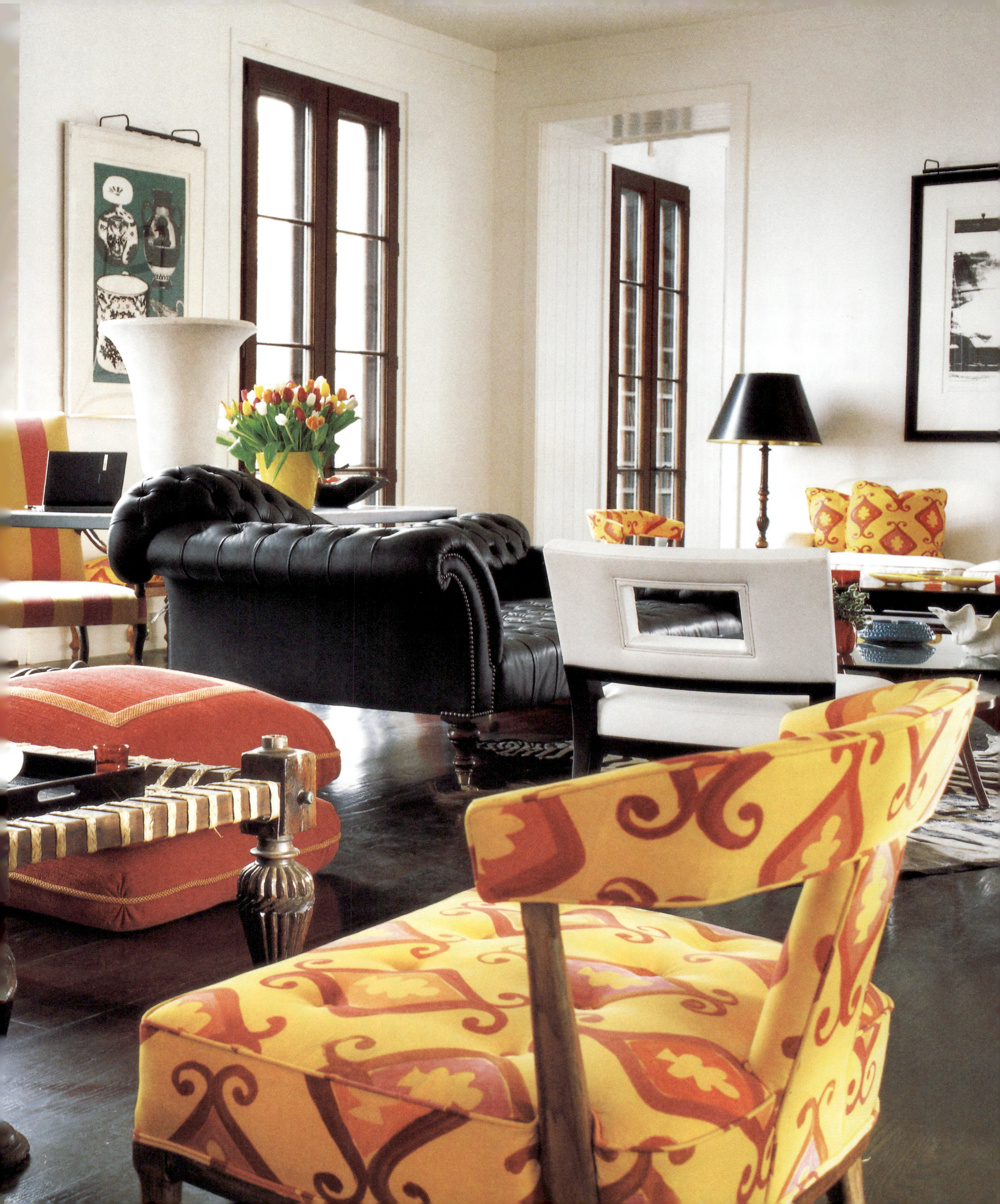

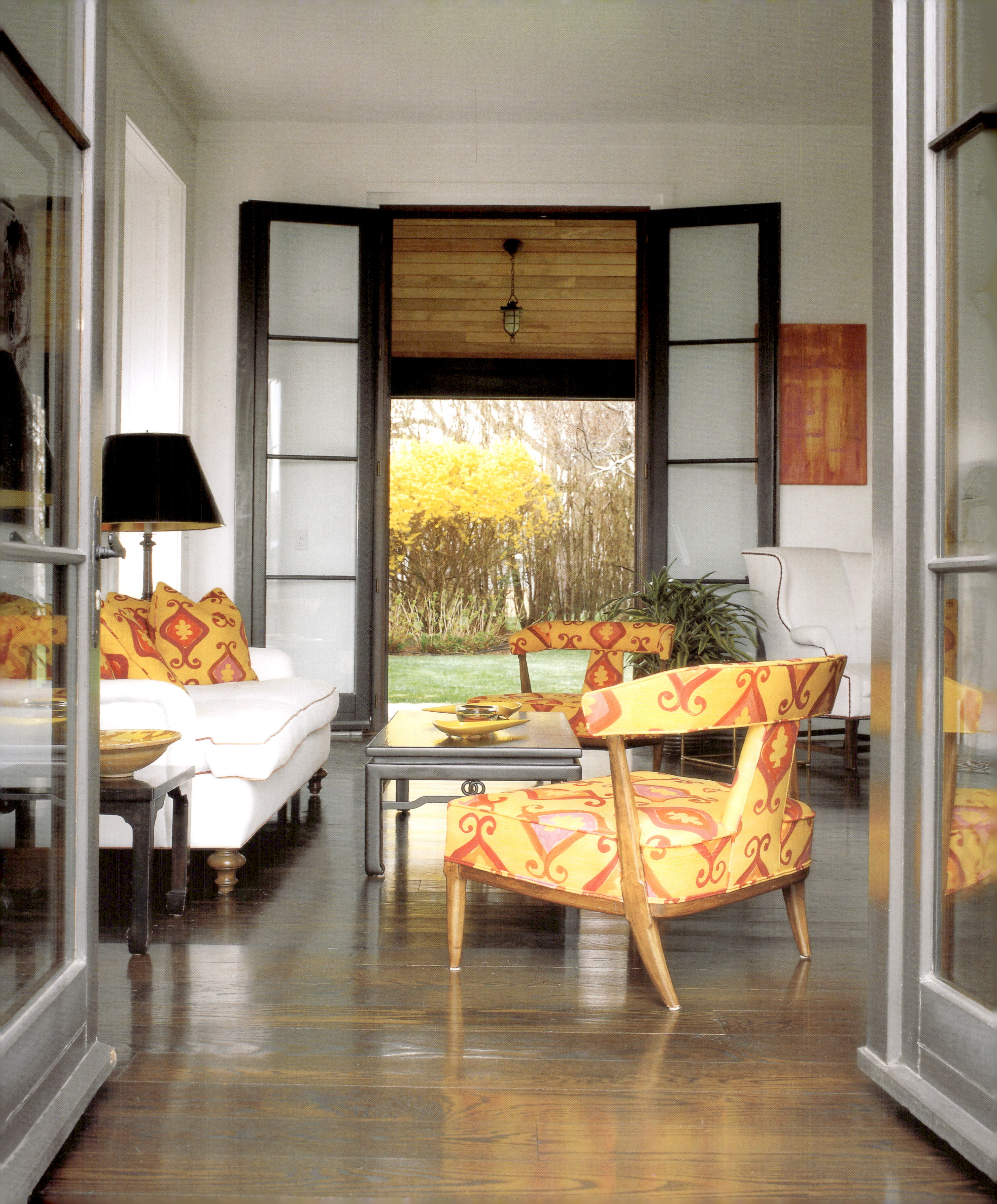

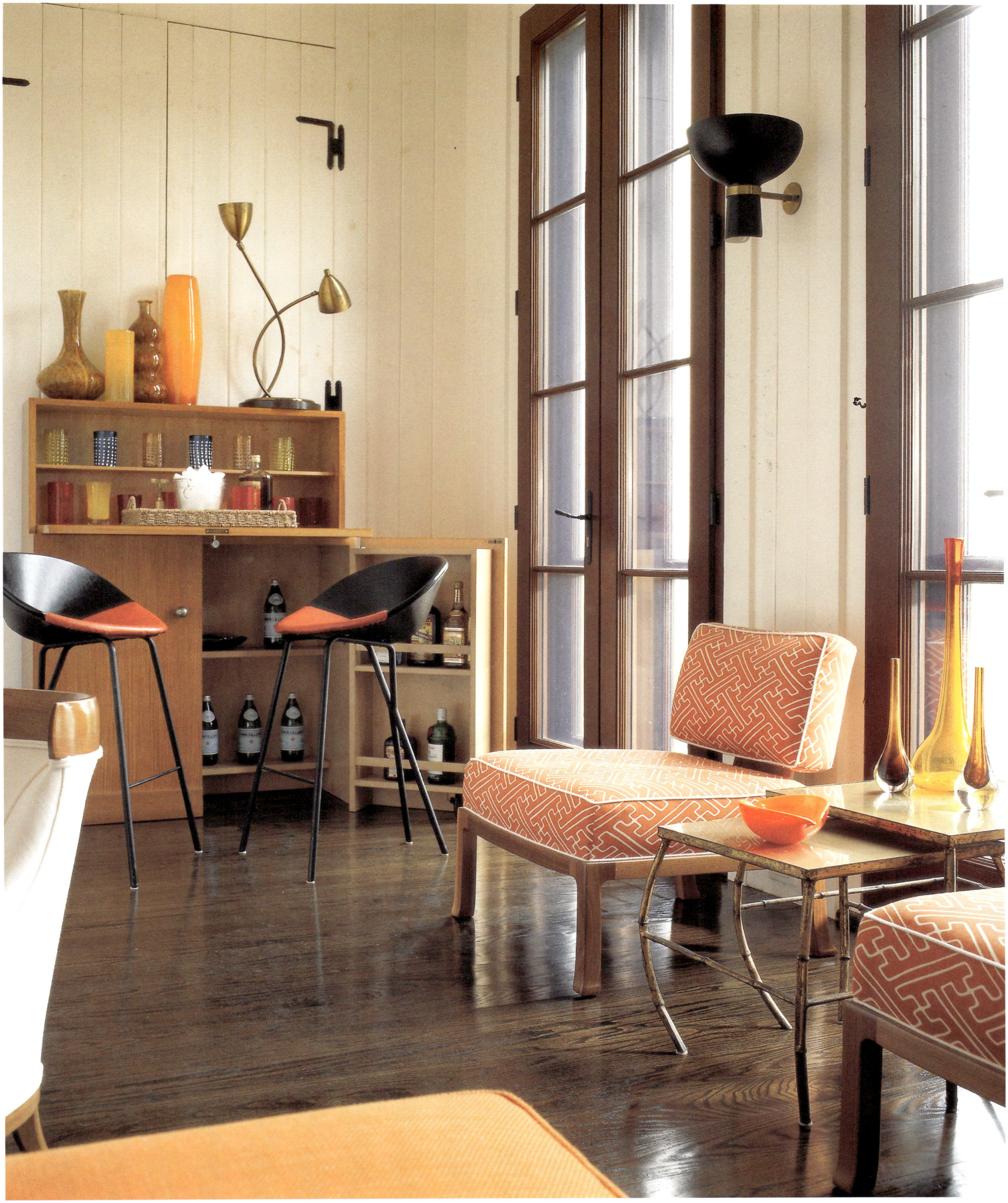

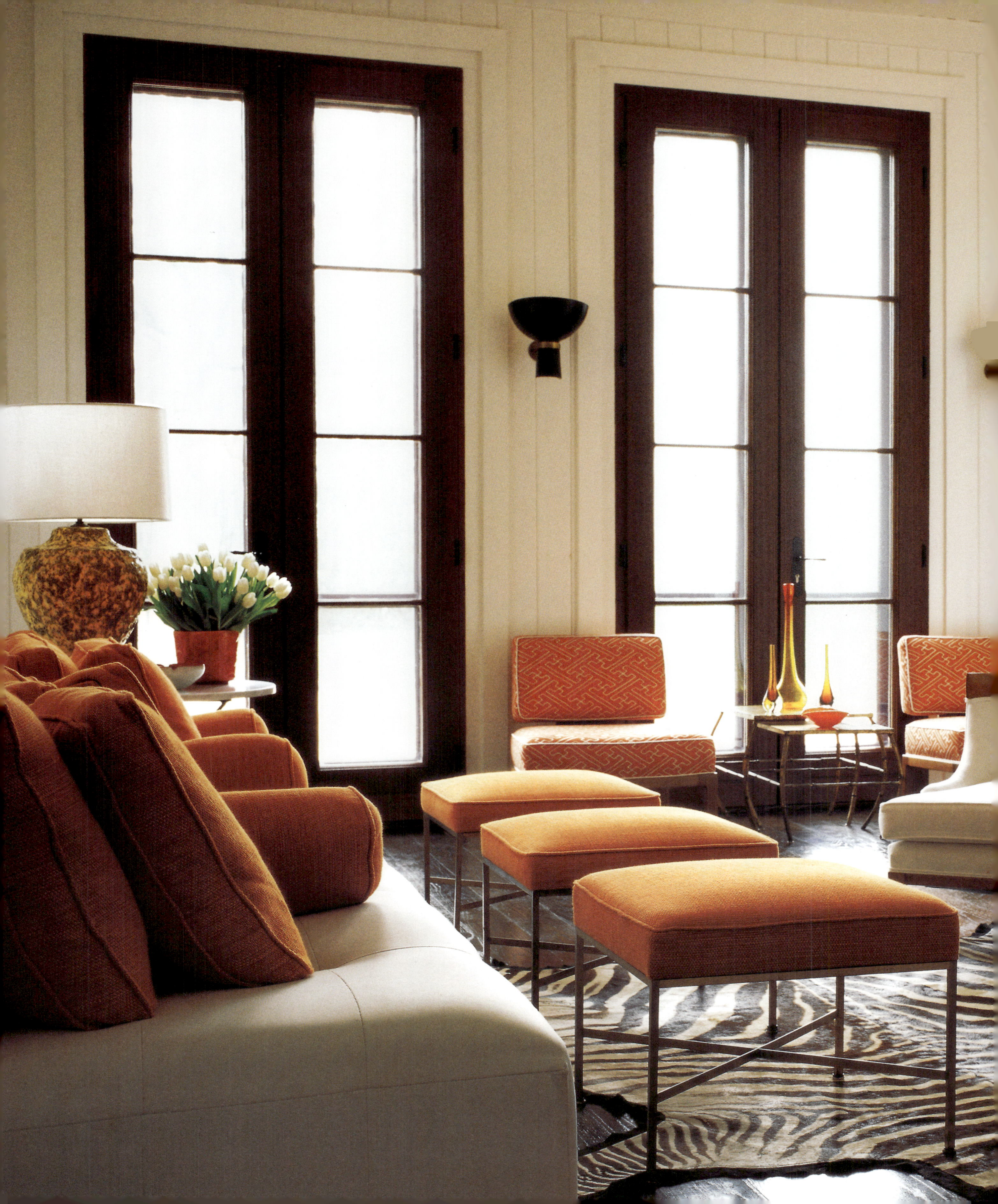

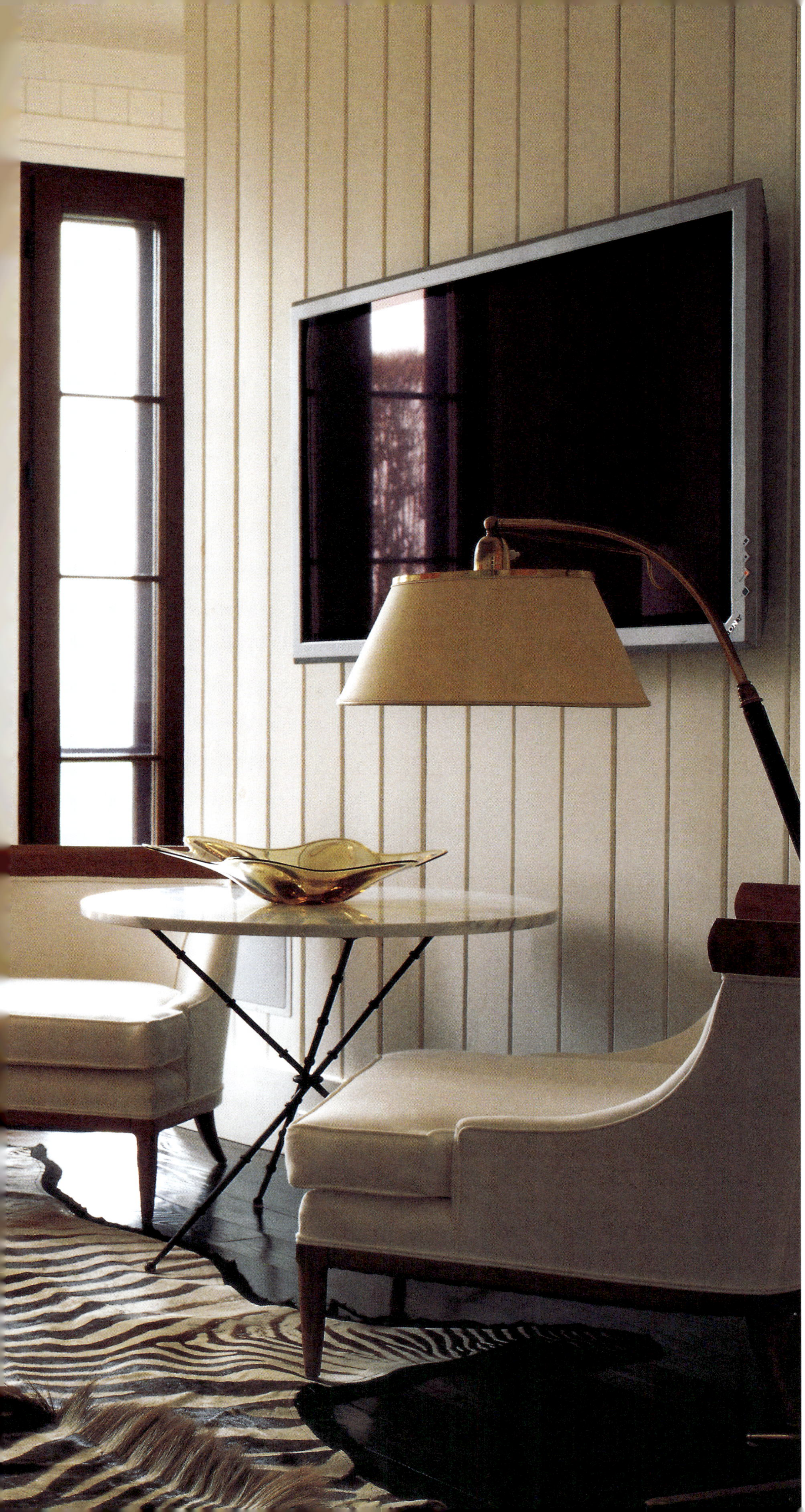

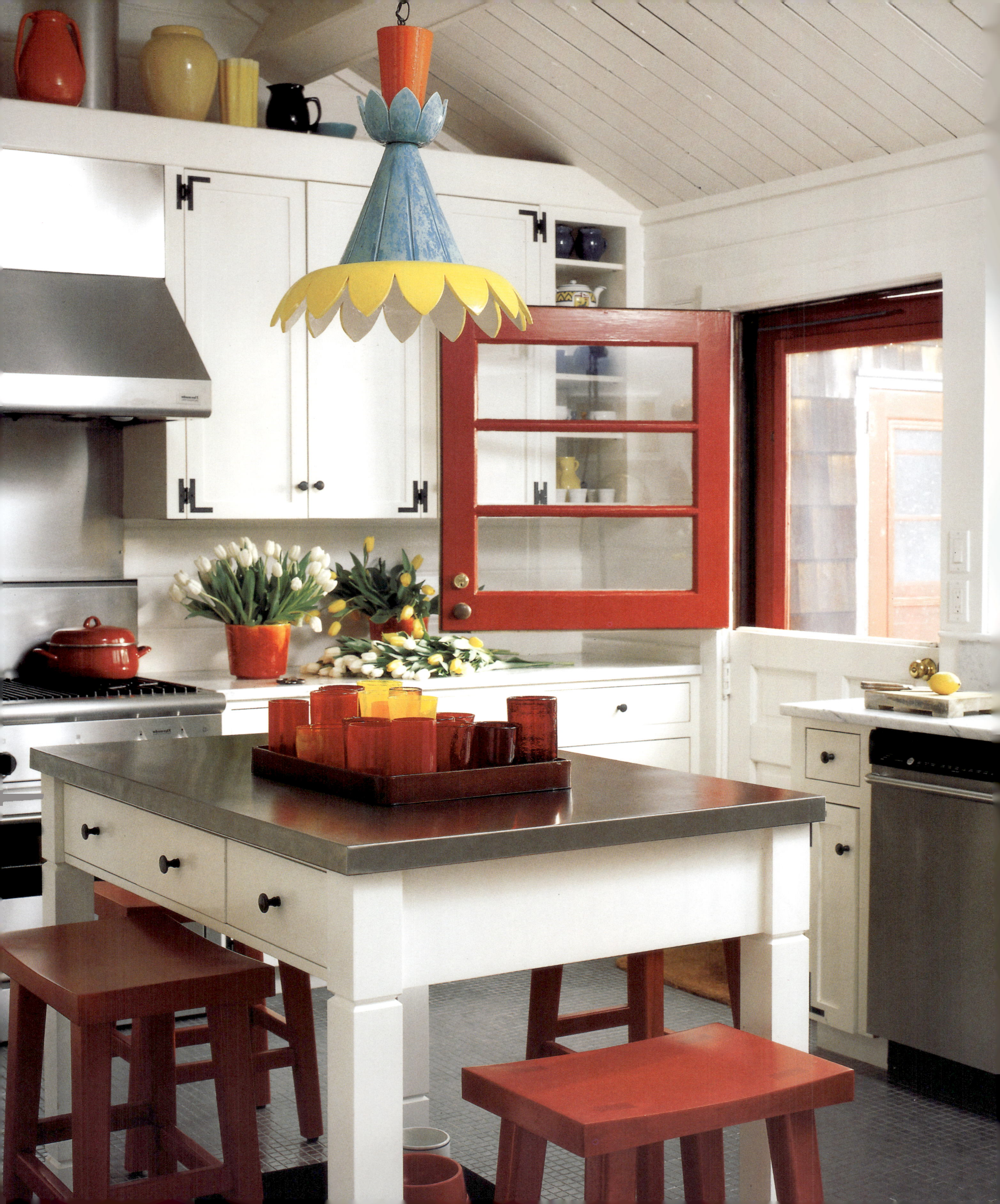

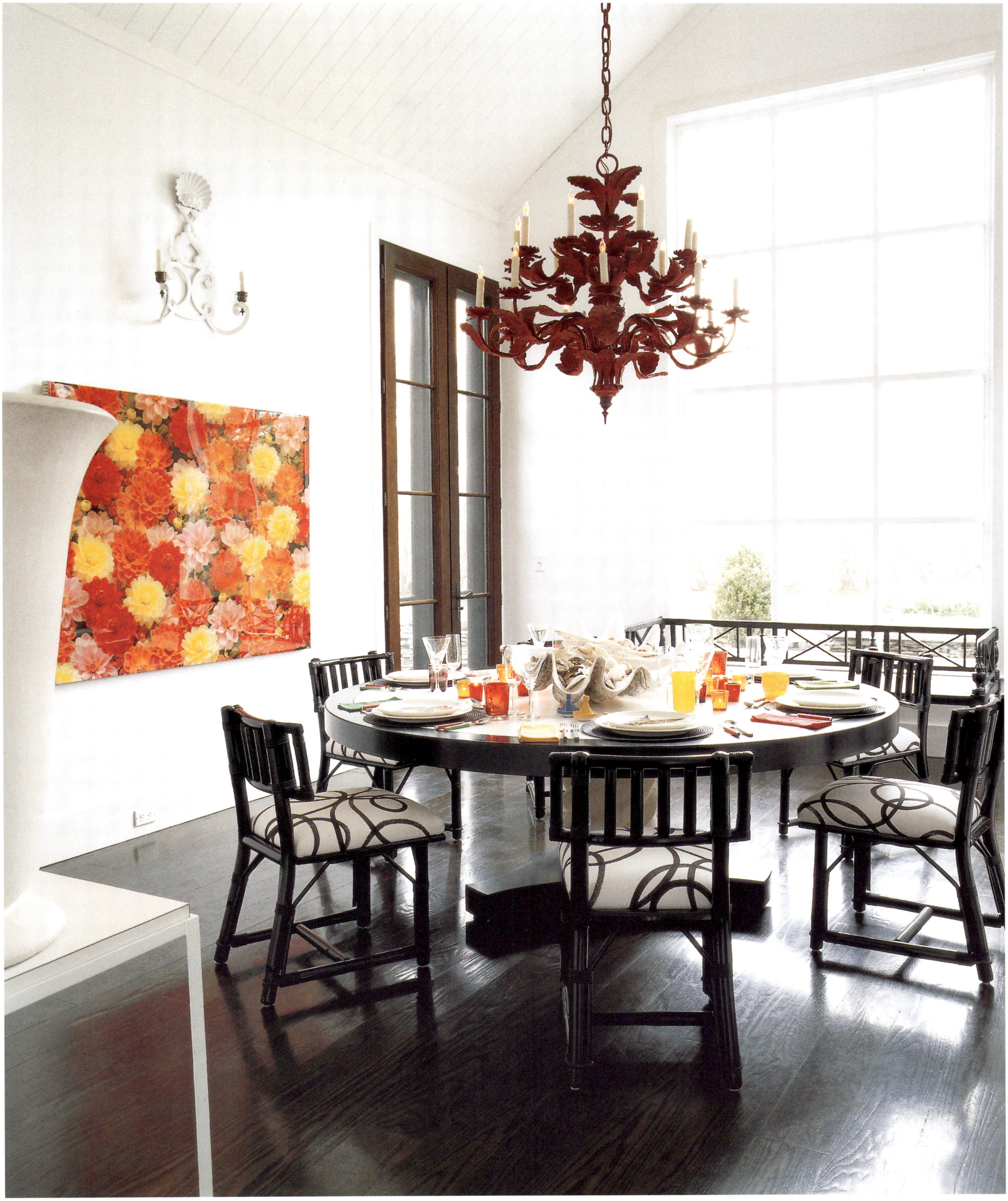

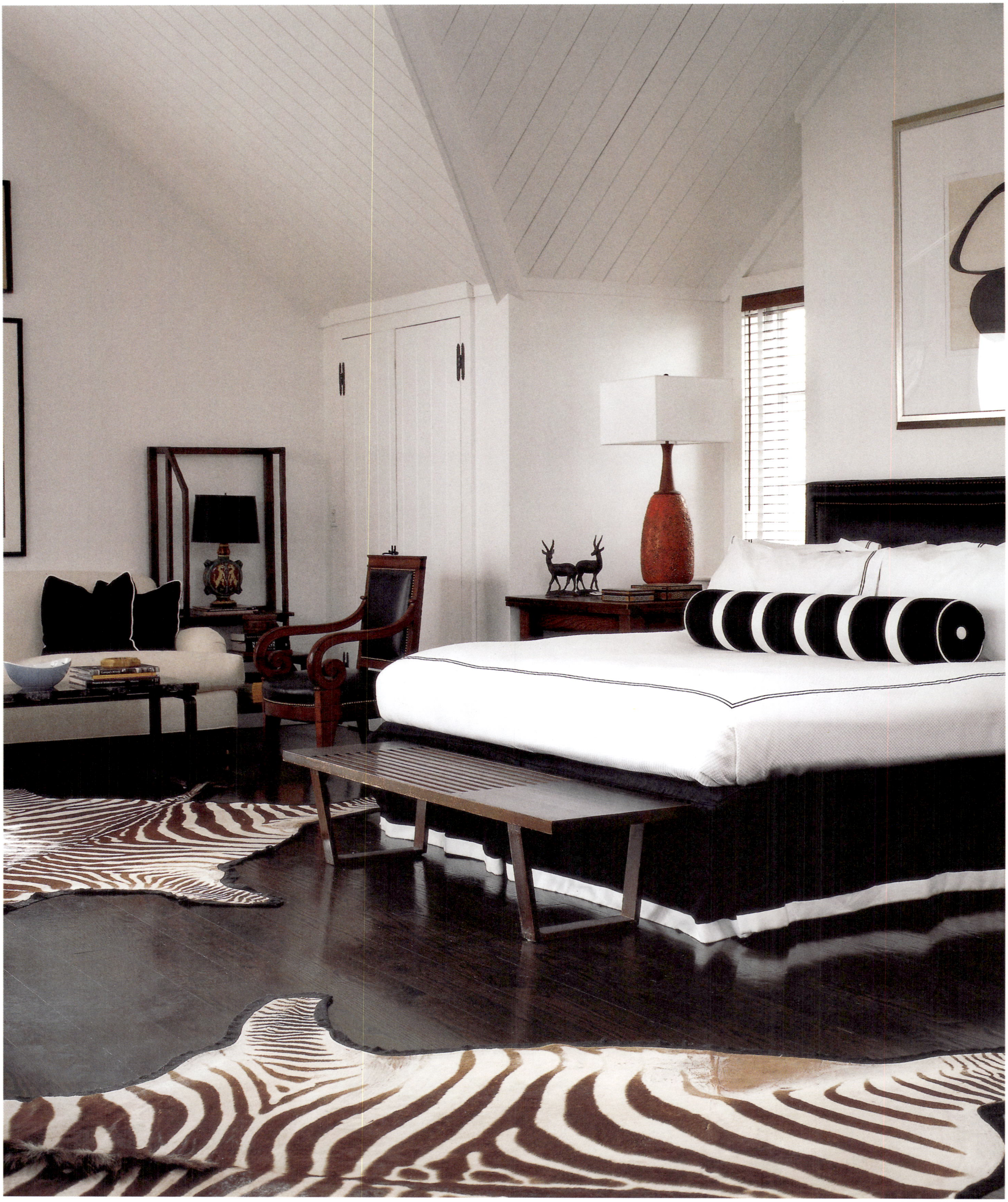

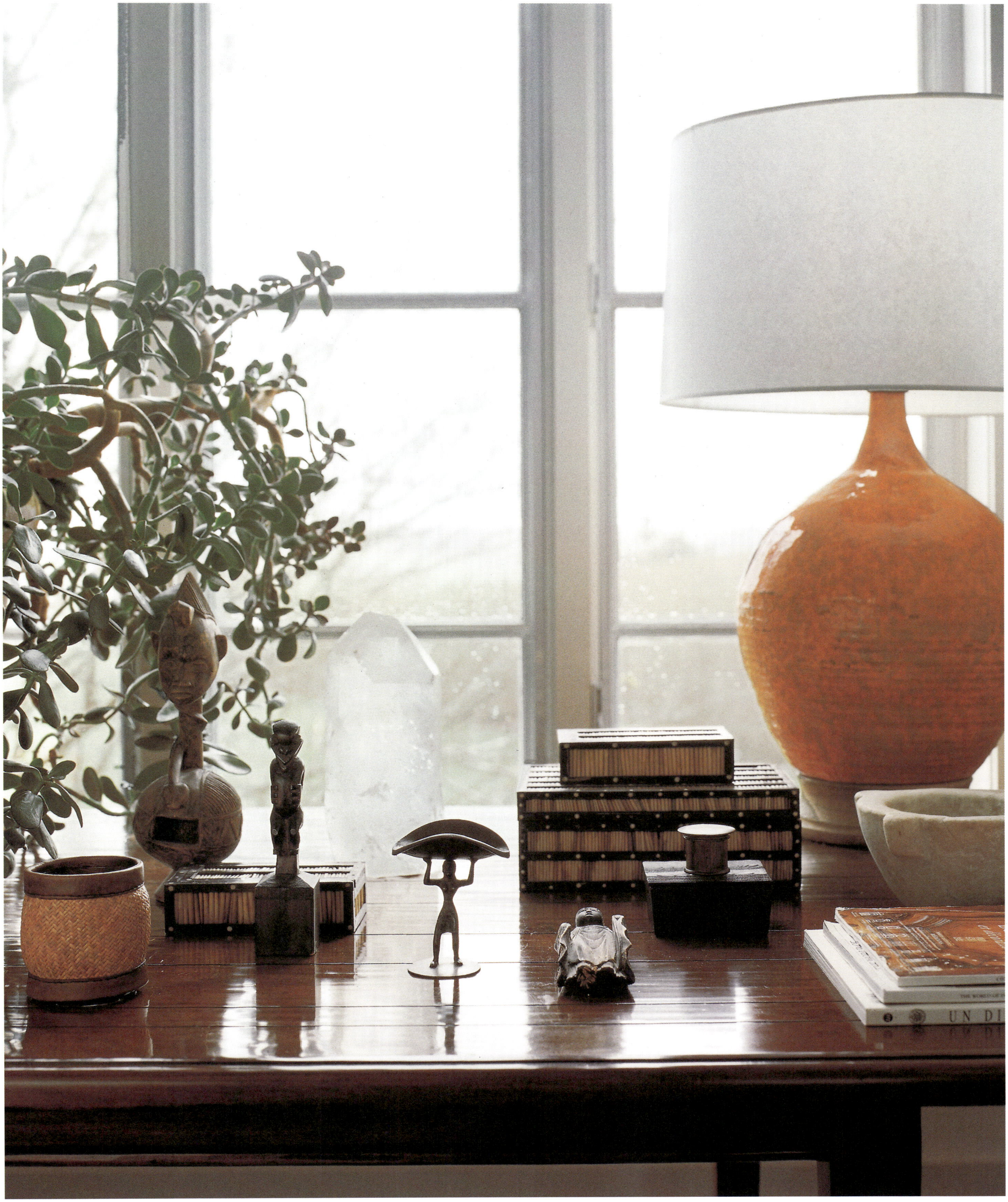

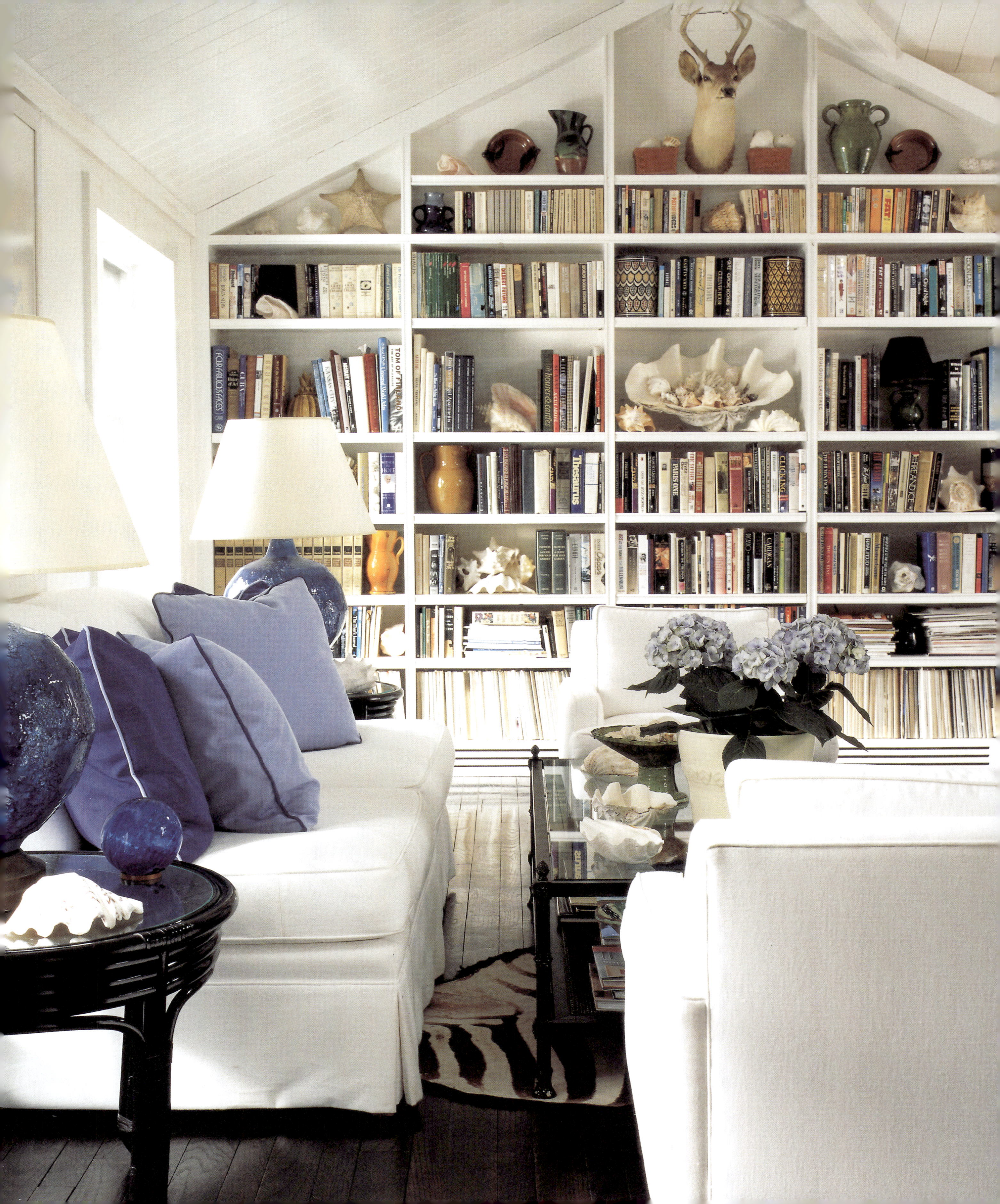
Thesaurus
CLICKING

vicente WOLF

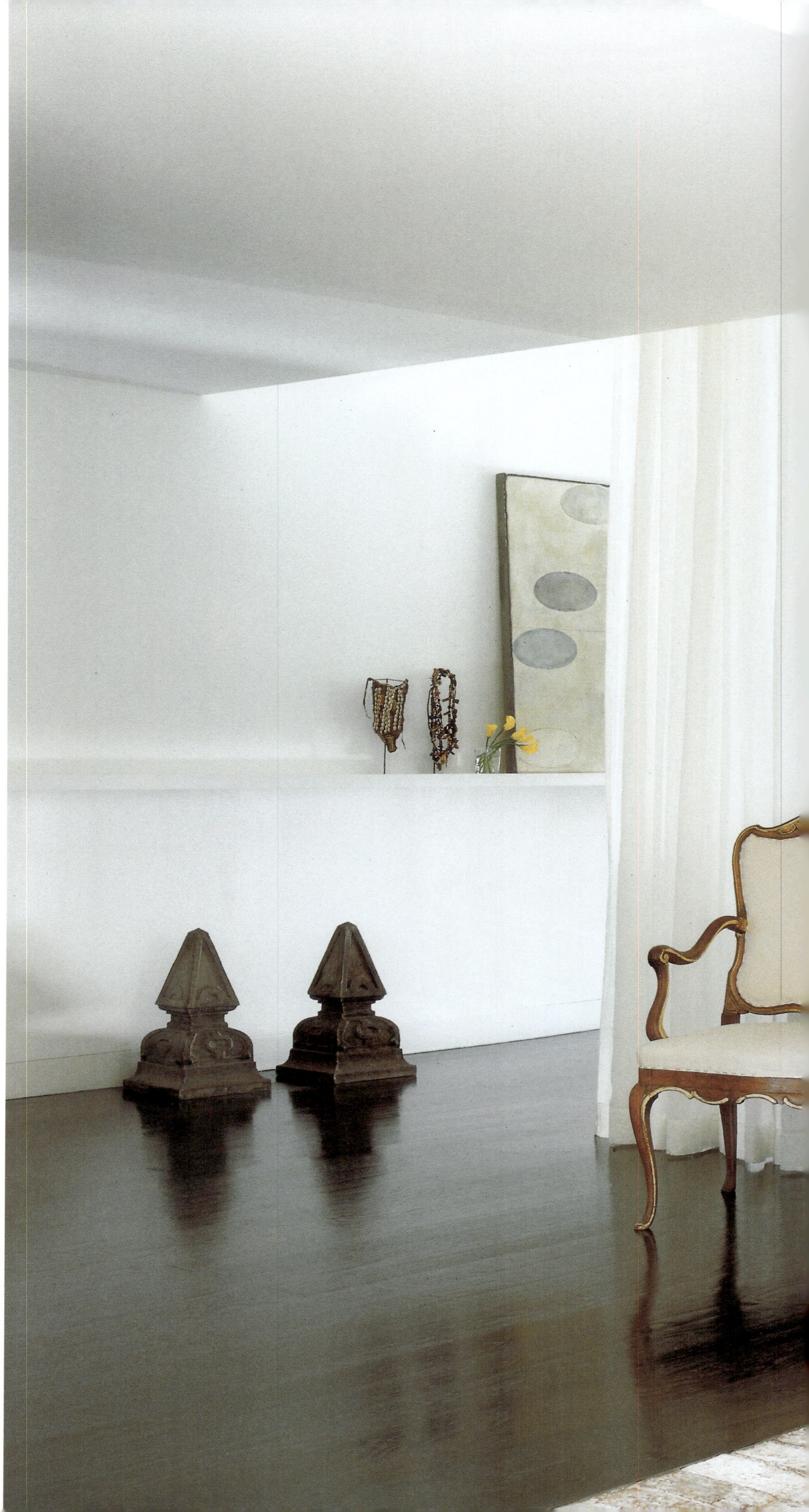

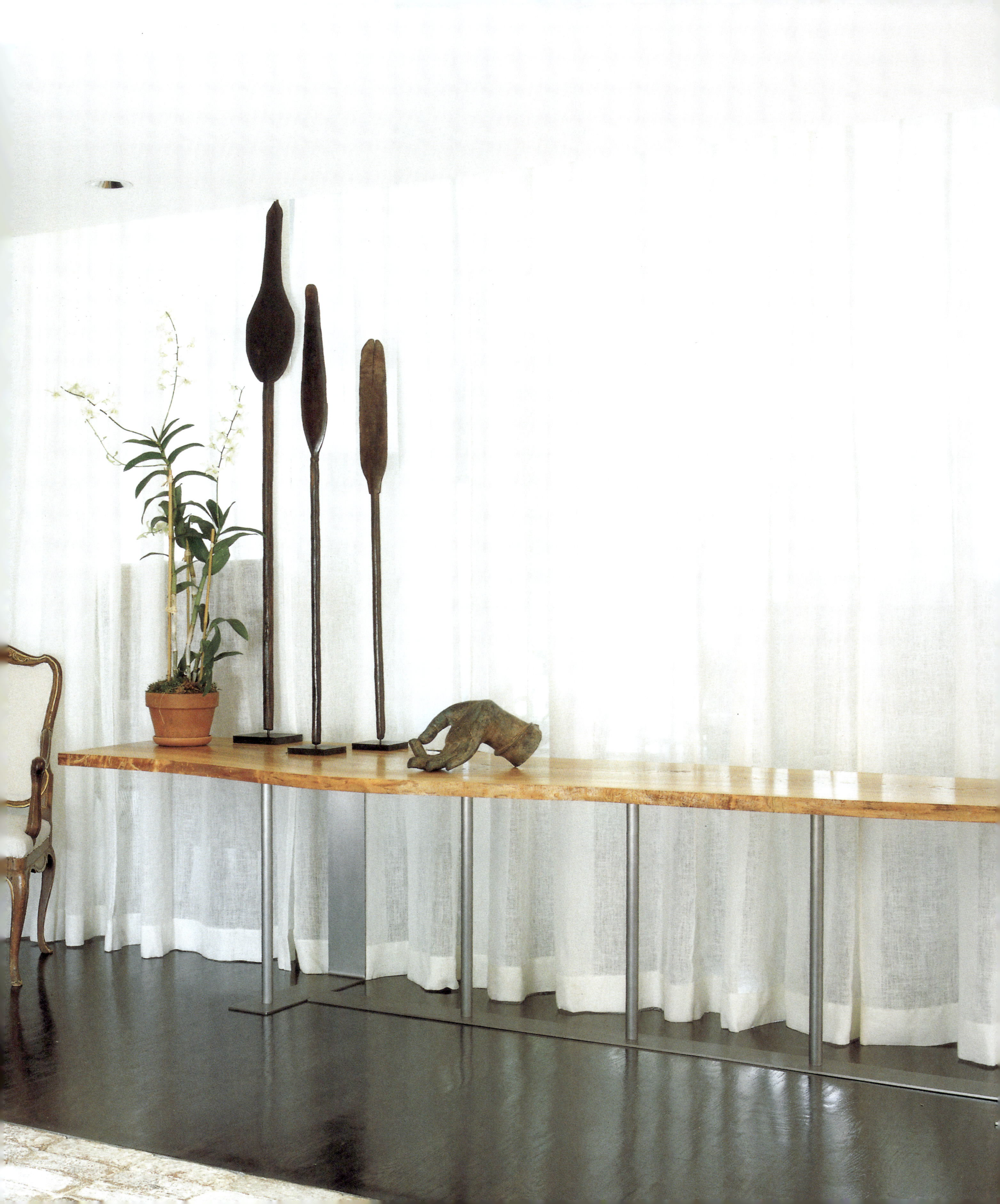

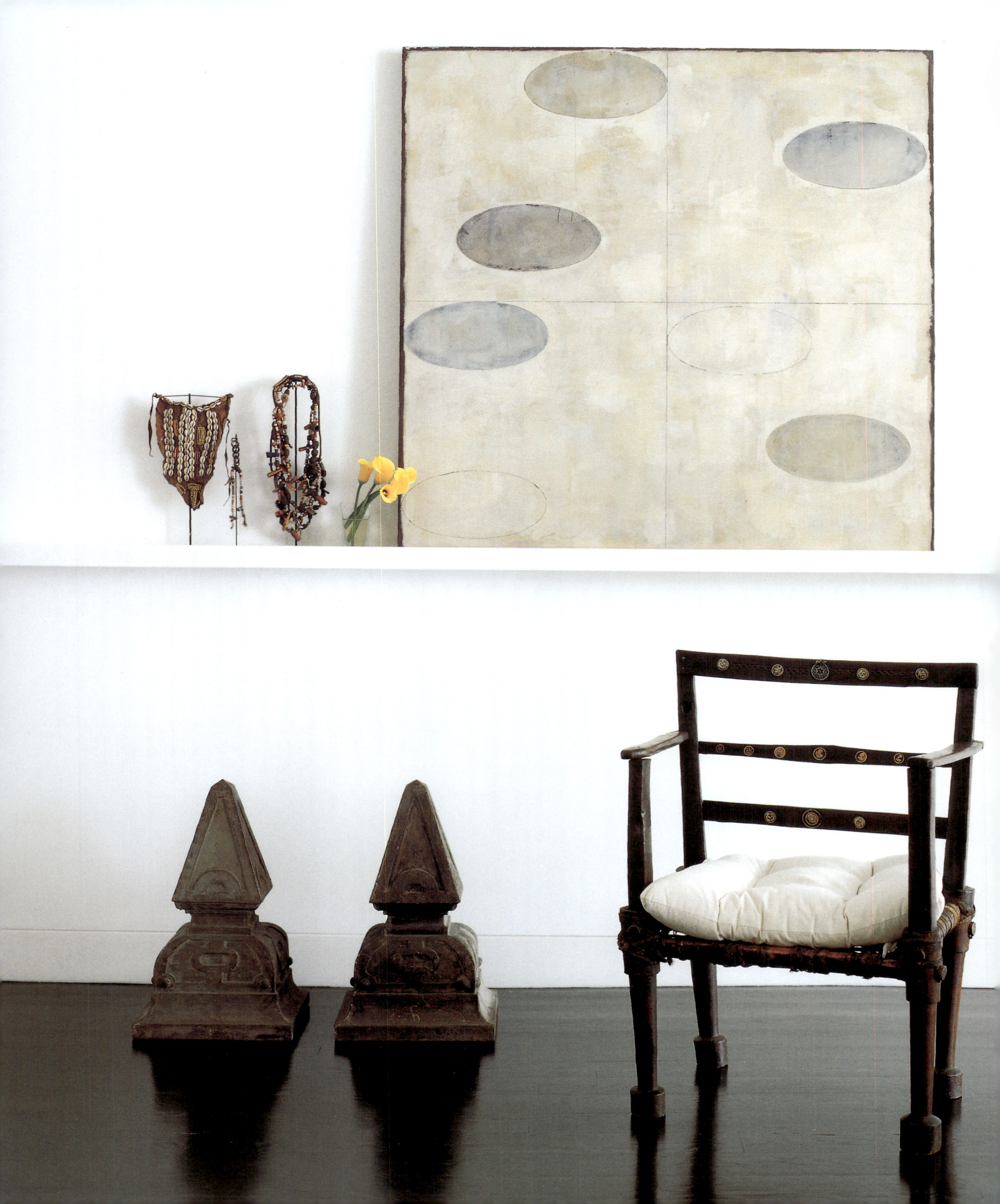

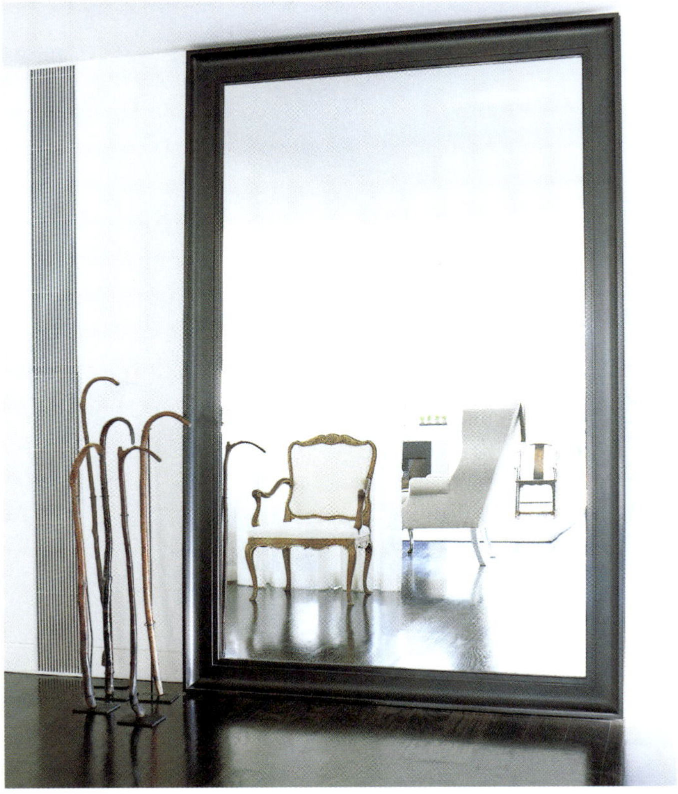

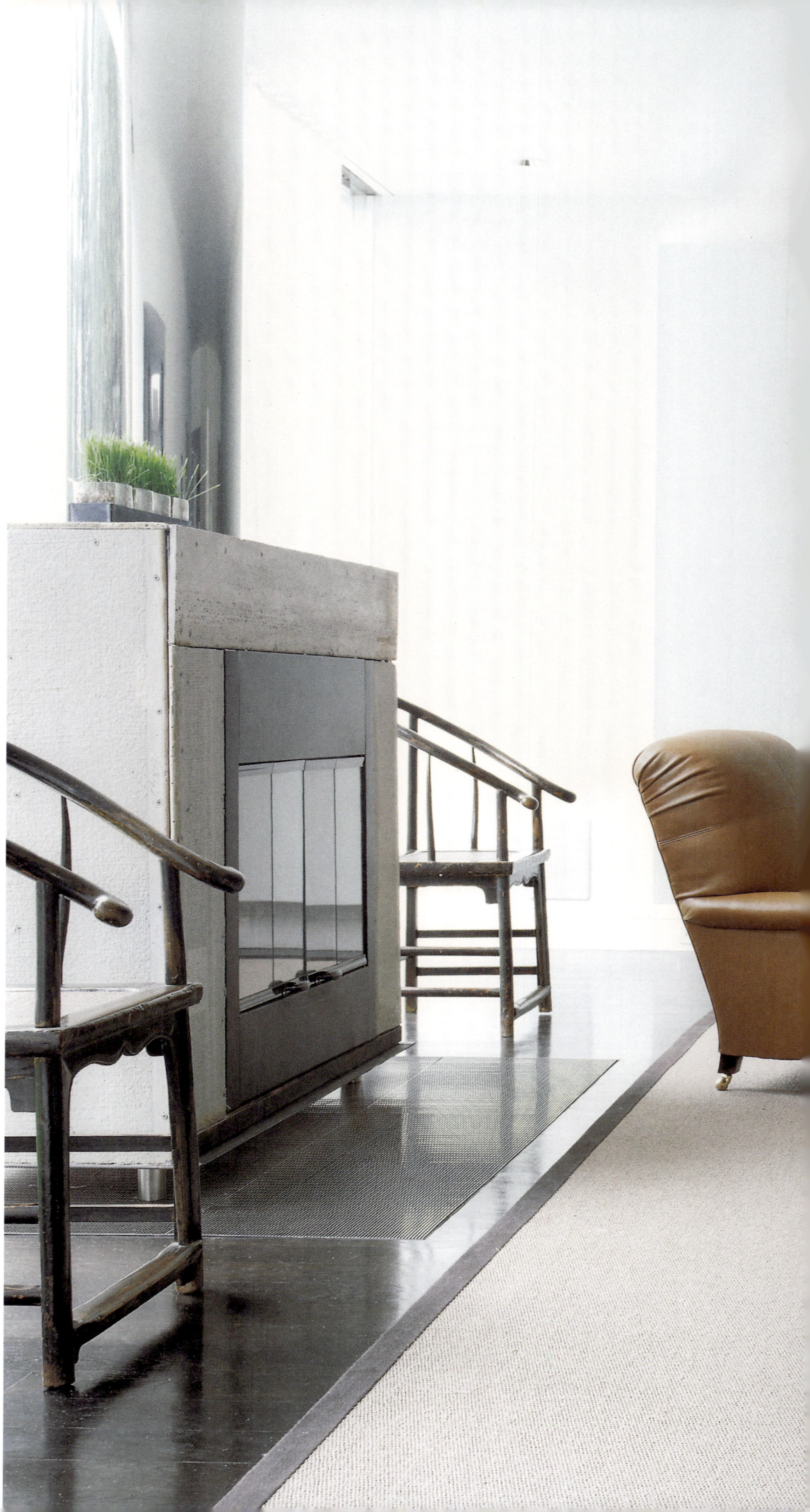

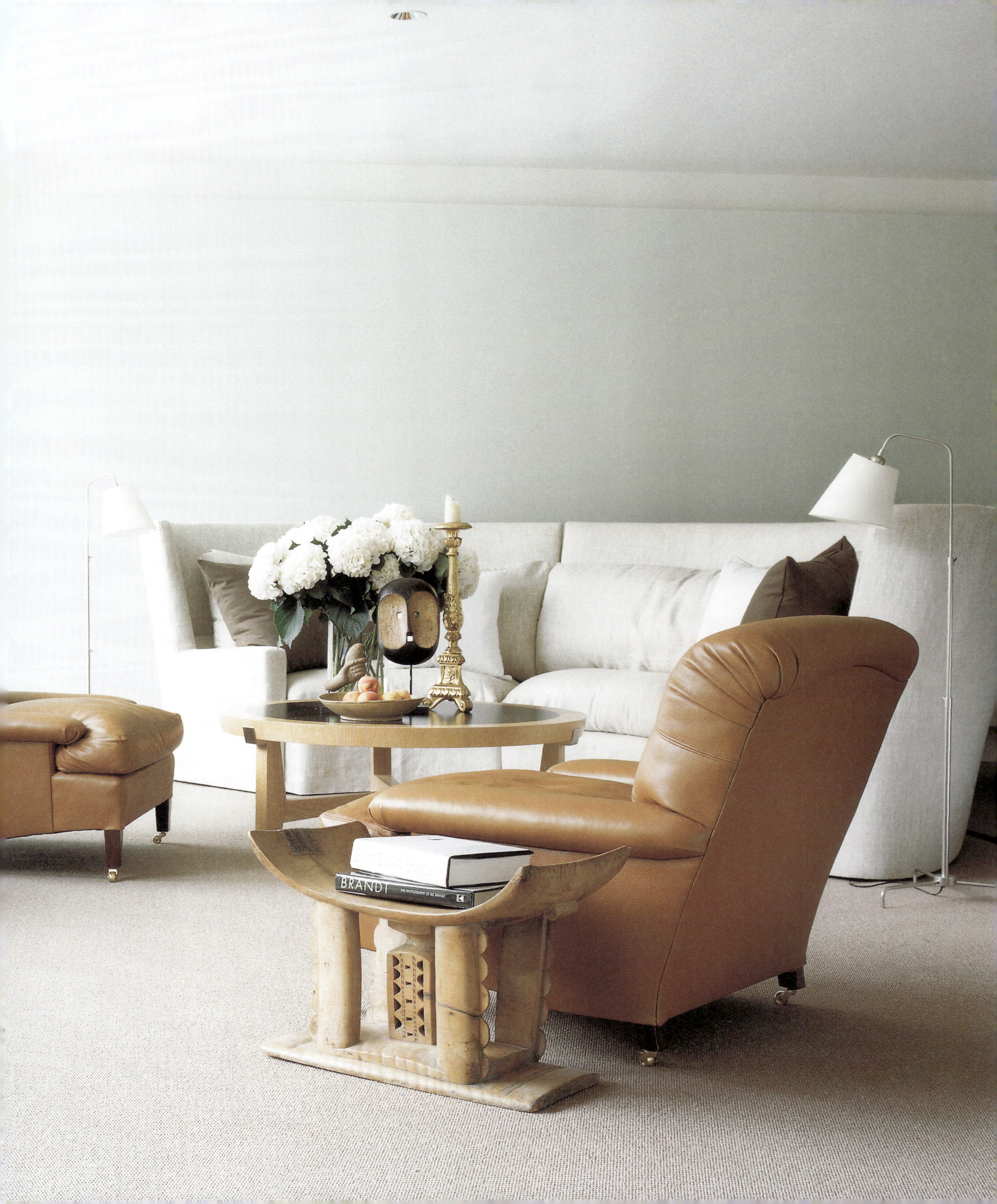
BRANDT
THE PHOTOGRAPHY OF BILL BRANDT

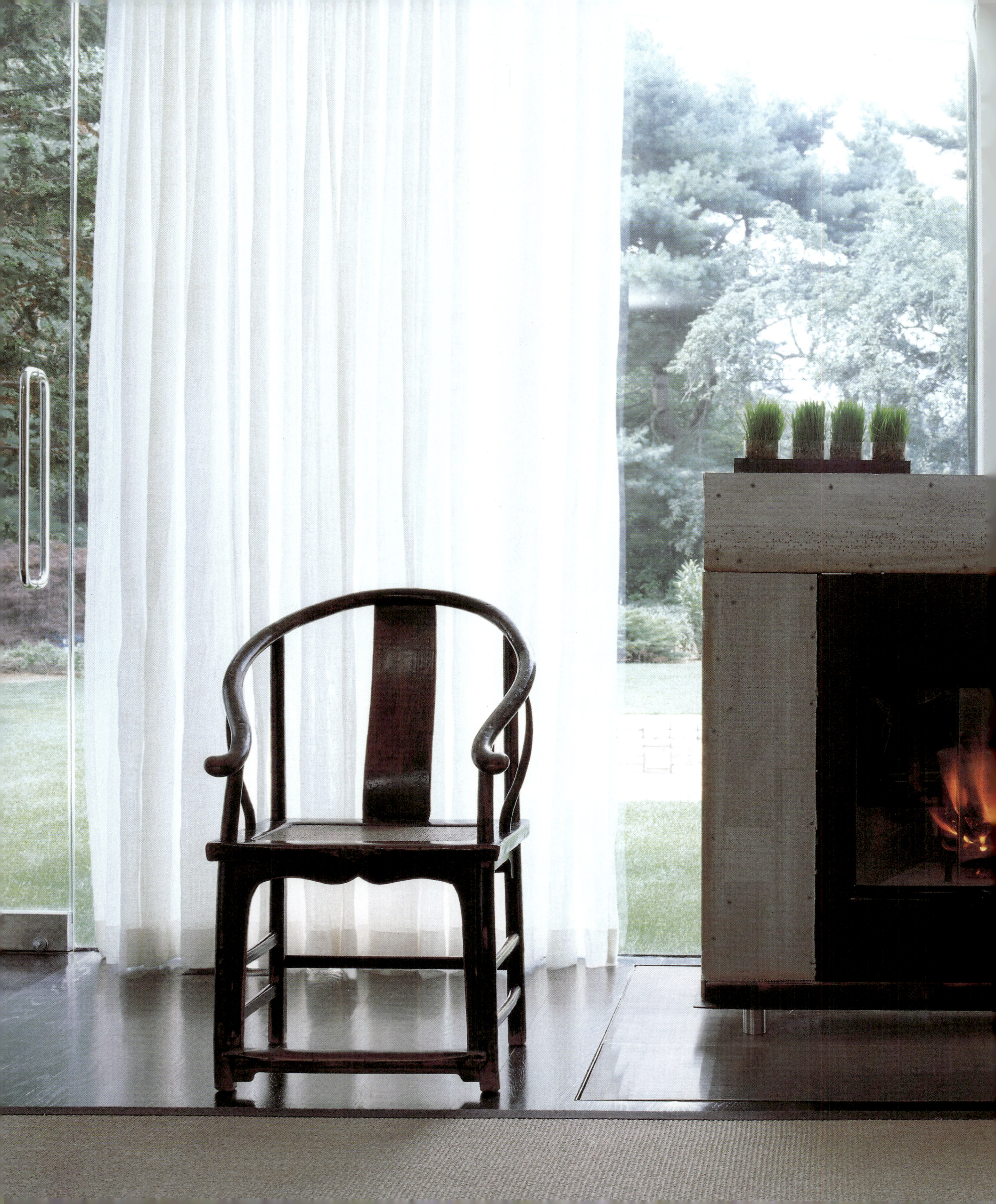

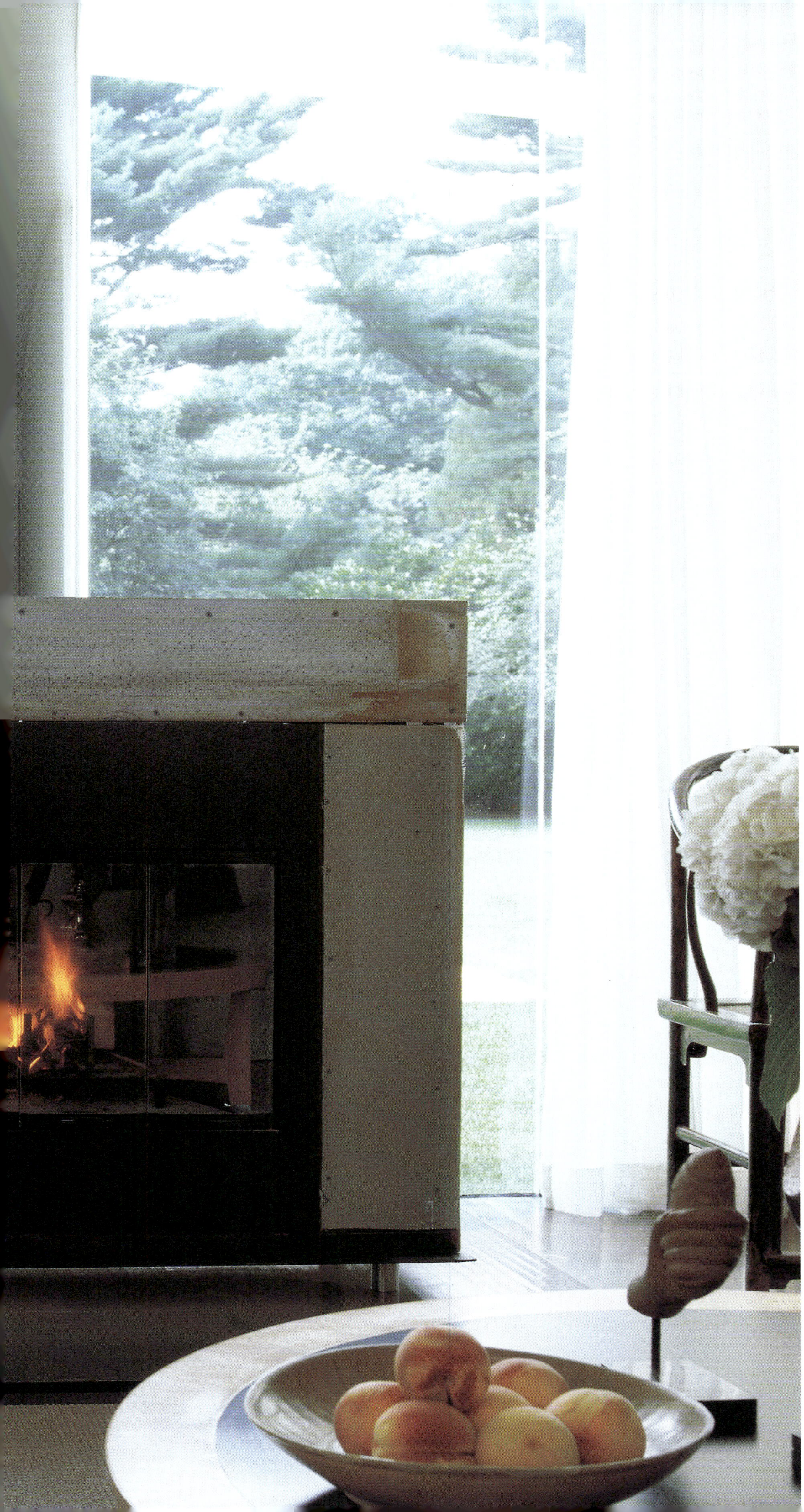

"The challenge with this project was to take a house that had been altered many times and make it cohesive. I wanted to create a space that reflected the themes of yin and yang, traditional and modern, but with a sense of elegance and comfort."

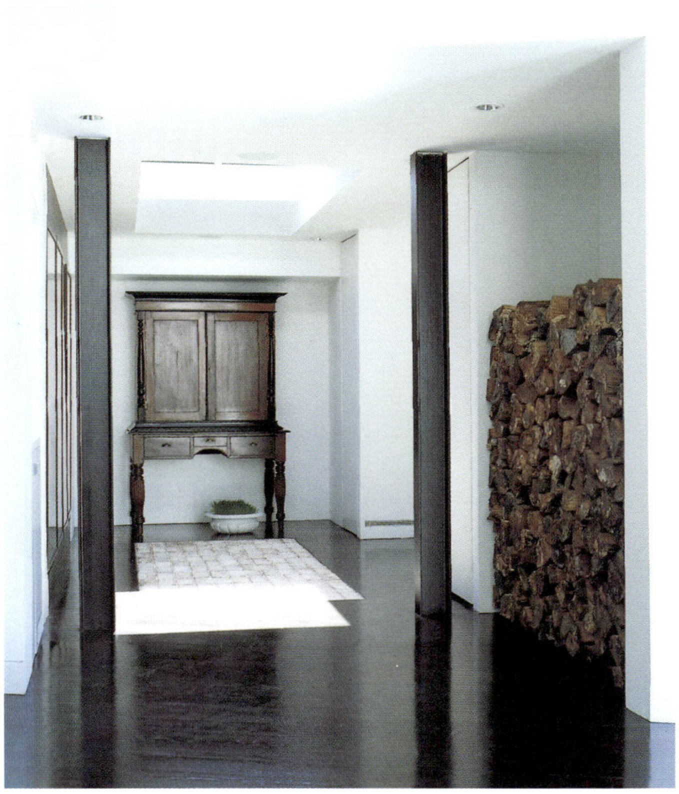

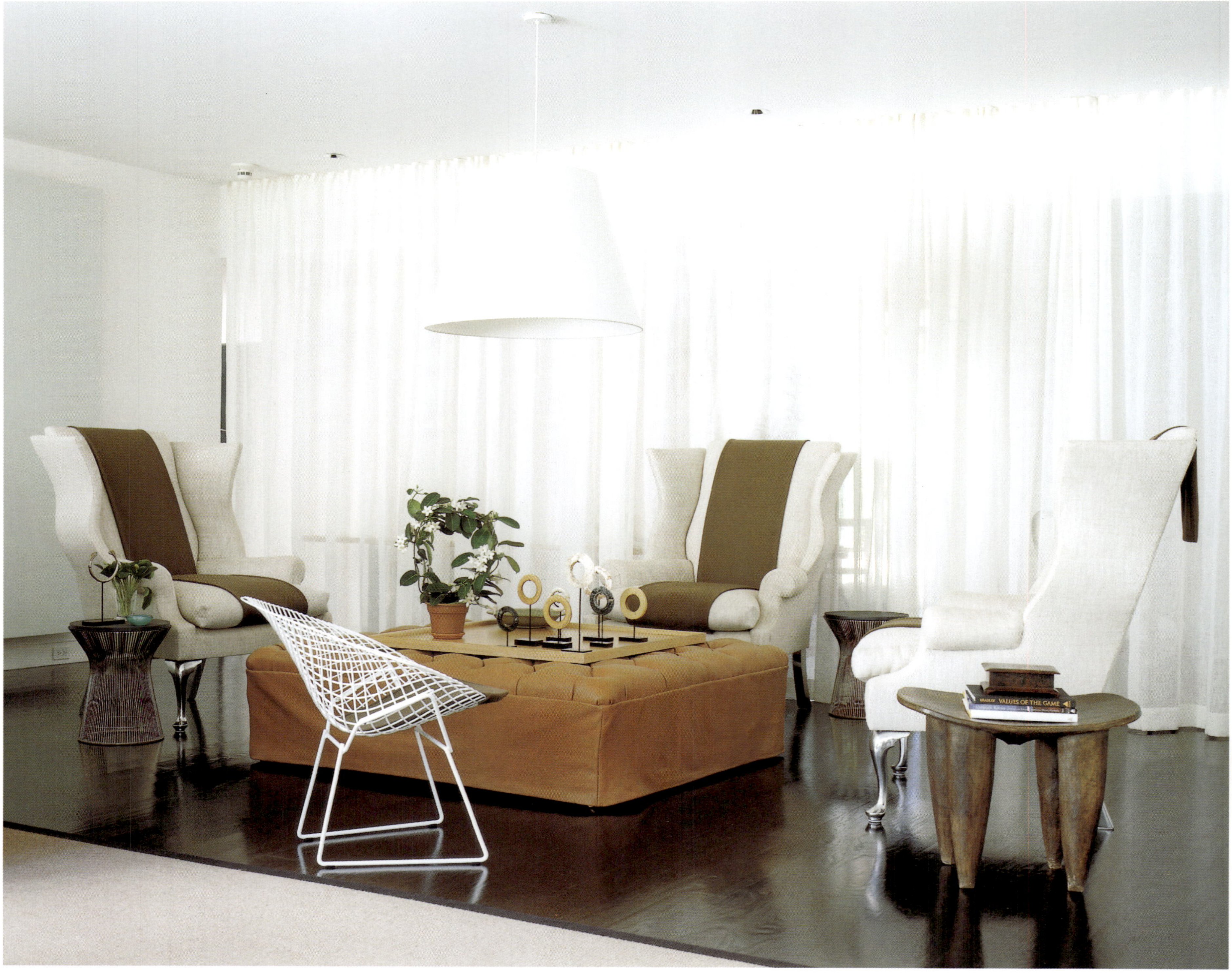
VALUES OF THE GAME

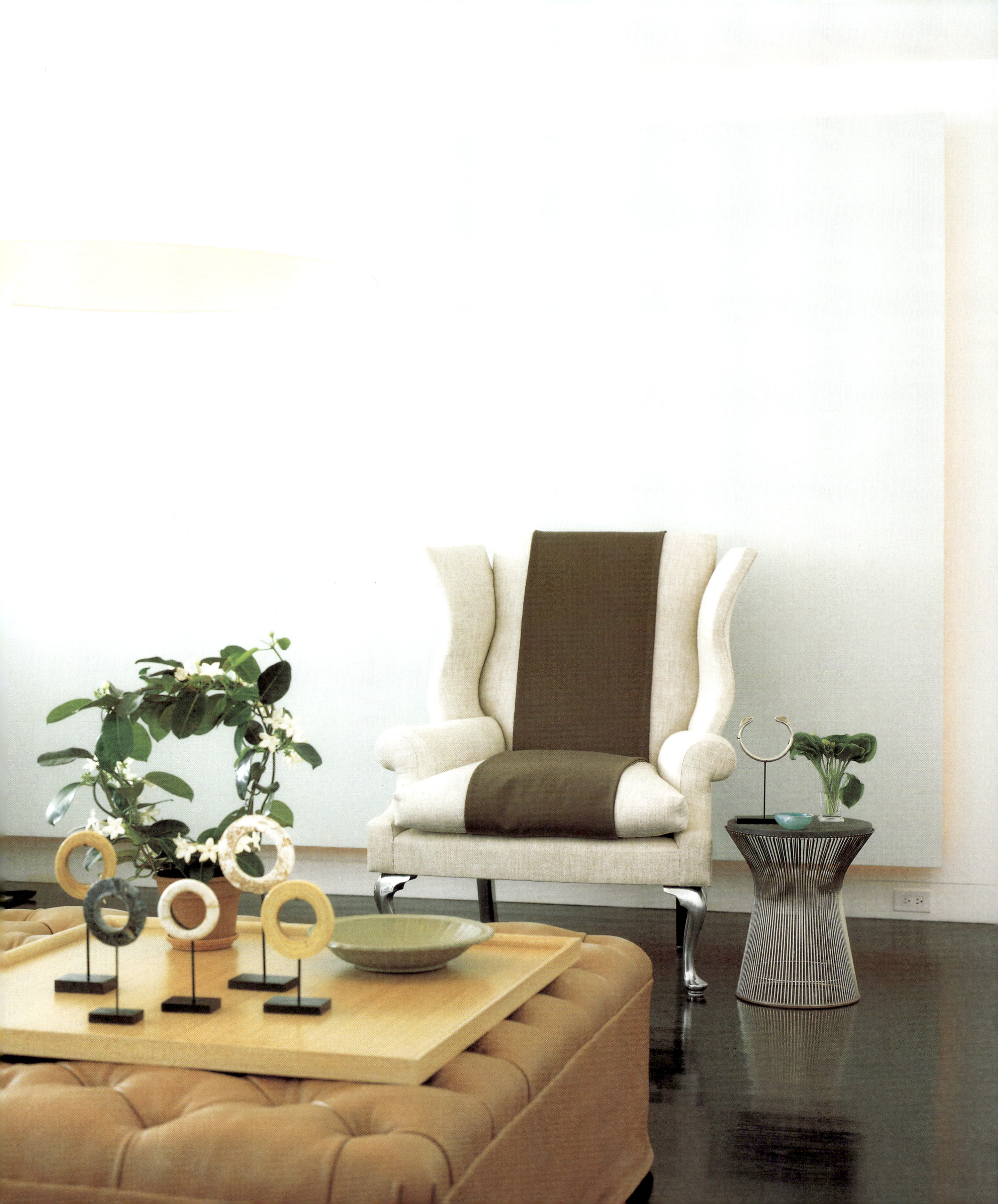

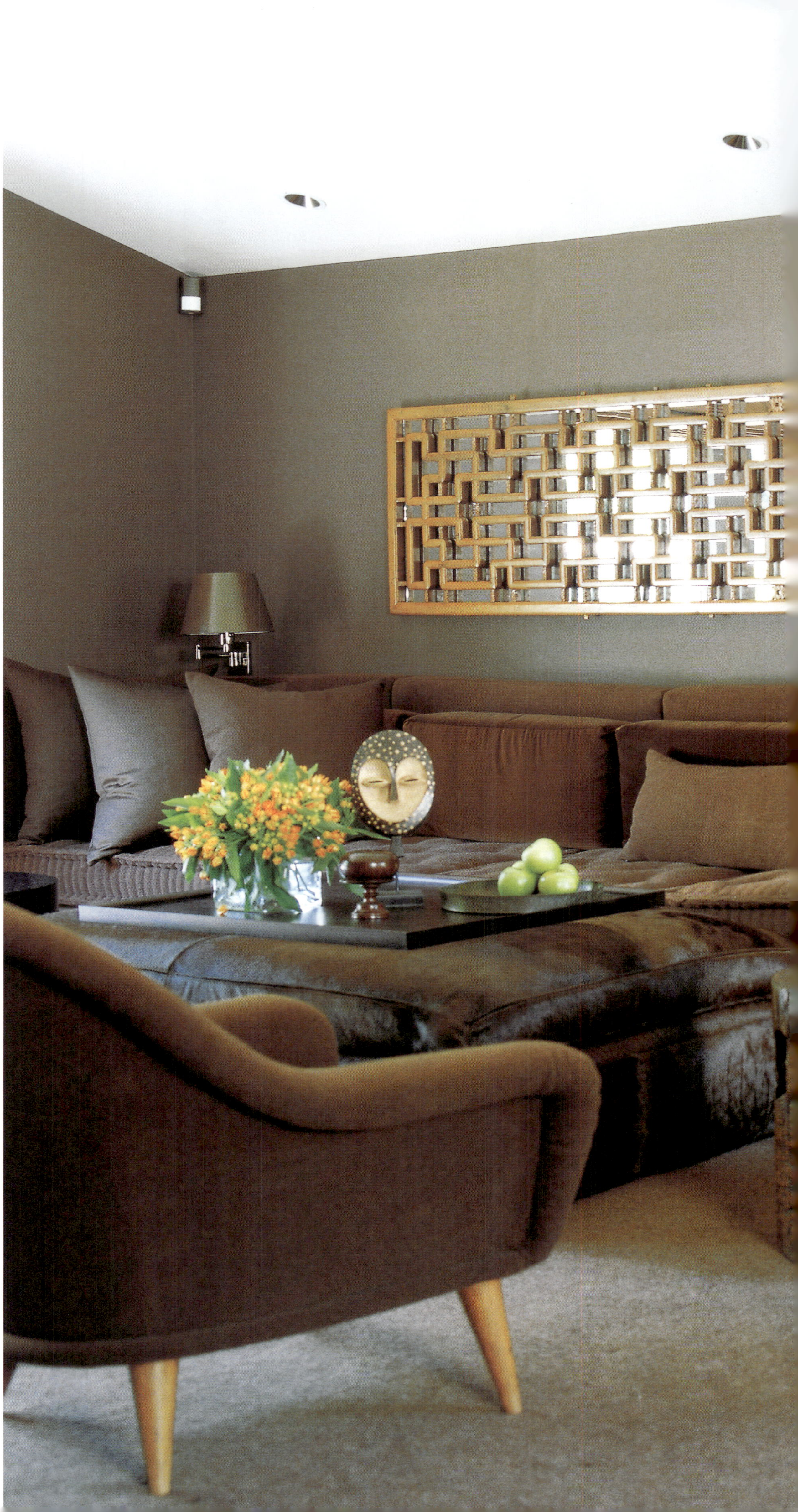

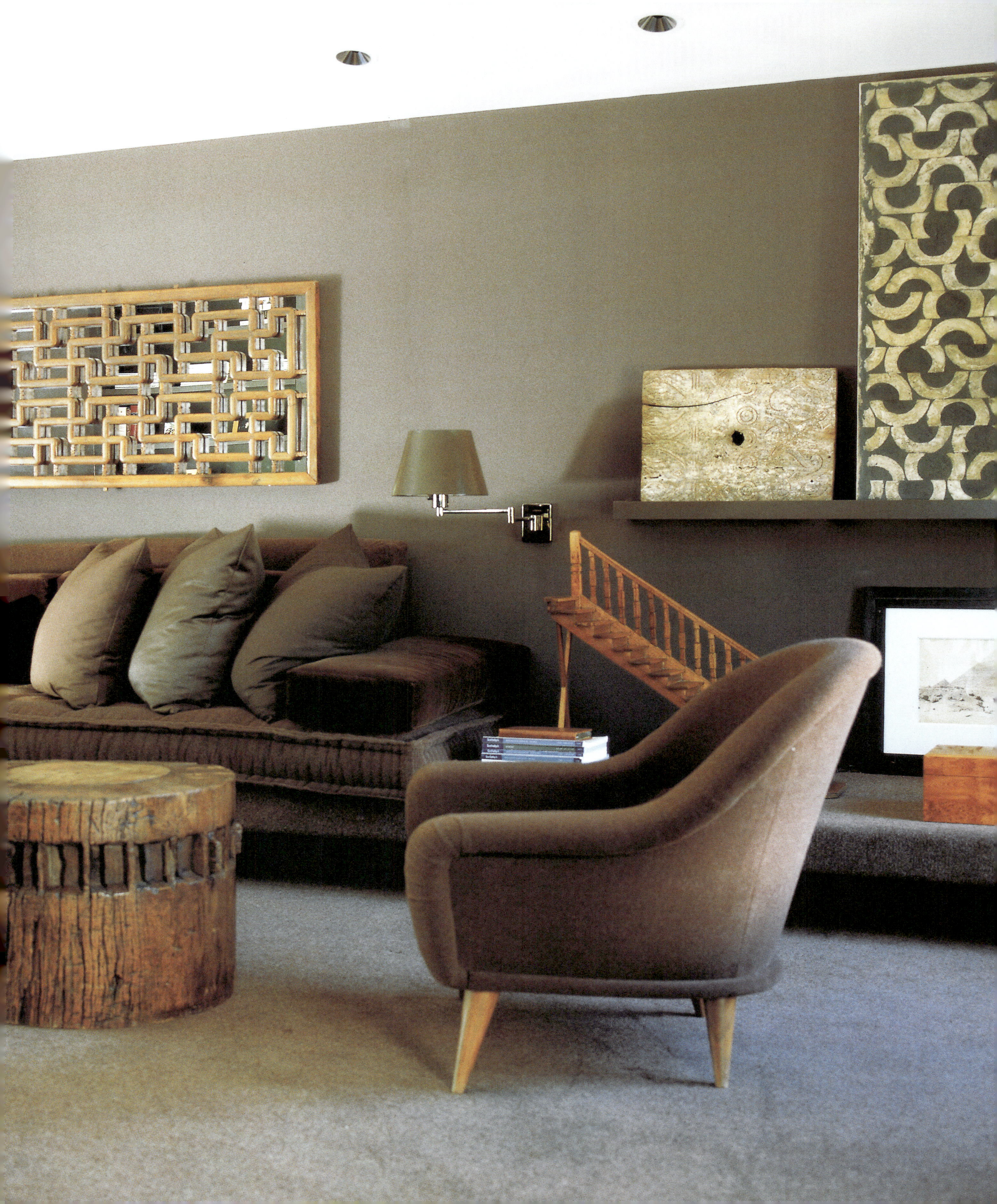

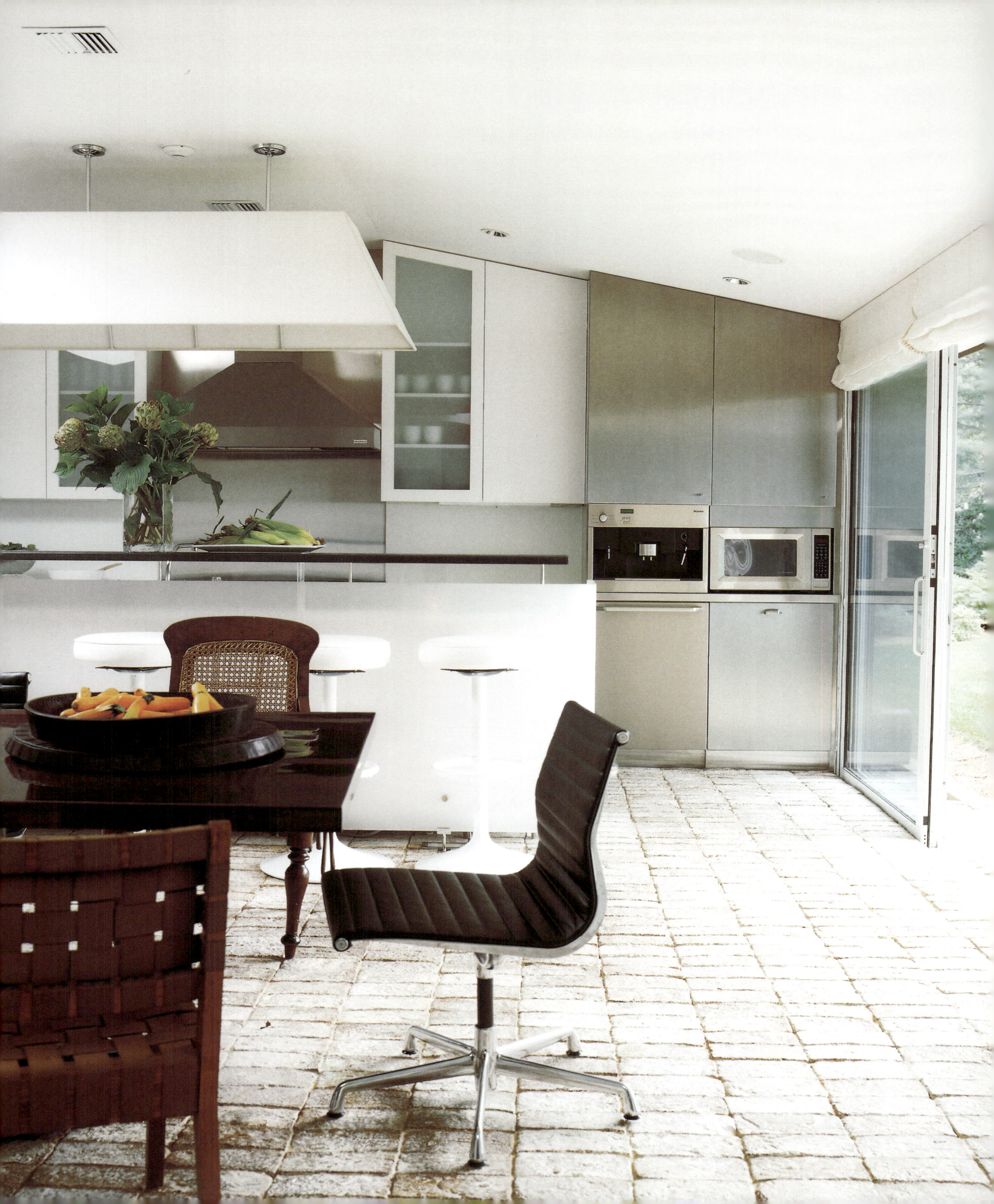

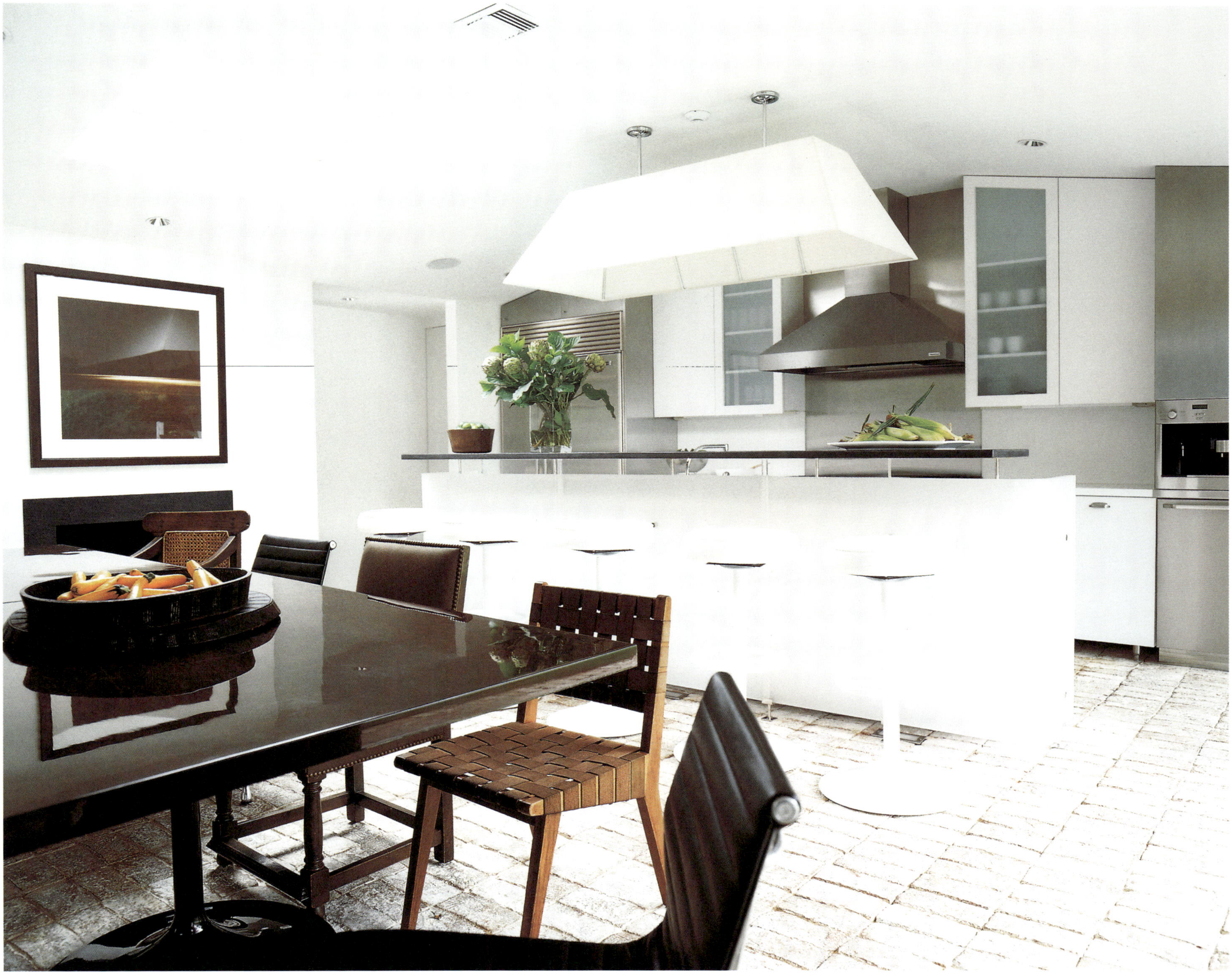

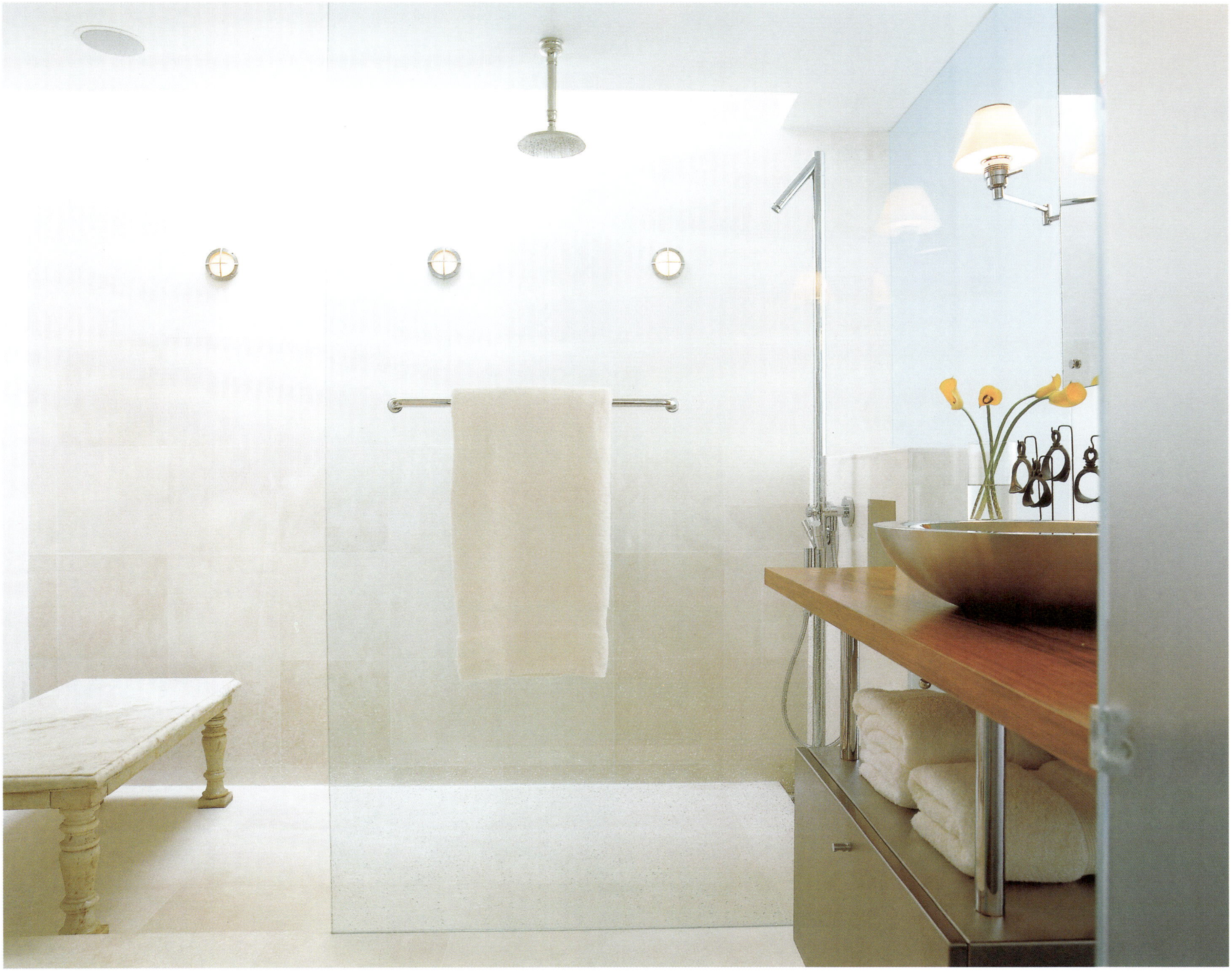

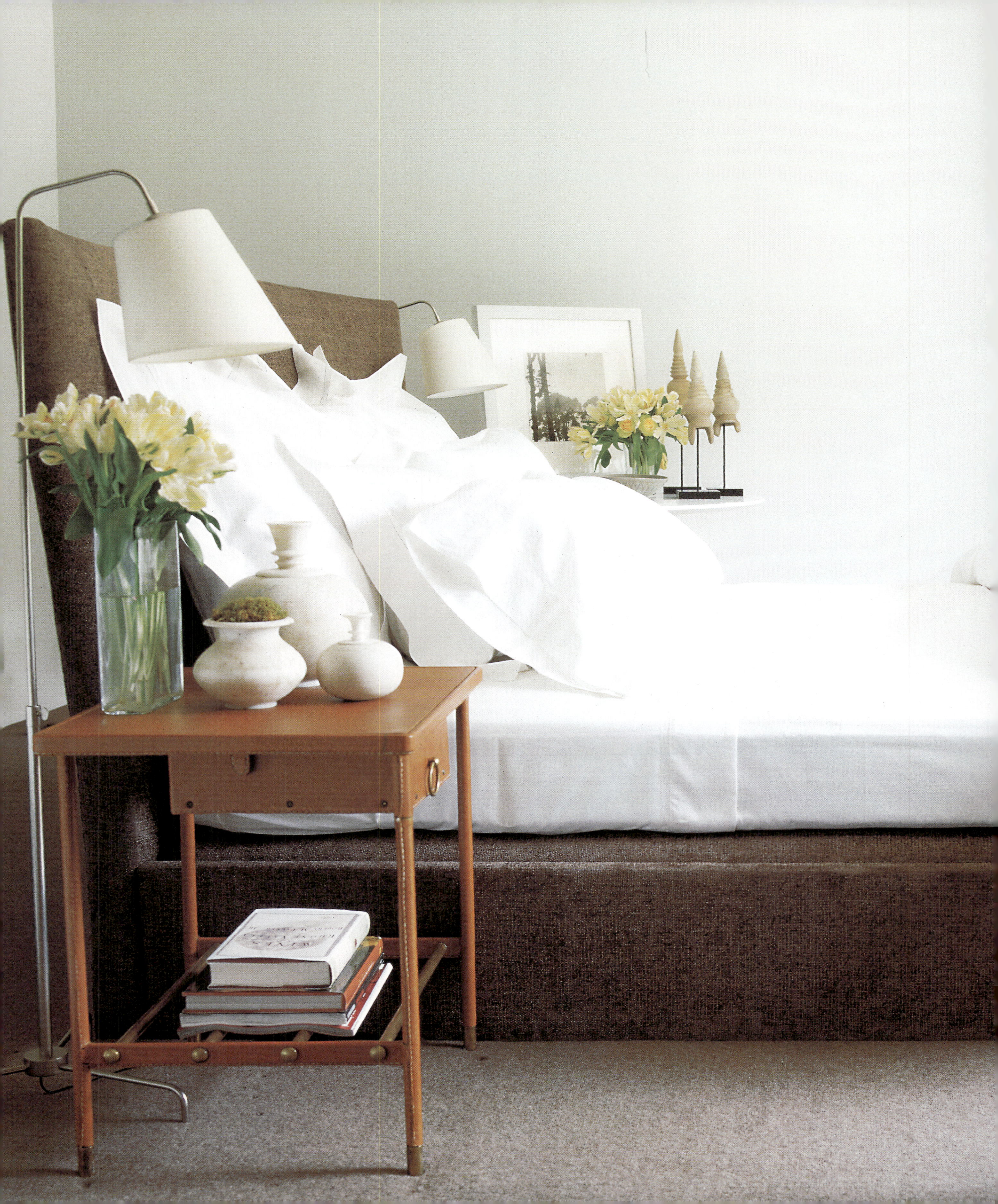

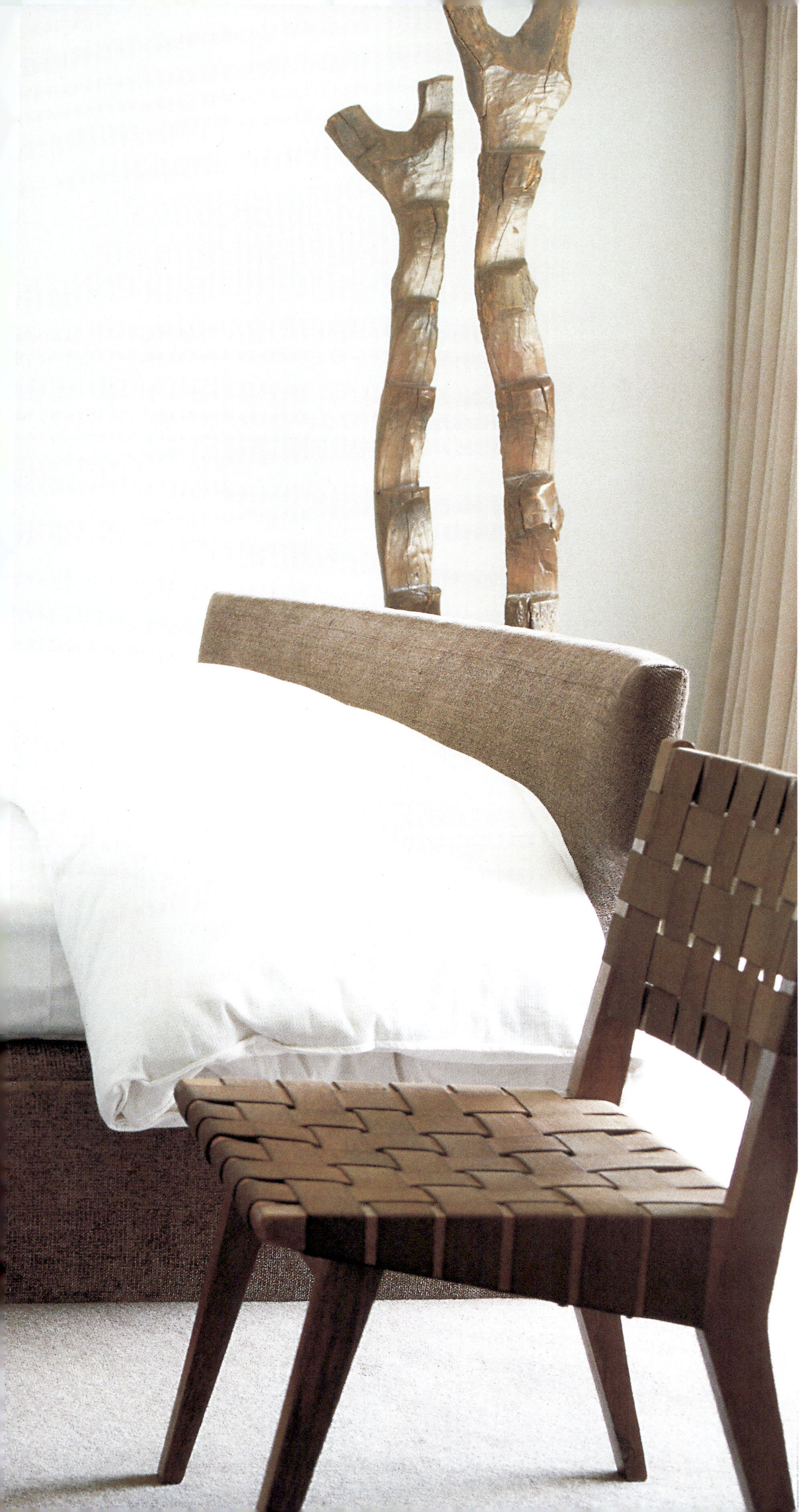

jonathan ADLER &
simon DOONAN

"For us, Shelter Island equals fun. We swim, we play with the dog, we bike, and frolic like children. This house, a 1970s rustic A-frame reflects this spirit. We painted everything on the inside white—floors, ceiling, Santa Fe hearth—and then added color with abandon. We think it's the perfect embodiment of the fun of the Hamptons."

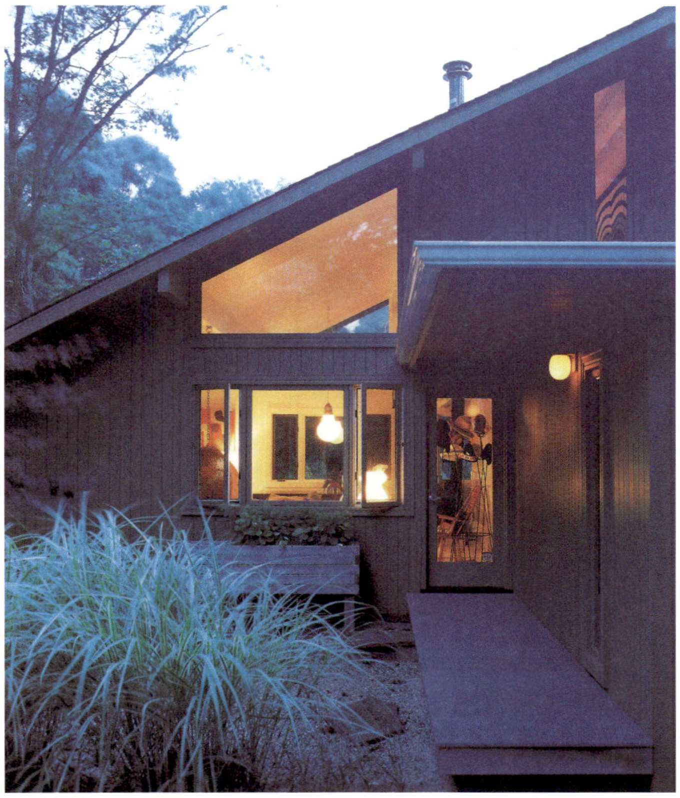

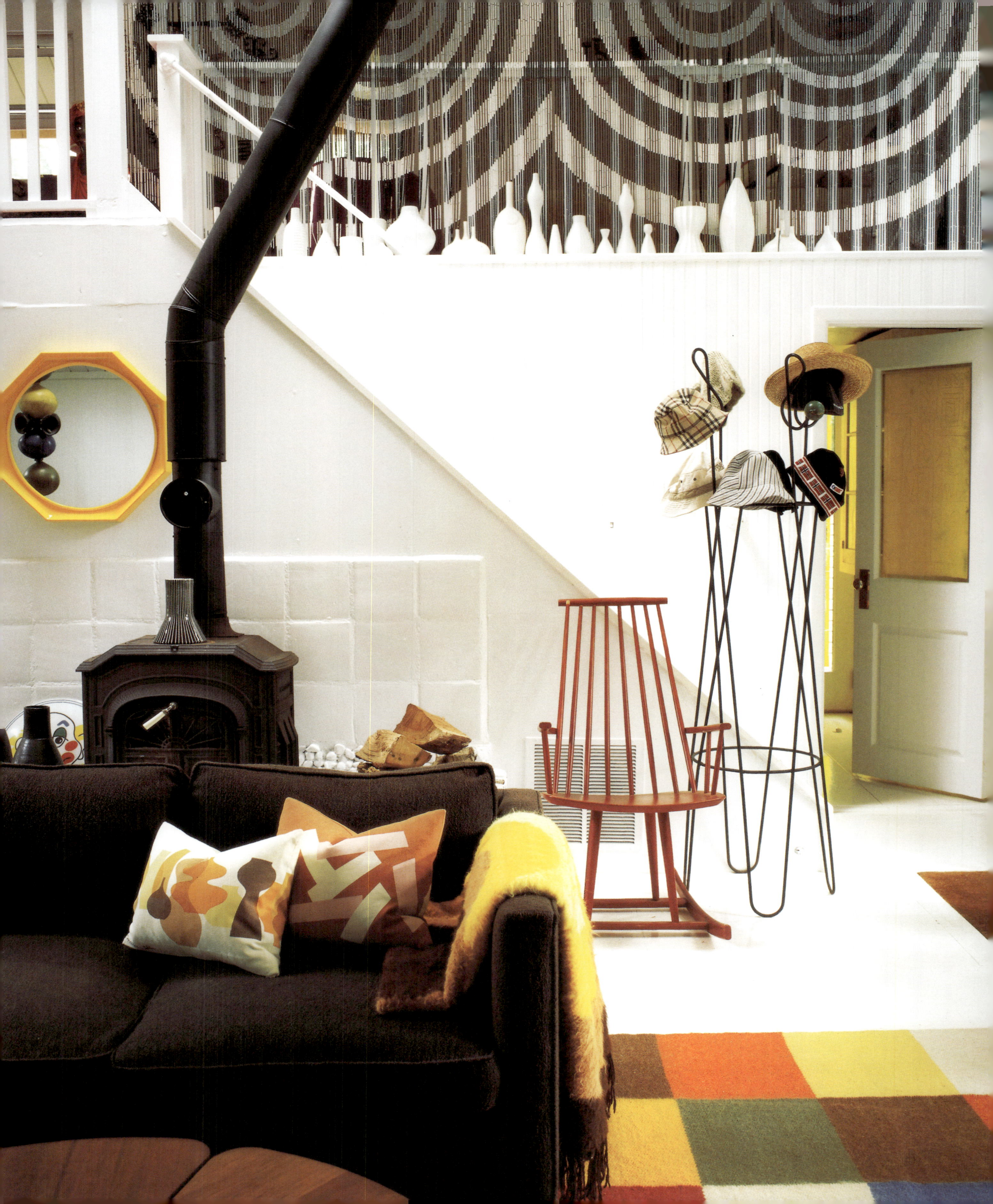

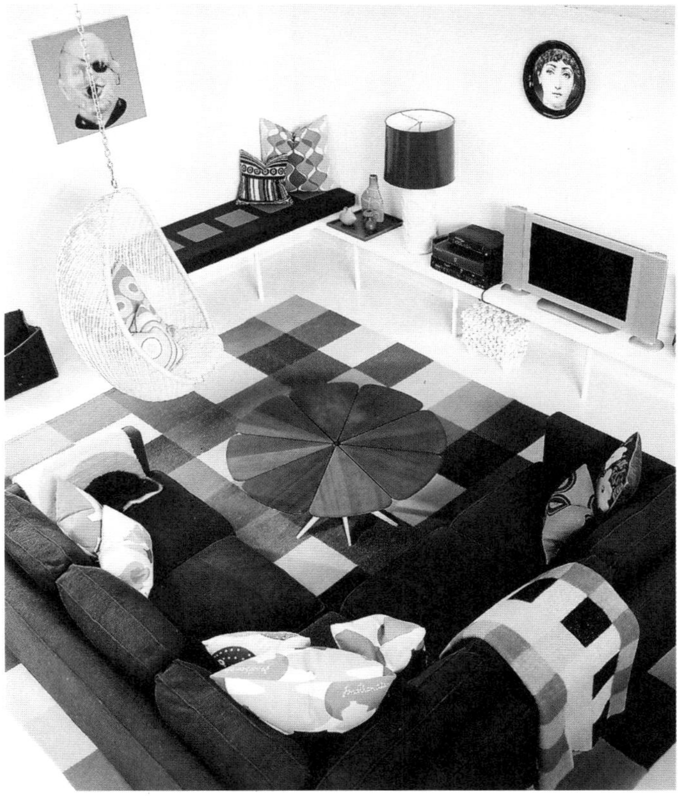

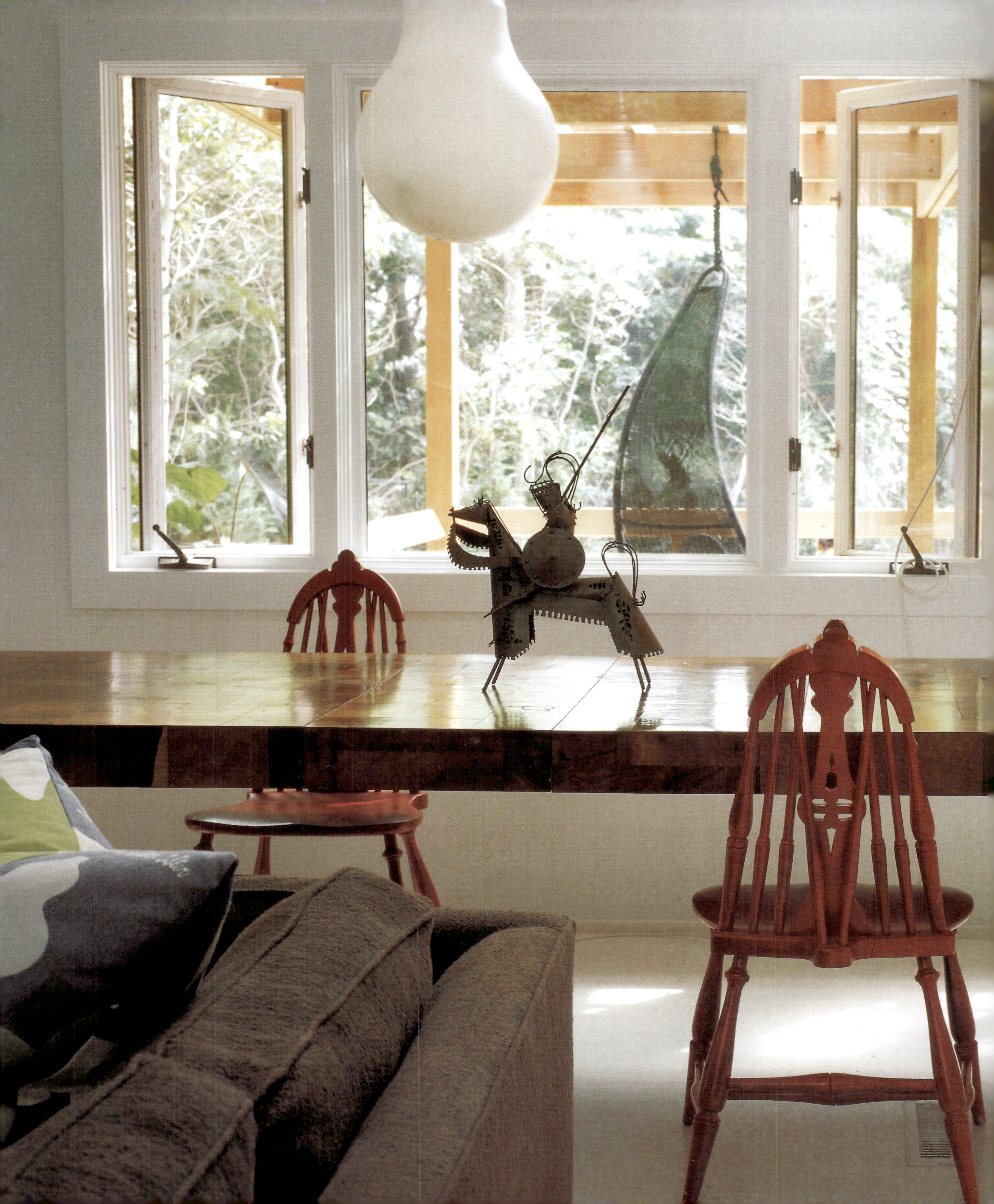

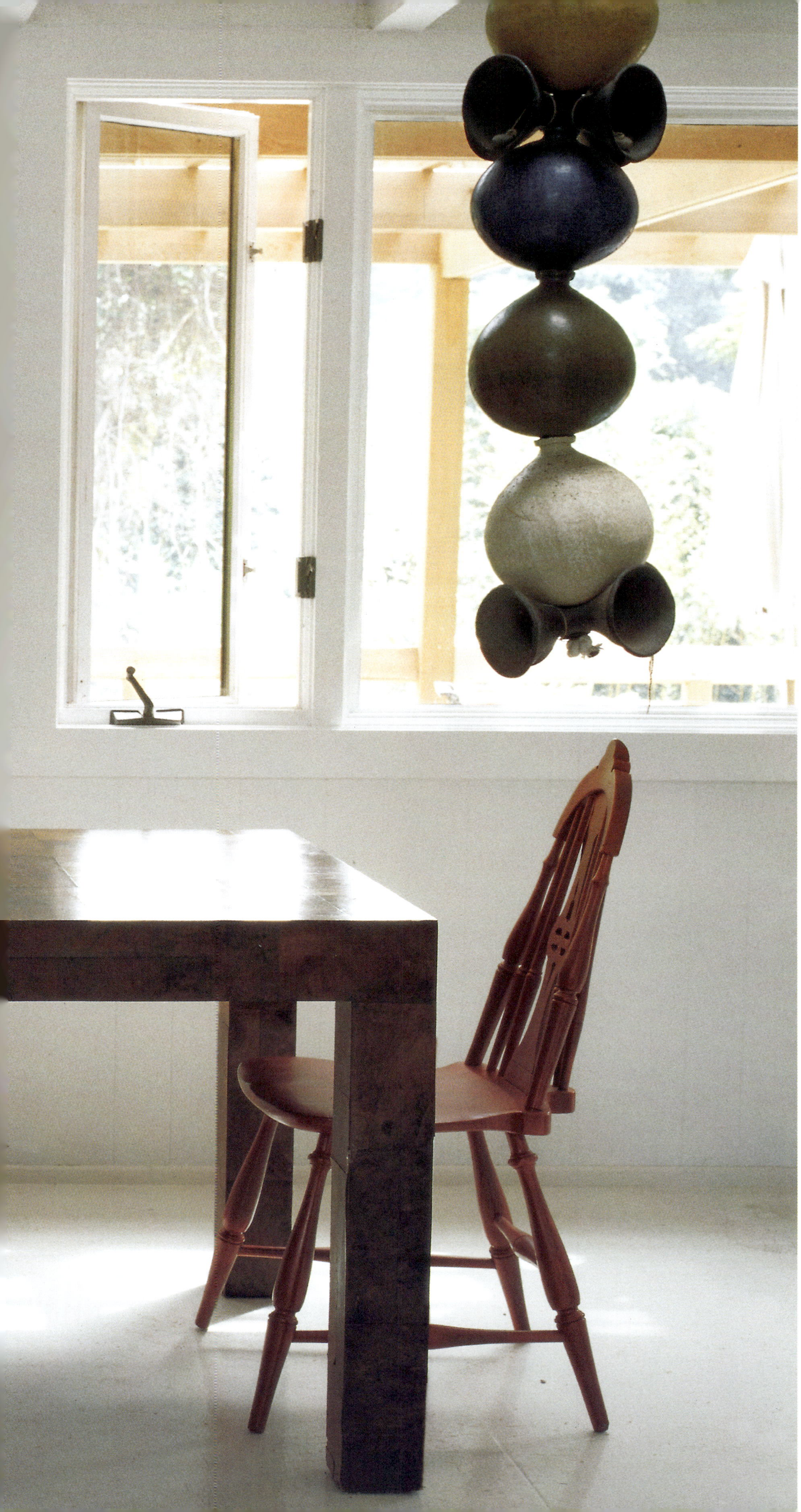

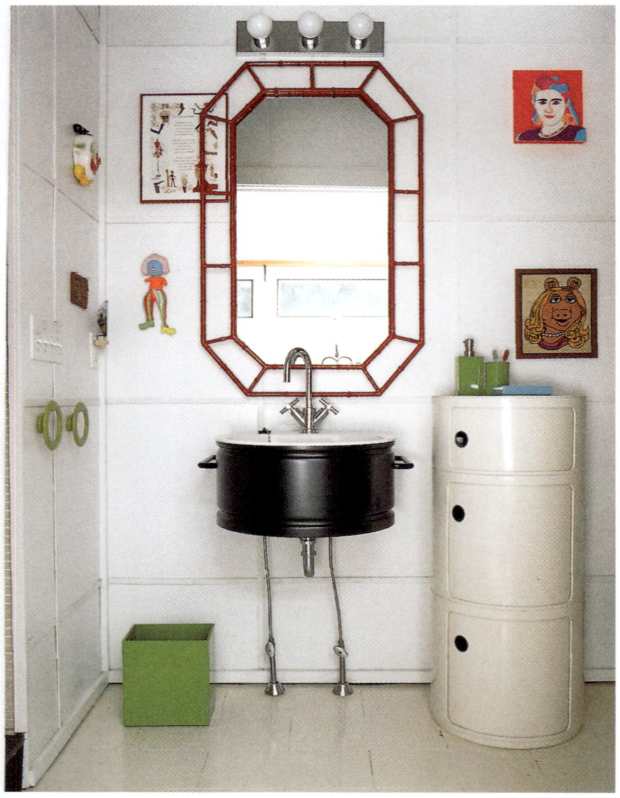

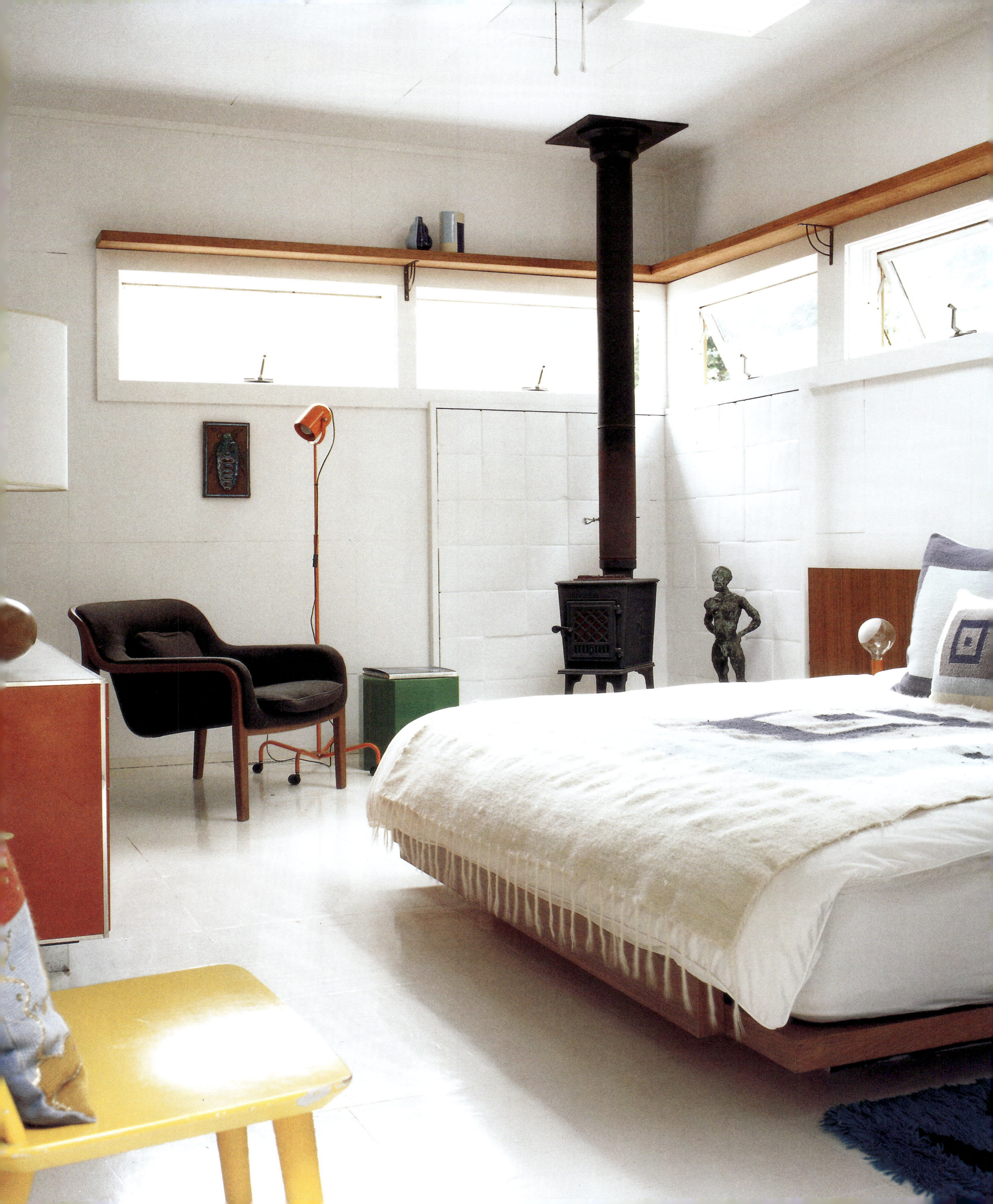

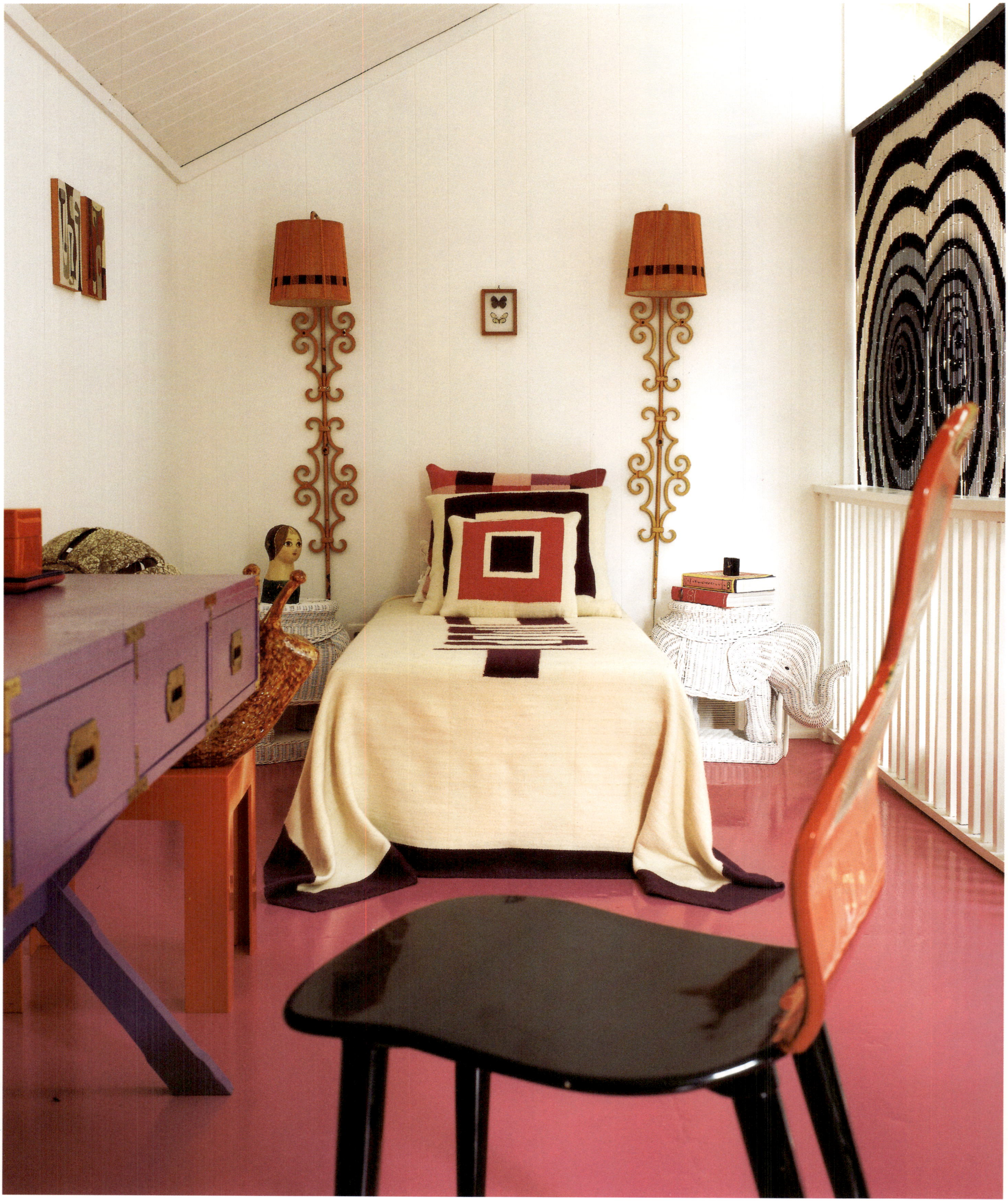

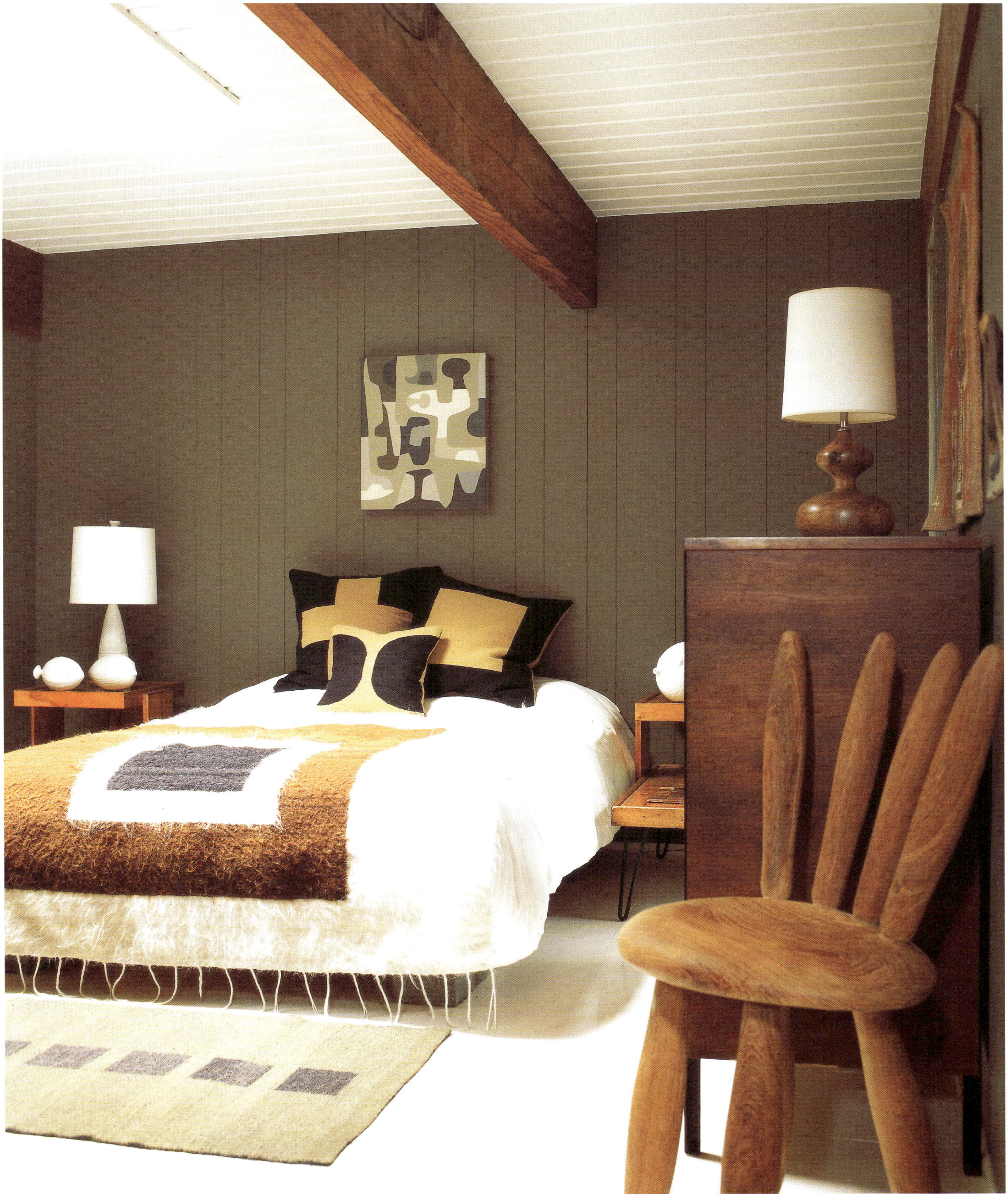

credits

joe NAHEM [PAGE 12-37]
INTERIORS: Joe Nahem for Fox-Nahem Design
ARCHITECTURE: Joe D'Urso
LANDSCAPE ARCHITECT: Edmund Hollander Landscape Architect Design, P.C.

Born and raised in New York City, Nahem graduated from Parsons School of Design in New York and Paris where he studied under celebrated designers Joe D'Urso and John Saladino. In 1980, together with his late partner Tom Fox, he founded Fox-Nahem Design. Their work was first recognized by the *New York Times*, House & Home section and has been subsequently published in magazines such as *Architectural Digest*, *Elle Decor*, *Hamptons*, *House Beautiful*, *House & Garden*, and *Interior Design*.

Fox-Nahem Design has been fortunate to have worked with or on buildings by renowned architects such as Richard Meier, Robert Stern, and Stanford White. The company's completed projects include apartments in New York City, and houses in the Hamptons, Martha's Vineyard, Pennsylvania, Florida, California, and Massachusetts, as well as corporate offices.

steven GAMBREL [PAGE 38-55]
INTERIORS: Steven Gambrel

Gambrel established his New York-based design firm, S.R. Gambrel Inc. in 1995, only three years after earning an architecture degree at the University of Virginia. Whether he's designing a polished uptown duplex, a rambling country house, or a weekend beach house, Gambrel infuses each project with his passion for timeless, comfortable houses that improve with age. His work has been celebrated in magazines and newspapers such as *Elle Decor*, *House & Garden*, *Interior Design*, and the *New York Times*.

thomas O'BRIEN [PAGE 56-71]
INTERIORS: Thomas O'Brien, Aero Studios
ARCHITECTURE: Norman Jaffe

O'Brien received his BFA from The Cooper Union in New York City in 1986 and established his design firm, Aero Studios, in 1992. Conceived as a "studio," with all that term implies, his company designs, develops, and produces for a growing circuit of mediums and brands—Thomas O'Brien products, Aero store collections and antiques, Aero Studios interiors, and a new comprehensive home collection for Target, Vintage Modern/Thomas O'Brien. The coupling of public and private design practices is central to O'Brien's philosophy. He borrows from the 19th century European tradition of the gallerist, guided by personal and eclectic tastes, funneling his many interests through a distinctive filter of modernism.

jamie DRAKE [PAGE 72-85]
INTERIORS: Jamie Drake
LANDSCAPE ARCHITECT: Craig James Socia

Drake graduated from Parsons School of Design and launched his namesake firm immediately after graduation. Since then he has completed a vast array of projects for an impressive roster of clients. Drake's notable residential interiors include a Los Angeles showplace for Madonna, a Martha's Vineyard vacation retreat and Manhattan apartment for Phyllis and Victor Grann, and multiple projects for New York City Mayor, Michael Bloomberg, a Drake client for almost 20 years.

Drake's professional honors are numerous. Chief among them are the 2003 induction into The Interior Design Hall of Fame, the 2000 D&D Designers of Distinction Award, and a recent Partnership for the Homeless Director's Award.

Craig James Socia is a landscape designer based in East Hampton, New York. He is noted for his *twig-style* construction of follies, pergolas, arbors, gates, fences, and a complete line of furniture and benches made to fit the client's needs. His work has appeared in the *New York Times*, *Country Living*, *Home Style*, *Marie Claire Maison*, and *Hampton's Cottages & Gardens*.

jack CEGLIC [PAGE 86-101]
INTERIORS: CEGLIC (Jack Ceglic and Junichi Satoh)
ARCHITECTURE: CEGLIC (Jack Ceglic and Junichi Satoh)

CEGLIC is an architecture, interior, and graphic design firm based in New York City. CEGLIC's residential clients include Joel Dean, Joe Mantello, Ron Rifken, Robi Baitz, and Perri Wolfman. Jack Ceglic was responsible for the design of the stores and cafes for Dean & DeLuca as well as their corporate identity and packaging. His associate, Junichi Satoh, joined the firm in 1994 and holds a BFA in graphic design and a Masters degree in architecture from Rhode Island School of Design.

waldo FERNANDEZ [PAGE 102-119]
INTERIORS: Waldo Fernandez
ARCHITECTURE: Waldo Fernandez

Born in Cuba, Fernandez relocated to the United States as a teenager and was encouraged by his family to explore his passion for design and the arts. He enrolled at UCLA to study art and architecture and was soon thereafter hired by Walter Scott as an assistant set designer for 20th Century Fox. Fernandez's set designs included furniture commissions, which caught on immediately and got him recognition in the field. Fernandez's first major interior design job was for film director John Schlessinger; ever since, his clientele has included celebrities from the entertainment industry. His showroom, Waldo's Designs, has been open at the Almont Drive location in Los Angeles for more than 28 years and carries a reproduction furniture line. His staff includes architectural and interior designers.

mark ZEFF [PAGE 120-133]
INTERIORS: Mark Zeff
ARCHITECTURE: Mark Zeff
Zeff is a native of South Africa and a scholar from the United Kingdom, where he studied furniture design and architecture. In 1985, Zeff started his own architectural design firm, Zeffdesign, in New York City. Today, Zeffdesign has completed major international commercial, residential, retail, hospitality, and corporate image projects. Some of the most noteworthy accomplishments include the architecture, interior design, and brand identity for The Red Cat and The Harrison in New York City; the architecture, interior design, branding, and graphics for Town Hall in San Francisco; and several residential interior and architecture projects, including residences for Annie Liebovitz and the Manhattan home of Hilary Swank. Zeff's work has been featured in numerous books and magazines including *Elle Decor*, *Food & Wine*, *Gotham* (New York Top 100 Designers), *Hamptons*, *House Beautiful* (America's Top 100 Designers), *House & Garden*, the *New York Times*, *US Weekly*, *Vanity Fair*, and *Vogue* among others.

**tony INGRAO &
randy KEMPER** [PAGE 134-151]
INTERIORS: Tony Ingrao and Randy Kemper
ARCHITECTURE: Tony Ingrao and Randy Kemper
Ingrao Inc., an architecture, design, and decoration firm based in New York City, provides unique architectural and design services to a select group of private clients. Anthony Ingrao established his studio over 25 years ago and throughout the 1990s he built and decorated many estates throughout the United States. In 2003, he opened an exclusive high-end art and antiques gallery, Ingrao Antiques and Fine Art.

Randy Kemper, creative director of Ingrao, began his professional life as a fashion designer. He was selected by Hubert de Givenchy as a designer for his Paris couture house; later, Kemper launched his own design firm where he dressed many prominent women of society including First Lady Hillary Clinton. After closing his couture business, Kemper joined Ingrao where he has worked since 1998.

tom FLYNN [PAGE 152-165]
INTERIORS: Tom Flynn
ARCHITECTURE: Hut/Sacks
INTERIOR ARCHITECTURE: Tom Flynn
ARBOR DESIGN: Joe D'Urso
LANDSCAPE ARCHITECT: Edwina von Gal
During the mid 1980s through the mid 1990s, Flynn worked for Hasbro Toys as Director of Corporate Design where he helped reshape the company's corporate aesthetic image through architecture, interior design, showroom design, graphic design, and fine arts acquisitions and commissions. Flynn later moved to East Hampton where he built a house on Georgica Pond and was a partner in the well-known store, Ruby Beets Antiques. Subsequently, one of his favorite and loyal customers, Martha Stewart, asked him to be a contributing editor for her publication *Martha Stewart Living*. Flynn worked as freelance design editor and stylist for a number of publications before joining Polo Ralph Lauren as a senior creative director. In 2003, Flynn began his design studio, Tom Flynn, Inc., based in Manhattan and East Hampton. His work has been published in *Martha Stewart Living*, *Elle Decor*, and the *New York Times Magazine*, among other magazines.

**bill SOFIELD &
dennis ANDERSON** [PAGE 166-185]
INTERIORS: Bill Sofield and Dennis Anderson
Sofield received his degree in architecture and urban planning from Princeton University, following an academic focus on art history and European cultural studies. He received the Helena Rubenstein Fellowship from the Whitney Museum of American Art in the 1980s and first established his design practice in 1989. In 1992, he co-founded Aero Studios.

The Bauhaus philosophy that piloted Aero—the belief that good design addresses the requirements of contemporary living with excellence in craft—was then fully realized in Studio Sofield, Inc., the interdisciplinary design workshop he established in New York's NoHo district in 1996. In 1999, he created a Los Angeles satellite office to provide more extensive design services to its west coast and international clients. With the express goal of integrating multiple design disciplines, Studio Sofield's vast portfolio ranges from residential, retail, hospitality, landscape, office, and furniture design to custom lighting and accessories.

Dennis Anderson grew up in High Point, North Carolina where his mother worked for one of the large furniture exposition buildings and had an influence on his early interest in design. After studying studio art and printmaking, Anderson became a photo stylist for Alderman Studios, one of the world's largest photographic venues. Twelve years ago he began consulting for Baker Furniture, and is currently responsible for styling their Milling Road collection at the High Point flagship and buying fabrics for the company's line.

robert STILIN [PAGE 186-199]
INTERIORS: Robert Stilin
ARCHITECTURE: Frank Greenwald
With nearly 15 years of experience running his own design firm in East Hampton, Stilin has built a reputation as a versatile interior designer whose work is custom tailored to the needs of each client and project. His projects include ones throughout the Hamptons, in Manhattan, Palm Beach, and the Pacific Northwest. His work has been featured in *Elle Decor*, *Food & Wine*, *Hamptons Cottages & Gardens*, *House & Garden*, and *House Beautiful*, among others. He was named the design director of the 2005 *Hamptons Cottages & Gardens* Idea House and also participated in the *House & Garden* Hampton Designer Showhouse.

enrico BONETTI &
dominic KOZERSKI [PAGE 200–213]
INTERIORS: Bonetti/Kozerski Studio
LANDSCAPE ARCHITECT: Bonetti/Kozerski Studio

Established in 2000, New York architecture studio Bonetti/Kozerski is led by partners Italian-born Enrico Bonetti and English-born Dominic Kozerski. With its roots in European education, the studio blurs the traditional boundaries of an architecture practice, resulting in a hybrid of design disciplines.

The studio has garnered international attention for its work in high-end residential and retail projects for clients, including fashion designers Donna Karan, Diane Von Furstenberg, and Cynthia Steffe. Recently completed projects include Donna Karan Collection stores in Tokyo, Dubai, and Singapore as well as new headquarters for the New York advertising firm Laird and Partners, an apartment in SoHo for hotelier André Balazs, a new David Barton gym in Chelsea, and a new flagship store for Tod's on Madison Avenue. Their work has been featured in many architectural and lifestyle publications, including *Abitare*, *Elle Decoration*, *Harpers Bazaar*, *Interni*, *Interior Design*, *New York Magazine*, the *New York Times*, and *Vogue*.

arthur DUNNAM [PAGE 214–225]
INTERIORS: Arthur Dunnam of Jed Johnson Associates
LANDSCAPE ARCHITECT: Joseph W. Tyree

Dunnam began his career in the office of Arthur Smith, partner of Billy Baldwin. In his six years there, he worked on many projects for Harding and Mary Wells Lawrence, whose extensive collection of international residences greatly influenced Dunnam's work. In 1986, Dunnam joined Jed Johnson Associates and has been a design director and senior associate there since 1997. His projects display a diverse array of styles, but he is perhaps best known for his individualistic interpretations for homes in the Hamptons. These Hamptons projects, including his own residence, have been published in magazines such as *Architectural Digest*, *House Beautiful*, and *House & Garden*.

michael HAVERLAND &
philip GALANES [PAGE 226–245]
INTERIORS: Michael Haverland and Philip Galanes
ARCHITECTURE: Michael Haverland

Haverland heads a small New York City-based practice and has taught at the Yale University School of Architecture for 10 years. His practice is committed to diverse work, including institutional, residential, commercial, and urban design projects, with specific experience in neighborhood planning, campus planning, housing, and public art. Each work of architecture is the result of a productive collaboration between the client and the firm—the work responds to each client's tastes and interests and the project's site without imposing a specific design agenda or style.

His design work has been widely published, including features in *Architecture*, *Architectural Record*, *House & Garden*, the *New York Times*, and *Oculus*. Haverland's work has also been honored with awards from the New York Chapter of the American Institute of Architects, the Congress for the New Urbanism, the Brick Industry Association, and the Association of Collegiate Schools of Architecture.

Philip Galanes consults on interior design projects for select clients. Recent projects include a house in East Hampton; interior design, furnishings, and art for an Edward Durrell Stone townhouse; and a guest house/garden pavilion in Greenwich Village. Previously, he worked as an entertainment lawyer at Paul Weiss Rifkind Wharton & Garrison, representing clients in film, theater, television, and fine art. In addition, his first novel, *Father's Day*, was published by Alfred A Knopf in June 2004 and he is at work on a second novel. Galanes lives in East Hampton and New York City.

thom FILICIA [PAGE 246–259]
INTERIORS: Thom Filicia Inc.
INTERIOR ARCHITECTURE: Thom Filicia Inc.

Founded in 1998, Thom Filicia Inc. (TFI) quickly gained celebrity for branding its unique aesthetic not only on residential projects, but hospitality and commercial assignments as well. Based in the heart of SoHo in New York City, TFI has attracted a diverse roster of prestigious clients ranging from leaders in fashion, entertainment, real estate, and finance. It was recently selected as the exclusive design firm for the US Pavilion at the 2005 World's Fair, and Thom Filicia was named one of *House Beautiful*'s top 100 American Designers. TFI has completed projects in New York City, the Hamptons, Connecticut, New Jersey, Arizona, Los Angeles, Miami, the Carribean, and other locations in the United States.

john BARMAN &
kelly GRAHAM [PAGE 260–275]
INTERIORS: John Barman and Kelly Graham of John Barman, Inc.

Barman's interior design career spans over 15 years and focuses on modern, high-end projects. His New York City-based design firm, John Barman, Inc. takes a very personal and individual approach to each project, with much of the inspiration coming from the client. Barman was honored as one of the "AD 100" by *Architectural Digest* magazine, "The City's Best 100 Architects and Decorators" by *New York* magazine, and has had his work featured in magazines such as *Architectural Digest*, *House & Garden*, the *New York Times*, and *W*, among many others.

Kelly Graham is the creative design director at John Barman, Inc. overseeing a variety of residential and commercial commissions. Prior to joining the firm, Graham enjoyed a long and prosperous career as a fashion designer, where he designed his own signature line of clothing for women.

vicente WOLF [PAGE 276-297]
INTERIORS: Vicente Wolf Associates

For the past 28 years, Wolf has been involved in the world of contemporary design. He heads his own company, Vicente Wolf Associates, located in New York City. It is from there that Wolf and his staff explore his passion for design guided by the principles of integrity and simplicity. He has completed a wide range of projects, including L'Impero restaurant in New York, the Registry stores in Chicago, the Luxe Hotel Rodeo Drive in Los Angeles, and the New York City apartment of Prince and Princess von Furstenberg. Beyond interior design projects, Wolf has designed furniture for Niedermaier, rugs for Tufenkian Carpets, and crystal, china, and stemware for Steuben, among many other lines of furniture and objects.

House Beautiful named Wolf one of the 10 most influential designers in the United States, and *Interior Design* magazine inducted Wolf in its Designer Hall of Fame. He was selected as one of the top 100 designers in both *Metropolitan Home*'s "Design 100" and *Architectural Digest*'s "AD 100." His first book, *Learning to See* (2002), focuses on personal style and travel.

jonathan ADLER & simon DOONAN [PAGE 298-309]
INTERIORS: Jonathan Adler and Simon Doonan
LANDSCAPE ARCHITECT: Buttercup Inc.

A graduate of the Rhode Island School of Design (RISD), Adler burst onto the design scene in 1994 when he sold his first collection of pottery to Barneys New York. In 1998, he opened his first store in SoHo, and has since opened six other locations throughout the United States. In 2002, Adler began his interior design practice and started a furniture collection.

Simon Doonan is the bestselling author of *Wacky Chicks* and *Confessions of a Window Dresser*. In addition to his role as creative director of Barneys New York, Doonan writes a column for the *New York Observer* and is a regular commentator on VH1, the Trio network, and *Full Frontal Fashion*.

endpapers
LANDSCAPE ARCHITECT: Edmund Hollander Landscape Architect Design, P.C.

Edmund Hollander Design, P.C. is one of the country's leading landscape architecture firms and has been involved with environmental planning and design projects for over a decade. Led by partners Edmund Hollander and Maryanne Connelly, the firm's experience covers a wide range of scales including estates and gardens, waterfront parks and developments, golf course restoration and planning, corporate headquarters, historic landscapes, horse farms, and urban rooftop gardens. The firm currently has 10 landscape architects, as well as an in-house horticulturist and ecological planner.

photography credits

joe NAHEM [PAGES 12-37]
Eric Piasecki, except Charles Mayer
Photography pages 14, 15, 30-37

steven GAMBREL [PAGES 38-55]
Eric Piasecki

thomas O'BRIEN [PAGES 56-71]
Laura Resen

jamie DRAKE [PAGES 72-85]
Minh + Wass, except Eric Piasecki
pages 74,75,82,84,85

jack CEGLIC [PAGES 86-101]
Eric Piasecki

waldo FERNANDEZ [PAGES 102-119]
Eric Piasecki

mark ZEFF [PAGES 120-133]
Eric Piasecki

tony INGRAO &
randy KEMPER [PAGES 134-151]
Eric Piasecki

tom FLYNN [PAGES 152-165]
Eric Piasecki

bill SOFIELD &
dennis ANDERSON [PAGES 166-185]
Toni Meneguzzo

robert STILIN [PAGES 186-199]
Joshua McHugh

enrico BONETTI &
dominic KOZERSKI [PAGES 200-213]
Paul Warchol Photography

arthur DUNNAM [PAGES 214-225]
Eric Piasecki

michael HAVERLAND &
philip GALANES [PAGES 226-245]
Billy Cunningham, except Chris Bausch pages
228, 238; Laurie Lambrecht 232, 239;
Eric Piasecki 243

thom FILICIA [PAGES 246-259]
Eric Piasecki

john BARMAN &
kelly GRAHAM [PAGES 260-275]
Eric Piasecki

vicente WOLF [PAGES 276-297]
Vicente Wolf

jonathan ADLER &
simon DOONAN [PAGES 298-309]
Eric Piasecki

endpapers
Charles Mayer Photography

dustjacket (inside)
Courtesy the designers

special thanks

I would like to thank all the designers for sharing their work with us and all the homeowners for letting us into their private worlds. There are many wonderful homes in the Hamptons, and this volume celebrates the design professionals who are defining, exploring, and challenging our notion of what the Hamptons are all about. Naturally, we could not include every designer working in the Hamptons, but those published here find deep inspiration in the beautiful natural surroundings, inspiration they often export to other projects in other places. We hope that the audience for this publication can share in this inspiration.

While many of the featured designers are part of the Hamptons community of friends and neighbors, they are all known to a much wider audience, and their work, as it is published and diffused, is having a profound impact on interior design across the country.

To a certain extent, all eyes are on the Hamptons, not only as a breeding ground for good taste, but as a point-of-entry into the inner circle of world-class designers. The work of these designers reveals a radical break from the preconceived notion that entry into that inner circle must take the form of by-the-sea cottages. Their work is about everything from a celebration of contemporary architecture to a Zen-inspired oasis. Personally, I am inspired by the variation and depth of creativity expressed here, and I hope this volume provides you with some insight into this wonderful place and the designers who are making it fabulous.

Within the design community we often speak of how design can influence lifestyles, and many of the projects here introduce us to innovative ways of experiencing the Hamptons.

Pierantonio Giacoppo

Copyright © 2006 Edizioni Press, Inc.

All rights reserved. No part of this book may be reproduced in any form without written permission of the copyright owners. All images in this book have been reproduced with the consent of the artists concerned and no responsibility is accepted by producer, publisher or printer for any infringement of copyright or otherwise, arising from the contents of this publication. Every effort has been made to ensure that credits comply with information supplied.

First published in the United States of America by Edizioni Press, Inc.
469 West 21st Street New York, New York 10011 USA www.edizionipress.com

ISBN: 1-931536-71-6
Library of Congress Catalogue Number: 2005936286

Graphic Design by Pace Kaminsky and Matthew Papa
Edited by Diana Lind
Editorial Assistant: Nancy Sul

Printed in China